Kay Bascom

Overcomers

CHRISTIANS UNDER PRESSURE:
STUDIES IN DISCRIMINATION AND PERSECUTION

On behalf of the International Institute of Religious Freedom
edited by Thomas Schirrmacher and Christof Sauer

Volume 2

Vol. 1   Bernhard Reitsma (Ed.). Fruitful Minorities – The Witness and Service of Christian Communities in Predominantly Islamic Societies

Vol. 2   Kay Bascom. Overcomers – God's Deliverance through the Ethiopian Revolution as Witnessed Primarily by the Kale Heywet Church Community

Kay Bascom

Overcomers

God's deliverance through the Ethiopian Revolution as witnessed primarily by the Kale Heywet Church community

WIPF & STOCK · Eugene, Oregon

Wipf and Stock Publishers
199 W 8th Ave, Suite 3
Eugene, OR 97401

Overcomers
God's deliverance through the Ethiopian Revolution as witnessed primarily by the Kale Heywet Church community
By Bascom, Kay
Copyright©2018 Verlag für Kultur und Wissenschaft
ISBN 13: 978-1-5326-6306-2
Publication date 7/10/2018
Previously published by Verlag für Kultur und Wissenschaft, 2018

Contents

Table of Maps vii
Table of Photographs vii
Abbreviations ix
Foreword and Acknowledgements xi

I. OLD SOVEREIGNTIES (FROM ANTIQUITY TO 1972)

1. "Negus"–What's in a Name? 3
2. Discovering Ancient Sovereignties 17
3. Meeting the North 27
4. Meeting the South 37

II. A CALL FOR ARMOR (DURING 1972–77)

5. Becoming Equipped 51
6. The Kingdom Crumbling 61
7. Mixed Reactions 79
8. Risks on Hostile Ground 87
9. Tearing Down, Building Up 97

III. FACING PRINCIPALITIES & POWERS (DURING 1977–78)

10. Facing the Cadres 113
11. Facing Disintegration 125
12. Facing the Red Terror 137
13. Facing Marxism 149
14. Facing Love and Hate 171

IV. WIELDING SWORD AND SHIELD (DURING 1978–81)

15. Vignettes across Addis Ababa 181
16. Gamo Gofa: Lessons from Prison 193
17. Wolaitta: Winds of Testing, Winds of Power 207
18. Kambaata / Hadiyya: "Daniels," "Josephs," and
    Community Development 223

V. HAVING DONE ALL, TO STAND (DURING 1981–85)

19. Into the Eighties 241
20. Encounters along the Sidamo Road 251
21. East Africa Writhing 267
22. The "Black Jew" Enigma 277

VI. PRAYING WITH ALL PRAYER (DURING 1985–89)

23. Free! 285
24. Deaths and Births 295
25. Two Sagas in Bale 303
26. Glimpsing the Kinship of Grief and Glory 315

VII. TROPHIES OF VICTORY (DURING 1989–94)

27. Surrounded 335
28. Breaking Forth 345
29. Consummation 359

Glossary 371
List of Informants and Recorded Testimonies 373
Bibliography 377
For Further Reading 382

Table of Maps

Area of Rift from Israel through Ethiopia	xiv
Major locations and roads mentioned in the text	50
Boundaries of Ethiopia's provinces	112
Addis Ababa: key locations and major routes	180

Table of Photographs

Negussie Kumbi with Coleman children	11
Sahle Tilahun at sixteen	32
Lakew Tesemma	65
Tekle Wolde Giorgis	68
Kedamo Mechato	71
Teshome Haile, Girma Abebe, and Solomon Beyene	90
Yohannes Bosana	101
Dr. Mulatu Baffa	117
Tadesse Ayissa	119
Belaynesh Dindamo and Hussein Yusef	141
Hsueh Yu Kwong, Kay Bascom, and Pastor Kedamo	154
Degu Deklaabo	194
Bassa Dea	197
Tesfaye Tole	200
Seta Wotango	212
Markina Meja	215
Desalegn Enaro and Waja Kabeto	217
Ekaso Eybero	218

Mahey Choramo	220
Sabiro Wesero, Daanna Meja Madero, and Abba Gole Nunamo	224
Fikre Nebiyehu	226
Girma Hanano	228
Girma Deresse and Werkwuha Makuria	230
Yoel Fughi	234
Mamo Belete	252
Werassa Hokotay and Hordofa Gidecho	253
Tsehaynesh Dori	255
Werku Gole	262
Yeshi Belachew	304
Asfaw Demisse	311
Aberash Takele and Sahle Tilahun	323
Timothy Niwar	325
Ethiopian Jewish regiment	327
Shiferaw Wolde Michael	349
Meresse Abraham	352
Negussie Kumbi and Fantaye Mogus	360
Negussie Kumbi	362

Photo Credits:

Cover photo of a conference at Soddo (probably in 1965) courtesy of Allan Kliever; photographs of Negussie Kumbi courtesy of the Coleman family; all other photographs courtesy of Kay Bascom.

Abbreviations

AAEJ	American Association for Ethiopian Jews
AD	*Anno Domini* (Christian Era [Gregorian calendar])
AEAM	Association of Evangelicals of Africa and Madagascar (now AEA: Association of Evangelicals in Africa)
aka	also known as
AM	*ante meridiem* (before midday)
BBC	British Broadcasting Company
BC	Before Christ
Br.	Brother
CD	Community Development
CIA	Central Intelligence Bureau (of USA)
COPWE	Committee for Organizing the Party of the Workers of Ethiopia
CRDA	Christian Relief and Development Agency
DMG	*Deutsche Missionsgemeinschaft* (now DMG Interpersonal)
ed.	edited by
EEC	European Economic Community
ELF	Eritrean Liberation Front
EPLF	Eritrean People's Liberation Front
EPRDF	Ethiopian People's Revolutionary Democratic Front
EPRP	Ethiopian Peoples Revolutionary Party
et al.	*et alii* (and other [authors])
EVASU	Evangelical Student Union (now EvaSUE: Evangelical Students' and Graduates' Union of Ethiopia)
f	following [page]
GBI	Grace Bible Institute
HIM	His Imperial Majesty
HQ	Headquarters

IEC	International Evangelical Church in Addis Ababa
IFES	International Fellowship of Evangelical Students
KGB	*Komitet gosudarstvennoy bezopasnosti* (Soviet State Security Committee, 1954–1991)
KHC	Kale Heywet Church
KHDP	Kale Heywet Development Program
KHMTC	Kale Heywet Ministry Training Center
KJV	Holy Bible: King James Version
LWF	Lutheran World Federation
MAF	Missionary Aviation Fellowship
NBC	National Broadcasting Company (USA)
NGO	Non-governmental organization
NIV	The Holy Bible: New International Version
OAU	Organization of African Unity (now AU: African Union)
PM	*Post meridiem* (after midday)
PMAC	Provisional Military Administrative Council
R & R	Relief and Rehabilitation
RSV	The Bible: Revised Standard Version
RVOG	Radio Voice of the Gospel (former Lutheran station in Addis Ababa)
SDA	Seventh Day Adventist
SIM	Sudan Interior Mission (now Serving In Mission)
TB	Tuberculosis
TPLF	Tigray People's Liberation Front
transl.	translated by
TTI	Teachers Training Institute
UN	United Nations
US	United States
USAID	United States Agency for International Development
Univ.	University
VOA	Voice of America
vol.	volume

Foreword and Acknowledgements

After years of silence under the heavy fist of communism, Ethiopians welcomed the opportunity to testify to the outside world about the wonderful works of God amongst them during those two decades of severe testing.

When freedom finally came, John Cumbers, Director of SIM[1] in East Africa during that period, did the initial work of returning to the country and interviewing Ethiopians in 1993. This historical material was envisioned as a gift to the Kale Heywet Church (KHC).[2] I was asked to assist him on the project when my husband and I returned to Ethiopia in 1994 to 1996. During the initial phase of gathering materials, Ethiopians graciously gave their testimonies to John Cumbers and myself. Mr. Cumbers chose to record the testimonies province by province. KHC executive officers checked early drafts of the material. It was published in 1995 under the title suggested by church leadership, *Count It All Joy*. That title is their testimony to the suffering church's being given God's eternal viewpoint, for they saw "the wrath of man" being turned to "the praise of God's glory."

This second treatment, called *Overcomers* (based on seven admonitions to overcome in Revelation 2 and 3), presents the history chronologically instead, in order to help readers less familiar with provincial contexts and the actual ordeal. After a bit of historical and geographical orientation, the story moves progressively through the Revolution years, combining the experiences of many Ethiopians

---

1. SIM had meant the "Sudan Interior Mission" since its inception in 1893. When SIM had been founded, *Soudan* meant the geographical belt south of the Sahara, rather than designating a country. Because the mission has expanded beyond Africa, the initials now refer to "Serving In Mission."

2. The name of this Ethiopian church with SIM background means "Word of Life Church."

and a few missionaries whose lives intersected each other during the *Derg* regime.[3]

This chronological treatment was enabled due to many people's encouragement and prayers. John Cumbers and Murray and Bea Coleman methodically went over the *Overcomers* manuscript, making valuable corrections and suggestions.[4] Most basic was my dear husband Charles' patience and input as well as the practical editing expertise of our writer sons, Johnathan and Timothy Bascom. Friends in our Christian community upheld the work in prayer.

However, the book that resulted was so long that a shortened story selected out of it was suggested for publishing. Negussie Kumbi's life became the story line used in a 150-page book titled *Hidden Triumph in Ethiopia*.[5] The larger tome was tabled, supposedly permanently.

Surprisingly, in 2017 I was contacted by Stefan Ritter, formerly a missionary in Ethiopia. It is his steady encouragement and editing expertise that has made this long unpublished book available, re-edited with the addition of photographs, listings of informants and recorded testimonies, as well as suggestions for further reading.

Temesgen Sahle and Dr. Johnathan Bascom graciously read through the manuscript and gave much helpful advice, as did Professor Tibebe Eshete, whose insightful endorsement on the cover is deeply appreciated. Technical assistance from Jay Herrmann, Connie Satzler, Claire Bishop, and Titus Vogt was invaluable. Last but not least, our heartfelt appreciation goes to Professor Thomas Schirrmacher and Professor Christof Sauer for giving this Ethiopian community's story an opportunity to reach a broader audience.

DEAR READER, SO MANY persons appear in *Overcomers* that you will need commitment to stick with the collage of their multiple stories.

---

3. The *Derg* literally meant "a committee of equals." The term was used roughly to designate the leadership of the Provisional Military Administrative Council (PMAC) during the Revolution.

4. Several stories in this book combine facts from two interviews, John Cumber's in 1993, and Kay Bascom's follow-up recorded in 1994. Similarities with variations appear from time to time throughout this book, done with both writers' agreement and permission.

5. K. Bascom, *Hidden Triumph in Ethiopia* (William Carey Library, 2001; Amharic version: SIM Press [Addis Ababa], 2001).

The "Informants" section at the end of this book (pp. 373–376) offers some help by listing the pages where the main characters play a major role.

The book's uneven coverage is due to my degree of intimacy with what was being reported: whether as a participant, a listener to firsthand interviews, or as a researcher working with written records. Regretfully, many people go unmentioned, men and especially women whose participation in this history was just as significant as those who are included. Most testimonies are from believers from the Ethiopian Kale Heywet Church community, but the book includes a wider perspective, for Ethiopia's various evangelical groups tended to melt together during their shared persecution.

Foreigners like myself long to broadcast this unique chapter in the Spirit's ongoing *Book of Acts*. Yet Ethiopians are best equipped to record their own history in depth.[6] Some have done so in Amharic books which have been published in recent years. For the *Overcomer's* collection, we are indebted to the Ethiopians John Cumbers and I interviewed. By opening their hearts to us, we were privileged to share their community's testimonies to God's faithfulness with English readers.

The Holy Spirit enabled Ethiopian believers to survive the Revolution as they stayed faithful to the true Lion of Judah to whom their history has been mysteriously anchored. Out of this faith community come stories that should not be lost, testimonies that challenge us as we run our own lap of life's race.

May the reader discover in these pages some of the unknown riches of Ethiopia—riches deposited by God's Spirit. The reality of His indwelling and empowering presence is available to His people throughout the world, as well.

Kay Bascom

---

6. For references see Tibebe E., *The Evangelical Movement in Ethiopia* (Baylor Univ. Press, 2009) and the bibliography at the end of this book (pp. 377–384).

MAP 1: AREA OF RIFT FROM ISRAEL TO ETHIOPIA (BEFORE AD 1991)

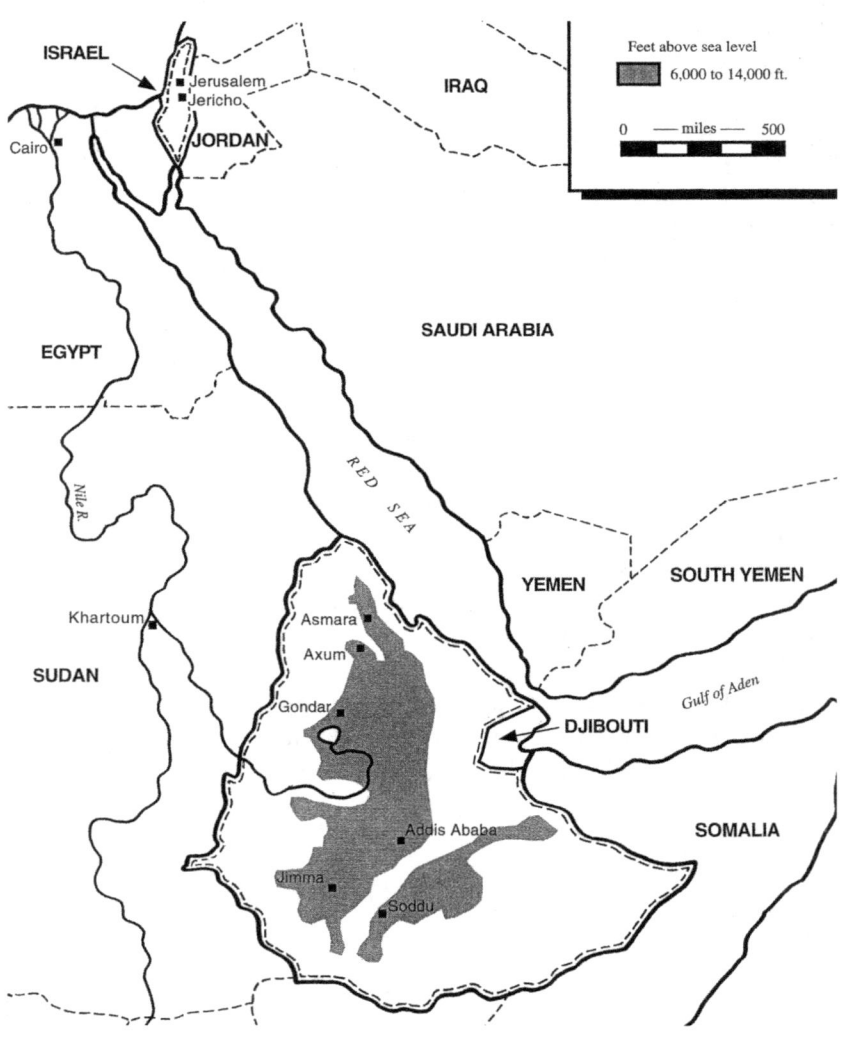

Source: Adapted from Shelemay & Berger (1986), *Jews,* by Johnathan Bascom.

Part I

OLD SOVEREIGNTIES

(From Antiquity to 1972)

*The name of the second river is the Gihon;
it winds through the entire land of Cush.*
                              (Genesis 2:13)

Chapter 1
"NEGUS"—WHAT'S IN A NAME?

The prisoner lay in a heap where the cadres dumped him. Was he unconscious or dead? Who cared? *Negus* was he? They'd teach him! Negussie's blood had dripped a trail from the torture room, and now oozed slowly from his lacerated body, dampening the prison floor.

What came to his clouded mind as consciousness flickered into his battered brain? Was it awareness of the trickle of blood blinding his eyes, pulsating from the battered soles of his feet, oozing from legs swollen to twice their size? Was it wonderment that he was for the moment still alive? Was it fear of another volley of the unrelenting blows that had exhausted even his torturers? Was it relief that the taunting voices had faded away? Was it incredulity that human beings could have done such a thing? Might it have been a stab of identification with thousands of other prisoners who had undergone this same kind of torture... or a visceral entrance into his Savior's suffering?

Across Ethiopia, people asked themselves, "How can humans do such things to fellow human beings?" In a country where "God be praised" had preceded everyday greetings, how could the Red Terror be happening? What had suddenly turned their society insane?

Few could remember when the King had not been the bannerbearer of Ethiopia. In 1928, Ras Tafari[1] of Harar was given the title *Negus* ("King"). In 1930, he was crowned Haile Selassie, Conquering Lion of Judah, *Nigusa Negest* ("King of Kings"). Progressive in his youth, the new emperor was an innovator in education and took preparatory steps for more representative government. Suddenly in

---
1. Note this title from which the Rastafarians of Jamaica take their name. P. Cotterell, *Cry Ethiopia* (MARC, 1988), 76–78, gives a brief explanation of this tie.

1936 Italy marched into Ethiopia. Haile Selassie went to the League of Nations and in an historic speech, warned them of an impending World War if they did not stop Mussolini. They didn't, and it came. The Ethiopian monarch became an internationally respected figure when he won his nation back from the Italians, with British help, in 1941. But the five-year Italian invasion had killed off the intelligentsia and slowed down progress. He began again. With education came an awakening to the wider world. Ethiopia still resembled a feudal state. Ambitions rose and corruption grew. Although the northern province of Eritrea had been granted autonomy in 1952 after World War II, the Emperor annexed it in 1962. Guerrilla activity eventually escalated into an all-out war of secession. Inattention to severe drought and famine in the north in 1972–73 raised more voices against the King.

A successor to a king requires kingly blood, and that posed another problem for the modern emperor. There were princesses, but Haile Selassie was unable to find a son to whom to pass on the kingdom. The heir apparent died in a car accident. Another son participated in an unsuccessful coup attempt. Time ran out.

IMPATIENT FOR FASTER CHANGES, student leaders found in Marxism-Leninism a tool designed for overturning the aging emperor. Although unrest had been multiplying underground, it was the Emperor's unseating in 1974 that openly signaled a total break with the past. The old Lion was captured by his own officers in a tiny Volkswagen "bug," imprisoned in his own Fourth Army Headquarters, and within months purportedly smothered in his own bed. So ended Ethiopia's venerable line of kings, the kingship, and one of the world's last "kingdoms."

So also ended life in Ethiopia in its former mode. Deep as were the traditions and patterns of three millennia, the Revolution displayed an amazing capacity to force over-night change. Political shoot-outs in the chambers of government and secret executions in the night hours rocked the capital with carnage judged as bloodthirsty as Lenin's overthrow of the Czar in 1917. In the ongoing Ethiopian Revolution, imprisonment, death, and terror spread to the far corners of the realm. In all but the remotest fringes of the great mountain massif, most areas were drawn into the major theater of modern times, their country's encounter with Marxism-Leninism. Old patterns of every kind were overturned—politics, land use, economy, religion—all were upended, catching the populace in the crevasses of a mammoth upheaval.

Under the eye of doctrinaire Marxism, Ethiopia's old greetings in the market place, interspersed with *Egziabihir yemesgen* ("God be praised") were no longer acceptable. In Revolutionary Ethiopia, the broad masses must understand that retaining allegiance to a "Kingdom not of this world" was politically incorrect and punishable. Nevertheless, with an ancient Orthodox Christian church in the north stretching back to the 4th century, and a new body of evangelical believers emerging in the south during the 20th century, such Party pronouncements were difficult to enforce. Some conformed their outer behavior to fit the system in order to stave off accusations on religious grounds. Others obeyed their earthly rulers as far as they felt they could in good conscience, but refused to deny their allegiance to the rule of the One they believed to be the true King of kings.

Thus a contest was enjoined between the two ideologies wrought out in the actions and reactions of individual lives, the contest between allegiance to Marx or to Christ. The former forbade the latter. The latter superseded the former. Other countries had seen the same contest. Now the battle of the "broad masses" was to be enjoined on new soil. Ethiopian earth would drink much blood under the Red Star, the Hammer and Sickle; the huge murals of Marx, Engels, and Lenin affixed on standards high above politicians and peasants in the "new" Ethiopia.

The tentacles of Marxism-Leninism reached out very quickly into the countryside, significantly changing the lives of almost everyone. Terror is an effective tool. Suddenly, who was in charge, what was allowed, and how dissent was handled, all shifted. Control passed into the hands of young cadres who were eager to be revolutionary. Often they relished and abused the absolute power they could wield over people through the barrel of a gun. The results betrayed an underlying tendency toward human depravity. Everybody lost. Victims went through horrors, but had no power of appeal. Torture corrupted the torturers, leaving them scarred within. Thousands were put through standard torture procedures.

Statistics don't feel, but a person does. Negussie's case was representative of the countless people who endured such tortures, or died at the hands of Marxism. A young single teacher in a village school, Negussie was a Christian. He didn't flaunt it, but he had made up his mind not to hide it either. Marxist-Leninist doctrine demanded stamping out Christianity, so over-night, Christians had been labeled "anti-revolutionary." Being accused of being "anti-revolutionary" was often all it took to put the accused in prison. Cadres in Negussie's area had watched for their chance, set the popular teacher up with false accusations, and took him off for "examination"—under torture.

The prisoner appeared to be simple to break, for childhood tuberculosis had left him with a hump on the spine, and he didn't act defiant. "It's your choice," they told him, sneering. "Deny that Christ of yours and go free now, or we'll break you with torture. It's your decision, not ours." One by one, Ethiopian Christians were facing such tests. Negussie heard the alternatives and prepared himself for torture. This is my turn, he told himself, having made his choice long before.

Negussie had become headmaster of a rural school a couple hours' drive from his hometown. The young man's strong character and warm love for students had led to early leadership, which caused some jealousy. Cadres sent in from the outside found the respect in which the young man was held to be irritating and threatening, for it put them in a poor light. Even his name seemed anti-revolutionary. Negussie meant "my king." He must be disposed of. How they maneuvered his arrest and what form of torture they used will be related later. But Negussie refused to recant, choosing death over denial of his Lord. Wary of the consequences, his accusers stopped just short of death and dumped his unconscious body in a prison cell, expecting the fool to rot away in ignominy.

What they could not see was the strength of this prisoner's "inner man," or his linkage with the wider family to which he belonged. Outside the local prison, believers heard of his treatment, and urged local Christians to stand with their brother in prayer. His earlier mentor, Pastor Kedamo, alerted his Addis Ababa congregation to pray. Students and faculty, who had known smiling Negussie as a staff member at their mission academy a couple years before, whispered the news of his capture to each other. Word of his imprisonment went across to Canada to the missionary family to whom he'd been like a son. The two hearts perhaps most wrenched were his sister's, and that of an anonymous young woman whose love for Negussie no one knew about, hardly even Negussie himself.

It is about Negussie's community that this book is written. Perhaps it could be called "a memoir of a faith community." Famine, war, death, and destruction have long been the sad news from Ethiopia. She has become a by-word for abject poverty. Yet hidden within her is one of the "wealthiest" communities in the world. Many hunger to hear good news about people like Negussie and others who came through the fire triumphantly. Such lives point us to the majestic worthiness of the God who enabled each of them to overcome.

These stories are representative of what countless people and their loved ones went through. Moving along with the various phases of the period of communist rule, each section of this book picks up the thread of Negussie's story, weaving his experience in among accounts from many other people's lives. Each story reveals a different hue of God's power and radiance which was displayed among those Ethiopians who, in their time, lived to the praise of God's glory.

Headlines and history books record facts. They tell us about the big people, about politicians and generals. Humanity is made up mostly of little people. It will be interesting to learn in the end who was "big" and "little," for Jesus said: "the last will be first, and the first will be last" (Matthew 20:16). And it will be sobering to learn just Who was being persecuted—in the light of the words of the ultimate King of kings—"I am Jesus, whom you are persecuting" (Acts 9:5b).

Many books have been written about the rise and demise of the big people during Ethiopia's Revolution. This one is mostly about the suffering and triumph of the little people. Negussie was one such, so we will start with his story, and go on to the wider community in whose lives we will be privileged to share. Their testimony to God's work among them constitutes a modern chapter of Acts.

IN A SMALL VILLAGE of central Ethiopia in 1952, a boy child opened his eyes on the world for the first time. His cries rang out in the humble mud hut of a peasant family who tilled their small acreage along a nearby stream. Life was elemental. By day, the baby could hear his mother grinding grain outside the door and smell her coffee roasting over a three-stoned fire in the center of their circular home. By night, he could hear the peaceful lowing of their cattle, which his father barricaded within, safe from hyenas that roamed abroad.

The couple named their son *Negussie*. It meant "my king." What might have encouraged these parents to give their tiny baby such a name? In Ethiopia, nearly every child's name has a meaning. Negussie[2] was not an unusual name, for the concept of royalty was ingrained in the country's culture. It reached back almost three thousand years to the national epic. A royal son had been born to Israel's King Solomon and Ethiopia's Queen of Sheba, their history said. Wasn't her visit to his court recorded in the Scriptures themselves, in 1 Kings, chapter 10? Somehow Ethiopia had developed a sequel to the biblical account—the birth of a child from that royal union—their King Menelik I. Factual or not, that epic has influenced the history of Ethiopia profoundly. It has been represented in her art and music, literature and politics throughout antiquity and continues today.

Negussie's parents had seen Haile Selassie come through victorious in bitter battle with the Italians just a decade before their baby's birth. His kingship had united the nation. Over the vast tangled mountains and dry savannas, provincial dukes[3] had fought for centuries for kingly control over Ethiopia, some of them from the Amharas of the central highlands, others from various other regions. In the 1920s, the duke named Ras Tafari—of the Amhara ethnic group—had risen above all the others to claim the title "King of Kings" *(Nigusa Negest)*. He used every opportunity to buttress his political power with historical credentials—reaching back to the Queen of Sheba's child to claim her line and appropriate for himself the Jewish title, "Lion of Judah." A Christian king, as most of his predecessors had been since the 4th century, the new Emperor made spiritual claim for his power as well, taking the regnal name Haile Selassie ("Power of the Trinity").

---

2. Depending on the phonetic system used to transfer sounds from Amharic's 250-symbol alphabet to English's 26, this may results in alternate English lettering for Amharic words. *Negussie* might be the chosen spelling by one person, or *Negusay* or *Neguse* or *Negusi* by another. The emphasis of Negussie's name is put on the middle syllable, and could be sounded out as *"Neh GOO see."*

3. The Ethiopian title for the equivalent of duke is *ras* and for king is *negus*.

Few rural Ethiopians were literate, but they knew their oral histories and ancestry. Around their fires at night, the stories were rehearsed. Baby Negussie's mother was of the Amharas, and his father of the Oromo. The family identified as Ethiopian Orthodox Christians but along with many, lived in syncretistic compromise with the fearful spirits of primal religions. It must have deeply grieved and even frightened the couple when their little "king's" development seemed stunted. His mother died in childbirth when ailing Negussie was about two. Although the mission clinic near the town of Wolisso was within minutes of their door, their fear of retaliation from the spirits kept the family from seeking help.

Later, an older stepmother took over the home and was not fond of the child with a deformed spine who sat hunched over in the shadows of their small hut. Often he perched crookedly on a little stool in the sunshine at the door of the compound. Sometimes the nurse from the SIM clinic would visit homes and would see little Negussie at his door, smiling brightly.

"Whose child are you?" she would ask.

"I'm God's child," was his unexpectedly happy response.

Stopping to visit a bit, the nurse could observe that the tiny boy showed signs of tuberculosis of the spine. Somehow she convinced the family that he could be helped if they allowed her to take him to the TB treatment center in the capital less than a hundred miles away. When Negussie was about four, it was arranged. Eventually the child returned from Addis Ababa with his TB arrested. At least his legs would grow, even if his torso could not fully develop.

Negussie stood out from other children, not so much because of his bent spine, but because of his sunny temperament. Very early he had been tried and had come forth shining, as gold. His illness and rejection were not to be the end of his refinement.

THE COLEMAN FAMILY, CANADIANS, came to Obbi station in 1962. By then Negussie was a bright fellow in the neighborhood, about twelve. The Coleman children bonded with him immediately, especially six-year old John who followed Negussie about incessantly, drawn like a magnet. John was a winsome boy, and a better friend than Negussie could hardly have been found. Negussie soon responded to what he learned of the Lord Jesus Christ in rainy season Bible classes. He began to develop spiritually, manifesting a gentle temperament and exemplary behavior.

Basking in Negussie's aura of cheerful friendliness was a gift to the lonely expatriate children. "He would keep us Coleman kids happy so graciously," John told some of us years later. "He'd teach us games to play, and where to find animals, and how to watch the birds. We'd spend hours on end together." Each evening, John and Negussie would bid each other good night under the big tree that soared above the mission compound and neighborhood homes. Moonlight outlined the grass roofs of round huts and threw rippling highlights on the few tin-roofed rectangular buildings that comprised their world.

The Colemans grew to love Negussie like a son. "He was always in and out of our home," Bea Coleman remembers, chuckling. "Neighborhood kids were a bit resentful, and nicknamed him 'the Minister of the Interior.' Yet at meal times, he would tactfully disappear." Negussie became a natural language teacher for the foreigners. He picked up their English, and they his Amharic and Oromo languages. The foreigners communicated in English among themselves, but the biggest hurdle was language. Missionaries were required to study the rudiments of Amharic, the national language, before being located "down-country." Oromo, the local language, was the Coleman's next linguistic challenge. Soft-spoken Murray Coleman managed the station and sought to encourage the fledgling church in the area. His wife seemed to have a gift for language, which stood her in good stead as she went around teaching, often traveling on horse or mule. Negussie's aid as an interpreter became so valuable that he seemed almost like a co-worker. He often explained usage's to them and advised them wisely in cultural matters. "He just seems to have an old man's head on a young child's shoulders," Bea would say to visitors, shaking her head.

Periodically the Colemans would depart for a furlough. At such times, the biblical "David-and-Jonathan" relationship between the two boys was poignantly acted out through the exchanging of gifts—a rare coin or some other treasure. On the Colemans' return, Negussie and John would continue to dream and plan together, sharing hopes and ambitions. That relationship was to have a powerful effect on John's whole life.

NEGUSSIE KUMBI WITH COLEMAN CHILDREN (OBBI, ABOUT 1966)

A German nurse named Christraude ("Chris") Ott came to the Obbi clinic when Negussie was about fifteen. She taught Negussie's Sunday Bible class, and noted that he had good answers and grasped the stories well, but even so, held back to give others a chance. She observed that he was a thoughtful, quiet boy, never calling attention to himself. He seemed graced with a natural cheerfulness and humility; furthermore, he evidenced an attitude that indicated that God's Spirit was quite active in him. Local families hardly owned a book or had the cash to buy one. Their wealth was in cattle. Chris decided to offer an Amharic Bible to any students who would memorize three hundred Bible verses. Negussie yearned to have his own copy of the Scriptures. Week by week he'd repeat an amazing number of verses word perfectly to Chris. In six short weeks he had won his Bible!

About that time, a strong fellowship was developing among the area youth. A new student named Alemu Beeftu[4] had entered the school. He was small of stature, but had been given a big name. Alemu means "the world." Only God knew how that characterization would someday be fulfilled. Negussie's father traced Alemu to actually be a distant cousin among his Oromo relatives. Alemu's passion to get an education had led him to the mission school, penniless, against his father's will. He came knowing no Amharic, and had hardly seen a white person before. He struggled to learn the language and keep up with the lessons, but his determination was fierce and his brilliance was soon unmistakable. Alemu's inclusion would soon develop a three-fold bond with John and Negussie.

Arrested by words in Psalm 15 read in a class one day, Alemu was riveted by the questions, "Who shall abide in thy tabernacle? Who shall dwell in thy holy hill?" The conviction that he must act immediately overwhelmed him. He understood the question in terms of his own deep personal need for cleansing before God. Put off by the teacher whom he questioned, he went to Mrs. Coleman and insisted that he wished to receive God's provision of salvation without delay. Right under the flagpole in the middle of the schoolyard, he committed his life to the Lord Jesus Christ as his Savior.

Soon after, Alemu, John, and Negussie all three took the step of baptism the same day along with others in a nearby stream. It was a time of joyful witness to their identification with Christ's death, burial, and resurrection, pictured by going under and arising from the waters. Had not the first-century "Ethiopian eunuch"[5] done the same (see Acts 8:26–40)? The official was reading Isaiah 53 in his chariot, and on questioning Philip, discovered that Jesus was the lamb of God pictured therein. Coming to water, the official had asked, "What is to prevent my being baptized?" This African stood alone in his conversion, and was baptized to confirm it.

---

4. The Ethiopian custom does not use a "family name," like "the Browns, the Smiths." A child's second name is simply his or her father's first name, whose second name was his grandfather's first name, and so on. In Ethiopia, daughters do not change to their husband's name at marriage.

5. The Greek word for "Ethiopian" refers to the area south of today's Egypt. The "Ethiopian" eunuch may have come from Nubia.

Centuries later, the practice of the Church in North Ethiopia was infant baptism. The Aksumite kingdom under Emperor Ezana had adopted Christianity in the fourth decade of the fourth century A.D. In the fifth century, the country opened itself to monks, mostly from Syria. These Saints "engaged in vigorous evangelistic activities that took them to many parts of the empire."[6] Eventually the Ethiopian Orthodox Church came to see itself as the ark of salvation.

On the other hand, the evangelization, which took place in the 20th century in southern Ethiopia, was not generally a broad "people movement." Individuals were believing that God had sent His Son to be their hope. Usually these first generation Christians had to stand alone in their primary belief, often against violent opposition from their families. Individual choice looked foreign to both primal and Orthodox community practices. Furthermore, foreign influences raised suspicion. When Alemu took the step of adult baptism, his family did not understand him. He was thrown out of his Orthodox aunt's home. How he survived from then on is a story in itself.

As they matured, each of the young men's futures was unfolding. John could go to Canada for college, but education was hard to get and difficult to afford in Ethiopia. Negussie was a conscientious student but it was Alemu who stood out as brilliant. Where could he get advanced training, or how afford it?

IN THE MID-SIXTIES, Christians around Wolisso town and the Obbi station were excited about a new biblical training institute which the Sudan Interior Mission had established a hundred miles southwest of them in the town of Jimma. "GBI" they called it, short for Grace Bible Institute.[7] Officials at the school offered Alemu a place in the Institute, but he had no money for entrance. They offered him a scholarship. Alemu argued that he hadn't even the funds for the bus trip to get there. Travel there would mean descending down into the Gibe River valley, crossing a bridge built by the Italians during their

---

6. See Tibebe (2009), *Movement*, 17.
7. Locating GBI at Jimma with its largely Muslim community was questioned by some. One rationale was that Jimma was the second largest city in the realm and a domestic flight hub of Ethiopian Airlines. Back in 1927, the first SIM party had set out to begin their work in Jimma, but had veered off to Wolaitta instead. See H. Wilmott, *The Doors Were Opened* (SIM, 1961).

occupation, and snaking up from the hot gorge to higher and gentler terrain before leveling out at some 4,000 feet in the lush Jimma area. It was John Coleman's little savings stash which helped him go. John's uncalculated investment would yield rich dividends in the future.

ALEMU GOT AN EXCELLENT biblical foundation at Grace Bible Institute, but Negussie got little formal theological education. Still, Negussie was shepherded too. Sometimes outstanding grass-root evangelists would circulate around speaking at conferences and counseling young believers. One such man was Ato Kedamo. (*Ato* is the Ethiopian term for "Mr.," an address showing respect.) He was from the Hadiyya area farther south and he traveled up to Wolisso periodically. A tall, broad shouldered man with tremendous gifts in speaking, Ato Kedamo's passion for the Lord was contagious. His twinkling eyes, expressive, staccato communication and skillful applications made his messages unforgettable. His ministry was highly sought in the countryside and the time would come when he'd be asked to pastor a large church in the capital.

The church to which he was called was not one of the many traditional Ethiopian Orthodox churches which dotted the city and had such ancient roots, but one which had emerged out of the new churches movement which had come to birth in southern Ethiopia in the 20th century. That this newer church's existence was tolerated will be explained in the context of a later chapter, which suggests what may have been the Emperor's strategy.

It was in 1972 that this congregation asked Kedamo to visit them as a pastor candidate. Years after his initial interview in Addis Ababa, he used to tell about his country-boy struggle with going to the capital. It was his habit to tell amusing stories, sometimes about his own foibles, as a vehicle for teaching some principle. When invited to the capital, he had just one suit to his name, a khaki one, made by a roadside tailor in Hossana town. He got it all pressed, but when he arrived in Addis Ababa in the cool season, he found men to be wearing stylish wool suits. He tried to put his best foot forward, but could not help speaking with a down-country Hadiyya accent, not impeccable Amharic. People snickered during the first five minutes of his candidating message, until the solidness of the content and dynamism of his preaching began to dawn on them. After all, he'd not been a student in formal government schools. In the end, he was called to the big city congregation. "Come and hear the preacher who never learned," he later joked about himself.

In those earlier days of his circuit riding through Wolisso, Kedamo was a role model for the three young men. None could have known that many years later, the matured Negussie would eventually get biblical education in preparation to assist Ato Kedamo in the significant ministry in Addis Ababa.

As the years passed, the three friends matured. Separation was not welcome, but adulthood challenged them all. Alemu graduated from Grace Bible Institute and took his first appointment. John left for college in Canada. Negussie looked for further education in Ethiopia.

During their twenties, John and Negussie wrote letters back and forth and pored over each word when the treasured message arrived. One consolation was to look forward to reunion when John would come "home" some summer. John's Canadian friends could hardly have understood the bond between this "Jonathan and David." They'd shared love of the same country, life in the same neighborhood, and had committed themselves to serve the same King. That kind of brotherhood goes far deeper than nation or ethnic designation.

> *Then they kissed each other and wept together—*
> *but David wept the most. Jonathan said to David,*
> *"Go in peace, for we have sworn friendship with each other*
> *in the name of the LORD, saying,*
> *The LORD is witness between you and me,*
> *and between your descendants and my descendants forever."*
> *(1 Samuel 20:41b, 42)*

Chapter 2

DISCOVERING ANCIENT SOVEREIGNTIES

Negussie was becoming an adult just as the unthinkable was about to take place, the dissolution of the Ethiopian kingship. To even begin to grasp the meaning of this event requires some appreciation of Ethiopia's venerable history. As foreigners arriving in this ancient land, we searched for keys to unlock her mysteries. Supplying some of them may help to contextualize this complex community, before we pick up Negussie's story.

Before my husband and I set foot on Ethiopian soil, we began to search for clues that would help us to understand this fascinating land. We learned that Ethiopia's exact identity or boundaries over the eons remains uncertain. A variety of leads can be followed. Chapter two of the Bible refers to "Cush" in earliest biblical times—when the term seemed to mean "beyond Egypt." Moses is recorded as taking an "Ethiopian wife" two thousand years before Christ. In King Solomon's time, "Sheba" may have referred to the vast region stretching from what we now call Sudan to Arabia. In the New Testament book of Acts, a key Ethiopian official asks to be baptized.

During modern times, "Abyssinia" or "Ethiopia" has referred to a nation state lying between the latitudes of 3 to 18 degrees North of the equator and 33 to 48 degrees East of the Prime Meridian. Ethiopia is in the center of "the Horn." Jutting out from the continent's land-mass, "the Horn of East Africa" is outlined by the narrower Red Sea which flows along the coasts of Egypt, Sudan, and Eritrea, and the wider Indian Ocean which is wrapped around Somalia.

Years later we were intrigued to discover that there is a dramatic geographical link between Ethiopia and Israel. Strangely, Ethiopia's broadest geographical contours are generated from Israel. Israel seems far away, located on a land bridge at the crossroads between Asia, Europe, and Africa. But down at the ancient city of Jericho (of Joshua's fame) a signpost reads: "The lowest town on earth." One of its listings points south to Israel's Great Salt Sea. That sea initiates a long geographical fissure extending 5,000 miles southwards, called "the Great Rift." The Rift cuts through Ethiopia, top to bottom. It gashes the earth's surface and creates natural water reservoirs from Israel's Dead Sea to Mozambique. The Rift stands out as Ethiopia's most dramatic land feature. In the north, mountain ranges fall off to the east and west from craggy heights that resemble the tan-green spine of a crocodile crouched north to south on desert sands. From stunning peaks up to 14,000 feet, the topography abruptly plunges eastward to the moonscape of the Danakil Desert, below sea level. The jagged pinnacles, deep gorges and flat buttes of the awesome Simien Mountains dissipate westward into the desert lowlands of Sudan. In the south of Ethiopia, between high but gentler mountain ranges, lies a string of Rift-created lakes in valleys that stretch on toward Tanzania's Serengeti plain.

These landforms we would see bit by bit in the future, but upon our arrival, the capital alone was more than we could take in. Like many a traveler wandering in its streets, we were puzzled by signs: "The Gihon Hotel," "Road to Nazareth," "Queen of Sheba Restaurant" or "St. Michael's Church." When we asked people their names, often they'd respond "Abraham, Yisak, Yakob, Dawit, Solomon, Matteos, Yohannes, Mariam, Marta," or the like. Was this Africa? While many Ethiopians wore western clothing on the city streets, some were in national garb woven from glistening white cotton which looked more Middle Eastern than African. At a restaurant, the menu was adjusted to the weekly fasting days of the Orthodox Church, devoid of meat. Foods are chosen in accordance with Old Covenant dietary laws, such as the avoidance of pig meat. The music we heard from radios didn't sound very "African," sometimes Jewish in tempo and tone. Where were we?

In gift shops, tourists were buying oil paintings, lampshades, silk scarves, or pamphlets, depicting the national epic, the *Kebra Negest* ("the Glory of Kings"), the story of the Queen of Sheba and King Solomon, who lived in the 10th century BC. Ethiopia's present king took his title from Solomon, calling himself "Lion of the Tribe of

Judah." We knew scripture enough to appreciate this biblical reference as a prophetic identification of the tribe from which the Messiah was to arise. But we wondered how this title commanded such a focus in modern Ethiopia. We went looking for the Emperor's Palace. Impressive! We stood at its iron-barred gate flanked by stone lions with crowns, and out on the grounds were real caged lions who roared, to our three sons' delight.

As we took a taxi around Addis Ababa, we discovered Ethiopian Orthodox churches to be the center of almost every neighborhood, although interspersed by an occasional hub around a mosque. The symbol of the cross appeared everywhere. Whether on churches, in shops, on magazines, or around necks, Ethiopian crosses seemed to symbolize the nation. They are repeated in multiple forms from art to advertising, from large crosses held up by the Orthodox priests, to tiny ones worn as jewelry. They are produced in gold, silver, brass, wood, and embroidery, with a great variety of designs. We began to wonder what these crosses really signified. Was it their national symbol? An art object? A receptacle of history? How much were these embellished crosses connected to the execution stake of the Lamb of God?

Old Covenant or New Covenant, Jewish and Christian symbols seemed to be interchanged with abandon. In a travelogue we ran onto an anecdote, which typified the "folk" understanding, we sometimes met. Travelers told of an exchange while dining in a lovely Ethiopian restaurant in Addis Ababa. They had just returned from seeing the famous rock churches at the 12th century site of Lalibela. King Lalibela had tried to create an Ethiopian "Jerusalem," having monolithic churches hewn out of red rock. The most famous is in the shape of a cross, and was excavated entirely below ground level. The graceful waitress, dressed in the white national costume embroidered with a lovely cross, heard about the travelers' trip. "Lalibela was a personal friend of Jesus Christ," she remarked proudly. "Oh, how could that be?" they asked with surprise, "for Christ was in the 1st century, and Lalibela the 12th!" Looking perplexed but proud, this daughter of the ancient empire raised her chin and before turning to go, stated categorically, "We were Christians in Ethiopia long before Christ."

AFTER GETTING THESE FIRST impressions, we kept looking for keys to unlock some of these enigmas. One was hidden from our eyes, yet seemed to be the golden key. This symbol seemed even more deeply fixed in the culture than the cross. Above all others in the myriad of ecclesiastical ceremonies and symbolism of the Ethiopian Orthodox Tewahedo Church, the Ark of the Covenant is the focal point. An Orthodox church is constituted a church by having its own replica of the Ark, much as a synagogue has a Torah.

Ethiopia has claimed to have had the original Ark for centuries. People ask, can this insistence remain today? Yale University Press in association with the Institute of Ethiopian Studies in 1993 published a beautiful collection of Ethiopian art called *African Zion*. In its opening chapter, called "Dreaming of Jerusalem," this statement summarizes the place of the Ark:

> The Ethiopian claim [...] involves the appropriation of the direct line of descent from King Solomon himself, and the assertion that the presence of God had been brought to Ethiopia in the Ark of the Covenant. This presence meant that the Ethiopian emperor ruled in a New Israel, and it gave him a preeminent position among Christian kings even above Constantine the Great, who may have possessed hundreds of relics but nothing to rival the Ark.[8]

Israelis may insist that the Ark is hidden beneath Jerusalem's Temple Site, but Ethiopia claims that it was secretly carried to Ethiopia during Solomon's time, that it has been moved to various places in Ethiopia and now rests in the city of Axum. Whether factual or not, Ethiopian writers demonstrate this confidence, one example of which was published in 1992:

> The original Holy Ark of the Covenant which was brought by Menelik from Jerusalem before the destruction of the Temple by Nebuchadnezzar is kept in the sanctuary of the church of Sion Mariam (S. Mary of Sion) at Aksum, the holiest of the holy churches of Ethiopia. This has made Aksum a source of religious inspiration to this day and Sion Mariam is considered the mother church of the more than 22,000 Ethiopian Orthodox churches with 250,000 clergy that exist in Ethiopia today.[9]

---

8. R. Grierson *et al.*, *African Zion* (Yale Univ. Press, 1993), pp. 4f.
9. Belai G., *Ethiopian Civilization* (Belai Giday, 1992), 15. Note the reference

Eventually it began to dawn on us that Israel was the root of all the symbols. Bit by bit we came to the conclusion that the Great Rift's finger pointing from Ethiopia north to Israel is a telling one, for more than geological reasons.[10] For centuries, Jerusalem has been in many senses the lodestar of Ethiopia.

We found that whether we studied the national epic, the historical sites, the ecclesiastical system, the art, the music, or even the greetings of Ethiopia, overtones of Israel are everywhere. Ethiopia bases the calendar on the lunar rather than the solar year, as did the Hebrews, and rather than Asia's "year of the rat" or the "horse," Ethiopia's are "the year of Matthew," or "Mark," "Luke," or "John."

Ethiopia boasts the longest Christian heritage of any nation in Africa, and constitutes probably the most Jewish country outside of Israel herself. With a history of relative kindness and peace toward Muslims, the Ethiopian populace joins in devotion to the shrines of Jerusalem, with only the largely unreached peoples on the fringes of the country unaware of that biblical nexus.

Lines of communication, immigration, and pilgrimage between Ethiopia and Israel have been recorded for three millennia. Understandably, ethnic and religious ties became knotted and mysterious to unwind.

King Lalibela is thought to have constructed his simulated Jerusalem in the mountains of northern Ethiopia as a substitute for the exhausting pilgrimages his people were making to the Holy City, sometimes dying on the way. Modern explorers rated the constellation of rock churches as one of "the wonders of the world." I saw them in an encyclopedia in my childhood. It would be long into our Ethiopian pilgrimage, however, before we would have the privilege of visiting there. When our prop plane landed on a dirt airstrip in the valley below Lalibela and our transit bus reached the little town, Charles and I began to see that if we got out of sight of the two or three modern hotels and the tin roofs of an occasional public building, it would seem as if time had stood still. The circular home construction out of local rocks, or the apparel of priests, or

---

to Zion/Sion. The mother church of Ethiopia is called "Mary of Zion," the Mother of the Messiah. Behind the Ark lies Israel.

10. See map on p. xiv.

the ecclesiastical Ge'ez language whispered in the vaulted monolithic churches, all seemed to differ little from when the underground structures were carved out of the rocks eight hundred years before.

Today, Ethiopians can fly to Lalibela, and they jet to Israel too. Thousands of pilgrims go yearly from Ethiopia to Israel, where they can find an Ethiopian Jewish synagogue or an Ethiopian Orthodox church or monastery that has been maintained for centuries. Years after our sons were grown, Charles and I sat one memorable day in the circular outer court of the old incense-scented Orthodox church, absorbing its total Ethiopian aura, yet we were in Jerusalem. In the Old City, Ethiopian monks live on the roof above the Ethiopian Orthodox chapel, the door of which opens onto the courtyard shared with the Church of the Holy Sepulchre. A monk who was concerned about a sick brother discovered Charles was a doctor and spoke Amharic, so promptly asked for a medical consultation on the roof. After a delightful interchange, the kindly monks led us from their high perch down through the back entrance into their ancient holy shrine, a more intimate exposure than we'd ever been allowed in their homeland.

JEWISH TIES WITH ISRAEL are even older than Christian. Ethiopia's ancient and mysterious community of "Black Jews" has been an enigma many have sought to solve. This community's 20th century pilgrimage has been fascinating. They made world news with Israel's daring airlifts of thousands of *Beta Israel* ("House of Israel") to the Holy Land in 1984 and 1991. These deliverances became known as "Operation Moses" and "Operation Solomon."[11] Israel called it "the essence of what the State of Israel is about," and proudly quoted the Ethiopian Jewish proverb, "The hungry go to food, the thirsty go to water, but I go to Jerusalem."

Had this community once harbored the Ark? They say it was taken from Ethiopian monks who were keeping it on an island in Lake Tana to Axum in the Christian era. Axum has been the heart of Ethiopian Orthodoxy since the rule of King Ezana. Axum's history stretches back centuries before that, claiming the palace ruins

---

11. See accounts in T. Parffit, *Operation Moses* (Weidenfeld and Nicolson, 1985); K. Shelemay and N. Berger, *The Jews of Ethiopia* (Jewish Museum etc., 1986); R. Gruber, *Rescue* (Atheneum, 1987).

of the Queen of Sheba, and a ruin of an ancient temple at nearby Yeha. Fascination with the Ark has brought mystics and adventurers to Ethiopia for centuries. As recent as the 1990s, writer Graham Hancock's own quest for the Ark unfolds like a gripping mystery story, 600 pages long.[12]

Like many others, we too eventually flew over the great Simien Mountains to Axum, the dusty streets of which still seem to breathe with the mists of antiquity. We were moved to see and touch the solid reality of Axum's colossal stone stelae, inexplicably raised about the time of Christ. In the Sunday morning dawn, we stood on the roadside and witnessed long processions of the white-clad faithful circling the town behind priests, each carrying their own church's *tabot* (replica of the Ark), just as they have done for hundreds of years. As foreigners, we were allowed just close enough to the church that claims to house Solomon's Ark to glimpse its green dome through the trees. Only one priest is allowed to attend it, and he for life.

These roots passed on in sacred literature and art, in festivals and fasts, and reinforced by the wedding of church and state, underlie the enormous sense of pride among Ethiopians. It is as if they would say to the world, "Our history proves us supreme—we have lived by the best of both faiths, Jewish when God gave the Old Covenant, and Christian when He gave the New. Are we not the keepers of the Ark of the Covenant?" Surely they are a unique people, some would say an eschatological people.

On the other hand, while Ethiopia's best-known history revolves around the peoples of these Covenants, a vast area of the present nation is peopled by ethnic groups who are relative newcomers to the region, having migrated into what is called Ethiopia in the last 500 years. Away from the central highlands, out from Amhara influence where the Ark is venerated, out among the Muslims in the lowlands or among the traditional religionists, of the south, other images hold sway: minarets point skyward in the towns, and huge sacred trees soar above sites of spirit worship in remote regions. Jerusalem seems far away.

---

12. See G. Hancock, *The Sign and the Seal* (Simon & Schuster, 1993).

History doesn't supply all the keys to a country. Geography plays a powerful role as well. Reared amid the flat fields of Kansas, I grew up with geography based on a simple square grid. In Ethiopia, little could be marked plain "north, south, east, or west." It seemed just "up or down or winding." When trying to get a sense of physical direction in this complex terrain, I came to imagine the map of Ethiopia as a 1,000 by 1,500 mile diamond-shaped clock face with the capital, Addis Ababa, in the center. Precious few tarmac roads radiate out from the hub. These main roads do not resemble straight wheel spokes, but undulate over tangled mountain passes, down into deep river gorges and snake back up to breathtaking heights. Only an air route map with straight lines "like the crow flies" projects a hub-and-spoke pattern, radiating out from the capital to distant points around Ethiopia's circumference. With Addis Ababa as the clock's center, Asmara would lie where the clock hand points northward to twelve o'clock, Harar roughly along a hand pointing eastward toward three, Dilla southward toward six, Gambella westward toward nine.

Topographical features generally cut through Ethiopia vertically from north to south, the Rift's high spine and deep fault splitting east from west. Sociologically speaking, however, an intangible division is discernible by imagining a horizontal line cutting across the country from east to west, a little above the capital. This imaginary line (parallel to the equator, which runs through Kenya a little lower on the globe) divides the nation into "the north" and "the south." These two terms are repeatedly used not only as a physical distinction, but in discussions of the social, racial, political and religious history of this ancient land. Negussie's Wolisso town was positioned within the Oromo arc, and below the imaginary line, so it was considered to be "the south."

Much has been written about Ethiopia's northland. Were we to trace the capitals from which Ethiopian kings have ruled, locate sites of historic battles, visit Jewish communities or Orthodox shrines, they would overwhelmingly be positioned in the north. If we focus upon catastrophes for which Ethiopia is most known in the last half-century, her devastating famines and the Eritrean–Ethiopian War, both were largely suffered in the north. Only the upheaval of her Marxist-Leninist Revolution spread over the whole contemporary face of the country.

So what of the south? What of the southerners, the more numerous, usually deeper-complexioned peoples whose small acreages tilt along the angles of greener mountains, cluster in the verdant valleys of the central heartlands, or stretch out into bushlands roamed by nomads following their herds? Who knows much about them outside of Ethiopia, except for an occasional missionary or anthropologist? Who has cared what they have experienced over the ages, or suffered in the last quarter of this century when the world's media eye was on the north? How might we become aware of the predicament and the potential of these little-known people groups lost in the mists of rugged ranges and non-history?

Although this book is sensitive to northern predominance in Ethiopia's history and is intertwined with recent events that also took place in the north, it is largely written about people of the southern heartland and its fringe of primal people. Theirs is a fascinating story, one which is taking wings. Peasants and pastoralists have eked-out their existence across the vast face of Ethiopia for centuries. Their isolation and lack of literacy kept them unknown and unknowing. But a great awakening has occurred in southern Ethiopia this last half century. Something with more longevity than Marxism-Leninism has begun to change the present and the future of this great land. True, southerners who were sent to the northern battlefront served more often as gun fodder than as generals in the recent prolonged conflict over Eritrea. But like Negussie, many have been valiant in an unseen war. They have proved faithful to an unseen Captain. For those with eyes to see, His presence has been an unmistakable reality behind unexplainable victories won "not by might and not by power, but by God's Spirit."

> *When the queen of Sheba heard about the fame of Solomon*
> *and his relation to the name of the LORD,*
> *she came to test him with hard questions [...]*
> *When the queen of Sheba saw all the wisdom of Solomon*
> *and the palace he had built [...]*
> *She said to the king,*
> *"The report I heard in my own country*
> *about your achievements and your wisdom is true [...]*

*Praise be to the LORD your God,
who has delighted in you and placed you on the throne of Israel.
Because of the LORD's eternal love for Israel,
he has made you king, to maintain justice and righteousness." [...]
King Solomon gave the queen of Sheba all she desired and asked for,
besides what he had given her out of his royal bounty.
Then she left and returned with her retinue to her own country.*

(1 Kings 10:1, 4, 6, 9, 13)

Chapter 3
MEETING THE NORTH

In the center of a knot of thousands of white-clad people, turbaned priests robed with richly decorated capes stood on the porch steps. Each held up a ceremonial cross or a brilliantly colored velvet umbrella. They swayed slowly to a deep drumbeat, while their singing, half chant, half music, dignified the very air. Behind them stood the walls of the town's main Orthodox church. We'd seen it before, but not at such a moment of celebration.

Timket, they called this biggest holiday of the year. The word meant "baptism," and commemorates the baptism of Christ, or Epiphany in the Eastern church. Timket is the highest holiday of the Ethiopian Orthodox church year. Most of the town's populace was gathered to re-enact this scene which had been repeated over the realm every January for centuries. We'd never seen anything like it. Charles and I stood with our language class on the outskirts of the crowd, straining to take it all in.

Our school had been permitted to operate in this small northern city by permission of the King. Mina Moen, our language teacher, was using the occasion to orientate our class to the strange culture in which we found ourselves. We'd never been inside one of these churches scattered over the country, but we could see that their architecture was similar, often a six-sided structure with the raised cupola in the center. Three concentric circles comprise the building's architecture. The innermost hides away the church's Ark of the Covenant; the next comprises the premises of the priests and their activities; and the outside provides a court into which ordinary people could come. Ceremonies were usually directed from the porch encircling the building, before which the people stood, and were conducted in Ge'ez, the holy language of worship, much as Latin was used among

Catholics. Ge'ez was not understood by the populace, and sometimes not even by the priests. Like its derivative, Amharic, Ge'ez can be sounded out phonetically without the speaker's grasping the meaning. Just this once a year, on Timket, each church's replica of the Ark, called the *tabot*, would be brought out, veiled in cloth upon a priest's head and canopied by umbrellas. In fact, the Ark would spend the night in an open field of encampment. In the daytime, the people would be sprinkled with waters of baptism, a symbol of cleansing and recommitment.

We expatriates stood there as outsiders in many senses of the word. Few greeted us, for in the north the *missionoch* (Amharic puts -*och* at the end of the word to pluralize it) were generally unwelcome. It was understood that permission for language learning was all that the mission had been given, and we were not to approach people with "new religious ideas." Not eager to call attention to ourselves, our class did not stay long. The next year, perhaps, some of us could watch in comparative anonymity from a window or rooftop above an intersection in Addis Ababa. From there one can melt into thousands lining the streets and see the priestly clusters around each Ark as it passes by, hear their haunting music, and sometimes spot an enthusiastic celebrant dancing before an Ark, as King David did in his day. Of course Israel rallied to God's single Ark, for it was prescribed that there would be only one Tabernacle, and later, only one Temple. When moving camp, Israel's golden Ark was carried on poles by priests or drawn by oxen. Ethiopian Arks are small enough to be carried on a head. They are flat, perhaps to symbolize the tablet of the Law kept in the original Ark, but their dimensions do not reflect the presence of the seventh article of furniture in the Tabernacle as prescribed by God in the pattern given to Moses, the crowning cover of the Ark, which was called the Mercy Seat.[13]

As we walked back to our school after that first encounter with Timket, the twenty-some of us peppered Mina with questions about various elements of the pageantry. Since we were from half a doz-

---

13. Resting like a lid above the Ark (containing the tables of the Law) is the "Mercy Seat" (KJV term), or "atonement cover" as the NIV translates it. "There, above the cover between the two cherubim that are over the ark of the Testimony, I will meet with you and give you all my commands for the Israelites" (Exodus 25:22).

en English-speaking countries, our accents varied. She had tried to prepare us for the occasion, but we'd barely grasped what we were hearing. Our students from the British Commonwealth might have understood a little more than we two, but Orthodoxy was virtually unknown to American Christians, with our short New World history, our multitude of denominations, and our country's careful separation of church and state.

As we walked back to our walled-in compound, children shouted *ferenji* ("foreigner") and tossed an occasional rock at us as we passed along the dry, rocky path between rock-constructed homes. Mina explained that we were not to use the word "Coptic" any more, what the church had been called for centuries. The Ethiopian *Abuna*, highest church leader, had from the fourth century been appointed in Egypt. In 1959 that ended. The leader was now to be appointed in Ethiopia, and the church was not to be called "Coptic," which refers to Egypt, but to be called "Ethiopian Orthodox Tewahedo Church."

THIS ALEXANDRIAN BRANCH OF the Orthodox church had broken away from the Eastern Orthodox churches after the Council of Chalcedon in 451 AD. The disagreement involved the understanding of the nature of Christ, the Alexandrians not wishing to divide His nature into divine and human. That decision would keep them separated from Eastern Orthodoxy to this day. It would largely limit their view of Christ's role to a divine one. Over the years, not seeing Christ as a human mediator "who in all points was tempted like as we are" (Hebrews 4:15) would lead to a yearning for a human advocate, someone who could intercede with God. Christ's mother seemed to have become that intercessor for them. Mary was of all saints most adored. Thirty-three feasts honor Mary in a year.[14]

That doctrinal argument was not the only element that distinguished Ethiopian Orthodoxy from other Eastern Christian communions. What further distinguished Ethiopia's Orthodoxy was its unusual Jewishness. For instance, on the surface, the Timket holiday seemed less to celebrate Christ's baptism, found in the New Testament, than the Ark of the Covenant, found in the Old

---

14. Aymro W. and J. Motovu, *The Ethiopian Orthodox Church* (Ethiopian Orthodox Mission, 1970), 59.

Testament. Add to this the weight of the nationalistic factor, for the Ark is at the center of Ethiopia's epic about Solomon and Sheba, the authentication on which the kingship relied.

Observing the Ethiopian attitude of deep pride set me to wondering. Had they'd inherited an innate sense of being related to royal seed? Were they reflecting centuries of being in charge? Meeting such proud Ethiopians reinforced my conviction that reaction to skin color was simply a culturally conditioned bias. I relished their pride! I did not find the Amharas of Ethiopia's north burdened with that "chip on the shoulder" which can be sensed where subjugation has taken place. They'd hardly even been colonized.

LANGUAGE SCHOOL OPENED VARIOUS windows onto the Ethiopian culture. A culture's thinking comes through in the way they express things in language. The very contrast with our own forms awakened us to Ethiopian distinctives. We would say, "I dropped it." They would say "It fell from me." In English we could bluntly answer "yes" or "no." They could say a simple "yes" but Amharic had no single word stating "no." Hour after hour we studied grammar and usage and worked laboriously with Ethiopians, called "informants," nationals who were employed to drill us in simple conversations and correct our pronunciation. In the afternoons we ventured out from the school compound to visit in homes. "You should go to Indalla's house for one of your home visits," one informant named Birhanu suggested to language students. "Who is Indalla?" we asked. "Go and see," he said with a significant air of mystery.

Charles and I tagged along with someone who knew the route through the rocky paths between small huts, each enclosed in its own compound, across the one main tarmac road to continue winding through another maze of paths and alleys on the other side of town. Finally we arrived at a miserably dilapidated mud and straw house, its roof tilting as if almost ready to slide into the weedy garden around it. Chickens scattered as we ducked through the low door into the dark interior lit only by the door opening, one window and growing gaps in the construction.

When our eyes adjusted we began to realize a whole crowd of students was gathered in the little room, their attention fixed upon their host. We were brought up short to find him to be a sightless leper.

The students were asking him questions, and although he could not see to read, he was using scripture to answer them, passages he knew by memory. They hung on Indalla's every word, which was usually a statement from God's word. Most of the students had grown up in the Orthodox culture. The holy language of Ge'ez, in which Orthodox services were conducted, had entered their ears but had hardly been able to enter their minds. They were thirsty to know what God actually said to them—and in a language they could understand. We could not follow much Amharic yet, but we could feel the vibrancy of what was going on between the students and Indalla.

In time we learned the connection between our informant and Indalla. Birhanu had been an intelligent but searching son of an Orthodox priest, nearly desperate to find answers for life. On a street corner he'd seen the leper, Indalla—whose disease was no longer active—surrounded by an assortment of the ragtag orphans to whom he gave a home. The man was selling a magazine called "Word of Life." The two talked. Indalla sent the young seeker to someone who could, he thought, better minister to this young man in his quest. Indalla sent him to Mina, our language teacher, and the result was his discovery of the person of Christ and the beginning of a whole new life. The school was allowed no freedom to evangelize, but people by their own choice could come to the compound. Students were the ones who were more inclined to take the risk of investigating. Mina was a keen Bible teacher with deep concern for students, and could answer their questions in excellent Amharic. Many put their trust in the Savior.

As the shadows lengthened that memorable evening, we tore ourselves away from the unlikely man in the unlikely hut, whose chain of significance had years before led him to the Savior while at SIM's Shashemane Leprosarium in the south. His leprosy had been arrested, although his sight could not be restored. He was overjoyed to have found spiritual light and healing. His joy was infectious. Indalla's simple, transformed life, simply throbbed with reality. Students who were honestly seeking were not too proud to come to him. He spoke life to them in words and in song. I will never forget sitting in that dirt-floored hut watching that blind leper lead the "intelligentsia" of the town in lines of his favorite song: *B'zeya alem hazen, b'abatey bet, hool geezay desita b'Yesus sim!* It meant "In this

SAHLE TILAHUN AT SIXTEEN (DEBRE BERHAN, 1965)

world there is sadness, yet in my Father's house all the time [there is] joy, in Jesus' name!" Verse after verse added new key words listing what we can expect on earth: pain, sorrow, illness, tears, and death. Nevertheless, expect joy in our Father's house! This man had no eyes to see his own pitiful abode, but he clearly saw the security of his Father's house.

Encounters with believers such as these had a transforming effect on the foreigners passing through language school. We had come thinking ourselves to be the "haves" going to the "have-nots," the "educated" going to the "uneducated," the spiritually "initiated" going to those who had yet to hear. Over and over in individual Christians we found a freshness, a reality, and a power beyond our pale Western version of Christianity.

DIFFICULT AS LANGUAGE WAS, we were surprised by the depth of relationships that we developed with a handful of Ethiopians. Friendship and time seem graced with a different quality in Ethiopian culture than in the West. Even the greetings reveal this, for before anything else, inquiries as to the health and well being of each family member, sometimes even the cow, are made. People, not possessions, are primary. Furthermore, time is invested in relationships—time drinking coffee and just "being" together.

We language school students were not received with enthusiasm by the Orthodox townspeople, and we found ourselves to be lonely and hungry for personal relationships with our adopted countrymen. As it happened, night after night, a soft knock at the door of our two-room apartment would indicate the shy presence of a student who took a liking to our family. Sahle Tilahun was about seventeen, a slight lad, with wavy hair and a dimple in his chin. He called himself an orphan, though he later confided that wasn't the literal truth, but he lived like one. On his own since he was ten, he'd climbed up from his home deep in the canyon below Debre Berhan with people selling eggs, and never returned. He'd scrounged out a life as a shepherd boy until he won a teacher's heart and was allowed to enter school. When we met, he was in his sixth or seventh year of study.

Like us, he too was lonely, and more open with us than any Ethiopian I ever met. Sahle evidenced a disarming simplicity and childlike warmth that we found irresistible. Not seeming to be endowed with the usual Ethiopian reserve, Sahle's feelings broke through on his countenance: his eyes large in a sober face, or twinkling with mirth, or widening with wonder. They'd often flit here and there with nervous insecurity and then would grow lustrous when he sensed any response to his winsome sharing of himself.

Although his long stays sometimes exhausted us as parents who had to get up with children during the night, Sahle's excuse for coming by was to help us with our Amharic. Amharic has 250 some letters in an alphabet that is transcribed with symbols strange to the Western eye. We asked him to write key scripture verses on cards in his careful script. As a new believer, he was hungry to learn the very Scriptures we were asking him to help us pronounce.

How had Sahle turned up at the language school? Not very long before, the deep yearnings of his heart had led him to walk to the mission, as he put it, to "ask about the Lord." Mina was away at the time, so he approached a language school student on the grounds with the flat question, "Can you tell me about God?" It was the rainy season, and under an umbrella, the man explained what he could—with the English and Amharic they could piece together between them—and asked if Sahle wanted to place his trust in a very personal way in this Savior. Yes, he earnestly did! Sahle was led in a simple prayer and went away rejoicing—so much that he fairly leapt across the puddles!

The next day he returned for services, which happened to center upon Matthew 6, Jesus' teaching about trusting God's care and not worrying about even basic necessities. At that juncture of his life, Sahle actually had no provision for food to eat and owned little to wear. He took the Lord's promise literally and left the meeting full of faith, whispering to himself excitedly, "He's going to care for me and feed me like the birds!" He tried it out immediately. God honored his unquestioning faith that first day with unexpected invitations to share someone's lunch, and then someone else's supper. Next came a surprising offer of a room to live in. The assurance of his Lord's care began so to penetrate Sahle's heart that not worrying, but instead "seeking first his kingdom and his righteousness" (Matthew 6:33) became a life principle which was to be tested and proven again and again in future years.

Sahle came often to the mission. At Christmas time, he reached out to our little first-grader, who got to come home from boarding school. The school took a Saturday off to explore the deep canyon immediately behind the school compound. Loneliness gets keener at holiday times. The Ethiopian calendar, being lunar, celebrated Christmas in early January, leaving the expatriates in town feeling blank on December 25th. Mina carefully planned for both Christmases. To friends at home, I later wrote this summary:

> Ethiopian Christmas, January 8th, brought 200 some to our yard, surrounded by grass roofed homes, to see a dramatic outdoor Christmas play (Sahle played one part) presented by nationals, and to hear a personal word as to what this God Incarnate means to each, from a student, a mother, a teacher, and a blind leper (dear Indalla). What an opportunity, and what a sight across the grass—women in white *shammas*, some with bright parasols, keen eyed students, fathers in Khaki jodhpurs or an occasional business suit, barefoot children playing around the fringes. Afterward there were sweets and tea for our national staff, and gifts for each family, received with winsome soberness, and opened at home. If you happened to send us a card with a scene from the Christmas story, it is now probably on some Ethiopian wall, brightening the brown interior with its portrayal, a verse in Amharic inscribed thereon.

When our language course was cut short in January because Charles was needed at a hospital in the south, we bid Sahle good-bye, little expecting to see the young chap again. It was a poignant leave taking. We had hardly realized how hungry our hearts had been to relate to Ethiopians and how few we had shared with on this personal level. Only our Lord knew that He would be weaving our lives together with Sahle's repeatedly in the unknown future. And although Negussie down at Wolisso and Sahle up at Debre Berhan were very different people and were growing up in very different areas, as it would turn out, their lives would intersect each other's repeatedly as well.

Jesus said to them,
"[...] And there were many in Israel with leprosy
in the time of Elisha the prophet, yet not one of them was cleansed—
only Naaman the Syrian."
And all the people in the synagogue were furious
when they heard this.
                      (Luke 4:23a, 27–28)

Chapter 4

MEETING THE SOUTH

What a contrast from the cold rocky north when we arrived in the south. Driving down-country from the capital, we were amazed at the beauty of the gentler mountains and stream-fed valleys which increased with lushness the further south we traveled. The rectangular stone-and-thatch homes seen on the rocky crags of the north were, in the south, replaced by haystack-shaped dwellings covered with long grass from peak to ground, laid over an inner wooden pole frame. A door was the only opening, and homes were surrounded with small acreages planted with corn and *ensete* (false banana). Our destination was SIM's Soddo Hospital in the heart of the Wolaitta ethnic group, where a vibrant first-generation church had been born in the 1930s.

How had that happened? God apparently used the Emperor to unlock the door to mission work in his land. In the vacuum left after the death of King Menelik II, Ras Tafari from Harar proved to be the master of diplomatic counterpoint and rose to the top. As *Nigusa Negest* ("King of Kings") he consolidated his rule over an empire which included not only Amharas, but many other ethnic groups as well.

As head of state, the Ethiopian Emperor was wedded to the church too. The Orthodox hierarchy was solidly Amhara, and churches were placed in most cities of the Empire, accompanying the warrior landlords who were paid for their services with something like medieval fiefdoms. For many of the southerners, this resulted in enormous loss of their land to the ruling Amharas. A deep sense of subjugation was the result.

As a young man, Emperor Haile Selassie was a progressive ruler who sought to unite and modernize his nation and thereby bring his aloof culture into the twentieth century. While attempting this, he maneuvered continually in order to maintain power, playing off one faction against another, whether political, geographical or religious. These strategies no doubt contributed to his willingness to allow missionaries to enter Ethiopia, something which the Orthodox Church had largely blocked up to that time.

THE LITTLE CLINIC AT Wolisso near which Negussie was born around 1950 was present because the Emperor had in the 1920s been open to the offer of Dr. Thomas Lambie, to start a work in southern Ethiopia. Due to the convergence of many factors including swollen rivers and earlier friendships, the first mule party heading from Addis Ababa southwestward for Jimma veered south. The early arrivers found a welcome which led them to begin their work in the provinces of Wolaitta, Hadiyya, Kambaata, and Sidamo in the south central highlands. Most people in these areas were subjugated to landowners. The Emperor had given missions permission only to work with these peoples, most of whom had no written language, were illiterate, and lived in subservient fear of spirits and Satan.

Just when small groups of believers were gathering together, Italy marched into Ethiopia in 1936 to colonize it. Fledgling churches had to be left behind when the Italians forced foreigners out of the country. Around a hundred in Wolaitta had been baptized as Christians. They had only the book of Mark translated into their language, and very few of these southern peoples had yet learned to read.

While exiled in England, the Emperor enlisted the help of the British and was able to retake his country from Italy in 1941.[15] By 1945, missionaries were returning to the south to assess the damage. They expected to find only a tattered remnant of the body of believers they left behind. Instead, they discovered that during the Italian occupation, while missionaries were gone, some 10,000 had cast their lot with Jesus Christ! They'd been reached through Ethiopians who had proclaimed Him as Lord to their people. Westerners looked on in amazement as they uncovered what seemed to be a new chapter in the book of Acts.

---

15. The campaign is reported in detail in A. Mockler, *Haile Selassie's War* (Random House, 1984).

By the time the expatriates returned, unique forms of church life had developed within the congregations marked by lay leadership and indigenous music. Missionaries were welcomed—but not to evangelize so much as to train and heal and help facilitate the work of national evangelists who were already networking into other provinces with the gospel. It was in this context that we were invited to join the medical work at Soddo.

HAVING BEGUN TO DECIPHER symbols of cultural expression in the north, we looked for more clues in this southern context. People generally treated us with curiosity rather than hostility, and often with warmth. Setting up a household introduced us to more nuances of cultural language. The student who helped in our home coached me on standards of dress for women, such as the unacceptability of sleeveless blouses (immodest) or jeans (masculine). I tried to tie a silk scarf over my soft brown hair like the local women did, gathering it together at the nape of the neck. We both had to laugh when mine kept sliding off, not having firm ringlets to hold it up.

When we first arrived, the contrast between the primal and Christian communities astounded me. The hospital admission form included listing the patient's religion. Most patients answered with the word *Saitan* ("Satan"). The pervasive atmosphere of suffering overwhelmed me. When I looked out the window to see a paraplegic crawling past on the ground, or I answered the door, only to draw back from a face destroyed by yaws, I was afraid I could never smile again. Selma Bergsten, a seasoned missionary, sensed my struggle and began to tell me stories about local people, talking about so-and-so's history, their immediate family, uncles and aunts, their marriage, new baby, even their cow—which Selma had learned to inquire about— the kind of basic life elements which are common to people in every culture. When we started being invited to homes and were drawn into conversation around the fire while munching corn, or drinking coffee, life began to take on warmth again. Never mind the salt and butter Wolaittas put in coffee, we were coming to love the people. Often restless in a long national church service, our sons awaited the reward after the meeting. They followed their noses to the local home from which was emanating the delicious, spicy aroma of Ethiopia's national specialty, *injera* and *wat*.[16] Our sons, Johnathan, Tim, and Nat couldn't get enough of this Ethiopian feast!

As I began to know Christians, their joy overwhelmed me. On the other hand, it sometimes stabbed my heart. My first memory of the Blind School was watching a string of little students, hand in hand, picking their way across the stones of a stream on their way to the haystack church. Their voices rang out happily. Suddenly the familiar tune awakened me to the words, *Amlak cher l'nay* ("God is good to me").

Just like the first believers, I couldn't help wondering why these responsive traditional religionists had failed to hear about Christ until the 20th century, in a land which had been known as "Christian" since antiquity. I tried to view the question through Wolaitta eyes. Somehow Amhara-dominated Orthodoxy with its churches dotted over the land had seemed to belong to the rulers who had subjugated the southern peasantry. They had sometimes seen an Ark paraded around a church and might have learned there were feasts and fasts proclaimed on the church calendar, but most had not perceived any message for themselves, no message about a Savior. They began to grasp that good news from the foreign messengers in the 1930s and thereafter from those first converts whose lives had been transformed by the Spirit of God. A sense of freedom broke out. They no longer needed to grovel in fear and appeasement before spirits and witch doctors and above all, death.

When the first believers discovered that there had been nearly a 2,000-year gap between the Ethiopian eunuch in Acts 8 and this modern-day outpouring of the Spirit among themselves, they were puzzled. They asked the first missionaries, "How could it have taken you that long to reach us with this all-important message?" They looked out at their valleys and up at the mountain ranges which stretched on and on to one people group after another who were living in the bondage of fear and treachery toward each other. "We

---

16. *Injera* is made from *teff* flour, little of which is grown outside of Ethiopia. It is usually cooked as a soft sourdough pancake on a huge clay griddle about two feet across. It is folded like a napkin and one is given to each person. It is then used, bit by bit, to pick up mouthfuls of the *wat* sauces being served. *Wat* sauces are concocted in great variety, using beef, chicken, pork, or fish, and various vegetables such as lentils, cabbage, potatoes, and onions, all richly spiced with garlic and a variety of hot spices.

are not going to let it take that long for these people to know!" they announced.

And so it was that very early in the movement's development, a legion of lay evangelists moved by the Holy Spirit, not by foreign organizational strategies, went out on their mules and often bare feet across those rugged mountains at great personal cost—sometimes of their lives—to get the word of Jesus Christ to those who had not heard. No radios, newspapers, TV, telephones—just simple telling from person to person or messenger to group gathered under a tree or around a fire. Traditional religionists listened to the amazing and thrilling news of One stronger than the Satan whom they had struggled daily to appease. They came to understand that the Son of God loved rather than hated them, that He had visited the world in the flesh, died in hopeless mankind's place, and had risen to give life to all who would receive Him. Those who feared Satan too much, or made their living on witchcraft, fought the new message and all its proponents bitterly. Yet the new hope spread like fire on the mountains. Wolaitta Christians seemed gifted with a straightforward sense of responsibility to get the good news to others living in the darkness from which they felt they'd been delivered. They lost no time sending out messengers to neighboring and more distant unreached people groups.[17] Their stories are thrilling, and their zeal convicting. An expatriate Christian can hardly avoid comparing their material resources with the wealth and technology at the West's disposal. Nor can we fail to be convicted when we compare spiritual resources, and are found to be the ones wanting.

By the time our family arrived at the hospital in 1965, these evangelists had reached out from Soddo to different ethnic groups all around them. The original base was a beehive of activity, including

---

17. The Wolaitta story is told in R. Davis, *Fire on the Mountains* (Sudan Interior Mission, 1966). The story of Ethiopian evangelists fanning out beyond Wolaitta from the 1940s to 1970s is moved forward by R. Davis, *The Winds of God* (SIM International Publ., 1984). A. Brant, *In the Wake of Martyrs* (Omega Publ., 1992), tells how it spread from the Gedeo base. C. Duff, *Cords of Love* (Presbyterian and Reformed Publ., 1980), records the pre-Italian mission efforts in the Kambaata and Hadiyya area. H. Fuller, *Run While the Sun is Hot* (Moody Press, 1968), pp. 157–216 include observations on the 1960s Ethiopian church. P. Cotterell, *Born at Midnight* (Moody Press, 1973), offers illuminating insights on Ethiopia's rare chapter in mission history.

five types of schools: elementary, Bible, women's, and blind schools, plus medical assistant training. Soddo's 100-bed hospital and clinic served Amharas from town, people of the ruling class, and farmers. Local people usually focused on rituals to appease *Saitan*, while Amharas were usually Orthodox. A circular burn scar at each temple—a traditional eye treatment—usually identified a Wolaitta.

Although the new evangelical believers were a small minority in the province, their impact was tremendous. They had been released from age-old fears and bondages and had become open to change, rare in Ethiopian society. While known as a slave people only a few decades before, the Wolaitta believers were eager to learn to read. Literacy had been hard to sell in most of Ethiopia. The country in the 1960s had a literacy rate of under ten percent, and it had been only half of one percent in down-trodden Wolaitta. Government authorities were puzzled by the upsurge in educational interest in this remote area. They sent investigators from Addis Ababa. "Why do you want to read?" they quizzed a group of our Soddo students one day. The answer seemed elementary to Wolaitta believers: "To know what God has said to us!" That significant statement revealed one of Orthodoxy's weaknesses. They did not put the Scriptures in the hands of the people, hardly in the hands of priests, except in the cryptic Ge'ez.

We went wide-eyed to our first church service. Given three-legged stools, we were seated among a hundred or more people sitting on logs or mats in a large haystack-shaped church constructed similarly to their homes. The skeleton of upright beams was neatly thatched with cut grass which escalated from a central peak right down to the ground. The sights and sounds of worship in this setting awakened epiphanies of meaning for me, time and time again. I couldn't help thinking as I looked up at the huge center pole and T-beam roof supports, so like the rough crosses on Calvary. Music was a whole new experience with a five-tone scale and antiphonally sung lyrics. Their indigenous songs employed a solo caller's statement or question alternated with a congregational response. "Are you suffering want?" the soloist would ask; "He suffered too!" the congregation would answer. "Are you rejected?" was asked; "He was rejected too," was answered. There were songs of confident hope. The solo part asked, "What is His promise?" With one voice they affirmed, "He will come again!" And always, there were songs of praise, deeply moving the spirit. *Misganah, misganah, le-Yesus misganah* ("Praise, praise to Jesus, praise!").

Indigenous practices in worship awakened me to meanings to which I had grown callused, or had not experienced at all. Local "honey water" served as the communion element, for grapes did not grow in the area. In addition to preaching (with translation), antiphonal music, and the Lord's supper, this Christian community employed various movements throughout the service: confessions of sin, requests for intercession, professions of belief, and earnest prayer in prostrate position. By the time a three or four hour service closed, our spirits were well filled! However, our stomachs were empty and our appetites well primed to enjoy *injera* and *wat* around a woven basket-table in a hospitable elder's home. Sometimes a whole congregation shared a meal outside under trees, served on huge *ensete* leaves, similar to banana leaves. Our sons were delighted with such a picnic with its local form of disposable plates.

Seeing our first baptismal service amazed us. In the United States we were used to a handful being baptized, at best. We found the river lined with thousands of believers. They were rejoicing over 500 some adults and older youth from the wider area who were being baptized as a testimony to their identification with the Christ to whom they had come within the year! At a celebration like baptism, joy is magnified by communal ululation, the trilling "joy cry."

Joy was their distinctive. Wolaitta believers could be spotted on the road by the joy visible on their faces. Joy is quaintly expressed in speech by an Amharic idiom, *des yelal* ("it says joy!"). One evening, as a group went singing past our home in the full moonlight we could see that the procession was carrying a white, cloth-covered box crested with flowers and a cross. Even at funerals believers express their joy. A believer had died, and as is the necessity, his body was being buried the same day. *Den-dah-nah!*—we heard the Wolaitta words flowing toward us, then fading into the distance. It meant "he will arise!" What a contrast to the blood-chilling wail so often heard from the hospital when someone died. Unbelievers' funerals were marked by shrieking laments riveted on death and hopeless separation.

Charles' favorite hour at the hospital was nine-o'clock rounds, when the electricity was about to go off and lanterns were being lit. At lantern time, the few Christ followers would spontaneously begin to sing. In the quiet of the evening, someone might say to the patient next to him, "Would you like to know about the Lord Jesus?" Given the bedmates' permission, a testimony followed. Still handicapped by lack of vocabulary, Charles could not communicate in this way, but he took joy from the hospital's role in providing the Christians with a natural "maternity ward," where births from above, by the Spirit of God, took place.

THOSE WHO SPREAD THIS good news from Wolaitta were usually unassuming people. This young church was a laity led movement with local elders and evangelists who had ventured forth to carry the message, but usually the churches did not have a pattern of formal, paid pastors. One of the patriarchs in the Soddo area was Wandaro Dabaro from up on Humbo Mountain south of Soddo. Wandaro was one of the first ten believers to confess Christ in pre-Italian times some thirty years before. His testimony had in turn reached a powerful slave owner, Daanna[18] Meja Madero, who eventually became head of the "Table Elders" of the Wolaitta church—some 300 congregations by the time we came on the scene.

Sometimes these elders or traveling evangelists came to call on us. Their passion for Jesus and commitment to extending His kingdom put my own to shame. When Daanna Meja came to call in our home, tall and regal in his white garb, I came to respectful attention. When tattered and barefoot Ato Wandaro came, smiling through teeth missing since torture in prison days, the presence of Jesus was almost palpable. Sometimes Balotay came, having finally returned with her small son from working alone among a distant ethnic group who had never heard of Jesus. Her husband had been killed by those to whom he carried the gospel. Such men and women became my heroes and heroines.[19]

Soon after we arrived at Soddo, Daanna Meja and Wandaro and the other Table Elders were taken off to prison. I was horrified. In America, going to jail means you have committed a crime. Here, I learned, people could be taken off to jail for preaching about Jesus, much as Peter or Paul experienced in Acts. One evening, we heard

---

18. The title *daanna* means "judge, leader" (from Amharic *danya*).
19. Many of their stories may be found in Davis (1966), *Fire*.

deep men's voices singing triumphantly and went to look out the window. The elders had been released. They strode shoulder to shoulder down the path through our compound, joyfully singing. We were mystified as we watched people accept harassment from primal neighbors or Orthodox church / government leadership as "a privilege." We began to hear stories of earlier imprisonments. The believers were used to suffering for the name of Christ and had learned to "count it all joy," just as the Scriptures admonish (James 1:2).

We kept wondering why the Orthodox church and government found these dear Christians to be threatening. In later years, we grew to better understand the wider picture. Much as in the book of Acts, a move of the Spirit had brought thousands of untaught gentile converts into the Kingdom. They knew little of "Christendom," and couldn't fit neatly into the system. But they were on fire to obey their new Lord and take the message further. Their faith and freedom and zeal overwhelmed and threatened existing structures, whether sociological, theological, or political. Because they constituted more an organism than an organization, comprised as they were of scattered congregations without a single bishop, they appeared to be uncontrollable. Yet they seemed to be imbued with the same spirit, devoted to the same purpose, led by the same leader. Who is he, establishment leadership wondered, that he might be "contained"? Who but the Spirit of God!

New Christians from primal backgrounds are puzzled when the ancient church misunderstands their motives. For example, one damaging accusation has arisen in a number of local situations. Twice in one place, the devastating message came to expatriate Bible translators: "Your translator has just been taken to prison!" The explanation? "Orthodox priests have accused him of stealing their church's Ark." Such an accusation shows how these two Christian bodies speak past each other, as if on different radio wave lengths. A church's Ark is their most valued possession and is considered to be their connection with the power of God, in the Orthodox context. Among evangelical believers, the Bible would be the most valued possession and the Holy Spirit looked to as the source of power. Since it is the Ark which constitutes an Orthodox church to be a church, priests may have thought a new "church" would need one, and that they might steal theirs. But if an Ark went missing, who could have taken it?

Only priests are allowed in the Holy of Holies. Perhaps the charge was simply trumped up to stop the work of translation. Wherever the truth lies, the task of translation was set back significantly. On the other hand, the Ethiopian translator, carrying the word of God (printed or memorized) and indwelt by the Holy Spirit, would take his message and "power" to prison. Repeatedly, the accused would testify to Christ's work in his own life, and by the work of the Spirit, fellow prisoners would become believers during the incarceration.

OUR FIRST APRIL IN Wolaitta brought one of the most exciting events the province had experienced in a couple of decades. The Emperor was coming! In Soddo town, people busily whitewashed buildings on the street side. On a hill located between our compound and the town, which lay a few miles across a stream, the community leaders had built a huge *dass* (temporary structure) for the ceremonies. Out at the mission, the hospital was scrubbed as clean as possible and students in the various schools were preparing songs. Then he came. As we saw flowers presented at the hospital entrance, and heard row after row of sighted and blind students singing to their Emperor, we stood in awe of "His Imperial Majesty." The diminutive man exuded royalty even stepping out of a muddy Land Rover wearing a military uniform and general's cap.

We were surprised to be among those invited to the dinner given in the Emperor's honor on the following day, because we were expatriates in the area. The huge *dass* must have seated a thousand, most at long bare tables running to the back of the building, and a precious few at linen-clad round tables clustered in a crescent around a raised platform for the Emperor's throne. We felt guilty being seated at one of the close tables which would have been so cherished a place for an Ethiopian. Here we were, eating with gold cutlery on plates crested with an imprint of the Lion of Judah. We tried to coach our little son on proper decorum, seated dangerously close to the always-dignified Emperor. Alas, when the Emperor's chiwawa dog ran under our table, our three years old Tim shrieked with delight. The Emperor smiled! Then, half-way through the meal, a warrior draped with a lion skin dashed from the rear of the building straight at the Emperor, his spear poised to strike. I nearly fainted. His Imperial Majesty at the last moment of the attack suddenly smiled and then rose to present the man who had shown such daring with a monetary reward! We learned that this kind of "warrior drama" was customary in Ethiopia. The day was like being part of an unfamiliar fairy tale for me, but rich with long-savored tradition for the Ethiopians around us.

We had gone to the event in a Land Rover with Daanna Meja—the slave master turned Christian—who sat tall and stately in his brilliant white jodhpurs and shawl, his eyes fixed with sober expectancy. When the historic event finally came to a close, the *dass* emptied out, except for neighbors who entered freely to consume any leftovers. Our carload climbed into the vehicle and we began to lumber up and down the slippery red dirt road homeward. It had been so awesome an occasion that we foreigners hardly knew what to say, what to ask, how to proceed. Daanna Meja's eyes were meditative, glowing. Finally he broke the silence. "Think," he mused, "think! If this is what the coming of our Emperor meant, what will it be when our Lord comes, when the real Lion of Judah, the true King of Kings arrives?"

A KINGDOM REFLECTS ITS king. Human kings dwell in palaces, levy taxes, go to war, demand homage and if they survive assaults, they eventually grow old and die. Their kingdoms are left to sons or ministers, conquerors or assassins, who go on to play the royal part and demand that their subjects play theirs. Ethiopia had known a succession of such kings. Who would have thought it could be otherwise?

How different the King of kings! Jesus dwelt in humble shelters, dealt not with money or war, invited instead of demanded allegiance. Rather than instilling fear, He captured hearts simply by his character and his love. Here was a king who offered his gentle, wise, strong rule to any who would acknowledge his claim to God's ultimate Kingship. He extended peace rather than waged war; won worship rather than forced subservience; asked no taxes, while pointing out the needy; suffered no fear of displacement, never grew old or stupid, and could not die—except as He chose to do in his subjects' place, when the Word became flesh in the incarnation. His resurrection power gave hearty assurance to all who chose to embrace the King's destiny, a future which would include ultimate deliverance from the Enemy's goading dominion. This King alone made all his subjects equal heirs, and eternal heirs, inheritors of an everlasting Kingdom.

Such was the King who had won the allegiance of Negussie, John, Alemu, and Kedamo; of Indalla, Berhanu, and Sahle; of Daanna Meja, Wandaro, and countless Ethiopians. They considered the honor of serving the Servant King to be worth the price which He warned them to expect—probably to be hated, as He was. Each looked to Him for strength to endure and overcome until He welcomed them home. They had tasted the Kingdom and looked forward to its fulfillment as a sure reality in time, and as God's marvelous goal for the human race in eternity.

> *If the world hates you, keep in mind that it hated me first.*
> *If you belonged to the world, it would love you as its own.*
> *As it is, you do not belong to the world,*
> *but I have chosen you out of the world.*
> *That is why the world hates you.*
> *Remember the words I spoke to you:*
> *"No servant is greater than his master."*
> *If they persecuted me, they will persecute you also.*
> *If they obeyed my teaching, they will obey yours also.*
>
> *(John 15:18–20)*

Part II

A CALL FOR ARMOR

(During 1972–77)

Finally, be strong in the Lord and in his mighty power.
Put on the full armor of God
so that you can take your stand against the devil's schemes.
For our struggle is not against flesh and blood,
but against the rulers, against the authorities,
against the powers of this dark world
and against the spiritual forces of evil in the heavenly realms.
Therefore put on the full armor of God,
so that when the day of evil comes,
you may be able to stand your ground,
and after you have done everything, to stand.
(Ephesians 6:10–13)

MAP 2: MAJOR LOCATIONS AND ROADS MENTIONED IN THE TEXT (BEFORE AD 1991)

Source: Adapted from Brant (1992), *Martyrs*, by Johnathan Bascom.

Chapter 5

BECOMING EQUIPPED

While Negussie and Sahle's generation was coming of age, Ethiopia felt rumblings in the realm: scattered student unrest, rebellion up in Eritrea, struggles over the ethnic Somali grazing grounds in the Ogaden, plus Ethiopia's year-by-year agricultural combat with nature, especially in the arid north.

For Negussie, adulthood had come. His cluster of closest friends was breaking up. Alemu Beeftu had proven to be an outstanding student at Grace Bible Institute. John Coleman was studying in Canada, and the Colemans had been restationed at Shashamane down near the Rift lakes, leaving a big hole in Negussie's life. For a time, his aptitudes and training were employed in the mission grade school at Wolisso. In his early twenties now, Negussie yearned for more education too. Teaching was his gift, and to a Teachers Training Institute (TTI) it would eventually be arranged that he would go. These Institutes were located in a few cities of the country. Except for the one university in the capital, TTIs offered the highest level of education available. Students were not always placed in their home areas, so schools became cross-pollinating possibilities, where people from different ethnic and religious backgrounds shared experiences and developed new ideas.

Similar to other areas of the world, student centers in Ethiopia became natural hotbeds of dissent. Especially in the capital, the wider world came more into view. Agitation had been escalating since the mid-sixties. Students made proposals for change and facing the regime with opposition. First it was the country's feudalism they cried out against, then they called for educational reforms. Ethnic questions came onto their agenda. In response, the regime would close down schools in order to punish perceived student impertinence and to cancel their opportunities to gather daily. University and sometimes high school students would take to the streets in almost clockwork annual demonstrations. It was not unusual for students to be reading Chairman Mao's little red book in secret in those days. Two decades later, historian Bahru Zewde in his history of modern Ethiopia would write of the students: "As impassioned advocates of change, more than any other sector of the society, they proved to be the grave-diggers of the old regime and the generators of the Ethiopian Revolution."[20]

While Addis Ababa acted as the fulcrum of dissent, the movement burst out into the rural areas through the schools, and especially by means of a national program requiring students to give a year of service in the countryside to teach literacy. In actuality, it taught more than "literacy." It became a network for spreading dissent all over the country. Furthermore, severe measures of governmental retaliation against agitators drove many student leaders to flee the country. This in turn created an external student movement component which fanned the flames of protest from North America and Europe.

Another kind of retaliation toward non-conforming students was mounting too, by the Orthodox Church. The new evangelicalism which had recently come to Ethiopia appealed to the young and the educated. Most of the expatriate missions were not "Pentecostal" in the Western sense, either in theology or worship forms. However, a small Pentecostal movement did begin to take root in Addis Ababa, one which became highly disturbing to the church/state authorities. Occasional excesses in Pentecostal public meetings became the opportunity for the Orthodox leadership to complain and take measures to stamp the movement out. Raids and arrests were one method employed.

OUR YOUNG FRIEND FROM language school days, Sahle, got caught in one of these raids inadvertently in 1972. By then, he'd completed teacher's training in Debre Berhan, had taught a year in the northern province of Wollo, and was slated to teach the next year in the northern area of Munz. Young believers from Debre Berhan kept in touch with each other. While visiting an older Christian brother

---

20. Bahru Z., *A History of Modern Ethiopia* (James Curry etc., 2001), 220.

who was teaching at the Girls Christian Academy in the capital, Sahle was introduced to a young woman who caught his attention. Aberash Takele was a soft-spoken, graceful girl with a heart-shaped face. She had a slight tie with Sahle's circle, because it was a young woman from Debre Berhan who had encouraged Aberash to put her trust in the Lord, while the two were schoolmates at a TTI in Harar.

During a summer course held at the University in Addis Ababa to upgrade teachers, Sahle and Aberash started to spend time together as friends, fellow-believers who were inwardly considering marrying. He would take her to restaurants or go for walks, talking the time away.

"One day we decided to see if we could get some 'soul food'," as Sahle put it, by dropping in on a *Mulu Wongel* ("Full Gospel") meeting. They'd heard about a surge of activity among this group which was so abhorrent to the Orthodox leadership, and were curious. "Pentecostal," the group was called. Eventually the Orthodox began applying the derogatory term *Pente*[21] to any believer outside Orthodoxy, even though most evangelical believers were not actually Pentecostal at that time. Sahle and Aberash were curious about the "dangerous" group, and went to check it out. During the singing at this particular meeting, government police came storming in and ordered the congregation to stop. They made 250 some people present (many were young) file out of the building and climb into waiting trucks. Held at a police station for a whole week, the culprits were told they must confess that they had participated in an "illegal meeting." If they agreed, answering "yes," they would be allowed to pay a fine and could leave. It they answered "no," it would mean six months in jail. Sahle and Aberash both were among those who answered "no." "Such a meeting was not illegal, we were only worshipping," they insisted. They were sent off to Akaki Prison.

One of the first indignities Sahle faced was the head shaving. It was part of planned humiliation, designed to be painful both to the prisoner's head and morale. To Sahle's horror, he was thrown into a filthy room with 400 some men, some of whom were real criminals, even murderers. The conditions were unspeakable. At night,

---

21. *Pente* was meant to be a disparaging attribute which seemed to sum up the free church movement in the Orthodox thinking, no matter whether the term was welcome or applied to the group or individual so labeled.

the prisoners on the circumference of the room had to raise their legs and lean them against the wall—"like so much cordwood" as he described it—to make room for all to lie down. Sahle became utterly demoralized. Gentle Aberash was incarcerated with tough female prisoners along with other women arrested in the raid. When the young couple eventually spotted each other over a fence, both were bald. They were shocked and deeply embarrassed. At first they wanted to hide from each other, then they wanted to weep; finally they chose to laugh in helpless amusement. Talking together was difficult, although they sometimes were fortunate enough to pass briefly at the clinic. They tried arranging a meeting in the presence of guards but found such circumstances reduced them to tongue-tied disappointment.

As they months drew on, Sahle came down to the last possible week for getting to his appointment in time to teach in Munz. Mercifully, the release came. He made it there just in time to take his post. However, the new teacher found persecution there too. Munz was an Orthodox-dominated area and solidly Amhara. Anyone claiming to be Christian but not observably practicing the Orthodox faith was in trouble.

MEANWHILE, OVER AT JIMMA, beyond Negussie's town, a choice group of eager young people were eagerly becoming equipped for service at Grace Bible Institute (GBI), the school to which Alemu had gone. In the early seventies, teachers and students at the new Institute were bursting with enthusiasm and high hopes for the future.

While on furlough from Ethiopia, Ted Veer attended a seminary in Chicago. Ted was impressed with a fellow seminarian named Art Volkmann. The two were opposites: Ted was a spirited choleric with a crew cut; Art was a steady, thoughtful man with philosophical bent. Ted succeeded in recruiting Art to come out to teach at GBI. And so it was that in the latter half of 1973, with some trepidation, Art with his wife and little daughter headed out to join the teaching staff at GBI.

As their jet neared Ethiopia, night had fallen. Only a haze of lights betrayed the presence of Eritrea's capital, Asmara. In the pre-dawn haze, their jet passed over the latitude of Axum's stelae, scratching the sky. Below the clouds, roosters began to greet the sun, waking sparse households sleeping in their mud and thatched huts. Sunrise revealed a gigantic wrinkled patchwork blanket of fields surrounding compounds perched on small isolated plateaus. During time immemorial, the highlands had been cut into endless shapes as the yearly rains gathered into crisscrossing streams that ran into rivers that cut gorges awesome to behold, their steep angles accentuated by the mysterious shadows of dawn.

The tinkle and aroma of breakfast brought passengers alive. Ethiopian Airline hostesses moved down the aisles gracefully on high heels, in soft white cotton dresses with bright bands circling the hems, their smiling faces crowned with stylish black hairdos, their Caucasian features set in coffee-with-cream colored skin. Over the public address system in clipped Amharic and then in excellent English, the captain announced preparations to land at the Addis Ababa airport. Ethiopian pilots were cosmopolitan, often having been trained abroad by Trans World Airlines in those days. A circle of blue-green mountains cradling Addis Ababa came into view. Greener fields and tin roofs blurred past. A modest two-story white air terminal loomed into sight as a thud of wheels announced earth. Motors roared, brakes screeched, the metal bird shuddered and fell still. In ringing ears passengers heard the public announcement system "Welcome to Ethiopia!"

WITHIN DAYS, A WHIRLWIND orientation to Addis Ababa gave way to a long day's journey with Ted Veer, to Jimma. Ted was in his element, pouring out geographical highlights and mission history as their Land Rover rumbled through potholes, slowed down through Negussie's Wolisso town, sped down the Gibe River escarpment, and struggled up breathtaking pin-curves to level out and finally arrive by nightfall at Grace Bible Institute (GBI). Ted had been called in for a new assignment in Addis Ababa, so he had to leave the Volkmanns with fellow faculty members for their Jimma orientation, and head back to his family in the capital the next morning.

Not knowing Amharic was a handicap for Art, but he was needed too quickly to allow for language training. Fortunately for him, English was Ethiopia's second language, the one used in higher education. Although he could not see the future, Art would be instructing a handful of key people who were destined soon to lead Ethiopians believers through perilous times.

Fortunately, much is communicated non-verbally, and Art worked hard to get to know the individual characteristics of his students, some of whom were older than himself. When one is faced with a whole new ethnic community, at first everybody can seem to melt together, except for size. Big Werku Gole could always be spotted, a veritable giant of a man about six foot four. He was from the Gedeo area east of the Rift lakes, although Gedeos were not particularly known for height. Werku was an exception, as he was in many ways. *Werku* meant "gold," and he seemed to have a golden touch even at twenty-three. Ted told Art that he had often been amazed at Werku as he watched him during his freshman year. "Even then, nothing daunted him. He did not know or did not care about his limitations!" An aggressive but jovial extrovert, Werku's natural bent for leadership was obvious from the start. That characteristic would develop in future years as Werku went on to become a visionary leader of the Gedeo church.

Ato Tesfaye Tole (*Tesfaye* means "hope") was one of the most challenging students to Art. A number of GBI's first students were already mature Christians and were being prepared for further leadership. Tesfaye injected a powerful presence into GBI's student body, yet evidenced a quieter, more mature leadership than Werku's, for he was older. Of average height and sturdy build, Tesfaye's flashing eyes and black beard gave him the look of a prophet. Already a steady family man by then, Tesfaye arrived in Jimma as a seasoned believer who had learned to persevere under persecution in his early Christian life. Tesfaye had long been a teacher and had five children by the time he began his education at Grace Bible Institute. Bringing his whole family was too expensive, so they remained back in Chencha, the highland town above the city of Arba Minch two hundred kilometers ("as the crow flies") south of Jimma. Tesfaye had served as a Chencha teacher before he was married. He kept advancing academically through attending the mission's short summer courses designed to upgrade teachers. They were sometimes taught at Shashamane, where the Colemans now worked. Tesfaye proved to be a good student of the Word of God and very practical in his application. He was well respected, but a rebel to tradition. When teaching at Chencha, on a Saturday he would be out in his garden digging and planting *ensete* trees. Local people would comment, "Now that you are a teacher, you should not be digging!" He would reply that work was not a shame, it was something that needed to be done, and he was going to do it. That practical non-conformity helped shape Tesfaye into a fiery leader who stood rock firm and took the consequences during the coming days of testing.

Girma Hanano was a more jovial man. Girma's presence, like Tesfaye's, was a mature one, for he was married too, with a family back in Hadiyya. He'd already had to be separated from them while he found work teaching in Assab, way up on the Red Sea coast. Girma had worked there with Hans Hagen, a German missionary who was alert to building leadership. Girma was a born communicator, a real actor, and graced with a delightful wit which would brighten many a situation that would arise as days grew more and more sober in Ethiopia. A teacher and shepherd at heart, Girma would eventually strengthen many a student under his guidance as they faced the pressures of systematic repression during the military dictatorship.

One of the three GBI women students when Art taught was twinkling-eyed Belaynesh Dindamo, from the Hadiyya area—Pastor Kedamo's territory. Not as sophisticated as the two Eritrean ladies, Belaynesh was from a rural background. Her warm personality and bright mind would in future years lead her into outstanding leadership among Christian women.

Watching Belaynesh quietly, a student named Hussein Yusef was ready to graduate when Belaynesh was just beginning. This thin, slow-speaking man stood out for one telling reason, he came from a Muslim family. Converted to Christ as a young chap, he'd had to leave his home in the north early and make a way for himself. Already he had served as head master of the Christian school at Assab, along with missionary Hans Hagen and his fellow GBI student, Girma, who had also taught there. At about twenty-eight, it was beginning to be time for Hussein to marry and move on in further service. The time would come when Belaynesh would join him in that endeavor.

Ato Tekle Wolde Giorgis, a student over forty, generally took the role of "father" of the campus. A very serious family man with a deeply furrowed brow, Tekle was small in stature but large in influence. Tekle hailed from Saja, on the way to Jimma, 225 kilometers southwest of Addis Ababa. Tekle had already been a Bible school teacher and a close colleague of Ted Veer's at Saja station. Before GBI opened, Ted had worked seven years at Saja, and before that, at Chencha, where Ted had known the fiery Tesfaye as well. Ato Tekle could not know then that shortly after his GBI graduation, he would be chosen to serve as the new denomination's first General Secretary and called to the capital. That assignment would be difficult not only because his national church body was in its formative years, but because the coming political upheaval would demand watchful shepherding and consistent self-denial from Christian leadership.

That the country would take a sudden left turn was as yet hardly imagined. Art's students would turn out to be the mission-related church's most highly trained student generation, the last to have such an opportunity to do biblical studies openly for many years. GBI students would go forth over the country with purpose and preparation, people Art would long remember, like young Werku "the gold," Tesfaye the prophet, jovial Girma, smiling Belaynesh, quiet Hussein, and dignified Ato Tekle.

Up to Christmas time, classes clipped along, a good spirit pervaded the campus and all seemed right with the world. GBI's students were thirsty to become equipped for ministry and were little involved with the growing rebellion. That is, uninvolved until orders came to go on *zemecha*,[22] a campaign to spread literacy and development. This government-ordered service program drafted the upper level of Ethiopian students, including GBI's. Women were not exempted. Art tried to understand what was going on. He took photos of his classes, their garb changing from civilian one year, to khakis the next. Hussein watched Belaynesh have to interrupt her studies and be sent off on national service. Dislocation into a foreign area was threatening for most students, especially for women. All over the country, young people systematically had no choice but to take their turn, interrupting their curriculum plan. Young believers sometimes found the national field assignment a challenging op-

---

22. *Zemecha*: i.e. "Development through Cooperation, Enlightenment and Work Campaign."

portunity, sometimes a time of painful vulnerability, or both. Each would have his or her own story to tell.

May the God of peace,
who through the blood of the eternal covenant
brought back from the dead our Lord Jesus,
that great Shepherd of the sheep,
equip you with everything good for doing his will,
and may he work in us what is pleasing to him,
through Jesus Christ, to whom be glory for ever and ever.
Amen.

(Hebrews 13:20–21)

Chapter 6

THE KINGDOM CRUMBLING

Perhaps alert people in the capital had the best opportunity to sense the seriousness of the multiple battles being waged out of sight. News trickling in from far-flung areas painted a grim picture of the state of the nation. Reports were not easy to get.

Mission leaders tried to dovetail what national newspapers and European radio news offered with reports from missionaries located all over Ethiopia. Since SIM was the largest mission in Ethiopia, its Director was able to touch the pulse of many areas.

John Cumbers was providentially fitted for leadership "at such a time as this." Tall, slightly bent, and quite thin, John had a clipped British accent that added punch to his slightly military manner. He was a disciplined man who had first come to Ethiopia to do a technical job. He would have been aghast then to have thought he'd ever be a missionary.

Born in 1927, John had graduated from high school while still fifteen. He went into an air corps training scheme for aspiring pilots and was accepted into the Royal Air Force in 1945. However, World War II was ending, landing him in the accounts division of the Royal Air Force—which led to two years in Iraq. After discharge from the airforce, he went into the volunteer reserve as an air traffic control officer.

John was twenty-three when he was converted to Christ. Getting a religious reputation was not popular at work, but his cool head in emergencies quickly won him respect. In 1957 an appeal for trainers and managers of air traffic controllers for fledgling airfields led the young adventurer to the city of Asmara, in Ethiopia's north-most province, Eritrea. There John became liaison officer for the Chief of Civil Aviation.

He soon discovered fellowship with other Christians at Asmara's Gospel Center, where he began teaching Bible studies three times a week. His habit of giving out personally-subsidized Bibles here and there won him the Amharic nickname *Keshi* ("priest"). In Asmara John met Naomi Bell, widow of a young missionary doctor who had died of hepatitis contracted from a patient's autopsy the same year their first child was born. By 1957, Naomi was nursing at the SIM hospital just outside of Dessie, some two days' bus journey south of Asmara.

John took out time back in England to do two years at London Bible College and then earned a diploma in theology from London University. Eventually he spent time in the States in order to marry Naomi. John was accepted into SIM in 1961 through the London office. After Amharic language school, John and Naomi's career took them for one term far down into southern Ethiopia to the station at Burji, then back up north to direct the language school in Debre Berhan. Two children were born to the new union.

In 1969 John was called to Addis Ababa to become Field Secretary for SIM East Africa. With further responsibility, he continued to mature. A health problem threatened the family two years later, when John was found to have a faulty heart valve. After the famous Dr. Michael DeBakey inserted a metal valve in John's heart in Texas, John was going strong again. Soft-spoken, golden-haired Naomi always stood beside him valiantly, whether as wife, nurse, or private secretary. Her gentle kindliness with people and the ability to keep confidences admirably suited her for the role she played.

John was appointed in 1973 to the top job, Acting Director for SIM East Africa, which included the areas of Sudan and Somalia as well as Ethiopia. SIMers in Ethiopia alone numbered some 300 missionaries. He undertook his new role with the decisiveness and precision for which he was known.

As catastrophic events began to break loose, John's wry humor helped the administration keep an even keel in the tense situations in which they became increasingly enmeshed. We had enjoyed that humor a few years before when John was covering the language school while Mina Moen was away. He was an excellent teacher, but we especially enjoyed his quick wit and relaxed piano playing "off hours." When his responsibilities intensified as head of the mission during the Revolutionary period, that former light-hearted accompaniment to John's personality diminished, as so often happens to those whose destiny moves them upward into a leadership which can drain nearly every ounce of their energy.

John and Naomi lived day in and day out right at Headquarters (HQ), close to down-town Addis Ababa. The building was a pretty basic, two-story L-shaped structure. At least its brown shingled walls were brightened by flowering bougainvillea vines ablaze with fuchsia. The gate-side north end of the building included a chapel. From second floor windows, landmarks were easy to spot across the bowl-shaped metropolis—City Hall on the high crest of Churchill Avenue, the Palace grounds across on an eastern hill, the nearest mosque's minaret to the north. Spread out between thoroughfares which were marked by two or three story buildings, lay a hidden sea of small, tin-roofed dwellings, from which rose the crowing of roosters and the smoke of cooking fires in the morning, the din of radios and the barking of dogs in the evening. A four-way intersection right at Headquarters' gate brought forth a constant background of grinding gears, honking taxis, and the odor of diesel smoke. Headquarters served as a guesthouse for missionaries and travelers while also being home to a couple dozen people who worked in the mission offices and supply departments in a couple of accompanying buildings.

John was assisted in administrative tasks by Howard Borlase, a tall mustached Canadian, veteran of mission work in a number of countries. Howard's objectivity and characteristic wit provided a calming balance to John's more tense temperament. Neither of them could have done without Ato Lakew Tesemma, their faithful Ethiopian assistant. Ato Lakew was a bright-eyed little man. His stocky person was packed with energy and his quizzical conversation was spiced with wit. The man brightened the office halls as he joshed with people as he made his way out daily, carrying a brief-case full of foreigners' papers to process when he made his patience-testing round of government offices. He knew missionaries well; he'd lived among them since almost a boy. He read them, teased them, loved them, forgave them, and sometimes he rebuked them—tactfully. Ato Lakew was every inch a gentleman.

In 1973 "HEADQUARTERS," as the little fourth-of-a block property was called, began teeming with a whole new set of personnel—volunteer famine workers, kind of a college student invasion. Their arrival came as the result of a phone call a few months before to John Cumbers from Dr. Dietrich (aka Dieter) Schmoll, a German doctor running the mission hospital and leprosarium up north at Dessie. Choleric by nature, Dieter's high pitched staccato voice was both urgent and shaken: "John, you must *do* something; today I have seen some terrible sights in eastern Wello. We have discovered hundreds of people starving and there are dozens dying daily. Why hasn't there been any report of a famine?" He cut John off, hardly waiting for an answer. "People are lying beside the road in all directions; they have no strength even to approach the few vehicles which pass by."[23] Before Dieter slammed down the phone, John had promised to get some kind of famine relief organized.

But Dieter had glimpsed only the tip of the iceberg. Throughout 1973, increased starvation reports came pouring in. When Jonathan Dimbleby of the BBC was somehow able to get through to the north and make a TV documentary, the media leak yielded an escalation of concern. The footage surprised the Ethiopian authorities and shocked the world. Up to then, although the government had known about the situation, evidently it did not want to draw attention to what might be construed as neglect. The famine in Wollo in 1973 was finally reported to have left more than 100,000 dead.[24]

As did other missions, SIM worked hard to put together a substantial relief program. Such efforts demanded food supplies and logistics operations and an army of volunteers. Young people abroad were quick to respond, particularly Canadians whom George Middleton recruited. George had consistently been a man of vision, spearheading the development of Grace Bible Institute in Jimma and then the Youth Center in Asmara in the sixties. The inexperienced young college students who flooded in needed orientation. They had to be supplied, housed, transported and given periodic breaks in the capital from the emotionally shaking conditions met in the north. All this required additional administrative complexity which involved

---

23. J. Cumbers, *Living with the Red Terror* (Morris Publ., 1996), 6.
24. B. Thomson, *Ethiopia* (Robson Books, 1975), 16.

LAKEW TESEMMA (ADDIS ABABA, 1995)

foreign grants, customs, hauling grain from seaports and the like. Not the least complicated was trying to introduce nearly a hundred inexperienced short-termers without Amharic language capacity onto the turf of career personnel already engrossed in pre-existent involvements.[25] Newcomers had to be matched with Ethiopian counterparts. Efforts to help in the north issued in what became known as the Relief and Rehabilitation Program. The burgeoning entity called "R & R" would significantly alter the course of missionary work in Ethiopia.[26]

---

25. Some of the conflicts introduced by situations like these are dramatized in a short story titled "The Development Workers" in R. Taylor, *The Prisoner and Other Stories* (MARC Europe, 1987).

26. M. and E. Forsberg, *In Famine He Shall Redeem Thee* (Sudan Interior Mission, 1975), 111f.

66   Overcomers

ETHIOPIA FACED YET ANOTHER massive problem. Whereas the specter of disaster along Africa's encroaching Sahel desert region was gaining the attention of the western media, another less-known but very difficult situation farther north was destabilizing the region. Missionaries deployed in the south knew little about the struggle for independence being waged in Eritrea.[27] Federated as an autonomous unit under the sovereignty of the Ethiopian crown in 1952, Eritrea in 1962 was wholly integrated into the Ethiopian Empire as its 14th province. Haile Selassie dissolved the Eritrean constitution, removed their flag and changed the official language from the indigenous Tigrinya to Amharic. Having developed differently, partly due to the Italian colonial presence introduced into their province in the 1890s, Eritreans were not prepared to lose their autonomy. Nor could they agree on who should lead their resistance. A bitter internal war between two rebel fronts dissipated their momentum, but in 1973 the Eritrean People's Liberation Front (EPLF) superseded the Eritrean Liberation Front (ELF). This consolidation strengthened the insurgents' focus upon their goal of secession.

John Cumbers was more conversant with the Eritrean struggle than most foreigners were because of his having worked in Asmara in his pre-mission days. SIM manned only a handful of lonely stations in the hostile territory of the north. Between the ruggedness of the terrain and the resistance of various communities, only three or four nurse's clinics, the hospital and leprosarium at Dessie and a station at the port of Assab comprised the sparse SIM presence north of the Shewa Province which surrounded Addis Ababa. It was in the south that over three-fourths of the missionary staff was concentrated. That proportion was a natural outgrowth of policies specified after 1927, when the Emperor first gave SIM permission to work among populations in the south, while insisting that missionaries stay at arm's length from Orthodox Christian areas, more prevalent in the north.

The early seventies found SIM and its daughter church thriving across the south. There were dozens of elementary schools and Bible schools, a blind school, agricultural training, literacy and translation projects, a leprosarium, three hospitals, and a dresser training program at Soddo which flowered into the establishment of about thirty

---

27. See Mesghina G., *Eritrea* (Companion Press, 1989).

Ethiopian-manned clinics. How had this all developed? A brief recap: these works largely served the new evangelical churches which had been born in the 1930s before the Italian occupation.[28] During that five-year period from 1937 to 1942, the gospel had spread across the south like wildfire. After the war interlude, missionaries returned to continue training and serving the growing church. In the 1950s and 1960s, bases for pioneer evangelism were planted further southwest and southeast into the countryside. Missionaries in their particular locations were concentrating on multiplying outreach, providing education, and extending medical services. Busy in these endeavors, they avoided politics, hearing little more about the north than what news could be gleaned via BBC. Thus, most were barely cognizant of the gathering storm which would soon break out from northern skies to envelop the whole country.

But mission leaders were uneasy when 1974 dawned. With the Eritrean–Ethiopian War, with famine raging in the north, and with students multiplying dissent all over the country, who could know what would happen next? Day by day John Cumbers listened carefully to Ethiopian news broadcasts, cocked his ear to BBC and Voice of America, and scanned the newspapers. Headquarters did a shortwave radio check on each outstation on a daily basis. Although having to be discreet in wording, missionaries gave indications which helped him read the situation.

Mr. Cumbers' disciplines included keeping a private daily log. In early January of 1974, his diary recorded an Ethiopian Air Force strike at their headquarters in Debre Zeit—just a few miles from SIM's Bishoftu Lake property. At the same time, soldiers at Negele Borana revolted against their officers and took control of the area. Rumblings echoed throughout the country over the rising cost of everyday commodities and a 50% increase in price of gas. Meanwhile, hot discussion in the Teachers Union was keeping teachers out of the classroom as they debated proposed reform of the educational system. Students showed their own disapproval of the system by disrupting the public transport system. John was himself caught in

---

28. These churches were led by local elders. They were loosely knit congregations which shared similar SIM-roots and were guided by their area's "Table Elders," not ruled by a supreme bishop. Not until 1971 did these churches give themselves a name, The Ethiopian Kale Heywet Church (KHC).

TEKLE WOLDE GIORGIS (ADDIS ABABA, 1995)

a high school riot in Shashamane town as the bus in which he was traveling crossed through Arsi territory. The white-skinned Britisher was told to crouch on the floor, lest the sight of a foreigner inflame the mob. On February 18th the teachers began a strike and the taxis on which Addis Ababa business so depended stopped running. City busses and private cars were stoned. Foreigners were advised to stay inside.

Then came the demonstrations. John's diary noted that unlikely bedfellows were putting forth their grievances. Orthodox priests demonstrated in one parade, and 10,000 prostitutes demanded "more equitable remuneration" in another. Some 100,000 Muslims paraded through the streets calling for more freedom for Islam, and prisoners revolted in the Addis Ababa jail.[29] On a lesser scale of self-assertion, SIM employees formed a labor union which, through

---

29. Cumbers (1996), *Terror*, 7.

endless disputes, was to cost hundreds of missionary and employee man-hours over the next five years. Mission stations in the countryside began to feel the effects. At SIM's largest station just outside of Shashamane, rioters destroyed the principal's house and smashed windows of school buildings and missionary residences. By late February news came of the closure of Asmara's airport, the mutiny of the Ethiopian navy and trouble at the Air Force base in Debre Zeit quelled by paratroopers.

Collapse of the regime began when Prime Minister Akililu Habtewold was toppled and the entire cabinet resigned. His replacement, Endelkatchew Mekonnen, called in leaders of Christian missions and told them he wanted their fullest cooperation in remaking the country, specifically listing the need for medical assistance, literacy and community development.[30] On February 28th the army took over all important installations in Addis Ababa. British Broadcasting Corporation (BBC) and Voice of America reported the entire country to be under military control.

A bit late to be starting, SIM and KHC began urgent consultations. The church's first General Secretary, Ato Tekle Wolde Giorgis from Saja, just having graduated from Grace Bible Institute, was called into SIM's biannual council. Strained and often tense relationships were not uncommon as the two bodies navigated unfamiliar waters together, and apart. All were out of their depth, and called out to the only One who could walk on water.

WHAT WAS HAPPENING TO Haile Selassie's Ethiopia? Not many sovereigns in the world held the title "King" or "Emperor" by 1974. Ethiopia's had gained world respect as a statesman in the League of Nations during the Italian invasion and subsequent repulsion of Italy connected with World War II. England had been his refuge, and the United States a friend. The Emperor had engineered a fascinating career as "King of Kings, the Lion of Judah." The Lion's rule had lasted since 1930, amazing longevity for an earthbound king.

But it proved to be too long. This diminutive but powerful sovereign had finally succeeded in realizing the unitary state of which Emperor Tewodros had dreamed (reigned 1855–68). Yet his

---

30. Cumbers (1996), *Terror*, 9.

inattention to the seeds of the disaster latent in feudalism brought forth an eventual harvest of revolt. The fact that reforms were slow to come and that the Emperor's successor was not installed, not even decided upon, rankled people who were growing too informed and too determined to be put off much longer.

The students were playing a larger role than most realized. Historian Bahru Zewde would later evaluate that "despite the growing intensity of the confrontation, the outbreak of the Ethiopian Revolution in 1974 caught both the regime and the students unawares. The regime had scarcely thought the end was so near. The students, their years of opposition notwithstanding, had not yet formulated a clear and viable alternative."[31] However political opportunists in high places were quietly formulating plans. One by one in the middle of 1974, those closest to the Emperor were either arrested or escaped from the country. On June 27, 1974, a "Committee of Equals" (the *Derg*) was announced. When this first proclamation was issued on July 8, it indicated that the new ruling body was loyal to Haile Selassie. The daily paper began to herald the banner *Ethiopia Tikdem* ("Ethiopia first"). This slogan was to become the rallying cry for the nation throughout the years of the Revolution. Lieutenant Colonel Atnafu Abate was named chairman and a Major Mengistu Haile Mariam (who eventually came out on top) was named as Vice-Chairman of the 126-member Derg. Little was said concerning the policies of the "Committee of Equals." Observers on the outside thought the Derg showed promise of supplying reasonable direction to a peaceful transfer of power. Questions rose when July 26th's report announced the forced resignation of the Prime Minister. New appointments followed. By August 15th, the Crown Council and its Review Commission as well as the Central Court were dissolved. The international airport was reported closed.

John Cumbers' diary records the fateful day, September 12th—New Year's Day on the Ethiopian calendar:

> A Volkswagen "Bug" pulled up outside the gates of the Imperial Palace in Addis Ababa. Three army officers entered the Emperor's study and told him he was to accompany them. As they approached the little car, one of them tipped up the front seat and motioned to the Emperor. Haile

---

31. Bahru (2001), *History*, 226.

KEDAMO MECHATO (ADDIS ABABA, 1994/95)

Selassie the First, King of Kings and Conquering Lion of the Tribe of Judah, accustomed to Rolls Royce treatment, climbed into the back seat of the bug and made his journey into ignominy.[32]

That night, the Derg made a statement to the world. Emperor Haile Selassie had been deposed. The 1955 Constitution was revoked. Parliament was dissolved. Another sovereignty—one claiming supreme credentials—had come to an end.

At home after these announcements, Pastor Kedamo Mechato paced the floor. Kedamo was a big man in stature and in soul. By now, his urban church dearly loved their country pastor from Hadiyya. New to the capital and the world of politics, the man labored under a sense of his responsibility "at such a time as this." He was not uninformed

---

32. Cumbers (1996), *Terror*, 14.

as to the communist attitude toward religion. Kedamo felt he had to deal personally with what he could see coming:

> I gave myself to a day of prayer and fasting, October 3rd [1975]. But the Lord saw fit to withhold an answer from me. I went on throughout that night in prayer, beseeching God to reveal to me what was the right thing to do. October 4th came and still I had had no reply from God.
>
> As I was returning to my house from the prayer house God spoke to me. He reminded me of the words of the Lord Jesus Christ as He was to be crucified. "Not my will but Yours be done." In a flash the Lord enabled me to say, "Yes, Lord, if you want the prayer houses and the church to be closed down, so be it. If the Bible is to be banned, let it be so. If we are to be imprisoned, let it be so. Even if you want me to die for my faith, so be it." After I had heard these words from the Lord I was filled with tremendous peace and joy and a strong faith that He would protect us in whatever circumstances we found ourselves.[33]

Kedamo testified that from that day on, throughout the rest of their ordeals, he was not really anxious. Over and over again his flock were to go through the fire, but each time Kedamo stood like a rock among them.

God sometimes visited Pastor Kedamo with visions similar to those reported in scripture, an experience which was not uncommon among Christians in the dark days of the Revolution. "One day I was having a day of prayer when suddenly the room became full of light. I don't know whether it was a vision or a dream. Then I saw a bird like an eagle, except it had a man's face. A voice said, 'Take courage, don't be afraid, I will protect you, even as I promised you earlier.' I stood up to see more clearly where the voice was coming from, but the vision disappeared."[34]

Pastor Kedamo continued to lead his large congregation with bold courage. It became one of very few which, although repeatedly threatened with closure by the authorities, miraculously stayed open—often day and night—throughout the ongoing Revolution.

---

33. See J. Cumbers, *Count It All Joy* (Morris Publ., 1995), 212; Temesgen S., *"Come and See His Works"* (KHC Communications & Literature Dept., 2016).
34. Cumbers (1995), *Joy*, 212f.

DAILY LIFE COULD NOT stop even for a coup. Although their king had been deposed, the sun still rose morning by morning, people ate and slept, life went on. The very week of the Emperor's fall, Sahle and Aberash had arranged to be married. They'd planned to both teach in Munz. With the country so unstable, what should they do? Well, hadn't they survived six months in prison already? Didn't God know what the coup would really bring? Had He not always been faithful? With youthful enthusiasm and a firm confidence in God their Rock, the sweethearts took their vows. Their union was to pay a high price in the coming years, but their confidence in their Lord would be vindicated.

ALL OVER THE LAND, people in every station of life were questioning among themselves, "What will all this mean?" In Addis Ababa every day seemed to bring new rounds of consultations for the mission administration, sometimes with KHC leaders, sometimes with staff flown out from International Headquarters to investigate and advise, others with government or court officials who brought constant and unavoidable demands.

As foreigners under the protection of embassies, actual threat to life for expatriates was rare. Not so for Ethiopians, particularly leaders. The small-arms fire heard around the city at night did not prepare people for the news of November 24th involving a Christian statesman. John Cumbers remembers the week well. Lieutenant General Aman Mikael Andom, an Eritrean who had become Chairman of the Provisional Government, had believed that as a Christian it was of no value to his country if he were merely a titular head; he wanted to apply biblical principles to his new position. From the first day of his appointment this brought him into direct conflict with the "Inner Derg." As the appointed Head of State, when he learned of their plans to execute former politicians without trial, he confronted his subordinate, Mengistu Haile Mariam, and demanded that due processes of democracy be followed. After a day of fruitless arguing, he returned to his home. The walled compound was located near Tsehai Hospital, not far from the Mission headquarters. The next morning the General awoke to find his quarters surrounded by tanks. For a week he refused to surrender. The Saturday night of November 23rd, gunfire could be heard as far as Headquarters. But it was with shocked disbelief that it was learned on Sunday that a tank had bashed through the stone walls of General Aman Andom's compound. The troops broke into the house, only to find his body inside, already dead.[35]

What staggered the public even more was to learn the meaning of the repeated shots people heard coming from Akaki prison that Saturday morning, "bloody Saturday," as it came to be known. Many can still remember where they were when the truth reached them. Ted Veer still remembers where he was. He and two KHC men had been called to Jimma to settle some church problem. The night of November 23rd, they'd worked with the elders until late, finally reaching a resolution. The next morning the weary advisors took an early bus for Addis Ababa. Ted vividly remembers the scene. All was noisy confusion while buses were filling, diesel fumes choking the air. As their crowded vehicle lumbered onto the road, people settled into their seats and began to chat. Before long the loudspeaker system was abruptly turned up to give passengers the benefit of the 7 AM news. A stark announcement blared out unbelievable words: "fifty-nine ex-ministers, generals, and other former Haile Selassie appointees were executed at dawn." A sudden hush came over the bus. Almost all bowed their heads, stunned. Everything else seemed to hush in silent mourning, except for grinding of gears as the bus navigated the mountain road. After awhile, conversation resumed in hushed tones. Perhaps that was the public's first real revelation of what Ethiopia was facing.

Details were filled in eventually. The Derg had taken victims to one place and wiped out the old leadership in two hours' time. Some held the military titles *Dejjazmach* or *Gerazmach*, others were mayors; included was the Emperor's grandson. All had been thrown into a mass grave right there at Akaki prison.

The day after the executions, newspaper headlines heralded the Provisional Military Administrative Council's accusations against General Aman in such terms as "working against the philosophy of *Ethiopia Tikdem*," "plotting against the popular movement of the people," and "trying to divide the Provisional Military Administrative Council." As for the others executed, November 27th's *Ethiopian*

---

35. Cumbers (1996), *Terror*, 24–26.

Herald reported their crimes as "maladministration... selling secret documents of the country to foreign agents and attempting to disrupt the present Ethiopian popular movement."[36]

On December 20th, Ethiopia was declared a socialist state.

THERE WERE A FEW other government leaders who openly confessed their faith who became targeted for "elimination." Seven months before that "bloody Saturday," a highly respected public servant had been taken into detention, a man who had since the 1930s faithfully served at post after post as minister of various governmental departments and in ambassadorships abroad. Emmanuel Abraham, by then nearly sixty, was known as a Christian and over the years had suffered no little difficulty due to his principles. The distinguished diplomat also served as president of a large body of Protestant believers which had Lutheran roots, the Ethiopian Evangelical Church Mekane Yesus.[37] Mekane Yesus translates literally as "the place where Jesus dwells."

Top officials were being isolated in the power-plays taking place previous to the formal announcement of a coup. Along with other Imperial Ministers, in April of 1974, Emmanuel was taken to the 4th Army Camp, where eventually some sixty were crowded into Room 5. His memoirs would someday become available to provide careful details of the proceedings, who arrived when, and how they changed from "guests under protection" to prisoners with shaved heads, stripped of personal belongings, and allowed a bath only once a month.

Being men of rank, they felt a need for order, so they organized themselves carefully as an operating unit. Emmanuel was chosen to chair the five-member administrative committee. Housekeeping tasks were assigned, a spokesman to the Derg was chosen, classes were organized (Emmanuel gave Oromo language lessons), and the like, all of which improved the group's morale. "Whatever needed doing in the room was thus divided among them, and I am gratified to recall to this day that they did everything willingly and in a

---

36. Cumbers (1996), *Terror*, 25.
37. See G. Arén, *Evangelical Pioneers in Ethiopia* (EFS förlaget, 1978), G. Arén, *Envoys of the Gospel in Ethiopia* (EFS förlaget, 1999), and Fekadu G., *Evangelical Faith Movement in Ethiopia* (Lutheran Univ. Press, 2009).

spirit of mutual understanding and respect. It is my belief that the daily Gospel readings and prayers helped the process in an intangible manner."[38]

How did this spiritual element develop? Although stripped of personal books, a monk among them had been allowed to keep his Bible. Later a Gideon New Testament was procured by another prisoner during his hospitalization. Some of the prisoners asked Emmanuel to lead a group effort in a spiritual regard. He knew they needed to be spiritually armed with the Word of God. In Ato Emmanuel's wording:

> I perceived that it would be beneficial if they followed the Gospel reading beginning with the Gospel according to Luke, to be followed by the Acts of the Apostles. It was agreed. The reason for the suggestions was, except for a few persons (one Roman Catholic, two Muslims and myself), all the inmates were connected with the Orthodox Church and the majority were not accustomed to reading the Bible. I therefore felt it to be necessary that they should get acquainted with the basis of their religion. [...]
>
> I told them that I was apprehensive that disputes might arise with those who did not care to hear the Word and that it was not my wish that the Word of God should be made an occasion for differences but for harmony. I therefore advised them to exercise patience until such time as all the inmates had found a settled mind and a quiet spirit.[39]

When that awaited openness came, "realizing that the prospect for an early release was growing dim, they agreed it was time for them to collect their minds and turn to the Lord. Thereupon, they asked me to read the Scripture and offer prayers."[40] Emmanuel began reading a chapter or two each day, discussing the content; he found his fellow inmates very open and spiritually hungry. Since there was an Orthodox Priest among them, Emmanuel felt it fitting to ask him to conduct prayer in accordance with the rites of the Orthodox Church on Sundays, and later, this became a daily practice. In this way, the Imperial Ministers prepared themselves for what was to come.

---

38. Emmanuel A., *Reminiscences of My Life* (Lunde forlag, 1995), 234.
39. Emmanuel (1995), *Reminiscences*, 236.
40. Emmanuel (1995), *Reminiscences*, 236.

Then came the order on October 23rd to be ready for transfer at 2 AM. They found themselves removed to "Room 1 and Room 2" in a basement which turned out actually to be under the Throne Room of the Menelik Palace. A long month later, the morning of November 23rd, twenty-seven men were taken away from Room 1, and others were heard being removed from Room 2. Emmanuel waited and waited for his name to be called. It never came. Their fellow prisoners did not return. Those who remained eventually learned that their fifty-nine fellow inmates had been massacred on that "bloody Saturday," by political decision of the Derg.

Somehow spared with no charges against himself, Emmanuel was released two months later. His preservation made possible much further Christian service and the eventual publishing of a detailed record of a long era of diplomatic history, an account in which God was given the glory.

> *Jesus knew their thoughts and said to them,*
> *"Every kingdom divided against itself will be ruined,*
> *and every city or household divided against itself will not stand."*
> *(Matthew 12:25)*

Chapter 7

MIXED REACTIONS

Perceptions about the coup varied widely. To many, the Emperor had been seen as a leader, a hero, a father. To others, his regime had meant misuse by landowners, poverty, and subservience. Outside Ethiopia, Sudan was giving asylum to escapees from the Derg. Sudan's president Nimeiry was accused of plotting to overthrow Ethiopia's fledgling revolution. Western countries were receiving Ethiopian students seeking political asylum. Those already studying abroad feared to return, especially if they were of the previously ruling Amharas and thereby identified with the deposed government. In the Ethiopian capital, students swelled with pride over bringing about change. They looked to the future with bright hopes.

Ato Tekle Wolde Giorgis remembers being impressed with the drastic change in political structure, but as yet he recognized little evidence of the Marxist-Leninist philosophy which would put pressure on Christians as it would sweep through the land later. In the countryside, young church leaders were among those who looked to the future with excitement. Often they were the first chosen for leadership by the revolutionaries. A fiery young Kambaatan Christian remembers making enthusiastic speeches touting communism, unaware where it would lead. In Gedeo territory, long-suffering peasants ground down by high-handed landlords were quick to take up the cry, "Down with the Amhara landlords!" A Chencha evangelist out in Gamu Gofa says he remembers first receiving the new era with joy. However, most rural people had no access to a radio or newspaper, so many in isolated communities did not know for months what had happened in Addis Ababa.

The fallout from the coup issued in a whirlwind of change that began sweeping through every social institution and across all the provinces. Missions bent in the wind as assaults came from every direction. The day of the Emperor's capture, John and Naomi Cumbers were packing up for Ethiopia after a short furlough in the States. When John arrived back in his office on September 17th, he was faced a with barrage of meetings, nearly all explosive. At that point, SIM employees numbered more than 1400, counting those in Addis Ababa and over the countryside. John observed later that it was doubtful that many of them had heard of the Communist Party, much less of the *Manifesto*.

A few employees of missions decided to take advantage of the explosive atmosphere. SIM employed 309 teachers alone, serving at 40 schools. Because clinics or hospitals were sometimes located on the same stations with schools, the attitude of teachers inevitably affected other employees.

Mr. Cumbers was called to Soddo, "grandfather" station to them all, for his very first round. A friendly teacher from Wolaitta happened to be in Addis Ababa when the call came. The preview of organized dissatisfaction which he painted left John weak in the knees. With Ted Veer and Ato Tekle, John set out for the day's trip to Soddo, by now one of SIM's largest centers. Over a dozen missionaries, scores of patients, and hundreds of teachers and students were clustered around the mission compound near Soddo town. When the Addis Ababa staff arrived, the avalanche of accusations and demands which poured out were staggering. Had the Addis Ababa leaders known such confrontations were to become a part of everyday life for them for the next eight or nine years, John later admitted, they would have been tempted immediately to flee.

Day after day in the next few weeks, trips had to be made to face uproars at station after station. Accusatory attitudes were spilling over from employees to the church people, whose representatives sometimes turned up brandishing their own list of demands. Poor lone Ato Tekle tried to counsel the disheartened foreigners as they rumbled along in their Land Rover from place to place. Overhead, Ethiopia's glorious sunshine lit up fields of golden meskel flowers (*meskel* means "cross") triumphant over the gathering gloom. "What you are hearing is not to be interpreted as the genuine voice of church leadership," Tekle tried to assure them, "much less as the opinion of the collective membership of the churches." It was, he insisted, just propaganda put out by the new political leaders in Addis Ababa, inciting a few gullible church elders in each location to blame their woes on the mission.

"How could these things be happening?" mission people asked themselves. They began to see that "freedom of speech" as encouraged by the new government meant that each employee was expected to act upon the propaganda which they heard in daily radio broadcasts. Missionaries were summarily labeled as "exploiters keeping workers in submission for a mere pittance." The party line insisted that missionaries were no better than any other foreigners; all were in the country "just to make money."

At station after station, the traveling team found that nearly all SIMers, including some of the humblest who had served most selflessly for years, ones unusually respected and loved, were strangely being accused of misconstrued motives and various "crimes against the people." Much soul-searching went on as each person examined his or her life and work. As they tried to ferret out the causes for these surprising human responses and threatening events, many were humbled, many confused, and many experienced deep grief. A few broke down under the pressure. All realized their need to depend more fully on the only One who knew the whole situation.

Quietly, books began circulating among educated Ethiopian Christians, books like *Tortured for Christ* from the experience of Christians under communism in Romania. Richard Wurmbrand had spent fourteen years in prison for his faith, and the experience was not wasted. His books have been used all over the world to inform believers and strengthen them for times of persecution. Ethiopian leaders began to gird themselves and take measures to prepare their people to go through the fire. The mission and the church began to seriously take counsel together. Leaders rightly ascertained that their young people would take the brunt of the suffering. And so it was that consultations with the youth began to be arranged.

There were plenty of issues to clarify and pray about. Many a young person from a Christian home saw the change of government as a promise of better things. They spoke enthusiastically about Marxism-Leninism, having no historical perspective available to them, and hoping for the best. Missionaries had access to information about what had recently happened to Christians under communism in China, in Russia, and in Eastern Europe. They talked to church people about the likelihood of foreigners being forced out, which would leave the church on her own. They even predicted the cessation of public worship, an unthinkable plight to Ethiopian believers, who were used to large public meetings and huge annual conferences.

Marxist-Leninist teaching tended to isolate the young from the old, a danger to the maturing of the church and to the fellowship of believers. In addition to changes in the political climate, the religious climate felt new winds blowing too. Questions were arising over the matter of speaking in tongues. The new freedom in music among second generation youth was threatening to the first-generation elders. Guitar music, youth choirs, and hand clapping seemed unruly to a church leadership who had developed indigenous antiphonal singing with its formal solo call and congregational response. Furthermore, many pastors and elders were not as literate as their young people, a hard situation in which to maintain authority. Graciously, God gave the church a couple of years to burn backfires and prepare for the oncoming blaze.

The social upheaval of the day was becoming turbulent between youth and age, between missionary and national, between civilians and cadres. No one could hide from governmental surveillance, for every house was given a number, every person was required to have his or her ID card, every roadway was barred by check points, every large group was systematically infiltrated. Organization was not the new regime's weakness!

AFTER GRADUATION FROM GBI, the promising leader, Werku Gole, was delegated to spend a year moving from one area to another, teaching and encouraging youth on the grass roots level. Towering young Werku was gifted for the task. A Christian youth association was formed, a body which was to wield great influence and produce much fruit for God in the coming years. Note that the term "youth" in Ethiopia is not equivalent to "teenagers" in the West. The social situation is quite different. Life expectancy is short and the young take early responsibility in the home or fields. Students vary in ages, depending on their age when they get the chance to start elementary education and how often their schooling is interrupted. A "young people association" thus is likely to have members running from the mid teens through the thirties. Of all age groups, youth came under the most severe pressure during the Revolution. Older, more experienced Christians awakened to the need to guide and prepare their young people. Special consultations were called at inconspicuous places, to which attendees filtered in from different directions at staggered hours, so as not to be noticed.

In the Spring of 1975, a significant consultation was held at a campsite which the mission had developed on the back side of Langano, one of the Rift Valley lakes a few hours drive south of the capital. The lake lay in a dry valley dotted with thorn trees and shrubs, in the midst of which a thin population of Arsi Oromo peasants lived. Representatives from the various provinces quietly made their way to the camp by public bus or in a missionary Land Rover. Turning off the tarmac, the travelers would weave among huge anthills and grazing goats, over three or four streams, to the site of a few buildings set back a bit from the sandy shore of the elongated lake.

THE 1975 CONSULTATION WAS pivotal for Roy Wisner, a heavy set American in his thirties who at that time was heading up Chencha station, high above Abaya, another Rift Valley lake. I tell this particular story with Roy's permission, as representative of the kinds of struggles missionaries and nationals began to face.

Chencha was the Wisners' first station in the south, after serving at three others in the north. It was one of the oldest stations, one of the first places reached by Wolaitta evangelists in the 1940s. Ato Tesfaye was a leading elder there. As a child, Tesfaye had served as a house helper on the station and had grown up to teach in its elementary school and its Bible school. After further upgrading his education at GBI, he'd rejoined his wife and five children, taking up top leadership at Chencha. Roy and Tesfaye were about the same age, and the men had developed a warm relationship. It took the two men a couple days to make the trip from their cool mountain in the Gamo area, and on through a gentler range in Wolaitta, to drop into the arid Arsi area and eventually wind into the camp at Langano, hot, dusty, and tired.

Roy had come in for some hard knocks in their three terms before. That spring he was still suffering the shock and bereavement of losing their child, who tragically had drowned in a wading pool on a vacation. When Roy and Jean took their remaining child and returned to Chencha in deep grief, they discovered that nearly every national family around them had lost at least one child, not by drowning, but by the harshness of life in such a place as Ethiopia. Roy had never been good at language, a real cross to him. But on the emotional level the surrounding community could understand their pain, and the experience of shared grief bonded the Wisners to them.

Unfortunately it seemed, Roy had been served a tough assignment at Chencha. The mission could foresee the inevitable. Leadership would have to be transferred to nationals, and many thought the transfer to be long overdue. Now the political situation was hurrying the need. Chencha was chosen as the pilot attempt, and Roy given two years in which to accomplish the ticklish task.

Roy studied the Nigerian model, where SIM had already "nationalized." At the Langano consultation, he took the director aside and proposed the Nigerian method to Mr. Cumbers. In Nigeria, they'd made a point to intentionally honor those put in leadership. They did it formally, with an elaborate ceremony. Perhaps particular pressures made Ethiopia a different situation. At any rate, as Roy remembers it, "The boss said 'No—do it, and do it quickly; just tell them the timetable.'"

Back in Chencha after the Langano consultation, Roy called the station leaders together in his living room and broke the news. When he would eventually leave for furlough, no new missionary would be sent, he said. They'd be on their own. A modest financial subsidy would tide the school and clinic over, and be decreased year by year. Roy swallowed and looked around. The group sat stunned. They did not look "honored." They exploded.

The angry scenario which followed is representative of what happened on many stations in Ethiopia as nationals reacted to what they saw as abandonment, an abandonment for which they felt they'd not been prepared. After conferring among themselves, the staff workers involved the church elders. The elders asked Roy to get on the radio and ask John Cumbers to come from Addis Ababa and talk with them. John responded, "No, preparing for Council meeting...

later." The elders conferred together again, and told Roy to tell Mr. Cumbers to come. John answered "No" firmly again. To Roy they responded with equal firmness: "You won't leave your home then, until the men from Addis come."

As happened to many missionaries in those days, the Wisners became hostages, first in a rather benign manner. However, escalation was easy to inspire. Police, cadres, and people with old scores to settle took advantage of the situation, adding their contributions to the equation. Almost everybody lined up against the Wisners. Roy was told that only Ato Tesfaye seemed to disapprove of how the local community was handling the situation. He publicly challenged the church to trust God in such an hour as this. Tesfaye was facing enormous pressure. Finally the elders ordered Roy to leave his family, get in his car, and go get John Cumbers. He left, and was allowed to take a single missionary out too. Somehow a helicopter was gotten in, and in a harrowing scene, Jean and little Tim were evacuated.

With his family safe, Roy took a time-out, a miserable one. Eventually he pulled himself together and then went through the unpleasant task of returning to pack up their things. While there, the elders made Roy do what some other missionaries were ordered to do in those days. As Roy was made to bow down to touch the floor before them, his forehead in the dust, he felt totally compromised. He did it, but he didn't understand why.

Cocky young cadres ordered him to sell everything on the spot, which forced him into the painful and embarrassing role of being a trader for a week. One day, at noon Roy got word that the government was coming again, in order to raise some issue over baboon poison. When? He could hardly face being taken hostage again. That night, a kindly Ethiopian who ran the clinic quietly sent in a meal. Perhaps it was a signal. As someone carried the tray back at eleven o'clock, Roy quietly drove out of Chencha compound and down the mountain under the cloak of night.

The Wisners were given work in the capital for a time after that, but when furlough time came, it seemed to bring a finality to their Ethiopian saga. There was little hope of things ever being the same again. As was the experience of many other missionaries who went through similar ordeals, they left with painful questions and deep wounds just under the surface.

Much later, as a counseling pastor in the United States, Roy would look back over their lives and affirm what came to be his stance: "God had an objective. I was being prepared by being betrayed. Ever since then, God has given me people in my life to whom I could say, 'I think I know how it feels.' He's given me a ministry of healing, of forgiving, of learning to love. I don't think the Ethiopians ever knew the pain we felt. But it helped me grow. It made them grow too. I look forward to heaven, when I can talk fluently with these people and we can celebrate what all God was doing."[41]

You intended to harm me, but God intended it for good [...]
(Genesis 50:20a)

---

41. Over twenty years later, Roy visited Chencha. At a large church conference, he witnessed a great time of celebration. Reconciliation and warm fellowship put a seal of blessing upon his relinquishment of resentment, an attitude he'd chosen years before.

Chapter 8

RISKS ON HOSTILE GROUND

Woe betide the student in a revolution. Students are a captive population and a ready resource to exploit. Students are gathered and identified. They are usually vigorous of body and malleable of mind. They dream dreams, entertain hopes, are usually willing to give their energies to some cause larger than themselves. When the leaders of the Revolution reshaped the national service program for their purposes, students were sent off on *zemecha* duty with the express agenda of indoctrinating the populace with Marxism-Leninism. The assignment was ambitious, the power given to youth considerable, heady to wield.

Power and fear were two sides of the coin. *Zemecha* students sometimes found themselves in foreign territories, in places where their ethnic background marked them as enemies. For some fifteen years already, Ethiopia and Eritrea had been fighting over whether that north-most province would be allowed to secede. Ethiopian soldiers and Eritrean guerrillas had died on both sides with the inevitable result that bitterness continued to escalate between the two entities. Predictably, an Ethiopian sent north to Eritrea for study or on *zemecha* was unwelcome, and an Eritrean who turned up in the south was uneasy, with good cause. Suspicion, mistreatment, jailings, and even death threatened those on hostile ground.

Out at Jimma, the Volkmanns began to notice the nervousness of their few Eritrean GBI students. In Jimma town, as in other places, Eritreans began to disappear from their work or schools. Eritreans reared outside Eritrea were in a particularly difficult position, for they were marked as Eritrean but were tied into relationships with non-Eritreans, people who didn't share their family roots. Political considerations began to strain old economic or personal ties. The possibility of mistreatment became so fearful that some stole away to the anonymity of cosmopolitan Addis or back north to Eritrea.

What seemed a safe move north for Eritreans could prove even more dangerous than being in the south, for at home everyone knew them or their relatives, and every able-bodied youth, male and sometimes female, was expected to join "the Front." Which front was one of the dilemmas, the ELF or the EPLF (Eritrean Liberation Front as opposed to Eritrean People's Liberation Front). Both tried to outdo each other in applying Marxist doctrine and conscripting fighters—without much consideration of the conscriptee's preference. As brothers and sisters and fathers and friends were killed in the field, those who survived grew increasingly committed to their not having died in vain.

Earnest Christians whose allegiance was to the Prince of Peace found themselves in an especially vulnerable position. Killing was repugnant to people who knew themselves to be just one among the all for whom Christ had given His life. Furthermore, those who had shared friendships with a wide spectrum of Christians had personally experienced the unity of believers, regardless of ethnic background. On the other hand, young people living "in the field" of warfare had been fed on Marxist-Leninist philosophy, to which the doctrine of love was anathema. An earnest Christian's effective witness to fellow Eritrean youth seemed truncated by unwillingness to fight shoulder to shoulder, taking up arms for the Eritrean cause, a cause which most saw as justified, and for which they were willing even to die. "This gun is my god," one young guerrilla growled at a witnessing believer, "and I will level it at you if I hear more of your God talk!"

Christians were torn asunder as they faced no-win choices. Some reluctantly joined a Front, able only to say "war is war." Some found a way to escape via the excuse of going abroad to study (but not being able to return), or else walking over the border to Sudan or Djibouti or Kenya (and if they made it, thereafter to find themselves to have become homeless, stateless, and often destitute refugees).

The option of going into hiding could be a living hell. The case of one young man who chose pacifism in civil war exemplifies what such a choice meant. He tried the route of going incognito in Eritrea, disguising his youth by dressing as a merchant, moving only at night, sleeping by day under cover of a bush or hidden in a cave. Death always hung over him—either by enemy strafing from the air, or by discovery among guerrilla fighters on the ground. They would not hesitate to kill a "neutral" Eritrean youth. He said that when he was asleep, nightmares filled his dreams: when awake, horrors punctuated his days. He could never forget the carnage he moved among, sometimes stumbling over an ant-eaten body with a watch still encircling the corpse's bony wrist.

IN THE REVERSE POSITION, southerners placed in the far north were especially in danger. Negussie was one such person. His golden opportunity for further education finally came. But somehow he was assigned to the Teachers' Training Institute in Asmara. What an adventure, to get to go to Eritrea, and yet, what would he find there, in the light of the civil war?

The brightest spot of the experience was the fellowship he discovered in the Asmara Youth Center recently started by Pastor Tsehaye Abai, an Eritrean, and George Middleton, the visionary who had earlier helped GBI get started. The city of Asmara was not only Eritrea's capital, it was her pride and was the prize all factions strove to control. Guerrilla activity seethed around the city, in which was ensconced the Ethiopian Army and airbase. Eritrea was taken up with a struggle between her different political factions.

The Youth Center provided an oasis from the war. What a collection of "enemies" came together there! City dwellers, Ethiopian military men from the base, orphanage youth from out at Dekemhare, an occasional Eritrean guerrilla, multi-national missionaries—they all learned there to experience contact with each other as people to enjoy rather than as positions to defend. The center and the KHC Immanuel Church which undergirded it, wrought friendships which endured throughout the political struggle because they were based upon a sovereignty which rose above ethnic loyalties, political doctrines or nation states. It was Christ, the supreme Brother, whose work of reconciliation had "broken down the dividing wall of hostility," as the Apostle Paul put it (Ephesians 2:14), between all "born in Adam." That bedrock fact superseded contemporary quarrels.

The center served a variety of young people. One cluster was Asmara students. Another was from Dekemhare. Two church groups maintained orphanages in that town about thirty kilometers out of

TESHOME HAILE, GIRMA ABEBE, AND SOLOMON BEYENE (KURIFTU, 1995)

the capital. Orphanages are a mercy anywhere, but especially so in a place where fathers are taken into battle and often lost. Eritrea's youth faced early conscription. Life was serious. Mesghina Gebre Medhin, a recent GBI graduate, directed the SIM/KHC home for about a hundred orphans and a school for many more. The teaching and leadership at Dekemhare was such that many young people developed an integrity that outshone their age-mates. Their lives drew young people to examine the claims of the Christ whom they so effectively followed. Young people in Asmara city were ripe to hear those claims.

A third cluster of young men were gathered at the Ethiopian Air Force Base about seven kilometers outside of the city. Measured politically in Eritrea, they could have been seen as "the enemy." Many came into Asmara over the weekends for recreation, bored and lonely. Some wandered into the center. It became a home-away-from-home for servicemen who took some interest in the Christian message and sought friendships there. On Friday nights a bunch of the soldiers would pile into a van sent out to the base, and would talk at the center till the wee hours of the morning. Many who just dropped in to the oasis discovered living water. Some got interested in helping out with the orphan ministry. Sometimes the Dekemhare youth would travel the mountain road to visit the big city activities. Other times groups from Asmara would travel out to the orphanage for weekend camp type meetings, bringing teaching, dramas and games. The Air Force men could get involved at either end.

AMONG THOSE SERVICEMEN TOUCHED by the center were three Master Sergeants from Shewa Province in the center of the country. Solomon Beyene, Girma Abebe, and Teshome Haile were all in their early twenties, unmarried, and had been trained as technicians at the Ethiopian Air Force headquarters in Debre Zeit, Bishoftu Lake's town. They listened carefully to George and Pastor Tsehaye open the scriptures and talk about the Lord Jesus. Teshome was the first of the trio to give himself to Christ. Solomon and Girma also soon came into a vital relationship with the Lord. The three began to study the scriptures and develop unusually warm hearts toward their Lord and toward fellow servicemen who they felt needed Him. As their lives unfolded, this "threefold cord" proved strong. Jesus told his disciples they were to become "fishers of men." These three drew many into the safe net of Christ's love, both in Asmara, and later in Shewa Province.

Fellowship at the center was warm, but the Marxist-Leninist ethos at the base was cold and calculated toward soldiers who were open about expressions of faith. Exposing themselves as Christians in the military often meant being accused, harassed, and cut out of the promotions and extra benefits awarded other men. Nevertheless, Solomon, Girma, and Teshome flatly accepted the challenge. "We have to pay the price for our Lord's service," Teshome would insist, unmoved by difficulties. They set themselves to build their King's kingdom no matter where their base of service might be, systematically caring for the body of Christ, however secretly they were required to minister, or however openly they were required to pay the price. That commitment brought forth solid fruit at the base, and later in Shewa when they were re-stationed at Debre Zeit.

IN OCTOBER OF 1974, Negussie wrote his childhood friend John in Canada from the Teachers Training Institute (TTI) in Asmara, where the Youth Center was being boon to this young man from the south.

While warfare circled the urban center, inside the capital city, life retained some semblance of normality. The three airmen from Debre Zeit were among the brothers he came to know in the Asmara fellowship. Negussie's sunny disposition cheered their war-strained nerves. At some point, Negussie picked up guitar playing, perhaps there.

But by January of 1975, Negussie's guarded letter to John was sent from Dekemhare, the orphanage town. It seemed Negussie and other southern students at TTI had to be taken out of Asmara for their safety. Although still in Eritrea, Dekemhare afforded the advantage of friends among the orphanage youth there. Again, growing pressures made that location a short-lived haven.

Within half a year, Negussie had to leave Eritrea, working southward to Addis Ababa. Such travel was not simple. Crossing rugged mountains and swollen rivers would be challenging to the fittest body. Bus tickets were prohibitive for an unpaid student, and bombing threatened the roads. A lonely traveler on foot never knew when he'd suddenly be confronted by an Ethiopian soldier, an Eritrean guerrilla, a nervous deserter, or a hardened bandit, not to mention wild animals or the ethnically suspicious peasants whose land had to be transversed.

When Negussie finally made it to Munz, an Amhara stronghold halfway to Addis Ababa (where Sahle taught, although Negussie probably had not met him yet), he felt safer. Yet, an unexpected incident left him nearly dead. Hearing the cries of a woman being beaten in the lodging where he slept, Negussie ran to the scene and begged her drunken lover to stop. Enraged, the man turned on the short-torsoed stranger and beat him nearly to a pulp, so badly that Negussie had to be hospitalized.

The battered lad finally made it to Addis Ababa in time to rendezvous with his childhood friend, John. Like a homing pigeon, John Coleman had taken the college summer break in Canada to come back to visit his family. By then his parents were not living in their old home in Wolisso, but at the Press compound in Addis Ababa.

The young men's reunion was ecstatic. What a rush of memories! They savored childhood experiences in Wolisso and filled each other in the best they could on what life had dealt them in their young adulthood. John's college experience had been a straightforward one in Canada. Visiting his parents in Addis Ababa, John got a clearer picture of the violence Ethiopians faced. After hearing about some of the dangers Negussie had survived in pursuit of his education, John was shaken. He was thankful for Negussie's protection, but he couldn't help feeling uneasy about his hero's future.

John remembers their final parting as one of the most poignant leave-takings of his life. The two stood at the Press gate trying to swallow the lumps in their throats, embracing from side to side repeatedly in the warm Ethiopian way. Finally they shook hands once, face to face, slowly, hard, in western manner. The rainy season seemed to weep with them that final day.

OUT AT JIMMA, THE Volkmanns were starting their second year. Some of the more mature students had graduated. As political tensions grew and the more hot-headed students influenced the atmosphere, Ato Tesfaye's sensibleness and Ato Tekle's fatherliness were sorely missed, with them gone home to their families in Chencha and Saja. Quiet Hussein had graduated, but after a summer up north among his Muslim relatives, he returned to Grace Bible Institute (GBI) to teach. He did not mind staying close to Belaynesh, the younger student from Kambaata. Unexpected separation came when the Derg ordered all 12th grade graduates out on *zemecha*. Hussein watched Belaynesh march out of the campus with the others in a khaki cap, shirt and trousers, so in contrast to her usual full-skirted gracefulness.

Art confessed to his wife, Sue, that he found one of the newer students to be his "thorn in the flesh" that second year. The young man had charismatic leanings, which in itself was difficult to handle among a student body from churches who held varying viewpoints about Pentecostal manifestations. The charismatic spirit which had begun to sweep over Ethiopia in the late sixties was coming into full bloom in the seventies. It was changing the forms of worship, the music sung, the doctrines promulgated, and the experiences sought among evangelicals all over the country. Passionate Shimeles was a disturbing presence and a constant challenge to the more philosophical Art, for Art recognized in the fiery youth a wholeheartedness and freshness which could not help but disturb a "tamer" expression of faith.

As the Revolution escalated, Shimeles put an unsettling question to Art: "You came here to die for us, didn't you?" Art wasn't sure he had come with that in mind. He was responsible for a wife and little Amy and their new baby, and he felt a moral responsibility in that direction, too. Even crossing Jimma town to the airfield didn't promise to be without incident in these volatile days.

With students being yanked out for *zemecha* and unsettling rumors flying in every direction, the campus grew more edgy. Most disturbing was the threat that the Institute had not long to live. The earlier pressures from Jimma's cold Muslim majority and angry Orthodox leadership were now joined by cadre leadership bent on closing down all Christian schools. Each semester threatened to be the last. Morning by morning, veiled news from outstations was gleaned via the missionary radio check. Sudden riots and local showdowns at mission hospitals and schools were glimpsed in vague form by all missionaries who were tuned in. Meanwhile, students listened to a steady diet of propaganda on Amharic broadcasts, reporting the latest proclamation or the supposed course of the Eritrean–Ethiopian War. The barrage filled the airwaves with accusations decrying the "unscrupulous imperialist," the "foreign-influenced Pente" or the "capitalist dog."

If missionaries were ordered out or chose to leave, some nationals could see that they stood to lose jobs or hoped-for positions. They wondered, "Who would favor me after my complicity with what the cadres call 'the capitalistic demons'?" After one school vacation, students returned particularly radicalized. A group of them presented a document in writing, demanding that every student be assured a job and a bicycle when they left the school. The administration stood firm against such intimidation, but the incident began to erode the trust relationship which teachers and students had previously taken for granted.

When terrible reports came of a massacre of three thousand Kullo Kontan people in the nearby area of Bonga, Art and Sue felt further threatened. That raid wasn't even Marxist-Leninist, just the savage Bodis on the rampage. Churches had been torched and seventy Christians had been among those murdered.

In Addis Ababa, John Cumbers could read the writing on the wall. He wasn't encouraging assignment of new missionaries to the Ethiopian field. In fact, he usually wasn't suggesting old-timers return when a furlough came due.

As the 1975 school term came to a close, the GBI faculty took stock. Their oldest students were graduating, many were scattered out on *zemecha*, and the school might never open for another school year. The Volkmanns hadn't had language school, so transferring them to an Amharic speaking area was a problem, not to mention the difficulty of finding a place which was welcoming rather than repelling missionaries! The Veers had gone on furlough. Along with many others, Art and Sue agonized over the decision. Reluctantly they elected a leave of absence, taking a faculty position back at the seminary in Chicago. No one knew where this government was heading, and perhaps in two years the wind would have blown one way or the other.

Like many others who took to the skies from the Addis Ababa airport that rainy season, their emotions ranged from deep disappointment to profound relief. As they rose above the beautiful mountains cradling Addis Ababa, so deceptively quiet from above, they could only ache and pray.

Like others who left, they would have to struggle with uneasy feelings of guilt. Physically back in the United States but emotionally deeply entwined in issues thousands of miles from the Chicago Loop, the Volkmanns felt isolated. They searched for any information they could get, but news was scant and neither missionaries nor nationals could write openly without risk. A terse August 25th radio report in Addis Ababa did make international news: "Haile Selassie has died in his sleep." The Emperor died, it was asserted by investigators long after the event, by suffocation.

What is happening to others, they wondered, especially to our students? Only when separated from Ethiopia did Art and Sue realize how much they'd changed in those two years, how foreign they felt in America, how bonded to Ethiopians they'd become. Like many others who had left, they were out of Ethiopia, but Ethiopia would never be out of them.

> *For he himself is our peace,*
> *who has made the two one and has destroyed the barrier,*
> *by abolishing in his flesh the law*
> *with its commandments and regulations.*
> *His purpose was to create in himself one new man out of the two,*

*thus making peace,
and in this one body to reconcile both of them to God
through the cross, by which he put to death their hostility.*
(Ephesians 2:14–16)

Chapter 9

TEARING DOWN, BUILDING UP

Bobagaya they called Bishoftu Lake in the local language. Even from the capital, one can get a distant view of the area by driving up the mountain rim on the north edge of the city to Entoto, a vantage point from which *Addis Ababa* ("New Flower") unfolds southward. Bishoftu Mountain looms purple in the distance beyond. From Entoto one can sight the most imposing cone to the south, Mount Zekwala, shaped like a huge trapezoid and surrounded by smaller volcanic structures. Among those cones, nestled on the edge of one of the crater lakes, is "Bishoftu," SIM's beloved retreat center, used by almost all mission groups in the country.

I still remember our first trip there as newcomers to Ethiopia. We peered out the car windows on the way, to get a sense of town and country. The scene is nearly the same today. A strange mixture of old and new, urban and rural, moves past you as you bump through to the outskirts of Addis Ababa on pot-holed asphalt streets crowded with pedestrians on their way to work or to draw water at the neighborhood tap. People and cars weave their way between herds of goats or sheep mindlessly moving to market. An occasional steer stands placidly on the narrow median running between opposing lanes of traffic. Belching diesel trucks rumble noisily along, through which blue taxis and passenger cars defensively weave. Signs spelled out in peculiar symbols indecipherable to Amharic-illiterate expatriates stare down at strangers who are unable to recognize Amharic words for "Stop" or "Go" or to count from one to ten in this strange language. On our first trip out, when "SHELL" loomed up over a gasoline station in English, it brought tears to my eyes, just to be given a token assurance that I could read something in this bewildering world.

A string of brave entrepreneurs sit by the roadside with tiny pyramids of eggs or potatoes or tomatoes carefully arranged on burlap for display. As neighborhood after neighborhood melts past, an occasional face emerges out of the mass—a herder struggling with an unruly donkey, a mother shielding a child from traffic, jovial students ambling along with book bags in hand. Beyond the convergence of railroad tracks, power lines, and towering granaries, the Debre Zeit road makes its way out of the city past stick-and-plastic stalls selling pottery, fruit, blankets, rough furniture, clothing, and the like.

As town gives way to country, a strange horizon of volcanic leftovers meets the eye: igneous rocks and boulders strewn carelessly over the roughly cultivated fields dotted unevenly by scrubby flat thorn trees. Way in the distance on the left rises Bishoftu Mountain, its mighty shoulders mysterious in purple-gray haze. On the right rise grassed-over cinder cones, angular pyramids and odd landforms resembling huge geometric symbols. Overhead, rain falls in one season, and in another, majestic white thunderheads rise heavenward in brilliant blue skies. One can hardly fail to be awed, driving wide-eyed through this sample of Ethiopia's fantastic beauty.

Ethiopia's major Air Base lies south of the town of *Debre Zeit*, which means "Mount of Olives." In Debre Zeit, a Bishoftu-bound vehicle turns eastward onto a dirt road lined with mud and straw or tin-roofed homes, partially hidden behind the compound fences which everyone builds. Eventually a green gate appears, marked "SIM Guesthouse."

Once inside the compound, a first glimpse reveals a panorama of trees and bushes ablaze with blossoms which surround the lounge and dining room, shade cabins, and give way to a tennis court bathed in sunlight, and paths sloping down to a boat dock bobbing with canoes. At the base lies a lovely shimmering circle of blue water cradled in the ancient volcanic cone. This natural reserve on the edge of the water is a virtual paradise for repose. Visitors can relax between palms and bamboo and watch iridescent birds darting between the huge lavender and red blossoms of jacaranda and flame trees, all scented with the delicate fragrance of snow-white frangipani flowering bushes. The more active can romp at the children's playground, swim in a protected lake-edge enclosure, canoe around the lake, or hike up Bishoftu Mountain.

Before the Revolution, the Bishoftu property was used by a broad spectrum of missionaries to save their health and sanity, provide family retreats, and conference accommodations. The quiet lake property could not know that soon its peace would increasingly be split by screaming jets above, that Bishoftu's gates would open to become a refuge for harassed Ethiopian Christians, its pool would host secret baptisms, and its cabins hear increasingly fervent prayers.

Down near the water stands one Ethiopian-style round hut with a grass roof. "Sharon Cottage" is written over its door. It holds precious memories for many who have met with God in that quiet place. In 1975, an unexpected birth took place in Sharon Cottage. The spot was hidden. Nine people were present. There were the three Ethiopian Air Force men who'd come alive to Christ in Asmara a few years before, and six were brand new believers. A church was being born.

Girma Abebe, Teshome Haile, and Solomon Beyene had been re-stationed back at the base in Debre Zeit and all three had married. The town was largely Orthodox and so not warm to evangelical Christians. Yet the three men were convinced that Christ, not a religious system, offered the only true answer to human need. They began praying earnestly about how to present his claims to people in their home area. For a while, they'd made the tedious trip to Addis Ababa on Sundays to the Fellowship Church, one which especially served the university community and drew students like Negussie and Sahle when they'd been in town. Still, going there regularly didn't seem to the three airmen to be benefiting their neighbors. Finally, with encouragement from the Addis Ababa fellowship, the three couples committed themselves to reaching people right where they were, no matter what it might cost them. From the six meeting in Sharon Cottage that memorable day, a church came into being. Ato Yohannes Bosana, a Wolaittan evangelist at the Youth Center in Addis Ababa often came to encourage the new body of believers. Before many months, the spiritual vitality of the little band began to convince people around them that Jesus was very alive and available. Many were beginning to realize they needed something!

The mission property on the lake might well have been confiscated by the government, for it was such a plum. God not only protected the cloistered haven repeatedly, He greatly "stretched out its tent cords." Bishoftu hosts in those years began using every opportunity they could find to encourage the national believers. Conferences and special meetings, training sessions, and clandestine baptisms doubled the activity at the place as its arms were opened to many an Ethiopian group.

The hosts led devotions with the local Ethiopian workers who tended the grounds and cooked the delicious meals served there. (It was *injera* and *wat* night that took first prize, for missionaries greatly relished Ethiopia's national meal.) A few workers came to real faith in a living Savior, among them a young fellow named Belay Wendafarash. Very early in his new life, Belay's earnest testimony demonstrated his gift for reaching people. It was decided to send the young man to the Saja Bible school, where Ted Veer and Ato Tekle had taught before their GBI days. The Revolution soon closed the Saja school, but Belay got a little training. He proceeded to systematically witness in the Bishoftu neighborhood around the lake. Many responded. He started a school which eventually built up to 250 children. As missionaries diminished in the country, the national believers swelled the guest list at the Lake, tipping the balance of who was getting the most use out of Bobagaya.

However, cadres harassed the Debre Zeit believers at every turn and repeatedly closed down their meeting places. A partial answer was found right inside the mission property by turning the small garden barn into a meeting place the *kebele* (neighborhood association) couldn't touch. Sergeant Girma rented a villa in town in which low-profile gatherings could be held, but his home was stoned. Sahle was accused by the cadres and nearly relieved of his job. Many families were treated with contempt and some found themselves in serious financial straits. All these trials only seemed to mold them into a more unified body in which God was noticeably glorified.

Eventually the need for a meeting place was solved creatively by the three air force families deciding to arrange adjacent housing way over on the far side of Debre Zeit. People would amble in quietly, one or two at a time, and in hushed tones without apprehension they maintained a full battery of church activities. Solomon, Girma, and Teshome's living rooms became the regular setting for

YOHANNES BOSANA (SODDO, 1994)

Sunday School classes, worship time, prayer meetings, and even a formal Bible school with classes three nights a week.

As pressure on students in Addis grew stronger and church after church was closed by the government, Bishoftu became one sanctuary to which young people could sometimes come, shut the gate, and finally relax in warm fellowship. Such a place was a rare refuge in the midst of much confusion those early years of the Revolution.

A FEW BELIEVERS IN the area joined with the fledgling church. Eventually one family was that of Sahle Tilahun and Aberash Takele, the students who had laughed at each other's shaved heads in prison together, and later married the week the Revolution took hold. They had left Munz. Sahle eventually became head master of a school in the Debre area. Aberash taught mathematics, and they had started a family. Somewhere in that progression we returned to Ethiopia, and Charles had a surprise reunion with Sahle. Malcolm Hunter arranged for Charles to fly down to Chencha with a new doctor, to introduce her to one of the sites where she would be touching down in a new airborne medical service Malcolm had devised. Meanwhile, our old friend Sahle had been called to help his mentor, Mina Moen, with a short course she was teaching at Chencha. Mina was the language teacher with whom he had enjoyed such a meaningful relationship during Debre Berhan days. Tom Fellows (Alex's son) was managing vehicles and talked Charles into driving an ailing mission vehicle to Addis Ababa, "for repairs." Sahle needed a ride home, and would go along "to help with the cultural bridging." Nationals always made travel through unfamiliar territory smoother, and in these days of hostility toward foreigners, a go-between was even more crucial. The two seemed a good team, and were happy to enjoy a ride together. Tom would not have known that the pair had a way of sparking each other's spontaneity to an almost dangerous degree. Hearing about it later, crisis after crisis, gave the mission one of the most hilarious evenings people had spent in a long time.

Chencha is located on the edge of an escarpment of several thousands of feet. When Tom admitted the clutch was bad and the brakes not too good and handed them a supply of clutch fluid, a more cautious pair might have refused to give it a try. "Just keep putting fluid in it," Tom advised them nonchalantly, being an accomplished mechanic, himself. Navigating a weary Land Rover down a mountain and across a desert stretch along 300 some kilometers of rutted roads, passing through threatening ethnic diversities—these foreseeable factors might have been sufficiently foreboding to others. Not to Sahle and "Uncle Charlie"—as Sahle began to call his companion after that momentous trip. Oh yes, Dr. MacDonald was also along for the ride, the physician from Scotland. She could hardly have guessed what she was getting into.

The three travelers made it down Chencha's steep descent. Propelling the Land Rover through the country side began to take on the flavor of a comic movie. Just "adding fluid" didn't make everything fine. Charles wasn't even sure where it went into, as it flowed down intravenous tubing into the bowels of the motor. He'd used intravenous tubing for medical procedures, not cars.

Checkpoints were particularly tricky. Picture the situation when approaching a town's road barrier guarded by undisciplined local militia men with weapons—places where foreigners hated to be noticed. With no clutch, they had to gear down to stop, going into neutral.

Then they had to answer threatening questions and sometimes be searched. To get started again, they had to elicit people from the crowd who would help push them to a speed fast enough to allow shifting into gear. Thankfully, Land Rover gears synchronize to allow shifts without a clutch, but only within a narrow window when engine and transmission are at the right speeds. At the critical point, Sahle, the lady doctor, and Charles, puffing along with the pushers, had to jump through the open car doors into their seats. If the gear caught, they breathed a prayer of thanks, and waved good-bye.

Alas, next the fan belt broke. They scratched their heads about how to devise one out in open country. Charlie tried a series of substitutes: a rope first, next his tie, then his belt, and when that gave out, they tried Dr. MacDonald's nylon panty-hose! One might imagine the gymnastics and abandonment involved to make all these adjustments, but such seemed necessary to retain movement, and perhaps to spare three lives.

Despite remembered stories of improvisations bringing on-the-spot deliverance, nothing really worked. No effective fan belt meant the engine heated up to intolerable levels. About every ten to fifteen miles they had to add water from somewhere, sometimes from rainwater left in a ditch. When the lights began to fail at dusk, it seemed to be the last straw. Reaching Shashamane town Saturday night was itself miraculous. But foreigners were not advised to sleep in the hostile environment of places like Shashamane in such times. SIM's leprosarium on the outskirts had been taken over by the government. Where were the travelers to go? Where but to the Seventh Day Adventist (SDA) property, just beyond!

Upon arrival inside the gate, all Charlie could think of was his desperate need for a cup of coffee. The lady in charge, seeing his disappointment to be told Seventh Day Adventists don't drink coffee, offered him herbal tea, assuring him it was "very good for the bladder." The three scruffy visitors were kindly fed and given bunks in dorms which were empty during students' vacation.

Sahle would rehearse the bedtime scene many times in the future. Used to very formal Ethiopian prayers, standing, or with foreheads on the ground, he was shocked when the good doctor just threw himself on the cot and said, "Sahle, let's just pray as we lay here." They did. Somehow, they bonded that night in such a way that Sahle would often call my husband "Uncle Charlie" in the future, when we were in private. Maybe the fact that the missionary had so little money on him that he had to borrow from Sahle along the way might have tilted customary protocol.

Sunday morning, the discrepancy between official days of worship worked out fortuitously for the stranded travelers. A black American mechanic working with the Seventh Day Adventists was happy to work on Sunday, for Saturday had been the Adventists' sabbath! The Land Rover got fixed enough to risk travel. Hearty thanks were expressed to the kind SDA helpers. Off they went, Charles and Sahle teaching Dr. Helen the words of Indalla's favorite song, learned from him in Debre Berhan: *B'Abate baet*. "In the world you'll have trouble, but in my Father's house, joy, in Jesus name!"

They made it back to Addis Ababa just in time for the Sunday night service at the SIM Chapel. Arriving breathless and askew, Charles' spontaneity hadn't yet worn off when he was asked to give a short report to the congregation. It was not a typical one, for when the travelers' testimony to God's deliverance unraveled in a tale involving brake fluid, his belt, her panty hose, "tea for the bladder," etc., it couldn't help but bring down the house. Perhaps it was worth the risk, if for no other reason that to provide a little comic relief to the period's consistently grim overtone. "Tis mercy all [...] that found out me," go the lines of a hymn which Charlie is still moved to sing when he remembers that trip!

CHANGE AND CONFUSION WERE the steady diet in those months. To begin with, a hundred thousand Ethiopians were sent out on *zemecha* to promulgate Marxist-Leninist doctrine. Meanwhile, as the famine in the north was receding, the band of Christian volunteers who had come from overseas slowly made their way home. The handling of religious issues was contradictory. In spite of the Derg's bold proclamation of "freedom of religion," evangelical churches were taken over. Political activists sparred back and forth. In response to an attempted coup, assassinations and mass murders increased.

Every mission station experienced its unique last days. Cadre harassment and organized methods of expulsion were routine. Some stations made peaceful transfers to nationals; other places were more turbulent. The staff at Dessie Hospital had to be evacuated. Dilla

Hospital was relinquished to the government after many difficulties. Leimo Hospital was closed. At the hospital at Soddo there were threats on missionary lives, and at Shashamane's the foreigners were put under house arrest.

War played its role in the confusion. In Asmara, Pastor Tsehaye Abai was abducted first by Eritrean guerrillas, then imprisoned by the Ethiopian forces. Somalia declared war on Ethiopia and enlisted the Gujjis to fight with them. Some of the precious few believers in the Bale area were among those caught in a vice between the Somali and Gujji and forces, which resulted in many being killed and precious fields being burned. Even the elements seemed to conspire. Out east near Somali, the Wabi Shebelle River flowing in desert terrain flooded Kelafo station, one of the few Christian outposts in Muslim territory. Isolated deaths shocked believers in various areas. Dr. Doug Hill was stabbed by a Muslim fanatic in the Ogaden, and Teseme Dube speared by witch doctors in Bonga. Beyond Ethiopia, a blow disheartened the wider church: news came of the drowning of Dr. Byang Kato, a Nigerian whose leadership had been so stellar among African evangelicals.[42]

In the midst of these dreadful events, people were just human beings, with all the fragility and fallibility humanness includes. At times, administrative decisions had to be made quickly, and misjudgments were made. At one point, pressure over mishandling of one accused missionary's case made John Cumbers so physically sick that he telephoned Dr. Davis at the SIM head office in the United States and offered to resign. "That won't help the situation one *iota* (bit)," Dr. Davis responded. "Call a special Council meeting." He counseled from the scriptures and assured John of prayer backing from colleagues around the world. After a grueling all-day Council, John took the blame for the whole mess. Still, such episodes leave scars. During all this, Naomi stood like a brick behind her husband, serving both as his secretary and as SIM Headquarters nurse. John marveled at God's grace to Naomi, at her stamina to keep up her daily work, care for the sick, and stand with him day and night.

---

42. Byang Kato led the Association of Evangelicals of Africa and Madagascar.

ATO TEKLE WOLDE GIORGIS, the head of the Kale Heywet Church (KHC), was caught in the middle between foreigner and national, a difficult position. The negotiations and emotional energy involved in the incessant takeovers, or handovers, were exhausting. The man rarely enjoyed the comfort of home, for the family remained in Saja while he worked and slept in his tiny second-floor office above the SIM chapel in Addis Ababa. At one point, weary Tekle recorded the losses: "To date, 33 upper level academic schools, 265 KHC lower schools, 1740 churches sealed, 27 SIM Bible schools closed, 97 KHC Bible schools closed."

Nevertheless, while things were breaking down in many places, there were those who set about building up. Ato Kedamo had met with God over the Revolution, and set about steadying his city flock. When her *zemecha* service was completed, Belaynesh and Hussein were married. After a short time with Hussein teaching while Belaynesh finished her interrupted course at Grace Bible Institute, they moved to the capital. They brought warm reinforcement to Ato Tekle. Just outside Addis Ababa, the fledgling Debre Zeit church was catching fire spiritually. In September of 1976, confusion over certain doctrines of the charismatic movement was assuaged by the timely input of Festo Kivengere and Sam Kamelasen, eminent spiritual leaders who aided reconciliation between groups during a World Vision pastors' conference.

WEIGHTY TO MANY WAS the thought of leaving Ethiopia with its 80–100 language groups, with only three major languages yet having complete Bible translations. Evelyn Brant conceived of an emergency strategy which came to be called the "Key Scriptures" project. Al and Evelyn Brant had pioneered among the Gedeo ethnic group.[43] In the late sixties, they had traveled to Nigeria to observe a movement which was sweeping through the Nigerian church, called New Life for All. Bringing the essential vision back, the Brants developed materials for Ethiopia and held conferences which led to a great evangelistic thrust all over the south. Naturally they saw the need for the scriptures in native languages for Ethiopia's burgeoning multiplicity of believers. Al Brant had been stuck with an illness

---

43. Their story is told in Brant (1992), *Wake*.

which demanded their departure, and so the Key Scriptures project was turned over to seasoned faithfuls with linguistic gifts, Mina Moen and Ruth Cremer.

After choosing 1600 key verses of Scripture, the aim was to quickly get just those few passages translated into ten major languages. Seven languages did see completion. This was a mammoth task for a valiant band of colleagues who struggled under difficult constraints. On the one hand, the missionaries were confined by the government to the capital, and on the other, the nationals were regularly blocked at checkpoints from travel. Contacts with foreigners became dangerous. Once the 1600 verses were finished in a language, catechisms and teaching notes were created for their use, all built upon those pivotal verses. A great leap forward was therefore accomplished, one, which in "normal times" might not have happened for decades. Such outcomes could not but raise questions as to God's mysterious purposes in spite of, or because of, the national shake-up.

Meanwhile, Al Brant's mantle was passing to his son, Howie. In his thirties, Howie and his wife were spearheading work at Zenzencho in Gurage territory. Howie and another Canadian missionary, Paul Balisky, grasped the great danger to youth, and their potential as well. Together they called a conference at Langano designed for youth and elders to work through some of their roles in a godly manner. They repeatedly stressed the proverb, "age for wisdom, youth for strength." Christian youth associations started an underground movement, organizing cells methodically. (The communists had a lot to teach Christians in the matters of organization!) Where churches were open, the young people organized prayer groups and choirs. Choirs became an internal mechanism that included not just "music practice" but praying, planning, worshipping, all of which molded the members into a unified body of mutual support.

FOR THE MISSION, THE prevailing phenomena seemed to be "contradiction." While a surgeon at Soddo was being bitterly accused by the Wolaitta community, a beautiful new hospital facility was being dedicated for them. Although education was a precious entity, especially Christian education, the situation at the Girls' Christian Academy turned into an ugly fight with a group of parents and teachers who wreaked economic and emotional havoc for those involved over a period of many months. While missionaries swung back and forth between opinions on what course the mission should take in this or that situation, John Cumbers came near to exhaustion. Some were threatened with physical attacks, some had panic attacks. The director was on the verge of a heart attack. Mr. Cumbers was getting less than five hours sleep each night. It is customary in Ethiopia for a person with a problem not to feel there is value in presenting his case to anyone except the chief executive. John was victimized by the custom. He began to realize that his lack of delegation was both dangerous and ridiculous, but he could hardly get a breather to think how to change the pattern. When Howard Borlase (one man who could be counted on to keep a sense of humor) suggested it was time for him to bow out of administration, John was horrified. Howard was eventually persuaded to stay. Murray Coleman's cool-headed assistance was also a lifesaver. Behind the scenes, a handful of faithful women held the fort in the offices, staying abreast of exacting diplomatic and administrative procedures.

At one point John asked the missionaries and Ethiopians who worked most closely with him to meet and make some suggestions for sharing the workload more. While some compliments were given, the essential result was humbling, for it voiced a complaint to be heard more and more strongly from the church as time went on: the mission's tendency to run the ship alone, not delegate enough, and not prepare others for leadership. In March of 1976 the two bodies held their first real staff meeting. When John Cumbers saw how much the Ethiopians appreciated the opportunity to share the burdens and to offer solutions, he wondered why he'd left it so long to include them in staff meetings. At one meeting a frank letter was presented, censuring missionaries for giving vocal expression to their private political opinions. By September the KHC Executive threatened to break away from SIM, citing the mission's empty promises and failure to train national leaders, while being caught up in its own agenda. John Cumbers could hardly believe his ears.

1976 gave way to 1977 with both the mission and church confused, fearful, and at low ebb. The mission seemed harried disunited, stumbling about under siege. The church seemed to feel threatened, immature and angry to be so. Both probably felt betrayed and abandoned by the other. Painful as it was, they became hammer and anvil to each other as God shaped and pounded those who stayed obedient to His workmanship. As He formed their courage and developed their maturity, they grew. Eventually they would learn to forgive. Without crisis, there is little opportunity for faith. More opportunity was coming.

> *There is a time for everything,*
> *and a season for every activity under heaven:*
> *a time to be born and a time to die,*
> *a time to plant and a time to uproot [...]*
> *a time to tear down and a time to build.*
> *(Ecclesiastes 3:1, 2, 3b)*

Part III

FACING PRINCIPALITIES AND POWERS

(During 1977–78)

*For our struggle is not against flesh and blood,
but against the rulers, against the authorities,
against the powers of this dark world and
against the spiritual forces of evil in the heavenly realms.*
(Ephesians 6:12)

MAP 3: BOUNDARIES OF ETHIOPIA'S PROVINCES (BEFORE AD 1991)

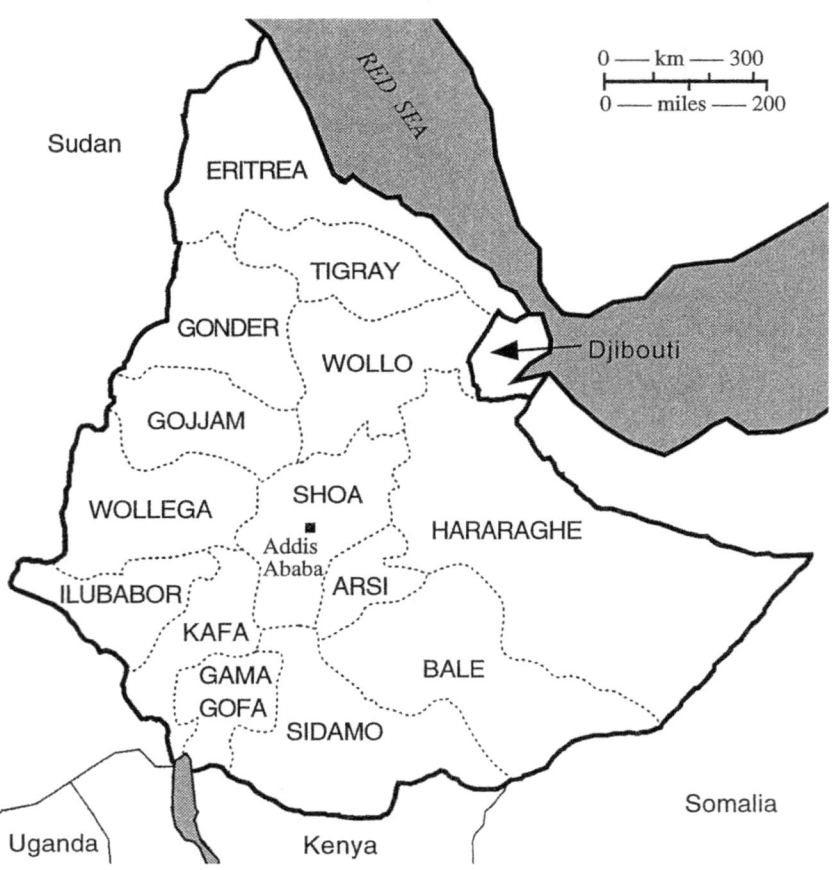

Source: Adapted from Parker (1995), *Ethiopia*, by Johnathan Bascom.

Chapter 10

FACING THE CADRES

Negussie looked over the dull brown fields around Wolisso with a sense of being back where he had started. In January, Ethiopia's lushness fades as ever-more bony cattle scrounge to find fodder. The harvest is over and the long months of dryness take their toll. Prayer goes up for "the small rains" in March to be adequate enough to avert the yearly possibility of famine. And yet another fear threatens, for without the cleansing ministry of rain, disease strikes and spreads more easily.

Added to these insecurities inflicted by nature, threats from fellow human beings escalated in 1977, as well. By then, Negussie had finished his teacher's training and had taken a position in his home area near Wolisso. A bit misshapen though he was, Negussie was a vibrant witness to Christ, making him a dangerous person in the estimation of local political leadership. He realized the axe might fall, but the young man continued to live normally, forthright about his faith. Negussie was unwilling to allow fear to get the victory over his life.

Fear was Ethiopia's overwhelming emotion in 1977. For some, it became sheer terror. A technique of Marxism-Leninism, fear was systematically instilled into all, whether bourgeois or proletariat. At the lowest level, young people were chosen by Party leaders as cadres to enforce communist doctrines in the local *kebele*, the neighborhood political association. *Kebele* headquarters numbered every house. Every individual was required to register for his or her personal identification number, in order to be issued a passbook. The identity booklet always had to be carried. It would be demanded at barricaded checkpoints on travel routes, or upon sudden arrest. Fear was fanned by many means, among them by cadre intimidation, by *kebele* action taken without right of appeal, and by high-handed

Party leadership. Such leaders might be committed to "the cause," or on the other hand, they might just be pursuing personal interests or settling old scores under the cloak of politically doctrinaire "purity."

Fear is experienced person by person. Multiplied throughout the society quite purposefully, its intensification in 1977 became known as "the Red Terror." Although the capital was home base to the process, it was felt throughout the country by students and peasants, by little people and big. Each will remember—or try to forget—his or her own experiences. The following three stories may serve to illustrate how a few individuals were meeting those fears.

L. (HIS NAME STILL must not be revealed) was one of six sons of a father who had become rich through owning several flour mills and a fleet of buses. L.'s family was nominally Orthodox. Highly idealistic, he went to the university and found in communism the hope that the world's problems would be answered by "the rich sharing with the poor." L.'s growing zeal for communism prompted Party leaders to appoint him to lead a team of *zemecha* campaigners to the south with the assignment of targeting Christians by terrorizing them and shutting down their churches.

Their technique was to take up positions in a church building early Sunday morning, and start haranguing the congregation, declaring loudly that religion had no part to play in the new Ethiopia. They ridiculed people for "praying to an invisible god," and tried to succeed in emptying the church.

One morning a simple peasant woman in a beleaguered congregation stood and said, "In spite of all that you have told us, we came here to pray to God and we're going to pray before we leave." Before anyone could stop her, she led in prayer. The campaigners were furious and hustled her off to the local police station. They charged the praying woman with resisting the Revolution. She withstood their abuse quietly, unmoved.

When she was released, her first act was to invite her accusers to her home for a meal. Angry as the young men were, home-cooked food sounded irresistible. Before inviting them to partake, she went ahead and thanked God for the food, in spite of their laughter to drown her out.

The campaigners worked in that area for many weeks, and kept trying to negate the humble peasant woman's influence. Neither their threats of imprisonment nor their weekly tirades in the churches succeeded in dispersing the believers. When the cadres were scheduled to depart, a local political leader was to be chosen by *kebele* vote. Who was elected but their thorn in the flesh, the praying woman herself! Years later, when L. told his story, he summarized: "We were defeated, she was victorious. I remember her face so clearly; never before or since have I seen such love in the face of any person."

Back at the university, L. relentlessly worked to make life intolerable for believers there. In the cafeteria one day, L. saw someone bow his head in prayer before eating. L. jumped up and screamed at him something about "thanking a non-existent deity for food which you bought yourself" and then struck the student a hard blow across the head.

Suddenly L. felt his body go numb. He stopped cold and asked himself, Why did I do that? The man had done nothing to me, and yet I hit him. Later, he recalled only a blur of finding himself back in his room, not eating, and not sleeping for days. The strongest memory was the recurring face of the praying woman appearing before his eyes, full of love. Finally he stumbled into a church one Sunday morning. With his head covered with his white shawl, he cried out to God for mercy. Although he knew nothing about the Bible yet, he dates his conversion to that moment. Later, God brought forth some believers whom the Spirit assisted to realize that this modern-day Saul could become a Paul. They began to nurture him in a secret Bible study.

Soon L. faced persecution at the university, but the most deadly danger turned out to be from his own brother, now a colonel in the army. The brother invited him to a drinking place, ordered a beer for them both, and when L. asked for something different, brought the accusation: "So it's true you've become a Christian!" L. sensed danger, rose to leave, and saw his brother reach for his revolver. He ran from the bar, praying for protection, dashed through traffic, crossed the road, and found himself blocked by a wall. By what he feels was supernatural power, he was able to scale the high wall and collapse on the other side.

L. really expected his brother to kill him. "An enemy of the regime" could be killed without fear of legal reprisal. The way L. disguised himself and escaped out of the city, how he got onto a bus southward, by what means he slipped across the paroled Kenya border and made it on, penniless, to Nairobi is a story of one divine deliverance after another, each episode strengthening his trust in God. L. found many careless-living Ethiopians in Nairobi, but he asked God to protect and direct him elsewhere. There were missionaries in Nairobi who were preparing radio programs to be broadcast back into Ethiopia after Radio Voice of the Gospel had been confiscated by the military regime on March 12, 1977. They happened upon L. and eventually employed him to read scripts in the Amharic language for radio broadcasting. L. was taking a risk by exposing his voice to identification, but in God's mysterious providence, "Paul's" voice became an instructor and comforter to Ethiopians whom "Saul" had persecuted.[44]

A SECOND EXAMPLE OF how Christians were meeting threats from the cadres involved being made "a spectacle." One of the most grizzly personalities during the Revolution was a man called Ali Musa, a notorious Muslim governor who during the Derg days at various times held the top position in Gamo Gofa, Bale, Gobba, and the Kefa area. His brutality broke out as he passed through the Shashamane area in 1977, killing nineteen innocent men and women. He had them buried in a mass grave dug by a bulldozer. This massacre agitated the Arsi Oromo peasant associations and *kebeles* to rise up violently to try to eliminate the so-called anti-revolutionaries.

One day they singled out a Kambaatan whom Pastor Kedamo knew well, Dr. Mulatu Baffa. He was a tall, erect man who had taken training in the United States, and was a respected administrator at Shashamane Leprosarium—the place to which the Colemans had moved from Negussie's town. The tenor of the day among employees had become dissent, accusation, and rebellion. Anyone trying to keep the discipline of a normal work ethic was branded as *adhari* ("one who pulls back"). One morning, Dr. Mulatu's turn for torment came. On the edge of the angry crowd which captured

---

44. See especially Acts 9:21 and 13:9.

DR. MULATU BAFFA (ADDIS ABABA, 1994)

him, the doctor's sister quietly accompanied him in his ordeal, praying all the way as her brother suffered. This is his experience in Dr. Mulatu's own words:

> On March 19, 1977, at 8 AM as I walked out to work, I found myself surrounded by over fifty men, many of them with guns and spears. They stripped me of my jacket, shoes, wrist watch, wedding ring, and any money that was in my pocket. The accusation was that I was *adhari*, anti-revolutionary. Then I was made to walk five kilometers bare footed on a hot asphalt road. As they marched and walked behind me chanting their false accusations, I was reminded of the words of Jesus as He walked to calvary's cross. "Father forgive them for they know not what they do." At that moment, I was encouraged by the Holy Spirit.
>
> During the procession, light and heavy weapons cracked along for many hours. It only takes one finger to the trigger to get the soul down. However the words of the great psalmist in chapter 23:4—"Even though I walk through the valley of the shadow of death I will fear no evil for you are with me"—gave me the assurance of His presence and peace of mind. Humanly thinking, it appeared to be my last moment, but with

God all things are possible. In a weak voice I tried to witness to Christ before the crowd. Among them there were those who were weeping and crying and those who were mocking. Twice I was slapped on the face.

Christians had been called to pray, even in the capital, so in the meanwhile, at home and in Addis Ababa, prayer and fasting took place throughout the day and night. Even some Orthodox church priests joined the prayer groups at home. Towards the evening as they walked me toward a cell at some distant farmers' area, the words of the psalmist again reassured me—Psalm 91:11–12: "For He will command his angels concerning you to guard you in all your ways; they will lift you up in their hands so that you will not strike your foot against a stone." Certainly his angels lifted me up and controlled every finger that carried the vicious weapons.

As our journey continued toward prison accompanied by about fifteen militia men with guns and spears, one of them took me aside and said, "I am Tulu. I will protect you and defend you. You do not know me but I know you. Some months ago I was at Alaba with my wife and child. My child was seriously sick to the point of death. You took my wife, my child and myself to Shashamane Hospital free of charge in your Land Rover. Thanks be to God, the child got well, and I shall never forget that favor. Therefore, I have a gun; should anything come to overtake me, I will give you this gun and you should defend yourself."

I said, "Tulu, thank you for your offer. Our Lord will not allow you to be overtaken by evil forces." When we arrived at the destination of my imprisonment, it was a one-room vacated farmhouse. With swollen and ulcerated feet, I moved into the cell. The night came and about midnight a gang of cadres came to take me out to torture and kill me. Sure enough, Ato Tulu was guarding from the outside and was arguing with the gang not to open the cell at night. As this was going on for about an hour, I was praying on the inside. In the Book of Ecclesiastes 11:1, the words of God rightly states, 'Cast your bread upon the waters for after many days you will find it again.' I certainly did not remember Ato Tulu or the occasion of his child and wife, but I know that God had provided a man for this moment. I was released three days later, unharmed.[45]

After the above experience, Dr. Mulatu felt it prudent to move his family to Addis Ababa. He went on to serve God in a wider way, taking more and more leadership in the KHC work, and eventually the top executive post. We may wonder what happened to the particular

---

45. Document submitted to the author, *Dr. Mulatu's personal testimony*.

TADESSE AYISSA (ADDIS ABABA, 1994)

leader who excited the doctor's ordeal? Strangely, the chief agitator committed suicide a few days later by jumping from a high bridge.

THIS THIRD STORY ILLUSTRATES again how Christians were meeting their fears. A slight young lad, only fifteen, stood surrounded by communist cadres, the newly invested power-holders in Marxist-Leninist Ethiopia. The town was Arba Minch in the lake valley below Chencha mountain, out in southwest Ethiopia. The belligerent young cadres had engineered a showdown. Tadesse stood in the midst of the angry group who were nearly all taller and older than their prey. The little dimple that sometimes appeared on one side of his lips trembled slightly.

Tadesse Ayissa had been a cadre target for months. How could this runt of a youth have such influence on the very young people the cadres were assigned to enlist for the revolutionary cause? Here and there Tadesse had turned up over the area telling any who would listen about the living Jesus, to whom he testified convincingly. Infuriated, they accused him: "You are brainwashing our youth with your idealistic teaching!"

Far up in the capital where the Revolution had occurred, university and high school students had played a significant role. The political machinery had soon deployed students down-country as carriers and enforcers of the new ideology. Youth could be dissuaded from unpopular viewpoints and quickly enlisted into the popular movement sweeping the country. Influence, indoctrination, persuasion—these were the political cadres' assignment in the new Ethiopia. It was heady stuff, having such authority, and wielding such power over people, both young and old. Cadres usually developed that brash arrogance and enjoyment of power to which human nature is prone.

This particular group of cadres assigned to Tadesse's area highhandedly hustled him off to jail. There they worked him over with a routine form of torture, beating the soles of the prisoner's feet with iron rods. The pain is excruciating and the injury is increased afterward by making the victim walk over thistles or thorns. Expecting this to be a conclusive lesson, they gave Tadesse a formal order: "Leave this Christianity, join us, and close your church work. Be still from now on about this 'good news about Jesus' or else take the consequences."

Tadesse refused to promise silence, and therefore surely did have to take the consequences. Ten of them took the slight figure to a storage hall that day, stripped him and ordered him to lie prostrate on the floor between a row of five cadres on each side. In turn they beat his naked body with rawhide whips. They were sure that this "disciplinary action" would make the rebel think hard before spreading any more of what they saw as counter-revolutionary teaching.

Since these cadres had been brought in from other areas, they could not have known what an unusual youth they were dealing with. Tadesse had come into an experience of faith in the Lord Jesus very early in his youth, and quickly had become an inspired teacher and leader. His testimony in the countryside and in marketplaces had resulted actually in hundreds of people turning from primal practices or beliefs to Christ. The young evangelist seemed to have a special gift for working with the youth of the area, teaching them, organizing them, and challenging them to share the marvelous news of Christ's forgiveness and love with others.

Shortly after the lashing torture, Tadesse again was caught encouraging people to give themselves to the Lord Jesus Christ. Again he was dragged into jail and made to strip and prepare for another beating. "Now, what is your intention?" they challenged. "Tell us what you plan to do!" "My... aim?" Tadesse answered slowly. "As long as I am alive, my aim is to learn God's word and to teach it. If someone stops me, I will die for this." The group stood quelled. Disquieted, they took counsel among themselves, and eventually released the unbending Tadesse. Their threats and the resulting opportunity for witness to his Lord only strengthened Tadesse's resolve to continue testifying.

Of course he was arrested again. This unbending counter-revolutionary had to be silenced, they reasoned. "We're not going to beat you this time," they announced to him. "This time we're going to kill you. This will be your last day." As he awaited their action, Tadesse managed to slip out a note which revealed his situation and begged urgently for prayer. The note was carried up to the KHC elders meeting that very day up on Chencha mountain, a meeting to which Tadesse had been called.

Late that afternoon about twenty determined cadres walked their prisoner to a windowless storage hall to settle the matter. Inwardly, Tadesse prepared himself to die. Outwardly, he stated his conviction to his accusers: "The beginner and finisher is only God. Whatever comes, I'll accept."

In the hall, they noticed a book in his pocket. "Take it out," one yelled, and grabbed what turned out to be a New Testament. In his hands it fell open to Romans 13, within which happened to be a passage commanding obedience to authorities. "We haven't obeyed, but have overthrown the Emperor," one spat out. "We are putting out reactionaries, and you are one of them."

"No, I only speak God's word, and God's word is not reactionary," Tadesse's soft voice answered.

"We don't believe in higher authorities!" they shouted back at him.

Going aside a few feet, the group took counsel. "The Bible has saturated his bones," one said. "He's so devoted he cannot deny. We can't convert him or brainwash him," insisted another. The consensus was inevitable: "We must kill him." Their decision should not be delayed.

A single bullet was the easiest way to dispose of an "enemy of the Revolution." But this embarrassingly small youth had angered them, shamed them. He seemed to have no fear. In fact, an aura of unconcerned confidence, almost pleasantness, surrounded his consistently peaceful face. Such a response was infuriating. One of them came up with a fitting method of retaliation. "Let's execute him somewhat like his hero!" He pointed to the wires above.

Back inside, they announced: "We've decided how to kill you. We'll see if your Jesus will save you. We're going to hang you into the electric wire. Take off your clothes." Tadesse obeyed. They stacked chairs on a table so that the bare electric wires hanging above could be reached. "Climb up there," they ordered him. "If Jesus was crucified on a cross, we've decided to hang you like your Jesus." The cadres were in their element, totally in control, and on the verge of eradicating this irritating little nonconformist.

The naked youth climbed up and took a footing on the top chair. He folded his arms and waited. Within himself Tadesse accepted the inevitability and the honor of such a death. After a few moments of quietness, he simply stated, "I am very happy to die like this."

Two or three times in his earlier experience with the Lord, Tadesse had seen visions similar to those recorded in the book of Acts. It was not strange to him, then, that God should visit him at such a moment. Darkness was coming on outside. It was that hour when electric lights appear dim and ineffective. But looking upward, the young stalwart saw a great light. He alone heard words spoken to him: "As I have done for the three in the fiery furnace, I will do for you" (see Daniel 3:25). In his spirit, Tadesse responded, "As you have done for them in their time, if you do the same now, I will go back and tell this miracle to the church. If you are calling me to die, I am willing to come to you."

Without hesitating, Tadesse took a deep breath—one which those who watched expected to be his last—and reached out purposefully toward the wires. The group stood transfixed. The instant he grabbed the wires, the lights in the building went off. In confusion, someone ran outside to see if a switch had been thrown. He returned shouting, "The whole town is dark! Everywhere! The electricity seems to have gone off at the main source."

"How did it go off?" they asked each other, shocked and afraid. "This is amazing." They scuffled around in the darkness, talking in muffled tones trying to decide what to do next. Finally they ordered their victim down from the scaffold. Shaking but overwhelmed with awe, Tadesse climbed down. He awaited their next verdict.

"Your Jesus is... something..." they admitted in the darkness. "We will have to make another decision." Hurriedly the group came up with a face-saving alternative. With assumed bravado they gave him two terse orders: "First, go back and close your church work. Secondly, if you ever preach again, get a paper from Addis Ababa's higher authorities to do it."

Tadesse made an answer: "I cannot accept your number one, but I will accept the second, to get permission from the head office. I have permission from God." "You stupid thing!" they retorted. "Get out!"

Tadesse swept up his clothes, dashed out the door and ran straight up Chencha mountain in the darkness. Usually a six-hour climb, he was so invigorated that he made it in three. Knocking at the door of the elders' council meeting (the place to which he had sent his plea for prayer), he burst into the room.

That night, a man fresh out of the fiery furnace delivered to that amazed group the first installment of his promise of testimony to the fourth Man, a witness which Tadesse would rehearse before the church all over Ethiopia in the days to come.

IN TIMES OF GREAT stress upon his people, God sometimes acts sovereignly to deliver. Tadesse's story is one which can be added to the contemporary Acts of the Holy Spirit. He came close to martyrdom—a man on a cross, a man to be admired. Instead, Tadesse points to the Man on the cross—God on a cross—the Man to be worshipped. As a missionary to India once wrote of Jesus: "He could not die in a room, confined to four walls. He had to die under the open skies, with the universe looking on and the whole earth shaking in cosmic shudder—God dying for man."

We are candles. "Thou art the Sunrise!"[46]

---

46. See S. Jones, *The Word Became Flesh* (Abingdon Press, 1963), 108 and "the Sunrise" on p. 116.

*Contend, L*ORD*, with those who contend with me [...]
Say to me, "I am your salvation."*

(Psalm 35:1a, 3b)

Chapter 11
FACING DISINTEGRATION

My most frightening hour in 1977 came not from outward danger, but the inner dread that sprung to life as I listened to a hard-hitting young church leader within the safe walls of Bishoftu. The mission had such a large staff that bringing everybody in for a conference required three installments at the lake property, two in March, one in April. "God our Rock" was the theme chosen for SIM Conference. The theme was suggested by the storms swirling around us. An avalanche of rain inundating the overflow tents of the third week's meeting dramatized the metaphor.

An Ethiopian speaker had been called to our conference by Mr. Cumbers to tell us how things were going from the nationals' perspective and to give us advice on coping with the situation. He'd been given free reign to speak bluntly, to face us on equal footing and "tell it like it is." For months, the administration had been facing the kind of frustration and anger I now saw mirrored in our speaker, but out at our remote station, I had not seen it. I'd not realized the resentment and hostility lurking just beneath the surface of some of our expatriate–missionary relationships. Added to the heat of real complaints was the incendiary fuel of the Marxist critique which an Ethiopian university graduate was bound to have tasted, even if ultimately to have rejected. Furthermore, his grievances against the mission were independent of Marxism-Leninism. His main complaint was simply aggravated by the threat of missionary departure: "We're not prepared for this, because you've not prepared us. You've not trained leaders as you should," he accused.

A university graduate himself, he resented the lack of attention to high-level leadership training, training which the Lutherans had emphasized more. It was no time to plead their more ample funding, or our mission's educational investment in lower level grass roots training which had benefited thousands. It was no time to point out discouragement from the high percentage of those sent to study abroad who did not return. Sensing the depth of the speaker's emotion, my heart froze within me. Except for the mysterious unity of the Body of Christ which God gives his people, I thought to myself, except for the forgiveness and forbearance only his Spirit can infuse, we were all wrecked—missionaries and nationals alike!

John Cumbers' diary in those days had tallied distresses affecting the mission from every quarter: KGB-type surveillance in church services… Ethiopia's military government enraged over Sudan's support of the Eritrean Liberation Front… Harold Bowman, an ACROSS missionary,[47] shot and killed in Sudan… evening curfew instituted in Addis Ababa… after a failed coup attempt, Teferi Benti and six other "imperialist lackey" Derg members executed… the government proposing to take the chaotic Shashamane Leprosarium off the mission's hands—for 100,000 Ethiopian Birr (the local monetary unit)… sixty Christian churches burned down by the Gujjis… stations caught in turmoil related to the Ogaden war… a five-day state visit from President Fidel Castro of Cuba… and Marxist confiscation of Radio Voice of the Gospel, the Lutheran station which served East Africa.[48]

HAVING THREE CONFERENCES demonstrated how fast things were moving. The administration could hardly keep up with all that was happening in between. Following the week of the first SIM Conference, Kelafo station in the Ogaden went off the air for four days and by the time Missionary Aviation Fellowship was able to fly in, the station head had nearly been killed and two single women had been raped by Somali soldiers. The day the second SIM Conference started, out east in Gode, a beloved veteran Presbyterian missionary, Dr. Don McClure, was killed.[49] Returning to Addis after the third

---

47. ACROSS is the acrostic for the interdenominational and international consortium known as the African Committee for Relief of Southern Sudan. Refugees from Sudan's war and Eritrea's crossed the borders of Ethiopia and Sudan both directions, complicating issues for both countries.

48. See Cumbers (1996), *Terror*, 70, 86–94, 111, 118–120.

49. The closing chapters of C. Partee, *Adventure in Africa* (Univ. Press of America, 2000), relate the McClure's final days.

SIM Conference, we learned that missionary Dr. Sam Cannata had been arrested.[50] For nationals, the "Red Terror" was beginning, leaving its hallmark on the streets at dawn: dead bodies with labels stuck on them, threatening passers-by with similar "elimination."

In April, John's diary noted western consulates were closed in Asmara... various "imperialist" American organizations like United States Information Service ordered out of Ethiopia; *Reuters* and the *Washington Post* expelled... Debre Berhan language school closed because of no incoming missionaries... Gamo Gofa mission station gates sealed, and missionaries forced out of Bakko, Kamba, and Hamer. Waka and other stations closed. Other missions, not just SIM, were targeted. Roman Catholics were also expelled from one area that spring.[51]

While all this was being served up on the expatriates' plate, those looking beyond the urgencies of the moment realized the strategic necessity to prepare the church for what was to come. Marxism-Leninism was obviously coming into full flower, avowedly anti-Christian. Missionaries were forcibly losing or giving up stations and scattering—all harbingers of abandonment to the church.

Two men with foresight were Paul Balisky and Howie Brant, both Canadians in their thirties. They invited two young people from each of the twenty-eight youth districts to a quiet consultation for a few days at the isolated property on Lake Langano near Shashamane. The mission risked calling the meeting and Ethiopian representatives from around the country risked coming. But what an encouragement for these brothers to meet each together! Some were GBI graduates, including Werku from Dilla, who was taking the lead in youth work along with others. Of course Ato Tekle, head of the Kale Heywet Church, and John Cumbers from SIM came down. "Paul was the genius behind the Langano youth meeting," Howie says, "and probably designed it as a Spiritual Life Conference, but I had developed an agenda." Wiry, dark-haired Paul seemed to be the quiet intellectual in the background, while robust, curly-locked Howie took the spirited speaking role.

---

50. S. Cannata *et al.*, *Truth on Trial* (Broadman Press, 1978) tells the story of Sam's sixteen days in prison in April of 1977.

51. See Cumbers (1996), *Terror*, 124f.

Howie had grown up in Ethiopia, been educated abroad, returned as a missionary, and in 1977 was stationed in Gurage territory. In his childhood, he'd seen Gedeo peasants chafing under serfdom, for the Amharas had made life difficult for them. Communist promises to redistribute land sounded to them like progress. Yet Howie felt he must give these young people some glimpse of what to expect from communism. He had been studying materials from Romania and Cuba, Russia and China. He felt it was time for those who had been given the advantage of a world perspective to speak, but wariness kept most informed people quiet at this time of terror in the country. He launched into his agenda with a passion. "I told them the story of communism," Howie recalls, "its political thrust, its theory: dialectical materialism, a classless society, and atheism the religion. I used the analogy of a bee: it attracts us with honey, but the sting is in the end." He gave examples from the underground churches' experience, using materials from Brother Andrew, Wurmbrand, Arthur Glasser, and the like. "It was powerful stuff. They left the meeting determined to start preparations for underground operations."

This conference was a turning point, perhaps a starting point, for the vigilance and creativity which was going to be required. "I'll never forget the closing meeting," Howie said. "It was in the main dining hall of the Langano Center. My text was 'Be thou faithful unto death' (Revelation 2:10). By then they all had the background of what I had taught throughout the time, and now at the end, the Spirit of the Lord was so strong that I gave no closing, invited nothing. I just sat down. Ato Tekle came forth and said, 'Now is the time to dedicate ourselves to the Lord.' All went to their knees, heads on the ground, and prayed perhaps half an hour, dedicating their lives unto death. When they rose, pools of tears dotted the floor."

ABOUT SIX WEEKS LATER, another meeting was held at the same place, a Spiritual Life conference for the *Andinet*, or General Assembly of the KHC. Leaders came from many areas, including Degu Deklaabo, a young man who would eventually have to take difficult leadership in remote Gamo Gofa, to the southwest. Asfaw Demisse came, a man used to rough treatment of evangelicals in Bale, to the southeast.

Ato Tekle had been so deeply affected by the previous meeting that he asked Howie to present the same series of lectures. "In the interim, things had been getting hot," Howie remembers. "Tensions could be cut with a knife. I realized that teaching like this might even mean that I might have to 'bite the bullet' myself. I went to John Cumbers and asked for his advice. Should I do this? Would I get the mission and church in trouble? We decided to go ahead. However, the elders didn't have the same receptivity as the youth. I got about a third of the way through the eight lectures, but the elders didn't want me to talk like this. Dr. Mulatu became particularly concerned. Might there not be plants in the group? Worse yet, I was a foreigner. Kedamo, Dr. Mulatu, John Cumbers, and I went off and consulted together. I told them I'd do whatever the church wanted. It came out that the Derg's Intelligence was probably aware of the meeting. Kedamo's advice was sought. His feeling was that the Lord would teach His church; therefore it would be better to talk about biblical things, not directly about communism. So that's what I did the rest of the time with them."

As it happened, within a few weeks a blow-up and house arrest at Howie's station led to his family's departure from the country by June. Missionaries were increasingly perplexed about what their role should be. They kept getting into difficulties with authorities. Ethiopian friends were sometimes at risk because of fraternizing or cooperating with the accused "imperialists." Are we doing more harm than good? some asked themselves. Much reflection continued on this question. Some answered yes, and some no.

ONE WHO LEFT (but years later returned to serve in Ethiopia) was Malcolm Hunter, a spirited British missionary of spontaneous and optimistic nature. He shared his 1977 experience as an example, he said, of how his own rash comments brought on trouble, how unwise words increased the stress of the church's situation.

Malcolm calls his experience of being disciplined at the hands of the church "a lesson in African justice." That scenario introduced other difficulties for the young optimist who from 1974–77 had served as District Superintendent of the stations in Gamo Gofa. Malcolm and Jean were flying by Missionary Aviation Fellowship back and forth over those mountains, touching down at half a dozen stations to supervise the work and to assist national evangelists working far out in distant regions. Big and warm as a husky St.

Bernard dog, Malcolm's expansive enthusiasm invigorated a team of young expatriate workers scattered out at lonely posts to which he flew or trekked with boundless energy along with the toughest nationals. Nevertheless, Malcolm was humbled at the hands of church elders in a way which a number of other missionaries also painfully experienced.

He reiterates how each time he visited the mission school at Chencha, he was caught in tension between two nationals, the school principal and a teacher he gives the pseudonym Tefa. Tefa became quite politicized by radio propaganda, and kept telling students about "these capitalists, these imperialists." He seemed somewhat irrational and unstable. Although he participated in the church, he was young and his behavior was incendiary among the students. Each time Malcolm came in, the principal would share some new trouble which Tefa seemed to have instigated. He tells how the matter came to a head:

I ASKED THE ELDERS to help Tefa and the principal make peace. They said that the next month they'd convene a proper appointment to deal with it. I prepared my case summarizing how bad I'd been told this man Tefa had been. At the hearing the elders said, "First of all, you must both put your heads on the floor and admit that you have divided the body of Christ; you have been in dispute." I thought, 'This is a bit unfair. It's the Headmaster's dispute.' "No," they said, "you haven't loved each other." So I got down on the ground. (They checked the dust on our foreheads to see if it were done properly!) Then I told the story of complaints the headmaster had given me. I told what I'd heard. Then Tefa gave his case: "These imperialists take our money, don't give our children good food, not the right education, not enough books, dominate, don't support the revolution, etc." The elders told both of us to go out to a side room and they'd discuss the case. We two spent an uncomfortable forty-five minutes together.

When we were called back in, they took my case first. They said I had not loved this man as Jesus would. "How can you expect us to listen to your teaching and preaching, if you don't love us like Jesus does? He's just a young man. He doesn't pretend to be a Bible teacher. How can you say these things? You are a bad example." They really made it hard for me. I was feeling lower and lower, my ears were beaten by this same tale for an hour. Then the young man got five minutes of "You did this, this, this..." and sat down. I thought, how totally unfair! I was humiliated.

"Now get up and embrace each other," they told us. I must confess I was feeling anything but forgiving. I was disgusted with Tefa and the whole group that had put me through the mill—made mincemeat of me! With a rotten attitude I put my arms around him. There was nothing very godly about it at all. About 11:30 that night I was allowed to leave. I walked outside, and back to where Jean was waiting. I told her, "I don't understand these Gamo people. They've just pulverized me... totally humiliated me. And I was trying to help their school. I don't know how I can face them after what they've done to me."

I was sitting there feeling thoroughly sorry for myself when in came dear old Ato Gembo, the first believer in Gamo. He was a godly man, a spiritual father to me, although illiterate. Ato Gembo put his arm around me. "Mr. Hunter," he said, "I'm so sorry we had to do that to you. I know that was so painful for you. But you agreed that we would deal with it and you would accept our way of dealing with it." I admitted, "Yes, I did, and I have to accept it. But I don't know why you did it like that."

Then he explained why: "In our culture, when we have a case, when we know who is not guilty, we have to make his case seem so bad that he'll have nothing to feel proud of, so that he'll feel ashamed, be humbled. So we take his case first, the one we know is least guilty. The most guilty, we take last. The more obvious his guilt is, the less time we have to spend with him. The least guilty party we have to work over until he feels really crushed. Now, in your way, in your culture, there is always a winner and loser. There's no way of making peace. One will come out justified, the other angry and resentful. There is then no way to bring reconciliation. We do it this way to reconcile people. Humble the least guilty at length, and the other who knows he's most guilty, he takes little time."

"That was a wonderful lesson in African justice," Malcolm affirmed. "It did crush me. But the explanation did at least ameliorate my pain."

THAT WAS NOT TO BE Malcolm's last struggle with authority. He eventually got into hot water with the government. As he was hurrying from Bulki Mountain to catch the plane down in the valley, he threw a starter motor that needed repair in an old sack. At the airport, authorities searched his gear and saw the motor, but more importantly, saw a civet cat skin that Malcolm hadn't noticed was in the bag. "Oh, this is serious! You're running wild animal skins," the authorities accused. Malcolm insisted he had no idea it was there. "This is a serious offense. You must go to police station." He missed his flight and was told he couldn't leave the area unless someone would "go *wass*" (security bond) for him. A Wolaittan friend was running a clinic at the airstrip town. Not without danger to himself, Ato Waja Kabeto kindly agreed to go *wass* until Malcolm returned the next month.

On Malcolm's return, they faced him with a more serious accusation. "Mr. Hunter, come straight to the police station, there's a serious charge against you. The last time you were here you were talking with some people in a tea shop and they accused you of opposing the Revolution." To his horror he remembered talking with two young fellows who were reading Mao's little red book. He'd facetiously asked, "Reading the New Testament?"—a similar appearing booklet. "Not the New Testament, but thoughts of Chairman Mao!" the two answered. "That's fine," Malcolm remarked. "I'm sure Chairman Mao has some splendid thoughts. But he's only a man and he'll soon be dead and forgotten."

"You are accused of opposing the Revolution! By Ethiopian law, the *hig* (rule) accuses you. We could shoot you. We're going to put you into prison, unless you can get Waja to go *wass* for you again." Malcolm realized this was getting too political to drag Ato Waja into a second time. A friendly official who tried to intercede became implicated in the delicate situation. Later, a letter came to Addis Ababa revealing the fact that the interceding man had been threatened with execution and that Malcolm was about to be charged with being a CIA agent. In the end, return to Gamo Gofa threatened to become very complicated.

There were other incidents that influenced Malcolm's evaluation of his position, including additional accusations invented by Chencha cadres, and physical threat to his wife and child while he was away. Malcolm said they realized things were breaking up, and he felt people like himself were becoming a problem to the church. He reasoned that the trouble he'd caused had to be factored into the situation. He felt the government took his blunders out on the church after he left Gamo Gofa.

Like many who loved and served Ethiopia, the Hunters reluctantly left the country. As missionaries struggled with what to do, some became convinced that retaliation against the church because of their presence should be minimized, by removing themselves. Some disagreed, seeing their presence as a positive support, and stayed on. Both decisions were difficult to live out.

WITHDRAWAL OF MISSIONARY SUPPORT services became another factor in the disintegration in process. In the spring of 1977, Good Shepherd Academy was confiscated, posing a major problem for families with high schoolers. Where could they enroll in an English speaking institution for the next school year? Kenya seemed to be the alternative, a whole country away from home.

Another problem which loomed large was transportation. Missionary Aviation Fellowship (MAF) was depended upon to get into remote areas beyond the airports of the Ethiopian Airlines. Stations three-day's hard trek apart could be reached in twenty minutes by plane, and an exhausting three-day car trip to the capital could be reduced to hours. MAF's services were a key factor in the whole system which had developed, as exemplified by Malcolm's assignment to cover a whole province characterized by rugged mountains and malarial valleys, few roads and a maze of foot-tracks across bushlands.

The government stepped up difficulties for MAF: flight permission blockages, cargo searches, riots on airfields, and threat of fleet confiscation. Often missionaries were denied permission to fly into the interior and many were leaving their down-country stations, so the demand for flight services was diminishing. Expecting their planes to be seized soon, MAF finally made the decision to leave Ethiopia in May. "Each station will be given just one opportunity to evacuate," they reluctantly told us. "Take it, for there will be no more flights. You'll be on your own from then on." Every station lived out its final chapter, documented by accounts collected later.[52] Each situation was unique, experienced by a handful of people at each location.

FOR US, THE DAY remains indelible. Only a few weeks before, Malcolm had settled us into Bulki, where Charles and Ann Donaldson, an Australian nurse, were to do mobile medical work by air. We called the place "Eagle's Nest," for it was perched on top of a mountain cliff at 9,000 feet, overlooking ranges in every direction, their peaks sometimes lost in clouds which flowed silently across valleys hidden far below. We'll never forget a moment when we first arrived. We walked into the empty house and surveyed the breath-taking mountain ranges beyond the dining room window.

It took three or four hours to make the mule trip to the base of the mountain, where Ethiopian Airlines landed spasmodically in those days. MAF frequently flew in supplies or transported Ethiopian evangelists, landing on our dog-leg airstrip, downhill coming in; up and over the cliff to get airborne, going out. MAF pilots were skilled at landing on dangerous strips, navigating through spectacular land forms, and fighting rains, fog, and down drafts among these wild peaks.

For days, our 7 AM radio check with Headquarters had me glued to the set, straining to catch from each location's veiled reports what was discernible over the static. Many were experiencing threats and riots around their station. We'd been told confidentially that MAF had decided to pull out of Ethiopia, and that we must be ready to leave on sudden notice when their one evacuation flight was offered to each station. My heart froze when our location's name and date was announced. We frantically scrambled to gather extra medicines for patients, prepared workers' last wages to be left behind, and filled boxes of supplies (precious Bibles, vernacular hymn books, a mimeograph machine, teaching supplies, etc.) to be taken under cover of night for distribution to various churches. I grieved that the four hundred Gideon New Testaments, so long blocked at the seaport, now would never be flown into this isolated outpost.

---

52. Australian missionary Alan Neal collected many of these later. Numerous accounts can be found in Cumbers (1996), *Terror*.

We packed a few suitcases according to specifications for the small load which the prop plane allowed. We needed to appear to be leaving on a round trip, to avoid a riot. That meant virtually everything which had built up over twenty years at that station had to be left behind. I tucked in a hand-painted china cup in which ladies before me must have served hundreds of cups of tea, Charles took a favorite book of spiritual verse left on a shelf by the Stinsons, Canadian missionaries. Good-byes dared not be said. The saddest hours of that night came as a result of an Headquarters' directive, designed to protect nationals from being implicated: "Burn the station records." As page after page of names of patients, students, and church members went up in flames in our living room fireplace, we wept. We wept over separation, over evil, over what our national friends would be facing, and over the lives poured out serving these beloved people by missionaries who had been stationed over the years at Bulki.

In the dawn, Charles went to the highest point above the house to pray. I gathered our luggage and left one empty cardboard box for the radio—to be dismantled after we heard the plane. Police always searched us at the airfield in those days, and detection of the radio was my greatest fear, a sure give-away of evacuation. As the little bird was honing in, we walked to the strip, praying for calmness. The familiar drone drew neighbors out of grass huts and from their fields to surround the plane. Out jumped the pilot. What would he announce with cheerful British accent, but that the motor was overheated and would require a twenty minute soak in a bucket of water! Would someone fetch water from a stream? As Ann and I waited tensely, Charles talked playfully with the children, almost enjoying the situation, it seemed to me. The pilot unloaded some boxes, probably the next six months' groceries we've ordered, I thought. Armed police soon arrived to inspect our luggage. Don't let them open the radio box, I prayed. To my astonishment, my dear doctor led the police chief to start the investigation at the very box containing the radio. It's all over, I thought.

The policemen looked inside the radio box... gave no reaction, and moved on to the next. I asked myself, Is he blind? Or did angels hide the evidence? Stunned, I watched the inspection continue... no accusations, no discovery, amazing.

After the three of us were loaded into the plane, I breathed a sigh of relief, thinking we were almost away. The pilot turned and confided what was in the boxes he'd unloaded: the Gideon New Testaments! I nearly screamed as Charles crawled out of the plane and quietly directed some believers in the crowd to deliver the precious cargo to the church elders. Then, to my amazement again, he pulled two Testaments out of one of the boxes and risked handing the forbidden book to the policemen. While they were examining them, the motor roared and we were off.

Gideon testaments come in many colors. These happened to be red—just the size and shape of Chairman Mao's little red book! My fear versus Charles' trust... Mao's hate versus Christ's love, I mused. I left better knowing Who would eventually win the battle raging over Ethiopia, "the battle of the red books."

> *The LORD is my rock, my fortress and my deliverer;*
> *my God is my rock, in whom I take refuge,*
> *my shield and the horn of my salvation.*
> *He is my stronghold, my refuge and my savior—*
> *from violent men you save me.*
>
> *(2 Samuel 22:2–3)*

Chapter 12

FACING THE RED TERROR

Most people who were in Ethiopia in 1977 remember where they were on May Day. My husband happened to be escorting our teenage son, Tim, back to school in the capital from our remote station on a public bus. It was only a few weeks before our surprise evacuation. Such a trip is always memorable for foreigners. Charles and Tim were a curiosity, jammed in with an overload of passengers jabbering in their local dialects, traveling the long hours from Jimma to Addis Ababa. Boxes, hides, cooped chickens and the like, stacked atop the bus, added a precarious tilt to the grinding vehicle as the driver—often jockeying with other vehicles for the lead—navigated valley stretches and hairpin curves at dangerous speeds. To the collection of animal, food, and diesel smells was added an assault to the ear—a loudspeaker screaming out whatever the radio was broadcasting.

By nature, Charles enjoys what C. S. Lewis called "the quiddity" of things. He has an unassuming, playful streak which usually wins him acceptance from children and adults in almost any setting, so he and Tim were happily chatting with fellow passengers as they rode along. Suddenly the crowd came to attention as the radio's martial music ceased and an authoritative voice spat out a harsh-toned message. The Amharic was delivered too fast for Charles to decipher. The father and son noted a swift chill in the atmosphere of the crowd, accompanied by cold stares, questioning eyebrows, and darkened pupils in the eyes of some of the men seated closest to the two. Murmurs of "Mengistu" helped Charles realize that Col. Mengistu Haile Mariam must be making a political speech. Mengistu's raging voice built up to a climax using the word *dem* ("blood") over and over again, punctuated by an echoed roar from what sounded like a mighty crowd.

It was a mercy that the two didn't know what they were hearing until they'd left their hostile co-travelers at the teeming Addis Ababa bus station and got back to the SIM compound.

In communist countries, May Day is no pastel springtime festival, it is a demonstration day for Laborers, and brings to mind the bloody birth of Russia's 1917 Revolution. The Party Chairman's speech to the cadence of *dem* was actually shouting "blood to the foreigners! Blood to the capitalists! Blood to the imperialists!" Each chant was accompanied by shattering a bottle of blood on the pavement beneath the reviewing stand, before thousands of Ethiopians who were gathered at the capital's Red Square parading ground. Some thought back to the square's original name—*Meskel Square* ("Square of the Cross")—and Jesus' blood which was voluntarily shed for communist and capitalist alike.

Starting in late 1976 on into 1978, blood spread its hue over the country, by means of butchery known as the "Red Terror." The causes for the undulating tides of killing, terror, resistance, and silencing, are too complicated for outsiders to fully grasp and are beyond this author's qualifications to presume to interpret. Most foreigners only saw fragments of the unbelievable carnage as they spotted bodies sprawled on the streets at dawn, often labeled with warnings designed to intimidate people passing by. Driving, or worse, walking through the city could be a terrible experience. People stayed off the streets and waited in terror night by night for the crash of an assault upon their own home.

Students who had in 1974 led the way for the Revolution now raised their voices, only to be struck down. Relatives were required to pay for the bullets used in the young person's execution before they could carry away the corpse of their son and daughter for burial. The army had supplied the force which made the Revolution possible and had systematically disarmed the people before they knew what was happening. One type of resistance did finally emerge, in the form of the terrifying Ethiopian Peoples Revolutionary Party (EPRP). In his book *Cry Ethiopia*, British missionary Peter Cotterell, who was on the scene, wrote of the Red and White Terror:

> The EPRP chose terror to oppose terror: they called their version the White Terror, and they launched it in September 1976. Now Marxist

murdered Marxist with a barbaric enthusiasm that friends of Ethiopia could scarcely believe existed. In four months came the army's response: Comrade Chairman Mengistu called for Red Terror, the 'Kay Shibbir', to counter the White Terror. The army was by now living in fear of the nightly murders, and with the encouragement they now had to meet violence with violence they abandoned all restraint. A new May Day protest was being planned by the students: five hundred of them were gunned down in a single day.[53]

Dr. Cotterell goes on to describe the growing terror from a third source, the *kebeles*, or communes, organized in all urban and rural districts.[54] They scrutinized everyone in their commune and held nightly interrogations of those who had been accused as "counter revolutionary." By morning, people were often executed by the *kebele* with no legal representation and no appeal allowed.

"Piano wire" strangling was one of the feared techniques. "Double torture" was a further technique that seared the mind and heart. It forced one prisoner to inflict the prescribed torture on a fellow victim.

By the middle of 1978, this sickening horror subsided. Conservative estimates placed the death toll as a result of the Red Terror and of deaths in prisons and *kebele* jails at about 30,000.[55] Ethiopian sources opposed to the military regime reported 2,000 students and teachers killed by security forces in a pre May Day 1978 massacre in Addis Ababa. Of course, this did not count deaths on the battlefields of the Ethio–Somali War (1977–78) or the ongoing Eritrean struggle. Up in Eritrea, people were doubly threatened, first by the Ethiopian army, and secondly by the struggle for supremacy between Eritrea's own liberation fronts, the ELF and the EPLF.[56] There, too, revolutionaries were killing revolutionaries. Marxism-Leninism mandates killing.

ALTHOUGH THE BLOODY INTENSITY did die down somewhat in Addis Ababa in late 1978, the precedent had been set. *Kebeles* in various

---

53. Cotterell (1988), *Ethiopia*, 114.
54. Cotterell (1988), *Ethiopia*, 115.
55. Cumbers (1996), *Terror*, 111.
56. The ELF (Eritrean Liberation Front) arose in the 1960s. The EPLF (Eritrean People's Liberation Front) emerged in the 70s. The latter won out in the 80s.

provinces spasmodically took advantage of local people, using similar patterns of intimidation, imprisonment, torture, and death. Powerful men like Ali Musa used their leadership to inflict suffering broadly. In other cases, little village moguls served the fiendish spirit in ways unfitting for humans. At Wendo Genet in Sidamo territory Christian teenagers were made sport of by cadres who engineered ultimate humiliation for a young person. The cadres would block the believers from leaving the school even to relieve themselves. Children of Ato Mamo Belete, a Christian pharmacist, and fifty-two other youth were confined to one room for a day without food and told, "As soon as you testify you have given up this false religion, we'll let you outside." The intestinal desperation many boys and girls felt made some capitulate: after they registered their names with shame, they were released. The rest were kept in that room all night. In the morning they were driven outside and beaten. The whipping caused them to lose control of their balance and bodies—while on-lookers jeered. An evil genius seemed to be orchestrating a cacophony over the land, using the depravity of man for all it was worth.

Addis Ababa newspapers blatantly reported arrests and executions around the country, justifying them in clipped terms straight out of Marxist-Leninist propaganda manuals, using awkward terminology unknown to Ethiopia before. We could not help seeing blatant foreign derivation in the translation of "broad masses" in Amharic, rendered *sefi hizb*, literally "wide people."

Messages quietly came into Ato Tekle's KHC office, or to SIM through missionaries, that people down-country were suffering incidents every day. Burials had to be attended, prisons had to be visited, government offices had to be approached to plead for justice, nearly always to no avail. Leadership slogged out hour after hour listening to complaints, going to frustrating hearings, and answering charges in courtrooms. John Cumbers' heart condition gave threatening signals.

ACROSS FROM HEADQUARTERS, the Black Lion Hospital was overflowing with war casualties, along with civilian patients. Hussein Yusef and Belaynesh Dindamo had married after Grace Bible Institute closed, and were living on the Mission Headquarters compound right across from the hospital. Belaynesh felt a burden to reach out

BELAYNESH DINDAMO AND HUSSEIN YUSEF (ADDIS ABABA, 1995)

with hope to suffering people. She undertook a dangerous ministry, carrying scripture portions into the hospital to give to patients. Often she was followed around the hospital. One day a cadre accosted her. Why was she here? Did she have permission? Was she CIA? Who paid her? "No one pays me," she answered kindly. "The word of God says to tell those who aren't in Jesus. He is the only way to find hope." The young cadre slapped her. "Why do you come to the hospital, bring that bad Bible, teaching people not to fight?" A real disturbance was developing on the ward, because patients complained when police forcibly took their gift New Testaments from them. A cadre got out a match, and ordered Belaynesh to light a Testament by her own hand. "You know, it is coming into Ethiopia legally," she reasoned with them. "Many others want these books. Why burn it? If you burn it, there are many Bibles in many places. The Lord doesn't allow His word to be stopped." They slapped her repeatedly during a long afternoon of harangue. At sunset they told her they were taking her to prison, where she would be killed. She begged to inform her family.

A shoe repair man on the street between the hospital and Headquarters saw them hustling her into a vehicle and took a message to Hussein. He called people to pray. When the cadres marched Belaynesh into the *kebele* headquarters, the authority there disappointed them when he accepted Belaynesh's explanation that she was not selling but giving these New Testaments out. He agreed that her act was not a crime, and infuriated the cadres. Hussein and a few others came, and Belaynesh was allowed to retrieve her precious identity card and go back to her children.

THE LOCATION OF THE mission compound across from the hospital made it a plum for the Ministry of Health to confiscate. They threatened to take it a number of times. One day when government officials came to examine it to take it over, the official had a deputy with him who knew Ato Lakew Tesemma, for Lakew visited many government offices in his line of duty. "What does 'IEC' mean?" the official whispered to the deputy to ask Lakew. Lakew explained to the deputy that IEC referred to an international group… "and they hardly have room for Ethiopians in their gatherings."[57] The two government men whispered to each other, "Then how can we take over this place?" and left. Ato Lakew rejoiced that he was used to keep SIM from losing the property.

In those days, Ethiopians were bonding together through a network of prayer raised for each other in each person's hour of need. Ato Lakew and others developed a system of alerting by telephone. Knowing that lines were tapped, and having chosen a scripture which indicated the situation, they would call the first person in a chain and simply say, for instance, "Regarding Mamo, Psalm 70:1–2" or "Tegayne, Psalm 41:9," "Ababa facing Jeremiah 22:12," or the like. The first one called would know or look up the scripture, and then pass on the alert in this brief, veiled way. Over and over, God protected. They were learning to use tools for survival. However, survival was not their primary goal. Rather, it was to complete their course, to the glory of God.

Out at Bishoftu, a conference was organized which was later remembered as "the Crown conference." It was one of the last open meetings allowed. Alemu Beeftu (Negussie and John Coleman's

---

57. IEC were the initials of the little chapel within the compound—meaning "International Evangelical Church."

schooldays friend) who became such a gifted graduate of Grace Bible Institute, was by then working with a church in Addis Ababa. Alemu gave a challenge to the believers as they were gathered by the ancient crater lake: "Hold onto your crown!"—an admonition from Christ's messages to the churches in Revelation. "Be faithful even to the point of death, and I will give you the crown of life," Christ had promised. Along with Alemu, a gifted apologist named Solomon Abate spoke, a man we were later to meet. These men, Pastor Kedamo and others, labored diligently for God's glory, that their generation of believers would keep their eyes on their eternal expectation of their Lord: "I am coming soon. Hold on to what you have, so that no one will take your crown."[58]

IN THE CAPITAL, many diplomats were expelled. Foreign business people were being harassed, accused, and brought to trial. The hundreds of expatriate missionaries who had been forced off their stations found themselves stuck in Addis Ababa with no permission to travel down-country, their stations closed and confiscated. Often a high price was extorted for the government's taking over an institution. Frequently the school or hospital seemed to have been manipulated into chaos, through propagandized breakdown of worker cooperation, in order to force expatriate leadership to beg for the institution to be transferred from mission control. Exit visas for the persons involved were denied, unless the huge amounts for "transfer" were paid. While this action was hard for the owner not to consider to be robbery plus extortion, it was true that the government had no provision for these institutions yet, and the national budget was assigned overwhelmingly to war.

Our family was among those marooned in the capital when we were deposited in Addis after evacuation from "Eagle's Nest." Charles found that no medical posts were left to the mission. Still, we hoped to serve somewhere, so we agreed to become house parents to the "Community Development House" young people at an Addis site which had been a coffee-company owner's compound. Since 1974, it had been used as a Rest and Rehabilitation base for community

---

58. See Revelation 3:11, the reigning Lord Jesus' admonition to the seven churches.

development workers during the famine. Our sixteen and thirteen year old sons were on school break. Tim's school had already been confiscated and Nat's was at risk. They appreciated being close to their parents during the Red Terror, and enjoyed getting to know the twenty-some Ethiopian and expatriate young people living there.

The Community Development workers lived in the big house on the compound, and we in the little house across the courtyard from it. Tim and Nat slept in an enclosed side porch, Charles and I in the one bedroom. Most nights, shots rang out from the compounds surrounding ours, making us repeatedly aware of yet more murders. One night the window against which Tim and Nat's double-deck bunk stood was suddenly shattered in the darkness. Glass sprayed over them in their beds. When the compound guard came running, we were relieved when the intruder turned out to be a thief rather than cadres.[59]

ALTHOUGH CROSSING THE CITY held dangers, a group of expatriate and Ethiopian Christian women continued to meet together in various homes on Friday mornings to study the Scriptures and pray. Their story presents one little microcosm which exemplifies what was happening over the capital.

The day I first attended, the aroma of coffee beckoned us to a buffet breakfast amid a babel of voices with various accents—Dutch, Irish, Ethiopian, Yankee, and even a drawl from the deep South. Having just come from our remote station where our nearest missionaries were three days' walk away, I was overwhelmed, yet delighted by this ground-swell of possible relationships.

The hostess, who had been a Miss America contestant a few years before, greeted us with practiced grace, concealing the strains under which, I later learned, she lived. Difficult circumstances in her life since bearing a handicapped child had led to her coming to know the Lord Jesus. Susan's voice caught as she presented a traditional brass cross to a striking woman in white pant suit sitting on a low hassock, the one she looked to as her spiritual mother. I learned that these crosses symbolized to the group a long procession of good-byes.

---

59. Tim Bascom's *Running to the Fire* (University of Iowa Press, 2015), 202–204 relates the story as experienced by a sixteen year old.

Over recent tense months, the group had been cut in half. And now this diplomat's wife in white, who had led their Bible studies, was herself bidding them good-bye.

Her last lesson was on Ephesians chapter five, on the fruits of the Spirit. I made it through the study feeling fairly normal, somehow imagining that my emotional fragility experienced in the down-country strain had been left behind. It was the prayer time at the end of the meeting that shattered me. A transparency unique to prayer occurred as each woman spoke of her concerns to the Father, in their various accents of English. I was unprepared for the soft voice from the corner of the room whispering, *Amlakachin hoy...* ("Oh, our God...") in Amharic. This woman's adoration hurled me back to a hundred such moments in grass houses, mud churches, or our own living room. Tears streamed down my face as I was overwhelmed by thankfulness and praise for the experience of knowing and loving these Ethiopian Christians who had taught me so much about our Lord. At times I'd thought I would be glad, relieved, to be out of the country, but at that moment I realized I would always long for these people, this country, wherever I might be.

The prayer time over, I scanned the group for the lady who had prayed in the Ethiopian tongue. There she sat in traditional white dress, upswept black hair, and above her high cheekbones, dark eyes I shall never forget—serene pools of sadness, framed in a soft, gentle smile. "Gentleness" was what she epitomized to me from the "fruits of the spirit." I learned that her husband had been in prison for months. In the meetings, she was so shy that she usually whispered her requests to a foreigner to voice to the group. Only in the quietness of prayer did she dare to speak out, not to us, but to her Father.

In June, I was asked to lead a study on some short book. With suffering all around us, 1 Peter seemed an appropriate choice. Yet the thought kept returning, Not 1 Peter yet, first concentrate on joy: Philippians. I suppose I was influenced by a principle I'd heard from Corrie Ten Boom, who lived through Nazi prison camps. "How do you live in difficult times?" she was asked in an interview. To answer the question she employed the example of an old gentleman who couldn't bear to read sad stories. When he read a book, he always jumped to the last chapter first, to see if he could stand reading it. "That is what we must do in the Last Days" she mused. "We read the last chapter of Revelation first, and then from that position of victory, we have the joy to live through the race that is set before us."

The theme of Philippians is usually summarized as "joy." As I pored over the book in the early morning hours, its central character, the Lord Jesus Christ, renewed and strengthened me, developing more of the joy Paul spoke of some fifteen times in the four short chapters. This prison epistle was a practical one for our group, every woman of whom was identifying with some friend, neighbor, or family member in prison. One Ethiopian member had spent a month there herself. As we identified with Paul's experience, we were exposed to attitudes God was giving him, and were helped to "count everything as loss, for the surpassing worth of knowing Him."

As the weeks stretched on, we shared burdens and saw God answer prayer. The husband of "Gentleness" was released. But another lady continued to slip out mid-meeting each Friday to stand in the queue outside the prison in the long line of women who hoped their men were still alive to receive the daily parcel of food upon which prisoners depended. We ached with her over her teenagers, now "re-educated" to despise their father. The youngest, a thin, distracted boy, seemed unable to get a hold on schoolwork after their family's frightening month in prison. We prayed. Answers came. New problems emerged. For some, release did not come. But there were sisters who cared.

As August came and more were leaving, we risked having a night together with our husbands coming too. A handsome Ethiopian military officer and his European fiancée who was visiting his country added a mysterious air of romance to the evening. What an assortment of nations and stations was represented! After a multi-cultural buffet, a rather impromptu program was emceed by "Miss America" with charm and humor. My good-natured husband risked starting things off with an old 1950-vintage melodrama, acting parts by changing hats and voices alternately to play all three characters: mean "Scarface the Villain," stalwart "Handsome Harry," and coquettish "Little Nell the Miller's Daughter," the heroine at risk. The audience cheered or booed the protagonists and oohed with Little Nell. A few lines in the script always caused me to color, but the woman whose husband was still in prison laughed till she cried, and whispered to me, "You know, once in a while, we need to forget everything."

With inhibitions considerably reduced, the sharing of readings and music from various cultures continued until late, for no one wanted it to end or to risk emerging onto the streets of the city after curfew hour. Reluctantly, some practical folk began to rise. It was the elderly Egyptian couple that brought us to the sharp realization that this moment was truly "good-bye" for some. The Khalils' construction business had been confiscated. Mr. Khalil insisted his wife must leave the country while she still could, and wait outside for him to somehow follow. They'd been inseparable and scarcely anyone there had failed to feast at the huge oval table in their home. It had been thrown open to weary missionaries and lonely expatriates from all over the world. The stout pair made their way tearfully around the room. None of us could have imagined how God would answer our prayers for his deliverance from the clever accusations and harrowing court cases designed for the bourgeoisie. His miraculous release came two weeks after her escape. It did not even require an exit visa. His heart simply stopped, right in Addis Ababa. They'd be reunited in heaven, not Egypt.

ONE FRIDAY MORNING A missionary just in from her station brought a story from down-country. Theresia Fellows had lived nearly thirty years of her life in situations similar to where I first met her on a lonely mountain top, treating eye diseases in the shade of a huge tree which the local people had previously worshipped. She'd washed diapers by hand, made do with little, and treated the sick, being the woman behind her man. Her husband, Alex, was a rugged Australian pioneer blessed with a quiet little wife who controlled her own longings in order to be his helpmate. A harrowing evacuation had delivered them into the city, the last place the Fellows would have chosen to live. She passed on to the gathered women one of the countless unwritten stories emerging out of "the Acts of the Spirit" in those days:

> At a grass church with a congregation made up of largely first and second generation Christians, a uniformed stranger arrived during a service. The congregation wondered, was it to forcibly conscript their young men for the wars in Eritrea or the Ogaden? Hundreds of southerners were being trucked to the capital, briefly trained to carry a gun, and sent to one of the fronts.

The defenseless peasants sat apprehensively in the church that day as the officer stepped to the front and blurted out, "Who in this room believes in the 'God' business?" Perhaps half the hands went up slowly in the silence. "The rest of you, leave!" he commanded. Those gone, another gruff question dared the remnant. "And who here believes in this 'Jesus Christ' stuff?" Silence. A few hands went up. "The rest of you are dismissed," he barked. When the last filed out, he ordered the door shut. With atheism being one of the articles of the Revolution, the little flock waited for their sentence.

With deep emotion, he spoke: "I, too, am a Christian."

Comforting them like a father, the officer encouraged and strengthened those remaining inside with the word of God. Finally, those who had waited outside were called back. "I am ashamed of you," he chided quietly, and proceeded to admonish them to stand firm in such days, for their common Lord.

My mind turned back to the account in Acts of Paul and the prison guard in Philippi. I surmised that the Ethiopian officer was risking the possibility of his own execution. I wondered if he felt like Paul when the Apostle wrote to the Philippians—"my joy and crown" (chapter 4:1)—of his impending death as an act of worship. Paul put it in the context of the Temple sacrifices. "But even if I am being poured out like a drink offering on the sacrifice and service coming from your faith, I am glad and rejoice with all of you. So you too should be glad and rejoice with me" (chapter 2:17–18). Joy, even in death.

> *My son, if sinners entice you, do not give in to them.*
> *If they say, "Come along with us;*
> *let's lie in wait for someone's blood,*
> *let's waylay some harmless soul;*
> *let's swallow them alive, like the grave,*
> *and whole, like those who go down to the pit;*
> *we will get all sorts of valuable things*
> *and fill our houses with plunder;*
> *throw in your lot with us, and we will share a common purse"—*
> *my son, do not go along with them, do not set foot on their paths,*
> *for their feet rush into sin, they are swift to shed blood.*
>
> *(Proverbs 1:10–16)*

Chapter 13

FACING MARXISM

That night when Sahle Tilahun stole into our Community Development compound as unnoticed as he could, he was on his way back to his wife, Aberash Takele, and his little ones. His light knock on our cottage door might have seemed like a replay of his visits as a high schooler when we were in language school over a decade before. But by now, Sahle was a family man and principal of a school in the Debre Zeit area. Charles had last seen Sahle a few months before, sharing that two-day escapade driving the faulty Land Rover from Chencha to Addis Ababa.

That was in February. By June, lightheartedness was forgotten, and a sober man stood at our door. The pressures of the new political climate were being forced upon teachers in a specific way, for they were expected to re-educate youth in accordance with Marxist-Leninist theory. Teachers received systematic lectures in dialectical materialism and were tested for compliance.[60] If hesitancy was shown, as had been the case with Sahle, the teacher was sent off to an intense re-education course. For Sahle it meant twenty days of brainwashing in Harar.

Unlike the usual Sahle, he left his coffee untouched and kept watching the door. He had always been a tender soul. His great dark eyes were wide and troubled as he whispered what they'd taught him—that his wife's love was purely a physical thing, nothing "spiritual" to stay "faithful" to. Men evolved from monkeys, they told them. The origin of matter was chance and necessity. "Must I believe in chance and not in God?" he had asked them. "Sahle needs

---

60. Dialectical materialism is the Marxian theory that maintains the material basis of reality, which is constantly changing in a dialectical process, a process which develops through the stages of thesis, antithesis and synthesis.

another course," they responded. All day they had to sit and listen to these propositions that nothing was really real except what was perceived through the five senses. That there was no creator, no judgment, no heaven or hell, no life after death, no reality outside what could be touched, tasted, heard, seen, and smelled. Sahle hesitated, challenged by theories he did not know how to refute, theories foreign to Ethiopian culture, theories insisted upon by people who held a gun in your face.

Men weren't the only ones tested in such ways. His beloved, graceful little Aberash was sent to Hawassa for re-education too. She was required to *fokere,* that is, to shout communist slogans—like "Down with the imperialists!" or "Down with God!"—while raising the left fist.[61] Aberash wouldn't comply, for she saw it as a form of cursing. Therefore she and one other stood alone in a gathering of 1,000, faced with public denouncement: "You are enemies. Down! Down with you!"

What was Sahle going to do? In all good conscience, he could not preach—were they not theological teachings?—these ideas to children who trusted their teachers and were at their mercy. What did Charles and I think? What did we know about such ideas? How could we help him, or fellow teachers like him? Even if we could help him think it all through, what was he going to do when he went back to Debre Zeit, back to surveillance by local authorities who would monitor his office and classrooms? What would happen to his children, if he and Aberash didn't act the part? He felt trapped. We talked, we prayed, we hugged him good-bye. He slipped out into the darkness.

Sahle had come to trust us over years of friendship, unlike our new Ethiopian friends to whom we'd so recently become house parents. These Community Development (CD) young people all spoke English and we had much in common, but they wondered whether they could trust us. They were bright-minded and well trained as engineers, accountants, mechanics, and secretaries, many of them college graduates and from various ethnic roots. Could they trust each other? Gebre, part Eritrean, had disappeared from his office. It was

---

61. *Fokere* literally meant, "to boast." These boasts were slogans required to be shouted by "the broad masses."

days before they found him—alive, but locked up in prison. Who exposed him? Who accused him? The CDers looked around wondering who would be next.

A SMART TAP AT our door another evening brought a man with receding hairline whom we'd never seen before. He introduced himself as "Solomon, an RVOG announcer." An attractive man who spoke beautiful English, Solomon Abate was obviously a fine choice for newscaster. It came out, however, that he felt his natural talent was being prostituted since RVOG (Radio Voice of the Gospel) had been confiscated and converted into being the country's major voice for Marxist-Leninist propaganda. He was miserable to be forced to read out news releases smartly stating "facts" he knew to be lies in terminology he abhorred. As we listened, we recognized he was expressing a background of reading and sophistication of understanding beyond any other national who had spoken to us on the sensitive subject of the Revolution. Furthermore, he seemed fearless to do so.

Solomon came again. He had been developing a series of lectures significant for these times. Solomon had been among the speakers at the "Hold On to your Crown" conference at Bishoftu. Werku from Dilla and Ato Tesfaye from Chencha were among those who heard him. Many were being helped by this man. He longed to share his understanding with young people who were confused over the political theories they were facing. His personal library and passionate study showed considerable depth. We learned that at great risk he was giving his "Bible and Science" lectures clandestinely. He never mentioned political terms, but simply built a biblical base, largely from the Old Testament, which buttressed a rebuttal to materialism. We thought of these CD young people we were growing to love, and wondered. Should we risk a meeting? Gatherings of over five people were forbidden, but weren't we a family living together?

While a guard was posted at the gate and the front door, one Sunday afternoon Solomon met with our "family" in the living room of the big house, the grand piano his podium. With the Bible in one hand and gesturing with the other, his Amharic poured out with precision and passion—all too quick in delivery and too advanced in vocabulary for us two foreigners to follow. The students listened intently, asked questions, took notes, and like dry wells, drank in

Scriptures and their implications. Four hours later as night was falling, the group reluctantly disbanded. Many told us they had learned more about the philosophical battle they were engaged in that day, than they had thus far grasped.

When the government raised our CD House rent to an impossible figure, the mission was forced to close it. What a strange last week it was. CD House employees were confused by the new government's labor union rules and were terrified that they might lose their only means of livelihood. They fought to keep the place open. Our household workers impounded all the national and foreign residents' packed-up goods behind lock and key. Yet they served us meals faithfully. The cook, tearful and wordless, hugged me in the hallways.

Being turned out was threatening for the residents, too. Young and educated Ethiopian youth were considered suspect and were fair game for imprisonment or death. After repeated exit visa rejections, one of our CD young men miraculously secured permission to study abroad. At a good-bye party at the Ethiopian Hotel the week of our closing, we were aware of two others who had confided that they too would "disappear" the same week, hoping to make it out of the country. Not knowing who might be a "plant" and betray them, they held in their secret and dared not say good-bye. Our eyes met over the table and locked, but our lips were sealed.

WHEN THE CD HOUSE finally closed, Charles, Tim, Nat and I ended back in one room at Headquarters, still with no medical post available. At least we had housing, but we worried about what was happening to each of our CD friends. How could we help them further? We realized that the battle with anti-God "principalities and powers" (Ephesians 6:12) is a spiritual one, so the needed weapons were also spiritual. The use of such weapons are best demonstrated by people who have learned to use them on the field of battle.

Western missionaries knew little about life under communism, so could only speak from research, not from personal experience. Besides, how could nationals trust a Westerner who had been reared in a capitalist framework to speak with understanding? Even if an experienced advisor were found, Ethiopians who got caught listening to a Westerner would be stoutly accused. Who was prepared to be of help?

God apparently arranged for the Macedonian call to "come over and help us" (Acts 16:9) to be heard by a certain godly Chinese couple who made themselves available for His deployment. Rev. Hsueh Yu Kwong and his wife Lily had been doing a refresher course in All Nations Christian College in England, where they had met students from Africa who drew them to investigate the Ethiopian situation. Yu Kwong was not new to Christian education, for after serving in the Sino–Japanese War (1937–45) and later graduating from Nanking University, he was able to get out of China in 1950, when he was about thirty. He, and later his wife as well, taught in theological institutions in Hong Kong, Taiwan, Malaysia, and the Philippines.

From outside China, the Hsuehs kept in touch with Christians on the mainland, some of whom were in prisons. Yu Kwong was deeply touched by the life and writings of Wang Ming-Dao, who did not register his group in the Three-Self Movement as demanded by the communist government.[62] Pastor Hsueh was also influenced by the writings of A. W. Tozer, and translated two of his books into Chinese, *Knowledge of the Holy* and *The Pursuit of God*. The latter has been printed twelve times in Hong Kong.

The Hsuehs had been praying about Africa. A surprise gift from a Christian couple in the United States made the trip financially possible. A friend wrote to Paul Balisky in Ethiopia (stationed at Grace Bible Institute in 1976) on behalf of Yu Kwong, introducing him as a Chinese Christian. "Our GBI students and staff have been praying that an Asian Christian would come!" Paul replied. Pastor Hsueh made his reconnaissance trip into Ethiopia in 1977. On his arrival, the tall, reserved Asian, seemed at peace. When Paul learned Yu Kwong's background, he thanked God. "You are the person we have been praying for!" They got acquainted as they drove out of Addis Ababa and on past Negussie's Wolisso town and Ato Tekle's Saja, down and up the other side of the Gibe River gorge, on the day-long trip to Jimma.

Paul canceled other GBI classes for three days, allowing the Chinese guest all the time possible with students. His key focus

---

62. "Three-Self" referred to self-governing, self-supporting, self-propagating—meaning free from "imperialist" ties, and "guided" by communist overseers. For a description of how the church in China was forced into this straightjacket of communist control, see L. Lyall, *Come Wind, Come Weather* (Moody Press, 1960).

HSUEH YU KWONG, KAY BASCOM, AND PASTOR KEDAMO (ADDIS ABABA, 1994)

during that first visit as taken from Matthew 19, in which John was the only Apostle who stayed close at the Lord's crucifixion. Who would remain, in Ethiopia? "The time has come that if you want to be faithful to God," he said, "you must pay the price."

When the time drew short, Paul Balisky insisted, "Your work here is not finished. You must come again!" Before Yu Kwong left Ethiopia, Murray Coleman found discrete ways for him to speak in Addis Ababa to senior secondary and college students, a graduate fellowship, a Mekane Yesus church, and the Gideons.

That became the first of Yu Kwong's six trips into Ethiopia. Back in Great Britain, Pastor Hsueh told his wife Lily they were invited for the next year. They prayed, finished their course, and returned to Malaysia, where Yu Kwong founded a new Bible seminary. During the 1978 Christmas holidays, the Hsuehs miraculously got entry visas. Tiny but strong, Lily's supportive presence and excellent English enhanced their ministry. John Cumbers drove them to Jimma, where students asked very sensitive questions, ones that missionaries couldn't answer. Obedience was a key issue. Fear was everywhere, for people were being arrested or were just disappearing. His answer was simple, but costly: "Fear God, fear no man."

For six weeks they traveled down-country. Paul Balisky and Murray Coleman were amused at some checkpoints, where they heard on-looking nationals whisper, "This Chinaman must be from the Derg. Pass him through!" Chinese, Russians, and Cubans were traveling in large numbers throughout Ethiopia in those days.[63] Over and over Pastor Hsueh's party was protected. In Addis Ababa, Ato Lakew and other trusted Christian leaders, assisted them. In one period of two days, the Hsuehs spoke to nine groups, including SIM, Finnish, and Baptist groups. In Gedeo, Ato Werku translated in Dilla. They visited Durame in Kambaata. In Wolaitta, Bruce Adams hosted them during the annual conference at Soddo. There they had the privilege of meeting Ato Wandaro and Daanna Meja, among the first Wolaitta believers, of whom they had heard and read. Mr. Hsueh did not speak, but gave a Bible study to leaders secretly after the conference. Yu Kwong often spoke from Isaiah 41, reaffirming God's admonitions: "Do not fear, for I am with you; do not be dismayed, for I am your God. I will strengthen you and help you; I will uphold you with my righteous right hand. All who rage against you will surely be ashamed and disgraced."

At one meeting in Addis Ababa, a dozen young people present had been in prison. Their Chinese brother's response was warm and simple: "It is worthy to suffer for Christ. God is with you. Remain faithful. Carry on." Yu Kwong encouraged Ethiopians in their hour of testing with testimonies from China's communist persecution. Wang Ming-Tau was twenty-three years in prison. Watchman Nee was to be released after fifteen years, but when he would not write a "repentance" document, he was kept in prison until he died. "He still speaks, even though he is dead."[64]

"We felt the presence of the Holy Spirit at every meeting," Pastor Hsueh reiterated years later. "Repeatedly we saw fruit from the previous visit. 'I wasn't a believer when you came last year and preached from John,' one young man told us, 'but now I am.' A frightened

---

63. By "March 1978 [...] The U.S. government announced there were now 10,000 Cubans, plus 50 MiG fighter jets and 500 Russian tanks in Ethiopia"—reported from his diary in Cumbers (1996), *Terror,* 169.

64. See the remark in Hebrews 11:4b, about Abel, among the heroes of the faith. Watchman Nee's messages were made into books while he was in prison. The best-known is W. Nee, *The Normal Christian Life* (Tyndale House Publ., 1980).

police chief came, thinking there would be no hope for him. I didn't talk to him personally, but the next year he was the interpreter as I spoke from Daniel. In 1978 the chairman of one meeting, when introducing me, said he had practically memorized all the points of my message the year before."

And so it was that God provided shepherds for Ethiopian believers. Through the Hsuehs and other Chinese Christians, the sharing of similar experiences served as a great encouragement to Ethiopians in their desperate hour. They rejoiced to discover their oneness in the Body of Christ, and the lack of waste in God's mysterious economy.

PASTOR HSUEH MADE IT to Jimma just in time, for before his second visit, GBI's closure had come. From the time Art and Sue Volkmann left, GBI's future had been precarious. Paul and Lila Balisky had been moved into the Jimma school. Paul came from a family of Ukrainian immigrants who had settled in Canada, and Lila had been reared by missionary parents in Kenya. The couple's family background and their own unique gifting made them a refreshing team. It was Paul who had worked with Howie Brant on the Langano conference to prepare Ethiopian youth for what was coming.

Before GBI's take-over, our family had spent a couple of weeks with Baliskys during an Elders' course which Paul devised. Christian leaders were under pressure from the government to show forth practical—not theological—contributions to society. Paul called in elders from all over the south to teach them practical skills which they could multiply in their communities—creating course blocks in carpentry, bee keeping, medical care, and the like.

Charles had one of the most stimulating opportunities of his life, teaching a course on simple first aid and providing preventive guidelines for pervasive health problems, such as intestinal parasites, skin and eye infections, broken bones and tuberculosis. Never had Charles seen such enthusiasm to learn. Daniel Scheel[65] finally had to turn the lights out in the shop late at night, the men were so thrilled to practice the basics of his carpentry course. They each took home a kit of tools.

---

65. Dan is the son of the Dr. Scheel who had first invited us to Ethiopia.

Meanwhile, our five missionary kids were home from school. The three Balisky boys showed our two sons the wealth of Jimma wildlife by day, and we all played games together at night, to keep the sons from undue focus on the political precariousness we adults felt. We declared a "creativity week," and challenged everyone to produce something artistic or musical to share the final day. What a repertoire came forth—from recital numbers to a gallery of art. Characteristic of his playfulness, Charles' masterpiece: a golden circle with a black dot on it, which he titled, tongue in cheek, "Fly on the Sun." Lila crowned the evening with a delicious culinary creation. When we heard of the Baliskys' banishment from Jimma later, I thought back to that night: With their dark heads turned to the piano which Lila played so magnificently, Paul had skillfully whistled, in high obbligato, the theme song of "Doctor Zhivago," a haunting melody for times like these.

When grace bible institute's count-down week struck the next year, the Balisky sons were home for Easter. The Farghers were co-workers by then, but Joyce and their daughters had not made it home before the take-over occurred. Brian Fargher was the only other mission staff man present to face the tense days along with the Baliskys and Ato Girma Hanano. A mature Kambaatan GBI student in the early seventies, Ato Girma by now was an instructor. His steadiness and sense of humor were priceless at this tense time.

Every station had its unique closing. At Jimma there were successive days of house searches, office ransackings, and confiscations, broken once by the *kebele* guards laying down their guns and playing volleyball with the "accused" GBI students! The scene typified the political drama all were being required to act out. The day before missionaries were given twenty-four hours to leave Grace Bible Institute, a grand invasion commenced with a swarm of police and soldiers in Land Rovers streaming through the gate. As Lila reported it:

> Some three thousand people bearing slogans, banners, and flags filed into the compound. The GBI students were made to sit outside the dining hall right in front of the parade. The marchers filed past the dining room and dorm, down across the volleyball court, up past Farghers' house and circled around the yard in front of our house. Even though we knew we were being protected, the sight was enough to leave one weak.

> We watched through the curtains. The crowd really wasn't very worked up—just a few. Loudspeakers blared, "Missionaries go home"...plus all the other stuff that had been on the posters previously. They also shouted, "We have found a new campus for our political school" and all the crowd would shout in response, "We have found it! We have found it!" The kids were upstairs and climbed up and sat in the open window. 90% of the crowd were completely taken with them and were smiling and waving to them. Really quite humorous. At one point there was a photographer on our front steps and we actually heard him tell the crowd, "Stop smiling and raise your left hands!"

Lila's report of that momentous week in March portrays escalating tensions. Hours of frustration or fear were punctuated with bursts of anger one moment, and a rush of pity the next. The foreigners and Ethiopian students shed tears of loss and sang songs of praise. Contradictions rose time and again—accusations in political jargon and quiet rebuttals in simple honesty. The courtesy and forgiveness extended by the attacked repeatedly confounded the attackers. When Lila boiled tea to serve to the soldiers, they declined, using an ancient cultural rationale: "It's a fast day today." What role does fasting play in a non-God, non-religious society, Lila wondered. Perhaps their excuse revealed how cosmetic this Party-line display really was.

In the end, the missionaries lost all but what was left in a couple of ransacked suitcases they were each allowed to take out. Yet they left physically unharmed. Classes were not resumed after Easter and it looked as if Grace Bible Institute was finished—its supplies, library, compound, and existence gone forever. Having lost home and assignment, security and future, staff and students looked to their very-present God. They continued to find Him well able to see them through such scenarios on earth.

AS FOR MISSIONARIES, August of 1977 demanded decision for those who had teenagers. Bingham Academy, teaching first through eighth grades, was still operational, but the government had confiscated Good Shepherd School, where our high schoolers attended, turning it into a military hospital. The mission begged sudden entrance for our students into Rift Valley Academy, the Africa Inland Mission school in Kenya, Ethiopia's neighbor to the south.

Many missionaries landed in Kenya temporarily when they were spun out of Ethiopia. A bit like refugees ourselves, having lost our homes and our work sites, we landed in various mission guesthouses in Nairobi. We walked the streets in disoriented confusion, pondering what to do next.

Divergent streams of people were pouring into Kenya in the mid-seventies from Ethiopia, Sudan, Somalia, Uganda, and more places. Ethiopia's dark hour was part of a mosaic over the whole Horn of Africa and beyond. "The Horn" was often in the news from a secular vantage point. One of the few who addressed Africa's plight from a Christian perspective was Brother Andrew from Holland, sometimes known as "God's smuggler" because he had labored to get Bibles behind the Iron Curtain.

Brother Andrew responded to the call to aid the suffering church which was inspired by Revelation 3:2: "Awake and strengthen what remains and is on the point of death." His vision took him wherever Christians were suffering, to the Soviet Union, Eastern Europe, China, and in the seventies, to Africa. The first chapter of his book, *Battle for Africa*, surveyed the tragedies across the continent from Angola to Zambia—a giant battleground ripe for revolution. He scrutinized the successes and failures of the missionary enterprise in Africa, and insisted that the church can survive under any political regime, but it cannot survive under apathy—its own apathy. He did not blame the success of communism for the problem as much as the failure of the church. "I have always distrusted those people who blame the communists for everything!" He explained his ministry in this way:

> People somehow expect me to be a vehement anti-communist, and I simply have never had the time nor the inclination to become a crusader against communism. I am not anti-communist; I am pro-Christian. I am pro-people. God called me to take the gospel to people, and whatever stands between them and me is my enemy. But I must tell you that communism is hard at work in the Revolution in Africa. Moscow, Peking, and Havana all have their hands in the African pot right up to their elbows. The clearer we are on that critical point, the more clearly we can see what the stakes in the battle for Africa really are. The African crisis cannot be fully understood in detachment from the events in his-

tory which have led up to it. It is a part of a larger pattern of worldwide agitation and violence that is generated and inspired by a persistent fight of communism against the church.[66]

His book briefly surveyed the wide range of operations over the continent in which the legacy of Marx and Lenin could be seen: military troops, arms and financial aid, propaganda, academic training, liberation movements, and terrorism.

To encourage Christians in Africa, "Open Doors with Brother Andrew" organized a "Love Africa" conference in 1978 in Malawi, attended by Ethiopians among others, out of which came the collection titled *Destined to Suffer?*[67] As a protected American, I was caught up short by the premise of a chapter by a Nigerian answering the title's question. Tokunboh Adeyemo titled his address: "Persecution: A Permanent Feature of the Church." Permanent: that jolted my thinking. I began to refocus my sights as I looked at the Scriptures, history and contemporary experience.

In Nairobi, Tokunboh Adeyemo maintained the office for the Association of Evangelicals of Africa and Madagascar (AEAM).[68] At the very heart of East Africa, Nairobi was more than the capital of one of the few stable nations on that continent. Head offices of countless international companies and agencies were housed in its skyscrapers towering above six-lane highways. Shops that could as well be in London lined its avenue, although its merchants had darker skins. Of course, there was a back side to Nairobi, areas Westerners would call slums. Each day from these districts thousands of refugees drifted down to the heart of the city searching for something to eat, something to do, and someone with whom to share their lonely, hope-diminished existence. Revolution, war, and oppression had shattered the lives they once knew at home in Ethiopia, Somalia or Uganda. From the airport of their nations' capitals came a sparser stream of countrymen on business to Nairobi—people still connected to their governments by an umbilical cord known as a passport.

---

66. Br. Andrew and C. Conn, *Battle for Africa* (F. H. Revell, 1977), 68f.
67. Br. Andrew, *Destined to Suffer?* (Open Doors with Br. Andrew, 1979).
68. Tokunboh Adeyemo succeeded Byang Kato as AEAM General Secretary. He was able to draw upon information from all over the continent, as well as his personal experience with the difficulties faced by the Christian minority in Muslim-dominated Nigeria.

As we walked the streets of Nairobi, we looked like Americans, but inwardly we felt Ethiopian. Although not destitute, missionaries displaced from their adoptive countries were also tasting the forced relinquishment and uprootedness of the refugee experience. Our radar system regularly spotted soul brothers among the myriad of peoples on the streets. It was not usual to find an Ethiopian in the various guesthouses foreigners frequented in the city. When we did, we assumed he had a passport and was not a refugee. Brief encounters with two such men gave us indelible glimpses of the crucible out of which each came.

WE WILL CALL THE first man "the zealot"—we purposely did not learn his name. He looked harmless enough in jeans and jacket, seated down the table from us in the Methodist guesthouse. I studied his face, high cheekbones, darting eyes, black ringlets above a receding hairline.

I cringed as an outspoken Britisher across the table outlined the Ethiopian revolution for an inquiring tourist. The Orthodox Amharas had brought it on themselves, he asserted. The lonely Ethiopian, who would seem to have the most authentic viewpoint at the table, started to speak, but swallowed, and nervously kept picking at his food. After the meal, he took my husband aside. Could he speak with us? When? Where?

We met in an empty lounge. He spoke quickly, looking over his shoulder with fear-conditioned regularity. "I am talking to you because you are friends of Ethiopia," he began. Desperate to share his burden with someone, even without knowing us, he poured out his story.

He was, himself, of the previous ruling ethnic group, but said he was disillusioned with his own people, the church, and the old regime, all inseparably intertwined and sweepingly discredited by the leftist Revolution that had come to birth.

A sensitive man, the Zealot had been tender to the famine that precipitated the unrest. At first he was in sympathy with the promised reforms, enthused about the goals of the Revolution. But then the alarming assassinations within the leadership had begun. The whole movement swung into a wild tangent, ripping the country apart. Russian and Chinese personnel and equipment poured in.

For men of bourgeois background, like himself, every day held the strain of being suspect. Politburo abductions from offices by day and raids on houses at night stabbed around his existence. The fear campaign which the revolutionaries fostered at all levels of national life isolated man from man. When his marriage crumbled, the Zealot's inner loneliness increased.

Struggling to extract some meaning out of the chaos, he joined with a small band of political zealots who met clandestinely to plot the ruler's assassination. Two were discovered and liquidated. Daily, he told us, he wondered when his number would be up in this game of truly Russian roulette. By then, many observers considered the Ethiopian military governor to be a helpless tool in Russian hands. To the Zealot, his country's total deliverance hung on the riddance of this one man. He told us how an exit visa had become available for a brief trip to Kenya under the guise of business. He'd come, desperately hoping to raise a resistance movement from outside Ethiopia.

He fell back in his chair, exhausted from reliving his experiences. The man was nearly manic. Pressing his hands to glistening temples, he groaned, "I can hardly stand these headaches." Sighing, he described his alternatives to us. It hadn't worked, this plan to raise a resistance group during these three short weeks in Kenya. America was his other hope. There were thousands of Ethiopians there, unable to return home. But the American visa, the money—they had not crystallized in time. His business firm had booked a flight for him to Addis Ababa the next day. Staying in Kenya longer would be illegal… unless he declared himself a refugee. At home he was already under suspicion and this trip to "the outside" may have made him more so. He figured he had a fifty-fifty chance of being intercepted at the Addis Ababa airport on arrival, being imprisoned, or shot. "Do you see any escape from this prison abyss, or worse?" he beseeched us.

Faces of refugees we'd met on the streets flashed into our minds, representative of thousands who had made the wrenching decision he was weighing. "Would you not choose at least to stay alive, in Kenya?" we asked him. I cannot remember the wording of his answer, but his thought was that swerving from his course would destroy his very reason for being. The slim chance of success in personally annihilating Mengistu, the target of his hatred, would seem too significant to be exchanged for the shelved status of a refugee.

When we questioned whether destroying the figurehead would solve Ethiopia's now insurmountable problems, he literally clasped his hands over his ears in torment and cried, "It will, it will!"

We sat silently, his pain pulsating among the three of us. What was there to say? Gently, we began to speak to him of the only kind of peace we knew to recommend. The fire in his eyes dimmed to a blind man's stare. Oh yes, he knew the Scriptures, the church. The church was hypocrisy, a tool of the old order, a sell-out to the new. The Spirit? New life? Peace? A relationship with God, rather than a religion? He knew nothing of such things. He tapped his heart. "I am not just battling over my country," he said in a dry whisper, "I am battling with God." He allowed us to pray for him, then left wearily, saying, "It has passed, a little." The next day he flew back into the jaws of Ethiopia.

A FEW WEEKS LATER, we were standing in the entryway of another guesthouse when a tall African in a blue business suit closed the gate to the street carefully behind him. He stood quietly in the shade of trees, grasping a small bag. We immediately recognized him as Ethiopian, and were drawn to him like a magnet. So was a young Ethiopian woman who had recently left her country. The questions poured out. "You've just come? How is it now? Is there peace anywhere?"

With a kindly patience no doubt learned from much listening, he slowly began. "The killings in the Addis Ababa streets are a bit diminished. The anti-revolutionaries are supposedly liquidated. Now it is the detention centers that are being filled—some 120,000 in them, they say. These aren't the regular prisons; they are all full. These are just high walled compounds in each *kebele* neighborhood, turned into jails."

I remembered our own uneasy visits to sectional headquarters in Addis—where every single citizen or alien had to be numbered and photographed, for the indispensable red identity booklet any traveler had to present at check points throughout the city and countryside.

"The women..." he went on, looking down, "you see the women on the streets, on busses, children hanging on their skirts, carrying food to their sons and daughters and husbands in various prisons. They weep. Some have too many areas to carry to in one day.

Some have to be left out." (Prisons do not extend food to prisoners in Ethiopia.) The Ethiopian woman gave me a stricken glance and then turned back to him.

She asked about a certain rural area. "No," he answered, "there is no peace even there. Cadre forces suddenly gathered up all the bureau heads in the province and jailed them. The people protested. Homes were burned. Simple farmers. The politburo acts, guerrillas react. The hardest thing is that there is no recourse to justice, no courts, nowhere to turn with a grievance. The man who is 'right' is the man with the gun. It is completely out of hand, beyond us."

We asked about a Lutheran training institute. "We lost everything except the books," he reported. "We're trying to get them moved to a basement and keep using them... till someone comes to burn them. You see, there can be no teaching in the schools now, no mention of God. When we call the people to church, the youth are called to political meetings at the exact same time. The children are marched in parades with small wooden guns, chanting hymns of war."

We'd heard rumor of a certain well-known Christian government leader's assassination. "Is it true?" we asked. He confirmed it. "It is strange," he commented bitterly. "We are forced to report for these military funerals. The gravestones have the hammer and sickle on the front, and the cross on the back! They read the obituary of the military 'hero.' It is all so deceitful. They murder their own men, announce it was done by anti-revolutionaries, and bury them with pomp and ceremony. Others just disappear. A real hero may simply be listed as dead."

The man literally groaned. "Don't ask me more. There is more I could tell you... but I cannot speak of it now. My wife and children are there. I'll soon return." He was deeply moved, but his voice did not break.

We stepped back, ashamed of our greedy questioning. He needed to rest, to forget it all. But this man was no escapist. He had learned to live with grief by inner resources. He brightened and seemed moved to say one thing more. "There is the other side of the coin. The Christian youth are growing stronger and stronger, even though it is hard for them. We have never seen such unity, such vitality, in the church.

"Recently we had meetings. To our surprise, delegates appeared from all over the city—from every type of Christian fellowship—as an expression of solidarity. Never have we known such an atmosphere of the Spirit permeating our meetings. When the conference began, two policemen appeared from Security. In private, one opened his lapel to reveal a Gideon New Testament. 'I, too, am a Christian,' he confessed. The other guard stood around looking through our books, listening, watching. Before it was over, he gave himself to Christ—and continues now in our fellowship."

Encouraged by his obvious joy in sharing the brighter side, we asked, "Is Solomon Abate still alive?"—the Solomon so gifted in steadying young Christians. He glanced heavenward with a gesture acknowledging God's intervention. "We prayed him out of his RVOG[69] job they were forcing him to do. His new work allows more writing and speaking time. He continues to be greatly used of God." My heart leapt. We had kept praying for Solomon, knowing they were always just a step behind him.

We asked about one other man—an outspoken Christian in the military—one we always expected to be killed. "His case is a continual miracle," our friend reported. "General Taye Tilahun is not only alive, but promoted. We hear he still opens his staff meetings with prayer. We don't know why they've let him live. They know he is honest! Christians are often trusted with responsibilities… while it is expedient. This man isn't plotting anything. Perhaps God has a special plan for him."

The roar of Nairobi traffic outside the gate echoed against the quietness of this man of sorrows, acquainted with grief. I stared at his unlined face etched with peace. "We must let you go," I said, rousing my thoughts from another world. I looked around for the crowd of witnesses I instinctively felt should have been exposed to this man, this testimony, but the four of us stood alone.

HAD THE BORDERS OF Ethiopia been able to speak in the seventies, they could tell countless stories of those who passed over or back with hopes raised or dashed, lives shattered or re-emerging. The borders were crossed in various ways. Soldiers were trucked across for war,

---

69. After the military takeover of the station in 1977 *Radio Voice of the Gospel* was actually renamed *Radio Voice of Revolutionary Ethiopia*.

businessmen flew out on ventures, others risked walking across on foot, propelled by fear or stolid refusal to participate. The last was the Prince's reason.

"L'ool," we will call him to protect his identity. *L'ool* means "prince," and a more princely man I cannot remember meeting. Tall and erect of body and handsome of face, his military bearing and warm-eyed graciousness were irresistible. L'ool had spent the early years of the seventies in university training in Europe, in preparation for taking a top command in the Ethiopian military. While there, this handsome prince had won the heart of a fellow student we will call "Jewel." When graduation time came, a weighty decision was required. "Don't come home," his family and friends had written him the year before. "Your life will be in danger, and the Ethiopia you will find is not the homeland you left. You will be appalled, and you will never fit into this system. You may even be executed." Repeatedly they begged him to stay out. Many of his generation of leaders had remained abroad, having "the good sense to accept the situation." L'ool thought differently. A deep man of principle, he could not imagine his country's having sent him abroad to prepare him for service, and his not making good his end of the bargain. Determined to pay back his education and persevere under hardship, he bid Jewel a poignant good-bye, with the hope but not the promise, that she could one day come to him.

Whether bidden or not, she did eventually come. This spirited young woman turned up in our Friday women's group one July day in 1977, her reason for coming to Ethiopia at this dangerous time a mystery to us. Eventually I was taken into her confidence. She had dared to come in order to meet L'ool's family, for they were considering marriage someday. At least she was, although his prior commitments were formidable. At first they tried every avenue to get permission to travel the hundreds of miles to his parents' home, but were blocked by red tape and denials at every turn. Travel across the city at night to meet after his assigned work was prohibitive. How were they even to use the few precious days of her visit? In times of war, the decorum of culture can become impractical. They took the only choice open to them, to share his apartment. "Don't worry, L'ool is firmly committed to abstaining from sexual relations before marriage," Jewel assured my maternal heart, but not hiding her own anguish. "My dear prince is truly a gentleman." I will never forget my last glimpse of the two at the Friday group's final party—bidding the hosts good-bye, he with the dignity of a general and she so small and vulnerable, despite her pluck. And then they stepped out into the rain.

When we were wandering in Nairobi trying to decide what to do next, I wrote to Jewel back in Europe, and wondered what would happen to the Prince. Patriotic as he was, Captain L'ool was not the kind of man who would compromise with "the powers that be" to stay in their good graces. I never expected to see either of them again, but I thought of them often as we made our own transition.

Ethiopian missionaries eventually drifted out of Kenya to serve in other countries or to regroup at home. Some found ways to stay close to Ethiopia. A contingent of us relocated in Sudan, one country to the west of Ethiopia. The Ethio–Sudanese border saw crossings both directions, some related to Ethiopia's civil war with Eritrea in the north, tying to secede; and others related to northern Sudan's attacks on the south, to subjugate non-Islamic peoples. Those fleeing either situation sought refuge in the opposite country, causing no small strain on international relations.

By the summer of 1978, Charles and I were studying Arabic in hot, dusty Khartoum, Sudan's capital. We were 1500 miles across swamps and deserts from our two younger sons, in school in Kenya. The mission headquarters, a flat two-story stucco guesthouse, included some improvised meeting spaces adjacent to the main building. Refugees from the east or south who had made it across the desert sands to Khartoum were helped to find their people in the worship services which they had asked to locate on the premises, conducting meetings in their particular languages. A Sunday visitor could walk through the gate and pass windows of one room after another, hearing not only English or Arabic, but the Ethiopians' Amharic, the Eritreans' Tigrinya, and the southern Sudanese tongues of the Uduk or Dinka. These Sudanese Christians had been driven from their homes by government soldiers bent on Islamization. Friday was Sudan's Muslim holy day, and so special services were arranged on Fridays as well.

One Friday evening at dusk, a guard with a puzzled look called us to the tiled porch which surround the guesthouse rooms. A tall, bent man stood in the shadows, his head and shoulders draped with an Ethiopian-style shawl, even though the heat was oppressive. I caught my breath when his gaunt face materialized out of the shadows. Captain L'ool! "Who... what... where... how...?" my questions tumbled out. "I can't talk now," he whispered with poise, "for the car is waiting at the gate. I'm being held in house arrest with only occasional hours outside, under guard. I will try to get in touch again."

"What, what have they done to you?" I kept asking the stillness as he glided away. As it turned out, we would see him in Khartoum two more times. This couple's sequel is another story, but I will share one thing he told us, the principle question that occupied his thoughts in the long hours of detention: Why? Having cooperated in the Ethiopian military to the limit of his moral choice, L'ool chose to remove himself from what he saw as evil. He would choose death over compromise, or life without a country, if God so willed. Having survived the long, excruciating journey through mountains and desert on foot, and having not been shot crossing the border, he had given himself up to Sudanese authorities. They thought him to be more of a crowning political plumb to keep in reserve for leverage than he felt himself to be. At least his accommodations were bearable, and his fellow prisoners represented an interesting variety of political positions, all of whom were reduced to argument rather than arms to slay each other.

Turning to the Word of God, Captain L'ool pored over the Scriptures, searching for God's purposes in the affairs of men. How vibrant his faith had been in his free years, I do not know. The fact that the woman he had meant to commit his life to was an earnest Christian gave one indication. During his detention, he grew in spirit. While their whole life seemed wrecked by external circumstances, L'ool turned to God for inner integration. As to the vicissitudes of Ethiopian politics, or world politics in the age of communism, his meditations led him to a way to view history. Man had been given many tests, many opportunities. Communism's total rejection of God provided one more grand test for man, perhaps one last clarion call before the reigning Messiah's return, a call for choice. He had made his.

For though we live in the world,
we do not wage war as the world does.
The weapons we fight with are not the weapons of the world.
On the contrary, they have divine power to demolish strongholds.
We demolish arguments and every pretension
that sets itself up against the knowledge of God,
and we take captive every thought to make it obedient to Christ.
(2 Corinthians 10:3–5)

Chapter 14

FACING LOVE AND HATE

Negussie's focus was pulled like a magnet toward the young woman across the room. She was among others he had met in the home just that night. Why did she stand out to him so? Of average height, with a strong face, was it her shy kind smile, or the almost liquid eyes? He'd been to "underground" meetings of Christians in Addis Ababa before. Guarded as they had to be, they were wonderful times, hours of worship and study and corporate encouragement in the difficult circumstances all were facing. Why should this one person emerge from the group, rising in his mind's eye after the meeting, continuing with him as he made the trip back to Wolisso, visiting his thoughts when the school day closed and he was trying to prepare for tomorrow's teaching. What did it mean, her strange lingering with him, so unfamiliar a presence in his bachelorhood?

Around twenty-seven by now, Negussie had maintained his singleness carefully, bent upon pleasing his Lord in all aspects of his life. What was God's purpose for this meeting? He spoke to Him about it. Could she ever be drawn to one such as himself? Might their paths cross again?

They did, very briefly, on his next trip to Addis Ababa. There she was again across the living room, so graceful and composed. They shared the experience of the group, his heart singing, while his fingers strummed on the guitar he loved to play, happy to be worshipping together through song in this simple way. Would she correspond with him, he quietly asked afterward. She would, she replied.

And Fantaye Mogus? She went home and pondered too. Only a month before their first meeting, she had specifically asked the Lord to someday bring to her a godly husband. She was only twenty-one. Her prayer was looking into the future, eager to commit this crucial area of her life to Him. Already, she was knowing loneliness in a home that did not appreciate her singular devotion to the Lord Jesus Christ.

Her Amhara family practiced Orthodoxy by keeping the festivals, fasts, and feasts prescribed by the church calendar—hundreds each year. Specific days were given to a myriad of biblical personages, angels, and martyrs, along with members of the Trinity. The Virgin Mary seemed to be the most venerated; her intercessions were considered most efficacious of all. Fantaye had often stood with the women outside the church (during her menstruation) or sometimes inside the vestibule, led by priests in chanting the ancient prayers.

In the privacy of her own home, however, she'd heard of the Lord Jesus' supremacy above all others, not only as the "one mediator between God and man," but as the one who had given His very life to care for her sins. She'd heard it from an invisible friend, one who read the word of God across the airwaves of her radio. And believing this testimony from the Scriptures, she'd received the Word-become-Flesh. Was He not alive from the dead, the Messiah Himself? Did He not bid her come to Him for her every need?

Fantaye had gone home from the evening of Negussie's first appearance strangely stirred. She rehearsed the evening. Across the room she had seen the visitor from Wolisso. Her eyes wandered over the group, but kept moving back to his countenance which radiated such unusual joy. Standing not much taller than herself, his stature, she confided later, "did not please my eyes." She wondered what had stunted his torso, for his face seemed deeply mature. The man so reflected the inner presence of the One she'd come to love, that she was instinctively drawn to him.

Thus began the keeping of her long secret, not voiced to others, or even to Negussie, for years. Yet as they met from time to time, her shy blush and warm eyes spoke volumes to him, stirring hope within him. Negussie began to make periodic trips to the little one-room post office in Wolisso town, hopeful not only for a letter from John in Canada, or Alemu, who had gone to study in the United States, but perhaps one from Fantaye as well.

Meanwhile, the Revolution nipped at everyone's personal life. It could not smash the stirrings of hearts, although it saddened them. For Fantaye, who had succeeded in finishing 12th grade, crossing the city to her Ministry of Health accounting job could be a terrible experience. Bloodied bodies lying on the streets in the early hours, unexpected roadblocks and credential inspections, mutually suspicious co-workers in the office—all these made the work world sober. The media reported local political executions and statistics on the battlefields of the Eritrean or Somali war fronts in strange jargonese. With much parading required of citizens, September brought the regime's grand inauguration of a "Cultural Revolution."

None of these subjects were safe for letters which might be censored, nor were they central to Fantaye and Negussie's developing friendship. Their relationship with the Lord was the central focus of their correspondence. Her letters came as priceless treasures to be read and reread again, lighting up his world darkened by the militant indoctrination they were all ordered to attend weekly, and the suspicion which its protocol fanned.

Negussie had seen what was happening in the north, knew about GBI's closing, and was experiencing daily intensification of communist control in his own area. It was clear that the basic tenets of Marxism-Leninism cut across his life-encompassing commitment to God. Such people as he could either avoid trouble by acquiescing publicly, or else risk suspicion and probable mistreatment if they did not hide their witness to Christ. Negussie complied with regulations as far as he felt he could, but decided not to compromise his faith into silence. He would share discreetly with those God sent to Him. He led a small Bible study for any interested, and shared Scriptures with those who appeared hungry to listen. He was careful not to flaunt his convictions in the classroom, but his life spoke unmistakably of an assurance and peace which was not shared or appreciated by local cadres, some of them former classmates, now taken up with the new movement. Furthermore, he'd been promoted, putting him in an enviable position. Negussie was popular, for students sensed his impartial attitudes and genuine interest in them. When some with sincere questions came to visit him in the evenings, he talked openly with them about the claims of the Lord Jesus Christ. That other teachers could become jealous was simple to deduce, and they watched for some way to get rid of him.

A method emerged. How better than putting him away in some backwater village? On his next visit to Addis Ababa, Negussie broke the news to Fantaye that he'd been moved to a tiny little school far off the Jimma road in the village of Amaya, where he knew no one. The demotion and isolation were hard to take for one so well-trained and gregarious. Even there, *kebele* leaders watched him with cool calculation, noting who visited him at night. In the lonely hours, he wrote John Coleman in Canada. Chris Ott, the German nurse who awarded him his first Bible, received a letter from Negussie during those lonely months. One line stood out: "I have chosen the way of the cross leading to glory." He seemed to sense what might be coming.

On their fourth meeting in the capital, Fantaye was delighted to supply Negussie with some Christian tracts, for he was always looking for ways to help his students and others to understand who Jesus could be to them. She wrote again after he left, but got no answer. She'd hoped to hear the tracts were finding their way into receptive hands. By now, their letters were going back and forth regularly, and sudden cessation from his end seemed unexplainable. He'd been at Amaya six months now. She risked making a phone call to get information, but was told curtly, "Negussie is not here." Alarmed, she waited for some word from him.

NEGUSSIE HAD BEEN PLEASED with the tracts and some New Testaments he had procured in Addis Ababa. Back at Amaya, a couple of teachers feigned interest in getting copies of scripture and came to his home, setting him up for arrest. Their initial charge? The anti-revolutionary act of giving out New Testaments. They hustled him off to a local jail, but not without rummaging through his belongings, which included letters from John Coleman and Fantaye. Once he was transferred to the Wolisso Police Station, those became the "evidence of his CIA connection" (although John was from Canada, not the United States), and "evidence of immoral relationship with a woman"—to add character assassination to political accusation. His enemies added *Pente* to his crimes. When taken to the District offices, he protested that he had no connections with foreign governments, but would confirm that he was a member of the Kingdom of God. "If you simply renounce this foreign religion you can be released" he was told. "I would rather die than deny my Lord," he flatly responded.

"Your choice," they leered. Negussie's physical handicap seemed to fan the confidence of his attackers. A police station is sometimes not a good place to be at the mercy of accusers, but with former restraints now removed under Marxism-Leninism, they became sites of uncontrolled mistreatment and torture. Inhuman experiments in brutality erupted in unbelievable forms. Cadres in power exercised the upper hand in ways designed to break the will of a dissenter and terrify those who heard chilling screams from the outside. The Red Terror deaths had given way to the black terror of torture, as if the depravity of man had been given free rein.

His interrogators took him to a room with two tables spanned by a pole—preparing him for an often-used torture technique. They tied his ankles together. They offered him one last chance to recant. They stuffed a gag in his mouth and told him to raise a finger when he had had enough. "You just recant, and we stop!" Next they bound his wrists and then bent him over to tie them to his ankles. The pole was thrust under his bound hands and feet, and then lifted up to span the table, leaving the victim hanging with head down and bare feet exposed upwards. A soldier of rank began beating the soles of Negussie's feet with a heavy cane. When the man grew tired, he pulled out Negussie's gag and threatened, "Are you ready to recant?" By this time huge blood blisters had formed on the teacher's feet, but Negussie gasped out, "I'm ready to die for my Lord Jesus Christ." A cadre became infuriated and started kicking Negussie's head like a football. He took hold of the ends of the ropes and strung them between the prisoner's fingers and toes, pulling them tight to cut the flesh. He picked up a club and lashed out at the feet again, bursting the blisters. Blood spurted all over Negussie's body. As the cadre beat on in a diabolical frenzy, the soldier feared for the victim's life, not wanting to explain a corpse on their hands. Negussie's legs had already swelled up like tree trunks. They finally stopped. The battered prisoner was unable to stand. Cadres had to carry him over to dump him in the prison.

As he lay in his blood, might his mind have flitted over the cry of Christ on the cross, from Psalm 22, "My God, my God, why have you forsaken me?" This Psalm he may have memorized went on:

> I am a worm and not a man, scorned by men and despised by the people. All who see me mock me; they hurl insults, shaking their heads: 'He trusts in the LORD; let the LORD rescue him. Let him deliver him, since he delights in him.' [...] Do not be far from me, for trouble is near and there is no one to help. [...] I am poured out like water and all my bones are out of joint. My heart has turned to wax; it has melted away within me. My strength is dried up like a potsherd, and my tongue sticks to the roof of my mouth; you lay me in the dust of death. Dogs have surrounded me; a band of evil men has encircled me, they have pierced my hands and my feet.

As he focused upon the Savior, Negussie's soul and body began to be revived. For many weeks, he was unable to walk, obliged to depend upon prisoners to carry him even to the toilet, a filthy area where he was thrown down. He faced unspeakable suffering in those first days after his ordeal, although he testified to being miraculously shielded from pain during the initial torture itself. "I thought I was dead, but the Lord wanted me to live," he would affirm later. Somehow, counting himself already dead freed Negussie to live without fear. His inward peace made fellow-prisoners thirsty for what he had.

Finally Negussie was able to slip out a message with someone going to Addis, telling Fantaye that he was in prison. As soon as she could arrange an absence which would not reveal to anyone her destination, she took courage to arrange a secret trip to Wolisso. She carried a little parcel of fruit as a gift. At the jail, they refused to allow her to see him, but did not deny his presence there. She wept bitterly and begged the guards, "He's my brother. I can not go without seeing him!" They finally agreed to allow her five minutes with the prisoner.

Negussie could hardly believe his eyes, and wept for joy that she had come. "Be prepared, they want to question you," he whispered before they were torn apart. Few words could be exchanged, and what she learned of his suffering had to be pieced together later. Heartbroken at his battered appearance and helpless to aid his release, she stumbled out and quickly made her way back to Addis Ababa. There she knew no one to whom she felt she could turn. She could only pour out her heart to her closest Friend, and wait.

THE NEXT MONTHS WERE a nightmare of mistreatment for Negussie. Long years later, the marks of torture were yet visible on his body. Local friends hurt over his condition. Mulugeta Haile, a teacher who had also gone through the local brain-washing sessions, loved Negussie dearly. He ached over the beatings his dear friend took. "He seemed weak in body. They gave him no sympathy. Even for a healthy person it was hard, and so it seemed to me impossible for him to shoulder it. But by God's grace, he did. His testimony comforted people on the outside. The faith!"

Like other "Daniels" in other localities, Negussie's uncomplaining endurance in his "lions' den" deeply encouraged and emboldened local believers. As the Apostle Paul's chains made the Philippians more bold and confident, Negussie's imprisonment mysteriously ministered outside the walls. His very weakness magnified God's strength. Perhaps unaware of the chosen vessel he was becoming, Negussie's attitude was that life anywhere, whether bound or free, was simply a matter of obedience to his Lord.

Suffering had been introduced into Negussie's life early, through childhood beatings, through his early illness, and other struggles along the way. As a maturing Christian, he seemed to accept trials as a gift and offered them up to his Lord. Perhaps he was learning that suffering unites the believer to the cross at the heart of the Christian life. Strangely, it provides an authenticity for lifting up the crucified Savior to the world. Negussie's prison years raised the warm torch of Christ's love high in the darkness, drawing prisoners to Him, one by one.

That summer of 1979, John Coleman again made his way to Ethiopia to visit his family. Negussie's incarceration in Wolisso cut him to the heart. Yet, for an "imperialist" foreigner to visit him would only add more charges against him. Somehow Negussie managed to slip out a little package to the Colemans in Addis Ababa, containing a bit of handwork which prisoners were allowed to do. With hairpins, he had knit John a handsome brimmed hat. Along with what looked like directions titled "Six steps for washing, drying, blocking, and stretching the hat" came this hidden message:

To My Dear Friend John and all my Family:

Daily He gives me unspeakable joy and comfort. I am completely well and healthy. I have received the soap and flint you sent me. May God bless you. If God wills, I hope to see you after I receive the verdict. Acts 20:24, Philippians 1:20. I am sending this small gift to my dear brother John. I am your son Negussi Kumbi.

Added to his message, Negussie's two Scriptures spoke volumes:

However, I consider my life worth nothing to me,
if only I may finish the race and complete the task
the Lord Jesus has given me—
the task of testifying to the gospel of God's grace.
(Acts 20:24)

I eagerly expect and hope that I will in no way be ashamed,
but will have sufficient courage
so that now as always Christ will be exalted in my body,
whether by life or by death.
(Philippians 1:20)

Part IV

WIELDING SWORD AND SHIELD

(During 1978–81)

*And in addition to all this, take up the shield of faith [...]
and the sword of the Spirit, which is the word of God.*
(Ephesians 6:16a, 17b)

MAP 4: ADDIS ABABA: KEY LOCATIONS AND MAJOR ROADS (BEFORE AD 1991)

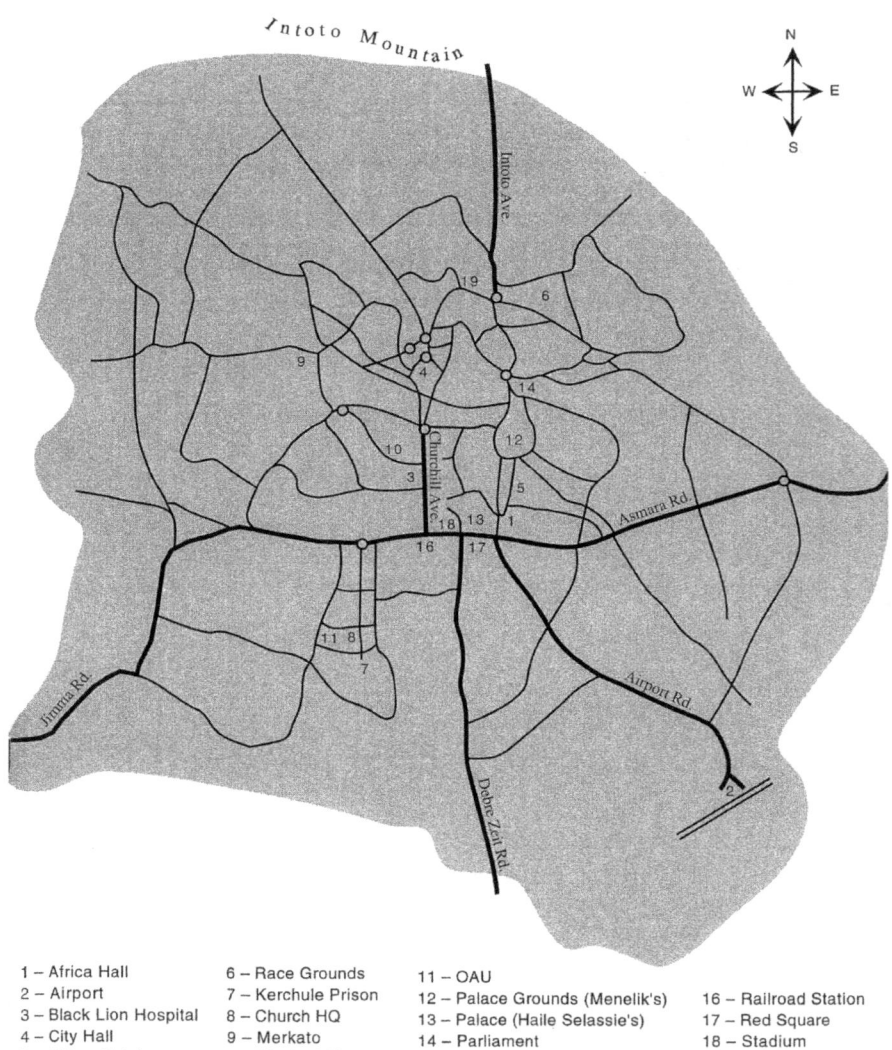

1 – Africa Hall
2 – Airport
3 – Black Lion Hospital
4 – City Hall
5 – Hilton Hotel
6 – Race Grounds
7 – Kerchule Prison
8 – Church HQ
9 – Merkato
10 – Mission HQ
11 – OAU
12 – Palace Grounds (Menelik's)
13 – Palace (Haile Selassie's)
14 – Parliament
15 – Piazza
16 – Railroad Station
17 – Red Square
18 – Stadium
19 – University

Source: Created by Johnathan Bascom in 1999.

Chapter 15

VIGNETTES ACROSS ADDIS ABABA

Fantaye's heart leapt when the news came: "Negussie's appeal will move him to Addis!" He'll be right here in my own city! she thought. Women go to the prisons every day to take food to their loved ones. Surely I could go sometimes too, even if it must be secretly.

With cadres trying out new forms of persuasion and due process of law evaporating, Negussie had decided that appealing his case to the Central Government might be the better part of wisdom. So it was that in January of 1979, he was moved to Addis Ababa and put in detention at an interrogation center which was located near the city's most sophisticated shopping area, the Piazza.

Although torture was employed less there, security was tighter. In fact, to go there to see him, Fantaye learned, would raise suspicion. After all, one of Negussie's charges involved "letters from a woman"—a woman not identified as his wife, or sister, or mother. Not even a cousin. Fantaye had not felt she lied when she begged in Wolisso to see "my brother." Was he not a brother to her through the familyhood of believers and their deepening friendship in Christ?

The Ministry of Health had assigned Fantaye to work outside in city in the wider Shewa province. On weekends back in her parents' home, she might shop in the Piazza. Going there was painful. To be in the midst of bustling crowds bent on business while her own heart was pulled like a magnet toward Negussie's prison was a struggle. He'd warned her in Wolisso that she might be questioned. She was afraid of complicating his case now by trying to visit him. She could only stare longingly at the walls behind which he was caged, keeping her distance.

When a summons for questioning was eventually delivered to her, she was frightened. As it turned out, the interrogators picked up no criminal evidence, and getting that over actually proved helpful. It cleared the air for her and helped to narrow down the charges against Negussie to "suspicion of being CIA." Even that charge was unreasonable, for John Coleman's letters came from Canada, not the United States. For three months, beatings stopped. Along with others there, Negussie's daily sufferings came from the very earthy experience of sharing a tiny room allowed little air with many unwashed human beings. On a regimented schedule, prisoners could be released from the stifling cell toward one destination, the reeking toilet. Rats added their own form of terror at night. Such was the life of prisoners incarcerated in overcrowded buildings across the capital. Among all the others, Negussie underwent the discipline of humiliation.

Automatic rifle fire at 10:40 PM outside the SIM compound brought John Cumbers rushing down the corridors yelling to everybody to put out lights and stay down. Within five minutes, the barrage gave way to deadly quiet, followed by the screech of departing vehicles. Ato Tekle and John crept quietly into the second-floor conference room. Tekle leaned out, and motioned John to come and look. This office building had been a late addition to the old Headquarters buildings, and used up most of the compound's front court. It crowded right up to the sidewalk of a busy intersection where five streets came together. Looking down, the men spotted just beneath their window seven bodies lined up against the base of the Headquarters building. A list of sins for which they'd been executed was pinned to each victim's chest. This was not the only time the SIM corner was used in this way. These stark reminders kept the populace aware of the Party's power, and their own vulnerability.

Chairman Mengistu Haile Mariam's politics in those days began to metamorphose along a zigzag between party line and his own increasingly independent line. On the one hand, in 1978 when Cubans apparently suggested that Ethiopia should set a date for moving from military to civilian rule, the Cuban ambassador was expelled. Cubans were not happy about losing soldiers in Ethiopia's northern war zone. Eritrean communists had been trained in Cuba, and after all, the

Cubans reasoned, Eritrea's struggle, after all, was for "self-determination," a Marxist-Leninist cause. On the other hand, Mengistu followed the Maoist lead by initiating a "Cultural Revolution" phase in Ethiopia. Headlines of the October 29th's *Ethiopian Herald* read:

> Nation Braces Up For Revolutionary Campaign [...]
> Proclamation Setting Up Framework To Revive National Economy[70]

Sterner economic measures were enforced therewith, often to the dismay of the broad masses, particularly the peasants whose traditional homes—usually clustered among trees or spaced along streams—were forcibly demolished. People were ordered to rebuild on bare hilltops in closely regimented gridiron schemes, "so that water and electricity may efficiently be routed to the populace"—pipes and lines that rarely seemed, however, to appear. By June of 1979, BBC reported that the government's proclamation on land reform would strip peasants of all but 1,000 square meters per householder, and that their cattle would become the property of the farmers association. Hopeful dreams of socialism were turning into painful actualities which destroyed patterns of life so long endemic to the culture.

In matters of war, citizens were told to gird up to defend the nation from enemies to the east and north: counter-offensives against Somalia in the Ogaden War, and on-going campaigns against the Eritrean rebels. Eritrea dared to ask the Organization of African Unity (OAU) to intervene in its struggle against the government in 1980, although the OAU's policy rigidly stuck to national borderlines precisely as they were "frozen" at the OAU's inception in 1963.[71] The province of Tigray agitated as well: a group who called themselves the Tigray People's Liberation Front was mentioned on international news in 1980. No one could have guessed the significance of that front. Eleven years later it would bring Mengistu's government down.

---

70. Cumbers (1996), *Terror,* 188.
71. The Organization of African Unity (OAU) was established in 1963. It was based in Ethiopia, fittingly symbolizing the role Ethiopia had played in the African independence movement. Ethiopia's victory over Italy in the battle of Adwa in 1896 symbolized for Africans their hoped-for victory over colonial domination:

At the turn of the decade, international relationships were bouncing back and forth like ping pong balls. In nearby Uganda, Idi Amin was overthrown by Tanzania in 1979. Ethiopia signed a 20-year accord with the Soviet Union. When America's USAID was terminated due to Ethiopia's deplorable human rights record in 1980, the US Ambassador was given 24 hours to leave the country. In 1981, Secretary of State Henry Kissinger visited Somali leader, Siad Barre, and arranged to send arms to Somalia, further exacerbating the USA's already strained relations with Ethiopia. From Poland, signs of unrest were reported. In the Eastern Block, self-evaluation was detectable; people were wondering where communism had gone wrong. Who could have guessed that this spirit of uprising would so soon spread across the world?

With propaganda continuing to label the Bible "anti-Revolutionary" and westerners "agents of capitalism," it was not unexpected that word came to John Cumbers that a high official at the Ministry of Labor had warned, "I hope SIM is preparing to take all its missionaries out of Ethiopia, because we are not granting them any more work permits." Already, SIM was down to twenty-seven work permits, bringing the staff including spouses to only forty.

For John Cumbers, the load of leadership plus constant uncertainties weighed heavily upon him. Furthermore as head of the mission, he was the major target of what might be called "extortion." Disputes over Shashamane Hospital in 1978 had implicated him in the worst of these situations, for he was barred from leaving the country unless a settlement (involving thousands of Ethiopian Birr) was forthcoming. For months he was virtually held hostage by the dispute, even though his health was deteriorating, and his crucial medical appointment in Houston was pending. The day after the employee case was settled, John was at last declared a free man. The next day, SIM Council made an historic decision, recommending to SIM head, Ian Hay, that the mission cease to operate in Ethiopia fifteen months in the future. "But the Lord had other ideas," John would later reminisce.

Rumors circulated that the government was about to take over the property of all Christian missions. As early as April of 1979, Radio Ethiopia had announced they were about to take SIM's Headquarters. Repeatedly, the Ministry of Health came to inspect the premises as if to take it. The recurrent threats created an emotional roller-coaster for missionaries, many of whom lived and worked there, or depended on the Mission Headquarters as home base while in Addis Ababa. The exceptions, the Adams, Fellows, and Winslows got clearance to live down-country at that time. Their work in literacy and development gave them an edge with government policies. Gerhard Bössler and Paul Balisky managed regular trips from the capital to the south, as well.

When furlough times arrived, departures which could be permanent were disheartening. When Howard Borlase disappeared from the offices, it was as if the sun had lost some rays. John wondered to whom he would turn for that hearty optimism that Howard had always provided when John was "having to reach up to touch bottom." Losing Murray Coleman's steady support at their furlough time in July of 1980 was another blow. When the Elys arrived in September to help with administration, John was bolstered up, for it was rare to be receiving rather than relinquishing staff now. Low in profile, but high in service were the faithful staff women who kept the offices and ministries organized and supported.

Serving by day as radio dispatcher, nicknamed "Marge the Sarge," Marge's nights were full too, for along with Brian Fargher she quietly engineered a budding underground evening Bible school, a Spartan form of Grace Bible Institute after the Jimma campus was taken. The school was never advertised and Marge checked out supposed "applicants" very carefully before revealing anything about this underground network for Biblical education. At first enrolling just a handful of students, the school grew steadily, opening up a key opportunity right inside the Headquarters compound. In November of 1979, crusty Australian trouble-shooter Alex Fellows (traveling with Ato Lakew's son) made a daring trip to Jimma to see what could be recovered from mission and school property impounded at the closed Grace Bible Institute (GBI) compound. John Cumbers tells the story:

> Alex successfully negotiated for the two vehicles, but what we wanted more than anything was the Grace Bible Institute library. Alex approached the authorities who told him that they had lost the key to the second-story room at GBI where the books were stored. That didn't

deter Alex for more than five minutes. Yared climbed through the window, pried open the door, and they soon had the books transferred to a commercial truck. Great was our rejoicing when all 5,000 books of the GBI library arrived in Addis Ababa.[72]

From 1978 on, Bark Fahnestock had been pastoring the SIM Chapel. Originally the chapel had mainly served SIM missionaries and a handful of English-speaking expatiates—business and diplomatic people. During the Revolution, many denominations' offices were closed, and the few missionaries who remained learned that their attendance at an Ethiopian church brought suspicion upon nationals. Therefore, staff from shrunken missions joined business people and diplomats in finding the SIM chapel to be their best option for Sunday worship. English speaking Ethiopians, many of them studying in the evening Bible school, were attracted as well. The result was the creation of a growing new congregation, one which would be transformed into the burgeoning International Evangelical Church.

ACROSS TOWN AT Bingham Academy, another closure loomed. Repeatedly the government threatened to confiscate the boarding school, now nearly empty. Must the mission let the beloved place go? As John Cumbers walked its grounds one day in 1979, he stood at the lower end of the compound looking at the original building, the graceful old eucalyptus trees, and well-marked paths that his own children had helped to flatten. "Are we really going to turn over this beautiful school to the government?" he asked himself.

At its peak, Bingham Academy had served some 150 children of SIM missionaries and other missions as well. The national staff, now idle but still holding on, put pressure on the mission through the labor union. John and his administrative team weighed their alternatives. They had one last trump left in their hand: the wider international community still needed primary schooling in English. In the end, Bingham began to serve families from all over the world, including children from the communist or Muslim world. Bingham's administration at least made it clear that children learned Bible verses in this school, and verses they did learn. The old saying, "a little

---

72. Cumbers (1996), *Terror*, 189.

child shall lead them," was exercised in many an unlikely home. And so a new and fruitful ministry rose out of the ashes.

After a short furlough in 1980, Mr. Cumbers sensed serious dissatisfaction among the missionaries, and talked about it with Naomi at night. A new threat of drought exacerbated their frustrations, for the government's destruction of the missions' infrastructure meant that it was difficult for them to distribute food. How could such a small staff meet the challenge? In the 1974 famine, there had been over 300 people and dozens of outstations to help with in the distribution. Now all that had been swept away: doctors and nurses, agriculturists and linguists, engineers and mechanics, Land Rovers and trucks, planes and airstrips—most of the mission infrastructure. Now most personnel were limited to the capital. Checkpoints sealed off the countryside, where famine threat was greatest. What frustration! In 1981, the staff was so small that all of them could be gathered into Bishoftu in one SIM Conference. They numbered only thirty-seven adults and ten children. Small for SIM, this was the largest body of expatriates left to a Protestant mission in Ethiopia.

EACH MISSION AROUND TOWN lived out their own ordeal. The Mekane Yesus Headquarters, large and modern, was confiscated in November of 1981. This was a great blow to that large body of believers. The same year, the Seventh Day Adventist compounds at Hawassa and Shashamane were taken. Five Catholics were deported in 1981. The Mennonite offices were closed. Their daughter church, which took the name *Meserete Kristos* ("Christ Foundation Church"), included about 5,000 believers when in 1982, all fourteen of the Meserete Kristos churches were closed.[73] Although the Ethiopian Orthodox churches were allowed to remain open, that huge Ethiopian institution was stripped of much property. On Party schedule, the early cooperation they'd requested of churches was giving way to systematic disposal of "the opiate of the people."

IN SPITE OF REPRESSION of the organizational aspects of the church, as an "organism," the body of Christ was burgeoning. Perhaps a line from Psalm 2 was applicable to the situation: "The One enthroned

---

73. See N. Hege, *Beyond Our Prayers* (Herald Press, 1998), 171.

in heaven laughs; the Lord scoffs at them." Ethiopian Christians, forced underground, were not dying out, but were multiplying like wildfire. For example, although Pastor Kedamo Mechato's congregation in Geja Sefir (area) was repeatedly harassed, it was one which did remain open, while the one in which Ato Lakew Tesemma served as a pastor in the Gofa Sefir was closed. The advice of Pastor Hsueh took hold: "Simply retool your groupings during the Marxist siege." This is how it worked: since the Party's contrived facade for religious toleration allowed a few Protestant churches in Addis Ababa to hold services, a few buildings were open. Those few opened their doors to others, often to congregations not of their own denomination, to use at odd times, and alternating between places. As a result, Christians wove back and forth among each other, eventually bonding together with little thought given to former denominational divisions. Many thought this to be one of the benefits of the Revolution.

In summary of the period, missionaries were taking less leadership, and nationals more, in the mission–church equation. New things happened. Ato Lakew and Dr. Mulatu Baffa were surprisingly granted visas to Great Britain for two months, perhaps because the government had its eye on incoming funds. In Europe the men promoted the needs of the Kale Heywet Church (KHC), especially the now flourishing Kale Heywet Development Program (KHDP). As Murray Coleman's field letter in 1980 explained, "KHDP is one of the remaining ministries under SIM that gives our presence credibility and through which we can work in the rural areas. The council therefore wishes to [...] insure that a worthwhile spiritual ministry is incorporated with it."[74]

Ato Tekle Wolde Giorgis was now five years into his KHC General Secretaryship. Day by day, he negotiated in cases involving mission and church institutions in courts and jails and prisons. The KHC was able to obtain a building of its own for $75,000 with the help of donors who wished to encourage the national church. This move to a compound away from SIM's headquarters marked a new stage of independence, ministry, and responsibility for the church.

Ever increasingly, Ato Tekle was challenged to keep the delicate financial balance between KHC's two departments: the Spiritual was

---

74. Cumbers (1996), *Terror*, 204.

struggling, the Development was booming. Dr. Mulatu was heading up the Kale Heywet Development Program, the aspect of the KHC which won government approval and gave increased opportunities to meet practical human needs. The downside became the competition between the two. The Spiritual Department, which shepherded Bible schools and church activities, continually struggled along on meager funding. On the other hand, water projects and famine relief brought in huge sums from media appeals made abroad. Development brought in technological equipment, disproportionate salaries, and thus a higher standard of living available to those who handled development funds. This attractive "genie" of foreign-funded development became a source of great and unexpected problems which would trouble the church in future years.

Negussie looked up at the wide sky and thanked God! Air... light... space... what luxuries! It was with excitement that he had been transferred from the crowded Interrogation Center to Kerchele, a big prison down in the southern part of Addis Ababa in the area called Akaki. Kerchele boasted an open prison yard. It was the dry season by then, and bright sunlight overhead could cheer prisoners as well as people who were free. Beware a south wind, however! The slaughter house area was nearby. Its stench swept over the exercise yard when the wind came from that direction. And the vultures which circled ominously above the general area increased the prisoners' sense of feeling like prey. Never mind: the golden dome of an Orthodox church building within the prison grounds pointed heavenward, beyond the vultures.

When the word of Negussie's transfer came to Fantaye, her feelings were mixed. So many took food there, that she could slip in unnoticed, she felt. But *Alem Bekany*, as Kerchele was nicknamed, meant "the end of the world for me." Will it be so for him? she wondered.

Fantaye considered carefully how to at least get sight of Negussie. She knew someone from his family would regularly be sent to deliver food to Negussie's new location. Fantaye decided a Sunday would be the best day to make her first attempt.

She had to board several busses to make connections to the Kerchele area to get to the prison gate that first Sunday morning. Her heart throbbed with both fear and anticipation. Trying to melt into the crowd of people carrying provisions, she hoped her little satchel of fruit fit into the scene. No one yet knew of her connection with Negussie, not even Almaz, his sister, who lived in Addis Ababa, and might well be the one carrying his food supply that morning. Could she avoid being noticed by Almaz? Fantaye could not claim to be a wife, nor a fiancée; she was just a friend. Would the authorities let her in? How does it work, she wondered. God help me!

She watched as people crowded up to a wire fence, while prisoners looked longingly from the other side for someone who had come for their own sake. Fantaye spotted a familiar face in the crowd: sure enough, Almaz. Fantaye stepped back out of sight. She watched while Almaz had a few moments handing Negussie his package, and observed her depart out the gate. Then she moved up into the front line and made herself noticeable, holding forth the little satchel of fruit. That first sight of her Negussie would never forget. She took his breath away. They met only momentarily as she handed the fruit over the fence, but more passed between them than an onlooker could ever know. From that day on, the fondest expectation of Negussie's week would be those few moments when they could meet each other through eye and heart, and perhaps speak a few words and be assured the other was well. Fantaye's family did not know just where she went each Sunday, for her church had been closed. After the prison stop, she attended a Bible study in a home, the low-key fellowship which went unnoticed across the city. This became the pattern of her week for longer than she could have guessed. When they parted weekly at the fence, they asked God for comfort. At their age, which should have been a time of beginning, here they were meeting at the end of the world.

Negussie knew better than the general public what the "end" and "the world" really meant and took no heed of his *Alem Bekany* address. He set about cheering prison mates with whom he shared the compound. Some were incarcerated as criminals. Others were there as "politically accused," such as himself. Here was a group of men badly in need of hope, and Negussie had abundant hope. What he had to offer was the risen Christ. It was not that he had to talk much, for the man's attitude and countenance was so different from the norm as to bring people to him instinctively, curious to figure out why the man could still smile. It was rare to be welcomed into another person's life, someone strangely free from obsession with his own situation. Many prisoners had given themselves to the Revolutionary cause, served it energetically, but had come out on the short end of the continuous jockeying for power that went on. Being accused by another revolutionary was a bitter pill to swallow from a comrade. It led many to ignominy or death, just as they had dealt the same to others. What an ironic boomerang to ruminate over in the long gray prison hours.

Negussie eventually discovered other believers among the prisoners, and three of them purposely teamed up for ministry within the prison. Whenever they sensed a searching heart, they shared the tools for survival which were serving them well. The Epistle to the Ephesians had taught them that God has provided the Christian with weapons. Their "sword" was to be the word of God, and their "shield" was to be faith. Negussie and his friends were testing out God's armory and by experience were proving the former to be their best offensive weapon, and the latter to be their mighty defense. One by one, prisoners watched these believers' lives and saw that faith in the word of God truly did answer assaults on the mind and spirit. Most cell-mates were as imprisoned by self-absorption, anger, and despair, as by locked gates.

Furthermore, each knew he might have to face "the final solution." No one knew who would be executed, or when. The threat was sobering, but it actually served people who were willing to grapple with ultimate issues. Were the Marxists-Leninists right, that life ends in the grave? Might there be life after death, as the ancient church, at least formally, had affirmed? During miserable nights, haunting questions would torment: When I am shot, will I be extinct... or judged? What will my destination be—a senseless body eaten by worms underground, as dialectical materialism teaches? Or might I find myself in heaven... or in hell... as God's word has warned? Who can stand up under the scrutiny of an all-knowing and holy God? Is hope possible for me? How can I prepare to die?

Negussie's small band shared the general suffering of prison life on the physical level, but they enjoyed a freedom of spirit which transcended the walls around them. They gave themselves to the needs of others, drew many into the fellowship of the Lord Jesus Christ, and labored to establish a strong foundation in new believers. As best they could, they quietly employed the ancient means of grace: prayer and study of God's word. Thus, many a prisoner found a depth of being and sharing which had been unknown to him previously. Some eventually emerged from prison as changed people, released from bondage both in body and in spirit, twice free.

Throughout his years in prison, Negussie walked through the valley of the shadow with some who were never released. Typical of these relationships was one he pursued with a certain man with whom he talked repeatedly. The man stoutly refused to receive the message which Negussie so earnestly shared. "No," he kept insisting, "no!" But the man had no peace. He surveyed his own despairing condition, so in contrast to the hope which Negussie's life authenticated. Finally, he made the choice to put his trust in the saving work of the Lord Jesus, the Christ. A great change began to come over this prisoner. Life took on a fullness he could not have believed could be his in such circumstances. Still, the hour of his summons finally came. He went to his believing brothers and broke the news. "I am to be executed. Yet, amazingly, I have peace, for I know where I am going." He embraced them, expecting to meet again, and took his place before the firing squad.

> *Remember those earlier days after you had received the light,*
> *when you stood your ground in a great contest in the face of suffering.*
> *Sometimes you were publicly exposed to insult and persecution;*
> *at other times you stood side by side with those who were so treated. You sympathized with those in prison*
> *and joyfully accepted the confiscation of your property,*
> *because you knew that you yourselves*
> *had better and lasting possessions.*
>
> (Hebrews 10:32–34)

Chapter 16

GAMO GOFA: LESSONS FROM PRISON

Gamo Gofa seemed to be the area hit hard first. That province spanned a wide, rugged area, including homelands of the Gamo and Gofa peoples, isolated from each other and isolated from the heartland by rugged land forms and ethnic diversity. Asked for their differentiation, one Gamo just said, "The Gofa kill, the Gamo don't." Gofas were known for raiding other ethnic groups. A prevalent cultural practice was killing a human as proof of manhood, preparatory to taking a wife.

Perhaps the imprisonments Christians underwent in Gamo Gofa stemmed from Ali Musa. After release from one of his first sentences, a leader named Zacharias Tsige made the hard trip from Gofa to Addis Ababa to ask the KHC Central Office for help.[75] A trip like that involved days of difficult travel. Planes were expensive and tickets not always available. Laps of the journey usually had to be made by catching an occasional public bus, riding a mule, or walking, shod or unshod. The terrain was rugged, traversed by ranges and rivers. A traveler had to pass through foreign areas, where threat could come from man as well as animal. When Zacharias finally reached the capital, Ato Tekle obtained a letter from the Ministry of Interior saying that the Bulki church was permitted to hold meetings. Zacharias made the long trip home and demanded an interview with Ali Musa himself, Gamo Gofa's Provincial Governor at the time.

"I figured I had nothing to lose by telling him exactly how I felt," Zacharias later related. I said, 'We have been prohibited from exercising our faith in a lawful manner, our churches have been closed and plundered; the Christians have been scattered. We are not breaking

---

75. For Zacharias' story compare Cumbers (1995), *Joy*, 97f.

DEGU DEKLAABO (ADDIS ABABA, 1994)

any laws, and here is a letter from the Ministry of Interior to prove it.' He took the letter from me and then started to curse me. 'You are nothing but a lot of foreign spies. I am sending you in the custody of the police to the district where this serious crime took place. That is where you are to be punished!'"

Zacharias went back to prison, this time in Arba Minch, for two more years. The response to his attempts to demand justice were typical of the treatment given to appeals. Throughout Gamo Gofa, arrests increased. Christians originating in various ethnic groups learned to know each other in prison. Three men whose experiences were intertwined in the growing "prison fellowship" were Degu, an Aari; Bassa, a Gamo from the Kucha area; and Ato Tesfaye, the Gamo who had taken up leadership again at Chencha after his years at Grace Bible Institute. Each has a unique but related story.

DEGU WAS A GENTLE person, an Aari among the Gofas. *Degu* meant "the good one." He had been born to a cruel father known as "clever in doing evil" and therefore bore a Gofa name which meant "the bad one." The son was first reached for Christ by an Aari evangelist, initially through a picture tract which demonstrated "Two Ways."

Hungry to learn, Degu Deklaabo mastered the Amharic alphabet within a couple of weeks, and virtually taught himself to read. He was directed to Jesus' story of the "two ways" in Matthew, and soon publicly testified to believing. The very next Sunday he was pushed forward as a leader in the church. Could he not actually read the Scriptures to them? A rare ability! Degu worked in the fields all day and began to teach children to read by firelight each evening. The national evangelist gave Degu a clear-cut assignment: "Pray, read verses, explain them to the children, pray again, then teach the alphabet." With the incentive of leadership, Degu was pushed to grow.

Eventually his hunger for the things of God led him up the mountain to the mission station, to enroll in the Bake Bible School. There the handsome young Degu met a student named Almaz, a young woman of homely countenance but beautiful spirit. When about twenty-four, he chose this deeply spiritual woman as his wife. Theirs was truly a love relationship, not generally the case with Ethiopian marriage patterns. Soon a little girl was born to the happy couple, just as the Revolution began up in Addis Ababa. By then Degu had become president of the Aari body of believers.

Quite quickly, the new regime reached out and touched the remotest corners of the realm. Because she could read, Almaz was chosen as secretary for the women's division of the Farmers Union. At their first leaders' meeting, a mildly intoxicating drink was given to the women, with the leader's apology, "When we go to Jinka we'll have *tella* to drink!"—stronger spirits. Almaz perceived this small detail in Party requirements to be indicative of the future. Strong pressure was regularly put upon abstainers, for drinking was considered to be a mark of submission to the Party. Almaz went home to Degu and wept. She had developed a passion for reaching the Banna, a fierce group in Gamo Gofa to whom the Wolaitta evangelist, Ato Mahey Choramo (aka Ato Mahare), was taking co-workers. "I wanted to go to the Bannas with the gospel. Rather than being forced to give my body over to intoxication, may the Lord take my soul!" Degu insisted, "No, no, we must pray, we must talk this over."

Almaz began to be sick with what was eventually identified as tuberculosis. She seemed to know it would be fatal. "My clothes are to go to the evangelists' wives" she said. Degu anxiously cared for her. Two months after the Farmers Union meeting, she gave birth. But before she'd even taken the baby to the breast, she died in Degu's arms.

Degu was inconsolable. Their relationship had been unusually tender. He remembered how when he'd come back from his work, she'd tenderly hugged and kissed him. "When Almaz was buried," he said later, "I knew nothing. I was overcome with grief, from the time they took the body until they returned."

In great distress, Degu begged, "Just let me go out to the desert and witness for the Lord." The elders judged that he would better recover by going to the upper level Bible School way over in Chencha, and sent him there in 1978. Ato Tesfaye Tole had finished at Grace Bible Institute and was teaching at Chencha again. Within three months, however, the government closed down the school.

Before going home, Degu traveled to Addis Ababa. In those years, men like Degu were indispensable to mission linguists, for they were trying frantically to complete the Key Scripture translations in many languages before being forced to leave. Degu was one who traveled up to Addis Ababa from time to time to secretly help with the Aari translation. When the Chencha school was closed, he traveled to his linguistic colleague Ruth Cremer in Addis Ababa, and then started back to Chencha to try to pick up his belongings before making the long trip home to Jinka.

At one of the checkpoints, his baggage was searched. Guards discovered an audio tape of a popular Christian singer. Degu hadn't even thought of the implications of the title or the picture on the cover. The guards, however, eager to fault an evangelical, decided the tape was treasonous. The Amharic caption, translated, meant "Through our gospel the whole world will yet be conquered." Furthermore, the picture showed a man with his right fist held high. The accepted way to show allegiance to Revolutionary Ethiopia was to raise the left first. The right fist was construed, in contrast, to mean allegiance to American imperialism. Furthermore, Degu was carrying a Bible—a sure sign of propagating religious teaching and not cooperating with the government. "We've just put out the white Americans and here this 'black American' is giving us trouble," the cadres grumbled.

Adding other trumped up changes, they arrested him and sent him to prison in Jinka. Other Aari and also Maale believers (the two main groups in the region) were detained there, and in other

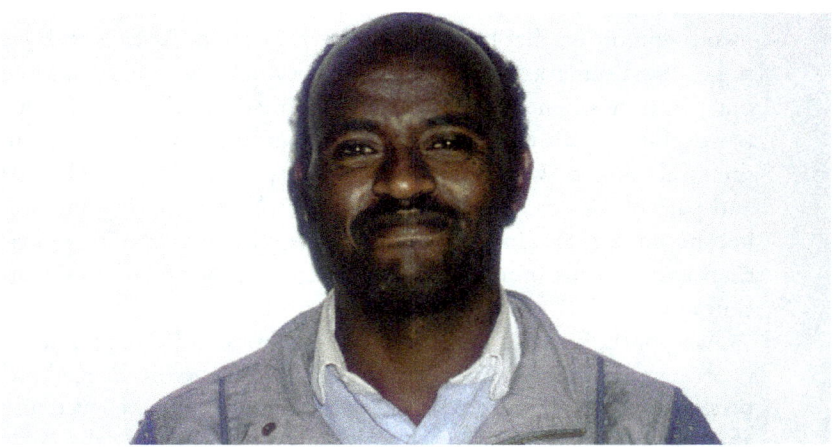

BASSA DEA (JINKA, 1994)

locations. It was difficult for church families to deliver food to all these places. In times of drought, small children especially suffered lack of food, including Degu's two little girls, motherless, and now it seemed, fatherless too.

A SECOND OF THE three men whose experiences tied together was Bassa Dea, a Kucha church leader in Gamo, many hours' walk northwest of Chencha. As Marxism-Leninism had crept into Ethiopia, Bassa had listened and watched and taken steps to inform himself. He'd paid the large sum of 20 Birr for a contraband copy of Wurmbrand's book from Romania and had obtained another about catacomb times under the Roman emperor Nero (reigned 54–68 AD). He could see where Ethiopia was heading, and where that would put believers.

When the news of Degu's incarceration in Gofa somehow got to Bassa, he managed to fly all the way to Jinka to visit Degu in prison. The two friends embraced, Degu about thirty, tall, square-jawed yet gentle; Bassa around thirty-five, muscular, with Roman nose and broad forehead. The older brother brought a gift of food and kindly encouraged Degu. Before he left, Bassa confided his own premonition that he was about to be arrested. As he was about to go, Bassa remarked, "I'd like to have a food basket like that fine one you have when I'm in prison!" It was made locally out of tightly woven grass, with a hinged lid. Degu sent someone to find one in the local market. "God be with you," they prayed as they embraced and parted. Three days after Bassa's return home carrying the basket, he was arrested in Kucha. He was kept there twenty-two days, then two months in another town, before being moved to detention in Chencha.

As a youth, Bassa had come to the Lord out of a *kalicha* family—people who practiced a type of witchcraft which involved "reading" messages in goat intestines. Eventually he'd married a believer, and after elementary and Bible school training, had become the Bible School teacher in Kucha. In the late seventies he'd played an administrative role with missionaries, traveling by plane with Malcolm Hunter. "Sometimes the Lord brings you up, sometimes down," he used to chuckle, referring to demotion from air to foot travel, when the missionaries left. Bassa had daughters old enough to carry food to the prison. When his case came up, the authorities called it "beyond their authority" and said they were sending him to the higher regional subdivision. They surprised him with a ten-day leave before the transfer to Chencha, and cheered him with the prediction that Ali Musa would likely kill him there.

Back home, Bassa found his children sick with whooping cough. The youngest, not yet one, hung near death. He and his wife, *Wudenesh* (meaning "she is precious"), took the baby to a clinic. "Go to Soddo Hospital," they were told. The long journey involved crossing a river. "Just after the crossing, the baby died in my arms," Bassa later recounted. "We stopped under the shade of a tree and realized she was surely dead. We prayed, and turned back. At the clinic, a worker buried the body. We walked the two hours to our home, talking. We'd never had a death in our immediate family before. I was a Bible School teacher, a church leader, and a pastor too. I'd taught my people not to cry at funerals, but rather to testify: 'Don't cry for me, cry for yourself, unbelievers, cry not for the dead.' I said to my wife, 'Now this is our turn. There will be no moaning, no crying.' Hard as it was, we dressed in good clothes, sat on a bench, and greeted people who came.

When the ten days were over, I didn't dare tell my oldest daughter I was going too far away for them to bring me food. She loved me so very much. She'll die if I tell them, I thought. I gave them gifts as we parted at the police station."

At Chencha prison, he found himself among about 400 detainees, many of whom were Christians. Some were women. Bassa was assigned to carry cattle feed from the prison to the town. Two prisoners had to carry a *quintal* load (220 pounds) on two sticks extended between their shoulders. "I wasn't used to such loads," Bassa recounted later, "and I could hardly stand it. I became so tired and so sick I was almost ready to die. Guards accused me, saying 'This Pente won't work!' The chief reassigned me to the stump detail. Digging up huge eucalyptus stumps was a favorite assignment for Christians. We were forced to work seven days a week, not allowed to rest every other day, like the common criminals. We felt like the Hebrews under Pharaoh. Old dry stumps were not as tough as newly cut ones. I still remember a brother interceding to get me an easier one."

When Bassa got to Chencha prison, who would he find incarcerated there but the fiery Ato Tesfaye Tole and eight local elders. In the long hours, Tesfaye thought back over his transformed life. He had been rescued from the idol worship his family practiced. Before he'd heard anything of Jesus, the lad had a dream two or three times when he was about twelve, in which he heard strange music, not the local kind he'd always known. Years later this dream became a confirmation to him when he first heard accordion and organ music at the mission. His introduction to the gospel came through a Wolaitta evangelist who came to his area, who taught the young Tesfaye to read, and led him into the Scriptures. When a few believed, resistance from the local population arose. They drove the believers out of their homes, plundered, beat, and jailed them. All but about ten turned back. Tesfaye had to flee, so walked a full day to Chencha, where missionaries gave him work. He entered the elementary school, later became a teacher, and eventually married Asteer. When he'd attended Grace Bible Institute, she cared for the children at home.

At forty-four when captured, Tesfaye had a long history with missionaries and major leadership among the Chencha believers. The fiery leader refused to hand over church property to cadres, and sixteen

TESFAYE TOLE (ADDIS ABABA, 1994)

elders were arrested over the matter. Their homes and churches were promptly plundered. Two of the sixteen were Tesfaye's brothers-in-law. Some were simple farmers and were soon allowed to leave, but eight remained jailed. It wasn't that Tesfaye was taken by surprise by the new political situation. He'd heard Roy Wisner and Howie Brant and Pastor Kedamo's warnings. He'd read Wurmbrand's *Tortured for Christ*. He'd struggled along with Malcolm Hunter's case a couple of years before, with its implications for the church.

Tesfaye had been reminded that biblical precedents apply to modern believers, too. He recalled responding to a clarion call to stand firm, a call delivered in music. He'd attended a concert in Arba Minch given by a man with his own first name, Tesfaye Gabiso, a well-known musician from Gedeo province. One song voiced words as if those of Daniel in the time of King Nebuchadnezzar. "I will never fall down and worship the golden image! I will never bow down!"[76]

---

76. See Daniel 3 for the story of the golden image to which Tesfaye Gabiso

Ato Tesfaye would quote the song emphatically, his fist striking agreement for himself, in his times. (The singer was soon arrested and was tortured terribly during his seven years in various prisons.)

Cadres ordered local people to refrain from helping either the Chencha prisoners or their families. The believers secretly left sacks of grain at Asteer's door, and the Central Office in the capital sometimes sent small sums to prisoners' families, so they were not completely destitute. The prisoners' wives purposefully dressed in their most "dignified citizen" clothing to walk to the jail on the edge of Chencha market. Guards took their food parcels, allowed just twice a week, but wouldn't let them visit their loved ones.

Later, Tesfaye would admit that early in his imprisonment, a spirit of bitterness began smoldering in his heart. The prison was dismal, enclosed by bamboo fences surrounding about ten cells built around an open court. The whole compound was located in a depressed area, surrounded by huge old eucalyptus trees, so prisoners could see little beyond the walls. The rainy seasons were the most miserable, with the rain and mud and cold at Chencha mountain's altitude of around 8,000 feet. Bedbugs, lice, mice and ticks made a night's sleep almost impossible.

At home, Asteer struggled to be mother and father to nine. The delivery of her tenth child became so difficult that she had to be taken to the Chencha hospital. They named the baby *Tageleny*—which meant "he struggled me" or "my life is a struggle." Ethiopian names, like Biblical ones, often tell a story.

One time Tesfaye and the elders were put to work digging a huge trench. "We have them digging their own grave," the tormentors used to tell the men's families, causing them much pain and fear. Even the children had to face persecution. Tesfaye's oldest son, Theophilos, along with other youth, was forced to hobble painfully on rocky paths on their elbows and knees to humiliate, injure, and exhaust them. "Why has all this happened," the father questioned, "not just to me and my family, but to all the church people?" His faith was wavering. All the attempts to get released, the letters to Addis Ababa, all came to nothing. *Baka!* ("enough!") he said to the Lord, tempted to give up.

---

referred in his song.

Strangely then, it seemed that his heart began healing, after giving up his own efforts to find a way out. The invisible bond grew between the believers as they shouldered their tasks together. When Bassa was sent from Kucha to the same prison where the eight Chencha elders were held, they warmly took him in. They organized a way to pass around the scripture they secretly had, hiding it in mats they made from grass they collected to protect themselves when trying to sleep with no beds on the damp ground. Talking much wasn't allowed, but during stump digging, they would enjoy their most uninterrupted chance for fellowship. Only the Christians were assigned to this hard task and were trusted to work hard without supervision. Therefore, they could at least talk among themselves. The warmth of their deepening fellowship with each other and the Lord was what they best remembered after the ordeal was over.

The men stood together when ordered to sign a "confession paper" which asked forgiveness for their "crimes" to secure release. They settled upon a standard answer to such pressuring: "We have not done anything wrong; we know that what we believe is right. The government is in the wrong and we will file suit against them if we are ever released. Our property and the church property has been illegally confiscated and we want it back." The other prisoners were astonished to hear them say such things. The prison officials showed some anxiety at their confidence, supposing they had influential friends in high places. "Of course we had the most influential friend of all— the Almighty God, our Father!" the believers affirmed.

AT ONE POINT, execution seemed imminent, but a strange thing happened. The weird story even reached the ears of the prisoners one day, it traveled so fast. Gamo Gofa had been terrorized by Ali Musa, the man who was known for burying people alive at Shashamane. For some reason, the man bitterly hated believers, and vowed to "eliminate" them. Traveling to Chencha to see that the believers were executed, he was stopped on the way by an employee friend from the Ministry of Agriculture. That man was also extremely anti-Christian and had boasted that "today is the last day for the Pentes of this area." The Agriculture employee wanted Ali Musa to make one stop and see a sophisticated irrigation system he'd designed, involving a watering hole. He jumped into the water to demonstrate the effectiveness of his invention, but he disappeared under the surface for a long time. Had he become entangled in weeds? His hand appeared in the air for a moment, then disappeared again. They called a swimmer to drag the man out, but he was unsuccessful. Even the governor himself reached into the murky depths to try to locate him. Shocked and distressed at this catastrophe, Ali Musa turned around and drove back to Arba Minch. Before he could remount his bloodthirsty campaign, a government order came out stating it was illegal to execute people without proper processes being carried out. The believers praised God for this mysterious intervention.

Unbelieving prisoners who saw these happenings and watched the lives of the believers. They wondered. Later, some confessed that it was the Christians' patience under suffering which baffled them. Their changeless strength and consistency made them ponder. They had stood firm. Some watched to see whether the Christians would be killed as expected, and admitted they were reserving judgment on the reality of God in relationship to whether these men were defeated or delivered. In later years, some of the very cadre antagonists who had tormented them came to the Lord, testifying that it was the lives of the eight which had made them consider the truth about God.

ONE DAY IN 1980, Ato Tekle Wolde Giorgis in his KHC office in Addis Ababa received a messenger bearing a note smuggled out from Tesfaye in Chencha. He unfolded the stained note. What code had his dear old friend selected to summarize his message? Only a verse and a short statement. Tekle studied the six words, trying to perceive what Tesfaye meant to convey. In the future, Ato Tekle would share what that message brought home to him, over and over again, to encourage others in their hour of trial. Tesfaye's six words were simply: "We are in prison for good." Not for evil, not for hurt, not for loss, but in reality, for good.

When Tesfaye was finally released, the prison years were not the end of his testing, for as a key figure among the Chencha believers, he continued to be harassed and threatened with arrest. That translated into having to stay out of the area from time to time, moving about like a fugitive and being separated from his family. He was much used of God, however, teaching and counseling in other locations. "God worked in our lives in ways that proved to me," Tesfaye said, "that He was working all things together for good, just as He'd promised in the book of Romans" (chapter 8:28–29). That confidence served Tesfaye well as he lived out the difficult years which were to follow.

Degu, too, would see the hand of God strangely using his personal tragedies for good in the next few years. After his release from the Jinka prison, another loss rocked the man. Fellow believers had tried to help his children. Terefe Alsi, another Aari who worked on the Key Scriptures, was arrested for transporting Bibles on his way home from Addis Ababa. He was carrying some little clothes for Degu's children, as well. It was too late. They'd been so poorly fed during Degu's imprisonment with no mother, that soon after their father's release, both little girls fell prey to illness and died.

There was a redeeming sequel, however. The man who had accused Degu of being "a black American" and had arrested him, later returned to the Lord. He had turned his back on Christ and on the believers during the Revolution, but repented later. "Whenever he sees me, he weeps and says he is sorry," Degu related this to Ruth Cremer. He actually sympathized with this ex-Marxist who seemed to hold himself responsible for the deaths of Degu's two daughters. Degu genuinely forgave and accepted the old enemy. Knowing they were mutual sinners before God, Degu could rejoice over this particular man's having entered the fellowship of those "justified freely by his [God's] grace through the redemption that came by Christ Jesus" (Romans 3:24).

Bassa would also come to count his season in prison as blessed. He said he got angry in the early days of his imprisonment, and then began to work it through with the Lord. "I remembered we hadn't suffered like Christ did. When you are training a donkey, you load it with leaves first. Later you load on a heavier burden. We load the donkey to teach it, loading it for learning. I began to take my load as a matter of training." Bassa came more alive to the Lord day by day as he experienced the warm brotherhood among the men with whom he was sharing this spiritual training there in Chencha prison. When asked what meant the very most to him about that time, he passionately affirms, "I took comfort *not* to be suffering imprisonment as a criminal, but for Christ, Himself. As the Spirit of God encourages us in the book of James [chapter 1:2], I came to truly 'count it all joy'."

> *Those who sow in tears will reap with songs of joy.*
> *He who goes out weeping, carrying seed to sow,*
> *will return with songs of joy, carrying sheaves with him.*
> *(Psalm 126:5-6)*

Chapter 17

WOLAITTA: WINDS OF TESTING, WINDS OF POWER

This letter from Ethiopia addressed to Dick McClellan, veteran missionary to Wolaitta and Gamo Gofa, reached Dick in Australia:

> Greetings. I want to give you this news urgently, but I don't know if it will reach you. The future is so uncertain. I am writing this secretly at 3 AM, thinking that this could be my last letter, but God knows all things. We are praising Him (and you rejoice too!) that His word is being fulfilled in us.
>
> Tomorrow I go to prison, with five other teachers including two girls. We never know if and when we will be released. Many of the Soddo church young people's singing group are already in prison. Yohannes Bosana was forced to flee to his home area on the other side of the mountain, but they have sent people to look for him there. The accusation is that the Christians are enemies of the Revolution if they don't shout the slogans of the Marxists and curse the enemies of the communists. And God's Word has come true in that the believers are divided. Over half of our Christian brothers say that it is OK to obey the government edict, but we take our stand on James 3:9–12 and insist that God's Word does not allow us to curse. Some church leaders have also joined the accusers and caused hundreds of young people to be taken into custody. Those seized have been beaten by clubs and whipped until their blood flows like water. The cadres force the prisoners by torturing them to say: 'The Bible is an imperialist book. Down with the Bible. Destroy it.'
>
> In Arba Minch all the churches are closed. Our town church was closed last week. Ato Waja Kabeto was taken in chains from Bulki to Arba Minch and three large vehicles filled with chained believers also went to prison there. These people seek us out, just to imprison and torture us; they have permission even to kill us. Therefore, it is as the Apostle Paul said, "If we remain it is glory to God; if we die it is gain to us."

Our country is very troubled and shaking. Therefore our prayer is for God to show His hand and do some marvelous miracles. AND YOU, PLEASE PRAY FOR US.

Truly, thoughts come on top of thoughts. We are weary but the Lord is working even now. We are distressed that some elders have gone with the world. Some fear persecution so they compromise, but we will be faithful unto death. PLEASE PRAY.

Your son, Eremiyas [Borko][77]

By such messages the larger body of Christ was called to prayer, in this case, especially for the spiritual battle going on in the church of Wolaitta. Could it be that Wolaitta, of all churches—the founding fathers who had sent evangelists with the word of God all over Gamo Gofa!—was now caught in the devices of the Enemy?

YES, IT WAS TRUE. Son of Daanna Meja, one of the first Wolaitta believers, Markina Meja was a leading elder during the Revolution years, but experienced many a heartbreak. Markina was tall and had a way of looking down with kindness upon the one with whom he spoke, answering slowly with measured thoughtfulness. He was often questioned about Wolaitta. With unhidden pain, he confessed the problem that internal divisions had done much more damage to the church than attacks from unbelievers on the outside.

The Wolaitta church seemed to enter the Derg years in a spiritually unhealthy state, unprepared to stand as one man in the face of clever strategies brought to bear from within and without. Divisions occurred between competing leaders, between the generations, and between principle and compromise. These cracks in spiritual armor made the Wolaitta church highly vulnerable to the devices used against this oldest and largest church body among the Kale Heywet congregations.

Nevertheless, God does discipline his true sons. He sometimes corrects his people through "severe mercies" wrought out by unwitting participants. The most sweeping of these prunings caught the believers' full attention when all churches which were still open, among the 728 in the province, were ordered closed in one day. It was as if judgment had fallen on the church like a thunderbolt.

---

77. Cumbers (1995), *Joy*, 108f.

It struck in 1983 and its effect lasted for years, forcing the church underground.

Although the record of the Wolaitta church was spotty during this season of leanness of soul, often a single individual stood firm and God established a precedent. For example, one of the first precedents fought for and won involved the believers' long-exercised practice of witnessing at the time of a burial. Such occasions gave a powerful message to the majority who were living without hope and were filled with fear of Satan and evil spirits especially in times of bereavement. Unbelieving neighbors in a communal society would not stay away from a funeral, and so a *lekso* (communal bereavement process) might provide their main exposure to the spoken gospel. A usual *lekso* (literally "weeping") stood in stark contrast to a believers' *lekso*, manifesting frenzied grief in contrast to quiet peace.

Even in a city atmosphere, the contrast could be marked. Ato Lakew Tesemma, John Cumbers' colleague, used to tell how he'd drop into a public *lekso* tent in Addis Ababa and quietly ask one of the distraught mourners, "Is the dear man now... in heaven or in hell?" "How should I know?!" was usually the amazed reply. "Oh, but we should know, we can know," Lakew would kindly respond. If the person showed interest, Lakew would begin to show how, from the word of God. Ato Lakew was obviously such a sincere gentleman that his unconventional approach often proved fruitful.

DOWN IN WOLAITTA, the burial issue arose early in the Marxist-Leninist period. A pastor in Wolaitta died, and the cadres went on the offensive, forbidding a Christian burial service. The pastor's daughter was adamant in her protest: "You may not bury my father until we have had a service of prayer, praise and singing to the Lord." In fact, she stood on top of the coffin and said that if they refused to permit the customary service, she would be buried with her father's coffin. For six days the battle line was drawn, and the body remained unburied. (Since embalming was not the custom, a corpse was always buried within a day.) The area's government officers were consulted and eventually came to discuss the shocking situation with local officials. The believers won the day. A witness was maintained which set a pattern for future believers' funerals in that district. In fact, such services, along with weddings, were often the only vehicle left for the spoken word to reach unbelievers after the churches were closed.

Weddings were the "churchless" church's other prime opportunity. During the struggle over freedom for public witness through weddings, one wedding went down in history in Wolaitta. Gam'a and Amarech's marriage was scheduled secretly, and held at 3:00 in the morning. Weddings aren't quick things in Ethiopia, and it was about 6 AM by the time Pastor Yohannes Bosana had delivered his message and was ready to proclaim the couple husband and wife. Suddenly, the house became surrounded by soldiers.[78] The bridegroom and the choir were all arrested, along with one particularly beloved guest, Ato Wandaro. A soldier barked at Wandaro, "You decrepit old man, isn't it better for you to die, or do something useful, rather than to be mixed up with all this religious nonsense?"

Wandaro Dabaro was one of the first Wolaitta believers, an elder of gentle nature who had literally won the people of his mountain to the Lord. Humbo Mountain with its slender, cone-shaped summit, would before long see one of the most exalted funerals ever known in Wolaitta, when Wandaro went to be with his Lord. But for now, the dear old saint was still working his fields and lovingly encouraging the youth. Ever smiling, Wandaro's now dimming eyes were framed by wrinkles. In the Wolaitta church's struggle between young and old Christians over the cursing issue, Wandaro had stood uncompromisingly with the young.

Wandaro went to prison with the bridal party, and it was two months before they were all released. Meanwhile the bride had been allowed to wait at her father's house. Authorities were prevailed upon to allow the couple to finish their vows. Rather than choosing secrecy this time, the group reconvened for the ceremony in the day time and afterward toured around town in cars and on motorcycles (rare to own, and probably borrowed), singing and testifying to the greatness of God. Soddo was a big town, surrounded by a dense population living in tin-roofed or "haystack" grass homes amid small plots of corn and *ensete*. Never mind the absence of phones: word travels fast. That was one wedding the whole area would long remember!

---

78. Yohannes was the first seized—one of many arrests for this spirited man who would go on to lead the youth movement in Addis Ababa in later years.

SOMETIMES GOD STRENGTHENED individual believers through dreams. Seta Wotango had a number of such experiences. This young man had grown up on Humbo Mountain and was a leader of the Wolaitta youth movement. In 1975, young people were joining the church like a flood. "At first we believers received the Revolution with joy," Seta recalls, "and cooperated enthusiastically in *kebele* government. The government had given the impression that there would be complete freedom to practice religion. But then false teachers entered our district. 'There is no God,' was the communistic teaching which began to cover Ethiopia like a cloud."

The situation Seta described was repeated throughout the provinces. Christians began to be accused. New prohibitions forbade the crossing from one *kebele* to another for a religious meeting. Citizens were ordered to parrot slogans like "Down with capitalism"… "Down with feudalism"… and even "Down with Jesus!" When some refused to comply with such demands, their boldness brought down trouble on the churches. Young people were whipped and put in prison. It was usually the older Christians who urged the young to stay in line to avoid trouble.

As a teacher in a government school, Seta said he was caught in the middle. He decided to testify to God on the students' behalf, and his own as well.

> This frankness brought me into sharp conflict with the teachers association, who accused me of poisoning the minds of the younger generation. I was branded as an enemy of the people. Then one day I had a dream. In my dream I was having a discussion with the other teachers on the 14th floor of a building. I told them, "Rather than discuss with you I'll jump out of the window." So in my dream, I did. On the way down I saw a young tree and grasped it. Slowly it let me down to the ground and then resumed its upright position. I puzzled as to what this dream could mean. [...]
>
> Soon afterwards, the monthly discussion forum of the teachers association came around. The leader started by expounding on the evolution of man. "Four gasses came together, and they amalgamated to produce the first form of life on earth. This in turn evolved into an animal and eventually into a man." Somebody asked what is the relation between plant life and animal life. Nobody had an opinion on that one until a certain man produced a Bible and began to read the Genesis story of creation.

SETA WOTANGO (SODDO, 1994)

The whole meeting burst into laughter. At this I felt very sorry for the man and was convicted that I had sat quiet for too long. So I raised my hand and said, "The Bible is the Word of God. In this world there are two kinds of people—materialists and idealists. Some of you here belong in one group; some in the other. Each has his own explanation of life, supporters, and book of reference. My conviction is that wisdom and understanding can only come from God's Word. Therefore I am sorry to hear you laugh at the man who read from the Bible."

I sat down and thought to myself, "Now I will be arrested and imprisoned." But five of the people whom I assumed to be my opponents said, "What he has said is true." I was amazed; but even more surprised that I walked out without being seized. Now I understood the meaning of the dream in which the sapling let me gently down to the ground.[79]

Seta seemed almost to be raised from the dead once. He escaped from various other situations, but eventually a thousand people from the farmers association were ordered to gather around a building where

---

79. See Cumbers (1995), *Joy*, 121f.

Seta was inside and yell "Let the Red Terror spread! Death to Seta!" When Seta appeared outside, the mob attacked him with sticks and violent kicking. When he finally went unconscious, they left him for dead. Relatives were called to bury him. To their amazement and his, life returned to his body. Weeks later when he was able to walk, he began to seek employment. Work was denied the "Pente" and he felt brought very low.

BELIEVERS LIVED THROUGH many a difficult experience together. On the fateful night of Gam'a and Amarech's wedding, Seta was there, and ended up in prison with the bridegroom, wedding party, and his dear old mentor, Wandaro. Even after the wedding was finally completed two months later, and their defiant point made by public celebration in Soddo town, Seta and many others went to jail repeatedly. Yohannes Bosana was incarcerated over and over again for his preaching and gifted singing, or due to the false accusation that he was a pacifist. Sometimes he would disappear for months, and when asked later where he'd been, he'd reply with a twinkle in his eye, "I've been a guest of the government."

Meanwhile, devout people prayed, especially the women. A number of Wolaitta's first women believers had worked years before along with one of the first Soddo missionaries, Selma Bergsten. During Derg days, these women were still quietly undergirding the Wolaitta church with prayer, fasting, and support to the evangelists in Gamo Gofa.[80] Wandaro's wife, Buchay, said they prayed in small groups for many hours each week during those days, mostly in secret at night. Behind the scenes, prayer strengthened earnest young stalwarts like Seta.

Missionaries played their part in Wolaitta's Christian community, too. They kept the wider church alerted to pray. Although the activities of most mission stations had been closed down, Soddo seemed to experience some slight immunity. Two or three foreign couples were allowed to stay. Linguistics was one area which won approval from the socialist government, so Bruce and Betty Adams were able to stay on and teach literacy, concurrently doing a valuable piece of

---

80. Stories of people like Balotay, Wandaro, and Daanna Meja were related by Selma Bergsten to Raymond Davis for creating the book, Davis (1966), *Fire*. Miss Bergsten had been among the original party which reached Soddo in 1927.

work translating the Wolaitta Scriptures. Alex and Theresia Fellows were allowed to base at the old Soddo station and move about some in Gamo Gofa. Paul Balisky for a time supervised a handicraft school which brought him to Soddo for monthly visits from Addis Ababa. Thus all missionary ties to the southern region were not broken.

MARKINA MEJA KEPT A record of remarkable instances which demonstrated God's power.[81] Power is the faith battle in much of Africa. In the West, the question of truth has been focal. In Africa, the pressing question is, where can we get the power to protect us against evil, illness, and death? Traditional religions generally work on the basis of appeasement—"paying" (through witch doctors) Satan and evil spirits to keep away. Those who discover that God is stronger than Satan, and that He is for them, rather than against them, often respond dramatically. The issue is one of power.

During the Derg days, God frequently shook Wolaitta, as if by the nape of the neck, through unusual manifestations of His power. Wake up! See Who is really in control, He seemed to be saying. Markina recorded instances of the hand of God getting the community's attention through strange happenings involving nature. One example:

> The *kebele's* standard operating procedure was to steal all the roofing tin from the churches and use it to cover the schools. In the Kindo Koysha district, a whirlwind came and ripped out the corrugated iron which had been the church's, depositing it some distance away. It was considerably bent, but the *kebele* leader ordered the people to collect it and to build a kitchen with it. Another whirlwind picked up the same iron and laid it at the side of the mountain. Again the leader commanded the people, "Go and collect the iron." They retorted, "This is God's iron, we're not touching it again. You go and get it!"

ONE OF THE MOST chilling episodes was confirmed by a number of witnesses. It happened at a church built on land given by a farmer named Ato Fancho, whose blind son was an evangelist. Markina records the story:

---

81. See Markina Meja, *Unbroken Covenant with God* (Guardian Books, 2008).

MARKINA MEJA (SODDO, 1994)

In the Bassoro district two cadres took the corrugated iron off the Shom'olo church roof and used it for roofing a school. Then for some reason they returned to the shell of a church and found the believers collecting money for the work of the evangelists. They said "We need this money for the work of the Communist Young People's Movement." One of the believers countered that with, "I have given ten Birr to the work of the Lord, how much are you willing to give to the Communist Young People's Movement?" One of the cadres retorted, "And I have put Jesus out of the church and instead have installed Mao, Marx and Lenin!" Then the two cadres turned and left, abandoning the idea of collecting the offerings of the church.

The third day after this was market day, and the senior man of the two cadres had too much to drink. Upon his return from the market late at night, he fell down in a stupor by the roadside. Hyenas consumed much of his body, but his fellow-cadres were able to identify him by recognizing a scar on a finger of his left hand. (*Left* was significant to people who reported this, for it was the left fist which was always raised to signify Marxist solidarity.) Furthermore, the second man was struck by a disease which caused his body to swell. After a time of much suffering and pain, he also died.

Another Wolaitta report:

> Three cadres riding a public bus were playing communist parodies of Christian hymns with an accordion they'd confiscated from a church. "Let Mao and Marx and Lenin live forever! Their words will never grow old," they sang with triumphant bravado. A believer on the bus said if they didn't stop, he'd get off. "You stupid Pente," sneered one, "go ahead and get off—that should worry us!" Before the objector could dismount, the driver failed to negotiate a turn and the bus went over a low cliff. The believer escaped harm, but of the three cadres, one was injured and two killed, including the singer. The pair were buried in the same grave.

SOMETIMES THE HAND OF God seemed to move through healings. One report was of a girl who had a "dumb spirit." Spiritual bondages similar to those evident in the time of Christ are commonly seen in Ethiopia in our century: spiritually-induced epilepsy, manifestations of deaf or dumb spirits, demon possession, and the like. Local people clearly distinguish these cases from physical impairments or insanity. Markina recorded: "This girl with the dumb spirit joined others who wanted to believe in Christ. She stretched out her hand to testify that she had received Christ, and as she lowered her hand she was able to speak again."

Of course, death is the final enemy. Various members of one Wolaitta church reported this: "A man died, and was being carried on a stretcher and carried to the burial ground. While he was being moved, the man later reported that while dead he had a dream that men in white were coming to get him. He awoke and asked to be released from the stretcher." Such public deliverances spoke volumes to the watching community.

IN SPITE OF THE spiritual decline which was experienced at this juncture in Wolaitta (and other areas as well), here and there a bright testimony was maintained. For example, powerful public witness was evident through the service of a number of men who had been trained at Soddo Hospital. When Charles worked at Soddo Hospital in the late sixties, some twenty-nine outclinics were manned by graduates, called "dressers," who cared for far-flung communities and distributed medicines made available from the hospital pharmacy. Huge

DESALEGN ENARO AND WAJA KABETO (SODDO, 1994)

supplies of pharmaceuticals were obtained yearly at low cost through groups abroad, enabling fees to be kept low enough to be affordable.

Ato Waja Kabeto was one of those who took their dresser training at Soddo with Dr. Barlow and Registered Nurse Pearl White. A short, solid man of practical bent and admirable character, Waja ran a pharmacy way out in Gamo Gofa. It was he who had "gone *wass*" (given security) for Malcolm Hunter. But as Eremiyas Borko's letter to Dick McClellan revealed, Waja was sent to Arba Minch in chains.

Ato Waja's and Ato Tesfaye's lives intertwined there briefly in 1981. Up at Chencha prison, Tesfaye became seriously ill, bleeding from the rectum. Tesfaye's account: "My wife, Asteer, somehow heard of my illness, and came to the prison. 'You must take my husband to the hospital,' she said to the commandant. 'If he dies you are responsible for raising his ten children!'" (Asteer couldn't believe she'd been so bold!) To her surprise, the commandant gave permission. The church members rallied around and collected the money needed for the fare to Arba Minch and for hospital fees. "The doctor was a gracious Christian man who gave me first class treatment," Tesfaye remembers, "and in ten days I was well again, and praising our great God." For the few days of Tesfaye's recuperation in Arba Minch, the prisoners Waja and Tesfaye were able to encourage one another. Ato Waja remembers one aspect of prison life with both pain and grate-

EKASO EYBERO (SODDO, 1994)

fulness. "The prison used pages of the Bible for toilet paper. So we could read it there, held on two sticks."

These highly-trained community leaders frequently came in for rough treatment, either due to jealousy over their training and reputation, or because of their refusal to compromise in order to move up higher. Desalegn Enaro, another Soddo dresser graduate, went on to get a master's in microbiology from the University of Addis Ababa. His could have had a brilliant career. Because he refused to compromise, he was hunted down and incarcerated. After the Derg's demise, it was Ato Desalegn and Ato Waja who would lay aside their high economic potential to lead the Wolaitta church during its re-emergence.

ANOTHER FAITHFUL REMNANT within the believing community remained steadfast while operating way out at a distance. Scores of Wolaitta evangelists had trod the mountains beyond their own ranges since they were reached in the 1930s,[82] bringing the good news

---

82. See D. McLellan's challenging accounts in *Warriors of Ethiopia* (Lost Coin Books, 2013) and *Messengers of Ethiopia* (Lost Coin Books, 2013).

to people who had never heard of the Incarnate God who had visited earth.

The mission infrastructure largely collapsed by 1978. A government decree had stopped MAF from flying, and their planes had left the country. Up to that point, Wolaitta evangelists had been helped by air back-up, bringing in supplies or evacuating sick family members. MAF's departure left these national missionaries in isolated, precarious positions. As a result, the sending church had called their Wolaitta evangelists home.

But a few refused to return, among them Ato Mahey Choramo and Ato Ekaso Eybero, who kept working in the Hamer area (wild and quite unreached) after the missionary planes had stopped flying in. "When we came to this part of the country it was in spiritual darkness," Ekaso reasoned. "We have no intention of letting the people drift back into that darkness. They still need much teaching, so we're staying." But he hadn't reckoned with the local people's opinion—people who as yet had not believed. The *kebele* leaders stirred them up to protest that Ekaso and the others would be a drain on their resources. "You see, we had no relatives there to help us," explained the sharp-featured Ekaso, "and according to them we had brought in a useless foreign religion which did not fit in with their way of living. I replied to them, 'You depend upon your cattle for life and strength; we depend upon our God.' They told me, 'Your foreigners have gone, and the water supply has stopped.' (We had a well and a pump which needed gasoline to run it.) My response to that was to remind them what we had always believed; that God, the creator or rain, could supply all the water we would need and theirs too." And He did. A long period of heavy rain came, and Ekaso claimed that "as far as the eye could see, water covered the earth. Wells and springs started. God answered our prayers in a wonderful manner." The stories of these evangelists read like a cross-section of the lives of the Old Testament prophets and New Testament Christians living in the time of Acts![83]

---

83. For more on the Wolaitta evangelists, see Mehari [aka Mahey] Ch. and B. Fargher, *Ethiopian Revivalist* (Enterprise Publ., 1997); P. Balisky, *Wolaitta Evangelists* (Pickwick Publ., 2009).

MAHEY CHORAMO (SODDO, 1994)

Life was at risk among the Bannas. It was difficult even to get food locally. Periodically Mahey or Ekaso would have to make a twelve day journey on foot through forest areas where wild animals roamed, to Kucha (Bassa's area). There it was possible to catch a bus for Wolaitta. Both were tall, muscular men, but this way of life wore the strongest down. "Always His angels protected us," Mahey testified.

Arrest was often just around the corner, whether through local, Revolutionary, or Orthodox provocation. Once when Mahey Choramo was in prison with forty-two other believers, his glasses were taken from him so that he could not read his Bible. He knew so many texts by heart, that he had little difficulty teaching the word. This demonstrated the importance of memorizing scripture for times when Bibles might be confiscated.

Mahey kept praying for the Muslim governor, Ali Musa, and other opponents. In some places the Orthodox priests violently opposed the evangelists' preaching. Somehow the Orthodox felt they were solely authorized to handle the Scriptures. "Why don't you go over to the Sudan where all the pagans are?" they suggested. "They are the ones who need your teaching, not the Christians in this town." Mahey, although gentle of speech, replied, "A true Christian is one who does the will of Christ. And God called me to preach in Ethiopia, not the Sudan!"

This sense of call was strong upon the Wolaitta evangelists. Mahey prayed that he might have a witness and see a living body of believers take root in each of the unreached people groups of southwest Ethiopia. Years later, when age and health would seem to preclude further travel, 1997 would see the faithful old veteran leading young evangelists into the area again, spearheading Wolaitta's fresh offensive to finish the job.

MARKINA PUT WOLAITTA'S EXPERIENCE during the Derg in a nutshell like this: "God loves Wolaitta very much and called us to be a witness for Him. Just before the persecution, the churches were sending out few evangelists, they were fighting, not loving each other. God judged us. Eventually, we Wolaitta believers realized our sin, cried to God, and confessed our ungodliness. Then God did miracles to send this government away."

> *My son, do not make light of the Lord's discipline, and do not lose heart when he rebukes you, because the Lord disciplines those he loves, and he punishes everyone he accepts as a son. [...]*
> *No discipline seems pleasant at the time, but painful.*
> *Later on, however, it produces a harvest of righteousness and peace for those who have been trained by it.*
> *(Hebrews 12:4b–6, 11)*

> *How beautiful on the mountains are the feet of those*
> *who bring good news, who proclaim peace,*
> *who bring good tidings, who proclaim salvation,*
> *who say to Zion, "Your God reigns!"*
> *(Isaiah 52:7)*

Chapter 18

KAMBAATA / HADIYYA: "DANIELS," "JOSEPHS," AND COMMUNITY DEVELOPMENT

A flashback: "They're out there dying of anthrax and don't even come to the hospital for help!" my husband lamented, throwing his arms in the air. It was our first month to be stationed at Leimo Hospital, which served the Kambaata and Hadiyya "cousin" groups just north of Wolaitta. An anthrax epidemic had struck and we learned by the grapevine that people, not only cattle, were dying. Charles practically had to beg folks to come to the clinic. They were not quick to conclude that we foreigners had superior medicine to offer. That characteristic would have a bearing on how much they could be moved, even by a new government.

Along with Wolaitta, these peoples of Kambaata and Hadiyya (who speak related languages) had been among the founding groups reached in the 1930s.[84] Therefore, most of their believers during Derg times were first-to-third-generation Christians. Strong Bible and elementary schools had come into being at Durame station in Kambaata and Hossana in Hadiyya. A small mission hospital was located at Leimo, seven kilometers from Hossana town across the low mountain grazing lands and small cultivated fields of this moderately populated area. Less easy-going than the Wolaitta folk, the Kambaata and Hadiyya people struck us as very much in charge of their own affairs.

---

84. For a record of SIM's 1927–38 pioneering in this area, see Duff (1980), *Cords*.

SABIRO WESERO, DAANNA MEJA MADERO, AND ABBA GOLE NUNAMO
(PHOTOGRAPH OF A WALL PICTURE AT KURIFTU)

We were awed by the elders of the Hadiyya church, Ato Abba Gole, Ato Sabiro, and Ato Shigute. *Abba* meant "father," and that's who Abba Gole was to the area. The broad man stood about six foot three, rode an immense white mule, and commanded one's full attention. Ato Shigute, in contrast, was short, bald, and hard of hearing. I still remember the day dear Shigute brought us a very special gift. From his little mule he unloaded a sack with utmost care and lovingly laid before us that which he had labored over for many months: a fine crop of potatoes. I could hardly eat them, they seemed so almost holy.

DURING THE DERG YEARS, the young people in Hadiyya came in for their share of mistreatment, beatings, imprisonments. Some even died as a result. During the Red Terror, if a father went to identify a body, he had to be careful not to show any emotions, or he would be accused of sympathizing with the "evil" the son or daughter had committed.

Parents and children were set against each other. If believing young people disobeyed restrictions by engaging in Bible study, prayer, or witnessing, their parents were warned that they themselves would have to take dire consequences. Some of the elders said they were not prepared to suffer for someone else's disobedience. In the heat of the atheistic government's struggle for the allegiance of youth, many students were coming alive to God. Public baptisms were out of the question, so they were conducted silently at a river in the middle of the night.

Makebo Wadolo, one who suffered as a teacher in the eighties, told of his pilgrimage. "My father and grandfather were witch doctors. As a child an evil spirit seized me. I became ill. They used to have to hold me. They killed sheep and a goat and laid the entrails on me. But when I went to a church school to learn the *fidel* (alphabet), I believed, and the evil spirits left. I was eight years old. My parents were so happy that I got release, that they didn't oppose me." That was long before the Revolution.

By Derg times, Makebo had become a government school teacher in Hossana, one of only three known as Christians on the staff. There were accusations and attempts to have the three posted to a remote area, but God protected them. "I kept thinking of the biblical account of Daniel's three friends in the furnace," Makebo explained. "No matter what, I knew God was able to protect and keep us. I promised the Lord—I drove a stake—saying, 'If you see that in the future I would deny You, kill me now.' He did keep me."

That principle could work the other way. A cadre who boarded a bus at Doyogena began arguing loudly that there was no God. He suggested that he could prove God didn't exist. "If there is a God, let him show me today by killing me," he boasted. The Toyota minibus made it as far as Hossana, but as it entered the town, the vehicle turned over. Nobody was hurt except the unbelieving cadre, who was killed outright.

CHRISTIANS WERE OFTEN THE first to be elected as *kebele* chairmen in the early years, for they were known as reliable leaders. One such was Fikre Nebiyehu, a very tall man, graced with humility. He was given a week to make his choice: "Deny God exists and continue as chairman, or go to prison." All week he prayed, and at the appointment, in spite of taunts from those who had turned back from believing, he affirmed, "I know there is one God and He is alive. There

FIKRE NEBIYEHU (HOSSANA, 1995)

is no way that I will deny Him. You can tie me up or even kill me, but I will not deny my Lord."

They gave him another week, and when he gave the same answer, previous churchgoers chided him for not just denying God with his lips even if believing in his heart. Fikre kept thinking of the text that said "If you deny me before men, I will deny you before my Father." He said to his old friends, "No matter if you made a mistake, I'll not make the same mistake. I will never deny the Lord." They threw him out that day, but then called him to an assembly with four hundred present. He was to face a sixteen-point list of complaints. One was that he carried a Bible. To that he admitted. Each additional accusation he answered with the unusual wisdom which only God could give. Sometimes he asked his accusers to produce a shred of evidence, and none could be brought forward. When the charade was over, a vote was taken. "Those of you who think this man is innocent of these charges, raise your hands." Fikre remembers the count: 388 people raised their hands. The Party leader was furious. "You people have chosen the Bible over the Party," he shouted. Fikre never did go to prison.

It is well to remember that prison was not a new experience for believers in Ethiopia. Years before the Marxist-Leninist ordeal, Ato Sabiro and Ato Abba Gole with a hundred other believers had been forced to make an infamous 1946 five-day walk to the regional capital chained together at their wrists. Theirs had been a fellowship of deep suffering, for some died on the way.

Ato Sabiro Wesero shared a glimpse into a purposeful arrangement Christians were making now during these Revolutionary days:

> [...] if a single believer was arrested, another Christian would go to the police and say, "Why don't you lock me up as well; I'm as guilty of preaching the gospel as he is." That way, the one in prison would have fellowship, and together the two men (or sometimes women) would be able to influence other prisoners for Christ. The Lord was so gracious, that many times the prison guards would hear the gospel and trust in Christ.[85]

Ato Girma Hanano, the Kambaatan who had studied and then taught at Grace Bible Institute, tells of his prison time with his characteristic honesty and humor. After GBI's closing, Girma took up leadership of the Bobicho Bible School just outside Hossana. Born in the area, he was well fitted for leadership there. Just before he was detained, his wife was due to deliver a baby. His incarceration was a strain on him, and on his large family. A real scholar and a highly disciplined leader, he found himself quite out of patience with being cooped up in one filthy suffocating room into which fifty-two believers, along with hardened criminals, were jammed. Girma lost his patience. He called for the guard, who did not come. A man of dramatic action, Girma started kicking the door. When someone came, the irate prisoner let loose a tirade: "Are we in Rhodesia or South Africa? Why do we have to put up with the company of these criminals? We've done nothing against our fellow-men that deserves this kind of treatment!" Actually, his exploding brought results, for improved "accommodations" were forthcoming.

Ato Girma was not to be outwitted. While he was in prison, the development department he administered ground to a halt. The church was helping destitute families in the area, in cooperation with World Vision. This was a practical ministry which concurrently kept

---

85. Cumbers (1995), *Joy*, 175.

GIRMA HANANO (ADDIS ABABA, 1995)

the Bible school open, the place where such compassion was taught. Officials came to Ato Girma in jail, asking him to sign checks to release funds from the World Vision account. "I am in prison for a crime I committed," he calmly replied. "How can a criminal sign a check? Either I am a development worker and can sign checks, or I'm a criminal and must remain in prison."

Eventually six of the top brass came to interview and intimidate him. "Yours is a false religion, Pente, a foreign influence. With your gift of oratory, if you had not been such a religious person you could have been a high-ranking member of the Party!" "You say this is a foreign religion," Girma countered. "Where did Islam come from? Arabia. Orthodox Christianity came from Greece and Egypt. Your Marxist ideology has been in this country for nine years at most. Our religion is found in the book known as the Bible, and it has been around for thousands of years." They barely let him finish speaking, and one shouted, "When we need to hear from you we know where to find you. Now GET OUT!" Girma was surprised to find they meant to get out completely—get out of the prison. That was the last time he was incarcerated.

IN HOSSANA TOWN, a couple named Girma Deresse (the one who became an artisan) and Werkwuha Makuria had quite a story. Both had been freed from the raw bondage Satan imposes on peoples long immersed in dark practices. Girma, a square shouldered man with mustache and a bright smile, shows himself to be a man of practicality and reason. But he might be very different, had his life not been transformed at nineteen. His father was a priest for the devil. Another witch doctor cursed their cow, and it died. Girma said that as a lad he asked, in frustration, "When will I be saved from these evil spirits? When will the witch doctor come to me, I ask you, my father? Will I die?"

Girma was searching. He entered an Orthodox priests' school for a year, but that still didn't help him find deliverance. "After your father dies, I'll use you as my instrument," said the witch doctor. What shall I do, Girma worried. Then God revealed Himself to Girma in a dream. He describes it in this way:

> A powerful devil spirit came and taunted me. "Where will you go from me?" he threatened. He came and controlled me. I shouted, "My Lord, help me!" That which caught me fell down. Then an angel spirit came to me and said, "God has helped you. Go and believe on Jesus Christ. Trust in Him. You are thinking rightly." I feared to become a believer. But I knew of some Christians who lived an hour's walk away. I hadn't yet heard God's word. After that dream, I went the next day to them. I heard the gospel, and believed! As a result, my family so hated me that they wouldn't even drink from the same cup. I had to leave home.

Girma went to town, learned a trade, and in two years entered Bible School at Bobicho just outside of Hossana. This was when the Derg was coming into power. Life for believers was becoming difficult. Girma went to Hawassa to learn metal work and carpentry—rare skills in Ethiopia. He became a gifted artisan, and seemed to have a knack for business.

Meanwhile the woman who would someday become his wife was having her own struggles. Werkwuha was her name. It means "Golden Water." Werkwuha is now as rational as you'd expect of an elder's wife, mother of five children, and manager of a large home. She calmly relates the fact that she was seized by an evil spirit when she was eight. Her parents took her to a *kalicha* (witch doctor) and

GIRMA DERESSE AND WERKWUHA MAKURIA (HOSSANA, 1994)

the bondage continued. Even unbelievers saw her condition, and suggested she be taken to Christians. When about eighteen, she went to listen at a church, but didn't believe. "Then the evil spirit came on me strongly. At home and at church, he threw me down. At the end of the third month, I accepted Christ. As the spirit left, he gave his name: 'My name is Five Thousand!'"

Girma was present, and heard the voice. "She used to go naked, cried, and wildly danced," he concurred. "Her father had taken her to the witch doctor, given money, and slaughtered many sheep. We believers prayed for her. She was released from the devil after three days of prayer and fasting. Then she was healed and completely freed."

Three years later, when the healed Werkwuha had finished tenth grade and Girma felt she was firmly established in the Scriptures, they married. However, with the Derg's terror campaign in operation, theirs became an unusual honeymoon. The day they married, five men with guns came to the house yelling, "Where is that Pente, Girma?" Girma slipped out the back door. The intruding men cudgeled the guests, and beat Girma's mother. A directive went out to the ninety-five farmers associations that if Girma was found, he must be handed over to authorities. Friends spirited his wife out under cover of darkness that night. Girma walked to Bobicho at midnight, then trudged on for nearly three hours to his birthplace, then to hers. Together then, they had to keep on the run for over a month. This "living on the run" was an experience many believers had in those days, at one time or another. Girma and his wife hid at the town of Sodere, many miles from home, in a sod shed. With only grass-stuffed jute bags for blankets and a leaky roof dripping above them, the weary bride got sick. "Oh God, when will I have a clean home? a bed?" she cried out in prayer. They determined to return to Hossana, even if it meant death. With thirty cents in their pockets, they started home. They hid in a the back of a house for two months, eating raw corn and drinking only water, until the search seemed to blow over.

Their property was almost confiscated, but always the Lord protected them and blessed Girma's building talents in such a way as to keep them fed. He built a house and put the business in her name, went to work far away in Illubabor Province, sent home money, and eventually returned. Each enterprise he undertook seemed to prosper. When the Hossana town church was closed in the early eighties for what turned out to be about five years, their large home became the church's meeting place, a privilege for which they had trusted God. Had they never been freed from bondage, how different their lives would have turned out.

THE CLOSING OF THE Hossana town church was a delicate matter, but an isolated case, for the Kambaata and Hadiyya churches largely escaped closure. Some thought the sheer numbers of believers, many of them influential, was the reason these churches survived. Some credited Lieutenant Petros Gebre,[86] the *awraja* administrator, who was reared by a godly mother and looked to the respected Ato Abba Gole as a mentor. Whenever he could, Petros seemed to protect Christians.

One exception occurred when Pastor Kedamo Mechato came to speak at a Christian conference which was attended by thousands. The Addis Ababa pastor had grown up in Kambaata. Kedamo chose to speak that day from Proverbs 18:10, "The name of the Lord is

---

86. Petros' titles ranged from Captain to Lieutenant to Colonel.

a strong tower; the righteous runs into it and is safe." He preached three messages from the text, focusing upon God's greatness, His kingship, and His holiness. Between meetings, Kedamo decided to walk half an hour to his mother's home to visit her.

Meanwhile, another man spoke from the book of Acts, choosing the chapter in which James was put to death and Peter was imprisoned. At the wrong moment, Lieutenant Petros, the district administrator, came past the conference grounds. Unfortunately, he had a political entourage with him and had to take some action. He called the thirty-two leading elders responsible for the conference and asked, "What's going on here?" Petros was obliged to arrest the men and they all headed for the administrative office.

By then, Kedamo had said good-bye to his mother and had started walking back to the meeting. "A few minutes later I saw a woman with two boys. She was shouting out something, but was too far away for me to hear. She sent the two boys over to tell me not to go back to the conference, because Lieutenant Petros was arresting all the leaders. I knew that it would only be a headache for the church in that district if I were to be arrested, so I thanked the boys and stayed on that side of the river. At the same time I praised the Lord that the message He had given me, 'the name of the Lord is a strong tower,' was being worked out in my own life."

Actually, Kedamo was quick to praise Lieutenant Petros. "The churches in Hadiyya and Kambaata have never been closed and that is to Petros' credit. Some of the things that he did to the church can be understood when one considers that he was a man under authority, carrying out orders from higher up in the organization." John Cumbers reminded critics that "the Lord had a few Daniels in the courts of the kings in those days and the people of Ethiopia can be thankful."

ADJACENT TO HADIYYA, the Kambaatan people struggled with government farming policies. Ato Segaro Seleto, a believer since 1944, related one personal incident with the farmers and producers cooperatives established in the area by the government. During Ethiopia's cultural revolution experiment, private ownership was done away with, and cooperative farming was enforced. Their own coffee trees and gardens had been forcibly cut out, to make room for communal field crops. "If you didn't work with the group, you got no food. We had to ask permission to do anything personal, like being away to attend a church council meeting. I cried out to the Lord, 'I don't want to take coffee from someone else's property. It's a sin! God, if you want me to live like this, change this system. If not, take me home. Have me killed.'" He told the church his prayer.

Soon a decree was made that whoever "volunteered" to stay in the farmers cooperative could stay. ("Volunteering" was a euphemism under the Derg, but amounted to an order or a dare.) Segaro went to a private place of prayer in the forest, knelt, and looked to heaven praying, "You are Lord. You are at hand to listen to our prayers." Then Segaro went to his wife and asked, "What is your choice in this option?" The couple made the dangerous choice not to "volunteer" but to try to stay private, along with just six families. They began to replant their gardens. Then another decree came out reversing the potential freedom. The couple decided to refuse. "We won't go in or else we'll flee," they decided. In the end, they stayed on their land and rode out the storm. Now aged, as Ato Segaro tells the story, he holds his lips tightly, with long-learned determination.

THE KAMBAATAN TENDENCY TO overcome from a position of power was evident in Ato Yoel Fughi's account of how they fared during the Derg. Ato Yoel was president of the Kambaata *mahiber* (fellowship) many years. "When the Revolution began in 1974," he said, "there had been no preparation on our part whatsoever. It was many months before we, or the missionaries associated with us, began to realize that the change in government was to mean great hardship for the church of the Lord Jesus Christ. Moreover, when the time came for the missionaries to leave, it was a great shock to us."

"At first the church was in confusion. After an early period dominated by cadre leadership sent in from the outside, the government eventually decided to choose officers from the local people. They were looking for honest, morally upright men and women to manage the affairs of the town and to serve the population selflessly. Where to find such people except in the church? So I was chosen for leadership positions in both the local and district administrations. For this reason the church had a considerable influence on the way things were run in the individual *kebeles*.

YOEL FUGHI (DURAME, 1994)

"One of the first matters we set straight concerned the keeping of the Lord's Day. We decided that no government meetings or public meetings would be held on Sundays. The higher government officials were quite angry when they heard this, but we were in a position of strength because the leading local and intermediate officials were all Christians. Cadres came in from outside and tried to disrupt the Christian meetings, and to turn the people against the Christian leaders of the local government. They circulated leaflets saying that *kebele* meetings would now be held on Sundays. We immediately sent around leaflets saying that Sunday would continue to be observed as the Lord's Day.

"But then the higher authorities stepped in. A decree came out of the Regional capital stating that all towns in the Region must observe Sunday as the day for political meetings. Things had taken a turn for the worst. But we decided that if the government could change its practices, so could we. We rang a bell at 6 AM on Sundays and expected every Christian to turn up at the church for worship. Our singing was the loudest we could make it, then we shared the Word of God and prayed until 8 AM. After a cup of coffee we would attend the mandatory political meeting.

"We never cease to be amazed as we look back on those days, that throughout Kambaata the churches were never closed. Of course there were still Christians in some of the leading government positions, but God had put us there, and he expected us to be faithful with the freedom He allowed. He tells us to obey the laws of Caesar except when they conflict with his teaching. We endeavored to follow that precept all the time, and we were blessed."

WHEN ASKED HOW GOD had worked in Kambaata specifically during the Revolution, Ato Tadesse Handeto (who seemed to serve as scribe), Ato Segaro, and the other elders added two other elements: miraculous interventions on the one hand, and carefully devised community development strategies on the other.

An example the elders gave of the first:

> The Lord intervened during the Derg. They were using capital punishment. Church leaders were in darkness, almost to be killed, and we had only the Lord to look to. They called it "free-step"—which meant "to kill." Ato Segaro was arrested. In 1978, the authorities were on the way to get him when their car tipped over. The accident permanently paralyzed the *awraja* Governor, Ato Paulos Bogale. They flew him to East Germany. In the car there were other passengers who were not killed, not even bruised. The car even could be driven, in spite of its having rolled and reversed direction in the road.

Another man said, "The news of how Paulos had tried to oppose the believers spread like wildfire throughout the eight districts. The militia people and the cadres, when they heard about the accident, let up on their persecution of the believers for a while. You could tell they thought this was the judgment of God on Paulos."

As to the second element, Community Development (CD), Kambaata Christians worked hard with what might be called "the development factor" during the Derg days. When the Christian elementary and Bible schools were being closed, the Durame leaders discovered one key to favor in the government's eyes: community development programs. Ato Tadesse Handeto went to Dr. Mulatu and

Mr. Cumbers with a letter, asking to start Community Development at Durame. The elders' explanation of the strategy:

> Our leaders were put in prison, but then we started a Community Development program at Durame. We made up a budget, got a tractor sent in with Mr. Winslow, and got leadership from our Daniel, who had been trained abroad. We did tangible things, efficiently, honestly— and as a result, those detained were freed. We worked with soil conservation, reforestation, cattle breeding, horticulture, health, water improvement, construction, and training. Community Development served as a means, not only an end, a means for keeping things open here. The Lord blessed because it was a holistic ministry, yet it was kept on track coupled with a gospel witness.

Ato Segaro made it clear that in his opinion their unity was based upon prayer. "We were of one mind, one heart among us, and in response God sent us this CD means."

The spirited Ato Girma Hanano responded similarly to inquiries about why there was not as much persecution of the church in Hadiyya / Kambaata as in most other places:

> The first was the personal relationship between Ato Abagoli [Abba Gole] and Lt. Petros Gebre. Even though the people under Petros were ordering the churches to be closed, his word overruled and they were never closed completely. Also, the Church was regarded as 'Abagoli's church.' For instance, when the new hospital was built in Hosaina, Abagoli persuaded the Mission and churches to collect quite a lot of money.

> The second reason was that we had a development program. When we were asked why our churches were still operating when all the Wolaytta churches were closed, we could say, 'We teach people to provide for the poor, we help the hungry, we employ people in the development program. We don't minister only to the souls of men and women, but to their bodies as well. We don't just help Christians, but, as far as is in our power, anybody who is needing help.'[87]

---

87. Cumbers (1995), *Joy*, 179f (quoting Girma Hanano's outline of the history of the Hadiyya KHC from 1978–1991).

THE IMPLICATIONS OF Community Development (CD) programs involved more than met the eye. In the capital, the mission's Community Development department was growing by leaps and bounds under Dr. Mulatu's leadership in the early eighties. At the new KHC property down near the prison in which Negussie was being held, huge railroad cars, now emptied of relief supplies, became offices and provided storage units. Community Development became ever more complicated. The mentality of "the relief and development industry" being created over the world by massive and ongoing international aid was manifesting a new phenomena which threatened local autonomy and self-reliance.[88] Organizational scrambles and alternate viewpoints over money matters arose. In Ethiopia, the decision was made to separate KHC and mission CD efforts. Whether for good or ill, the separation played out all down the line.

Missions had already been relieved of their institutions, but they still could interest compassionate agencies abroad in Ethiopia's needs. Pushed by the government to produce material benefits to stay in favor, national church bodies developed new physical ways to serve. They made major tangible contributions at the grass roots level. Yet these projects were often maintained at the high cost of becoming dependent upon foreign funds. While the broad masses of Ethiopia had no capital for such things, international funds from the compassionate west were forthcoming. Cries for help kept both givers and receivers from thinking through long term ramifications.

When the dire needs of another famine struck in 1984 and donors responded from all over the world, CD leaders in Addis Ababa began to discover that, like it or not, they had a tiger by the tail.

My son, if you accept my words and store up my commands within you, turning your ear to wisdom and applying your heart to understanding, and if you call out for insight and cry aloud for understanding, and if you look for it as for silver and search for it as treasure,

---

88. Much has been written about this aid "industry" phenomenon. One insightful vignette appears in the chapter called "The President" in Taylor (1987), *Prisoner*.

then you will understand the fear of the LORD
and find the knowledge of God.
For the LORD gives wisdom,
and from his mouth come knowledge and understanding.
He holds victory in store for the upright,
he is a shield to those whose walk is blameless,
for he guards the course of the just and protects the way of his faithful ones.
(Proverbs 2:1–8)

Part V

HAVING DONE ALL, TO STAND

(During 1981–85)

*Therefore put on the full armor of God,
so that when the day of evil comes,
you may be able to stand your ground,
and after you have done everything, to stand.*
                              (Ephesians 6:13)

Chapter 19

INTO THE EIGHTIES

Politics and nature compounded the suffering of East Africans as the eighties began. The Eritrean insurgency continued, and to that was added an external threat, the Somali war. Drought plagued not only Ethiopia, but the whole coastal region from Eritrea to Mozambique. June 30th, 1980 *Time* magazine titled its World page, "East Africa: A Harvest of Despair." Hearkening back to the famine of the seventies, it reported the new drought sweeping down through seven or more nations.

> In the Horn of Africa, more than 1.7 million refugees from the unresolved conflicts in Ethiopia's Eritrea, Tigre and Ogaden areas swelter in squalid relief camps, where thousands have already died from malnutrition and a host of hunger-related diseases [...] Says [...] a United Nations official in Nairobi: "From the Red Sea south, this area is on a collision course with disaster."

Back in America, we watched the news. During the eighties, most missionaries who had left Ethiopia had settled into work in other countries or were back in their country of origin. We strained to find Ethiopian reports and alert others to act or pray.

George Middleton had left Asmara, where Protestant churches had been closed, but as usual he set about creating new avenues for service. He drew together some young people to form a relief organization called "Emmanuel International." (*Emmanuel* means "God with us.") Mr. Middleton called us and talked to Charles about the desperate situation of various Ethiopians. In the east, a million had left the Ogaden and poured into Somalia.

Charles knew little about that region of Ethiopia, but had known missionaries who had been pushed out of that area. They had communicated passionate concern for those they'd had to leave, and had gone to Kenya to help Somali-speaking people there as best they could. He remembered the commitment of the Modrickers, still working away in Kenya at translating the Bible for Somalis. Charles had taken a position in Student Health at a university, one of the rare positions which could spare a doctor during the summer season. They'd agreed to let him take leave-without-pay should a summer opportunity arise to serve abroad.

So Charles went to Somalia. The stick huts of a few hundred hapless refugees spread across the desert landscape at Lugh, the camp assigned to the Emmanuel team. These were largely Muslim people out of Ethiopia's Ogaden, decimated by drought and war. Charles would never be the same after the Somali experience. On his return, I tried to enter into it, through pictures. One particularly burned into my memory—a beautiful, thin young woman in the lovely Somali-style blue gown, her emaciated baby in her lap. The mother's eyes, and the child's eyes, burning hot with suffering, were unforgettable.

Somalia had since 1977 tried to annex the Ogaden area of Ethiopia. As the Derg grew more desperate for help, they turned to the Soviet Union, since the USA had withdrawn benefits due to Ethiopia's human rights abuses. Somalia had previously been a Soviet client, but now Russia chose Ethiopia. Therefore Somalia abrogated their 1974 Treaty of Friendship with Moscow and expelled Soviet advisers. Around 17,000 Cuban troops leaving Angola came to assist the Ethiopian army. They repelled the Somali momentum by early 1978. In the process, the Derg had become a military client of Moscow and Cuba, a situation that caused significant international repercussions and resulted in a major realignment of power in the Horn of Africa.[89]

In 1982, Chairman Mengistu visited Moscow and met with Brezhnev. It was just a month before Brezhnev died. In Addis Ababa, John Cumbers read about Brezhnev's death in the news and noted in his diary, "His legacy, the 'Brezhnev Doctrine,' asserted the right of

---

89. See T. Ofcansky and L. Berry, *Ethiopia: A Country Study* (4th edition 1993), 59f, 256f.

any communist party to intervene in another socialist country where the government appeared to be diverting the nation towards capitalism. To uphold this principle the USSR [Union of Soviet Socialist Republics] invaded Afghanistan in 1979, and then suppressed Poland's Solidarity labor union in 1981. Bearing in mind these examples of Marxist dictatorial oppression, Col. Mengistu might have wondered where his relationship with the communist bloc would lead him and Ethiopia."[90] As John expected, that doctrine did result in major Russian intervention in Ethiopia.

When John had worked in Asmara as an air traffic controller years before, patience and alertness were qualities he had to develop—waiting, watching, guiding flights safely through the weather. Now he had to apply those skills to guiding a fleet of grounded missionaries. Even with the famine the nation was facing, the government did not return mission clinics or hospitals, landing fields or stations. The few missionaries still left under Mr. Cumbers' leadership had to slog along in hostile circumstances, often staying out of sight. Missionaries were torn, having to purposefully stay away from Ethiopian brethren, due to the threat to these nationals "by association." The threat of mission expulsion continued. The Baptist General Conference Mission's church building and homes were taken, and all remaining missionaries expelled from the Wollega province on Sudan's border. Now fifty-five, Mr. Cumbers' health seemed precarious. Once he had a transient ischemic attack while talking with Dr. Mulatu. Morale was difficult to maintain, his own included.

It was the national church which took the brunt of gearing up for disaster relief, struggling with mammoth budgets, distribution demands, and the expectations of a myriad of foreign donors. Dr. Mulatu headed up the Community Development work. Behind the scenes, missionaries helped find those donors, hosted their visiting field workers, and assisted as best they could. In Addis Ababa, the Christian Relief and Development Agency loosely coordinated the work of various humanitarian organizations, "NGOs" they were called, non-governmental organizations.

Foreign aid came more in finance than in personnel. Outside agencies were usually allowed only three-months visitors' visas for

---

90. Cumbers (1996), *Terror,* 238f.

relaying workers in to assess needs, administer projects, and briefly upgrade clinics and the like. Tearfund in the United Kingdom and DMG, another Christian group from Germany, financed many programs. World Vision in the United States undergirded projects helping orphans and supplying destitute families. World Relief and Emmanuel International, both Canadian based, also cooperated with the Kale Heywet Church in the countryside projects.

General Secretary Tekle Wolde Giorgis continued to carry the general oversight of the churches. Ato Hussein Yusef assisted him in Addis Ababa. Hussein's wife, Belaynesh Dindamo, eventually began to work with World Vision's staff, who needed well-trained Ethiopian colleagues. Many students who had built strong foundations through GBI training were led into wide areas of service. The church where Kedamo Mechato was the pastor, *Meserete Heywet* ("Foundation of Life"), remained open in spite of repeated threat of closure, providing a place of fellowship and growth for thousands of believers in Addis Ababa, some not from KHC backgrounds, but from various closed churches. By God's grace, the church near the SIM Press compound and the one adjacent to Bingham Academy remained operational. At mission's Headquarters, the underground Bible School swelled, as did the services of the International Evangelical Church, which was still left open, ostensibly for expatriates. Allowing an occasional church to stay open kept up the government's facade of religious freedom. At first predominantly attended by foreigners, the church filled up with so many nationals that three Sunday services became necessary to accommodate the crowds.

DAILY REVIEW OF THE varied situations around the country made the huge map of Ethiopia in the Director's office a frame of reference to scan. It became a constant focus for action or prayer. In the southwest, the Gamo Gofa Christians (people like Degu Deklaabo and Terefe Alsi at Jinka, Bassa Dea at Kucha, Tesfaye Tole at Chencha, and Waja Kabeto at Arba Minch) eventually were released from prison. They were weary, but had become stronger people. In Wolaitta, the church was closed, some defected, and drought came. In the heartland, Kambaatan Christians stayed in the saddle, strengthened by their Community Development involvement. The underground church grew in spite of persecution near Bishoftu and nearby Debre

Zeit. Somehow 200 gathered for a 15th anniversary of that congregation's inception.[91] To the west, life was hard for believers in the Kefa area, where Grace Bible Institute had been located. Some lost their lives.

East of the Rift Lakes, Gedeo went through "the Coffee Affair" and saw Ato Werku Gole and others of their leaders imprisoned. Up in the mountains of Bale, Ato Asfaw Demisse began a prayer meeting which lasted throughout the Revolution years. Not new to persecution in the southeasterly Bale area, Asfaw had begged his brothers for help for his small band at the 1977 Langano conference. The fierce Gujjis in the south and Somalis to the east sometimes went to war separately or joined together, bringing on periods of turmoil. Churches were sometimes burned. In the north, the church was still open in the Dessie Hospital area. On the Red Sea, in March of 1983, the local government ordered the KHC elementary school at Assab to cease operating.[92] In Eritrea, all Protestant churches were closed.

MEANWHILE GOD SENT PERIODIC encouragement. From Singapore, Pastor Hsueh and his wife Lily returned to Ethiopia for the fourth time for two weeks in 1984. This time they were not allowed to travel outside of Addis, but people were brought to them. "They are doing well," Yu Kwong reported to those who were praying in Asia, "and maturing after ten years of persecution." On this visit, the Hsuehs did not teach so much as listen to the Ethiopians' testimonies. Five or six at a time gathered in Ruth Cremer's room at the mission compound. She translated their stories. One told about a nailed church's door being ripped opened by a wind storm. Authorities feared to close it again. Another told of an area desperate for water, where unbelievers begged the Christians to pray for rain. "Not unless you repent," the believers answered. The unbelievers did attempt to repent. It rained like a pipe from heaven on that town, but not around it.

---

91. All was not easy in that area, however. Sahle Tilahun and Aberash Takele were ousted from their home there, and nearly relieved of their jobs.

92. The President of the Kale Heywet Church, who was also administrator in charge of the Assab oil refinery, made every effort to get that decision changed, but it remained

Many miracles were reported. "Mr. Hsueh," one of the group emphasized with awe, "we are living in the days of the Book of Acts!"[93]

Back in England Peter Cotterell, formerly a missionary in Ethiopia, watched for reports of the situation carefully and documented them.

> In October 1984 there came the worst news yet. Details were released by Keston College, the College dedicated to the task of monitoring the antireligious activities of the communist world, of mass closures of churches in Ethiopia. At the head of the list came Wolayta: all 748 of their churches were closed. Across the Rift Valley, in Wando all 177 churches were closed. In Yirga Chaffee, Sidamo province 90 were closed, 140 in Gedeo. The number mounted up... In total, 1,700 of the Word of Life churches were closed. Fewer than 1,100 were still open.[94]

Missionaries, when possible, wove their way cautiously among the down-country areas. Three or four couples managed to remain in Soddo and Durame west of the Rift Lakes. Gerhard Bössler began making rounds east of the lakes through Dilla and Yirga Cheffe as he traveled to the Gujjis, for whom he and Edith maintained a deep burden. Carolyn Ford worked in isolation on the language in Kele near the Gujjis, until she was forced out in 1984.

John Cumbers tried to visit Burji in the south, the place where he and Naomi had first been stationed. It was an isolated area, hard to reach from the capital. His repeated efforts met with permit problems, vehicle breakdowns, even police arrest one time, within short reach of their destination. The travel ban which resulted from that arrest became a serious problem for their son who was visiting from Tanzania. Vernon barely made it out of the country.

These travel blockages complicated life on the inside, but also made John Cumbers' East African superintendency difficult. Considering the strained relations between Ethiopia and Sudan, administering the whole East Africa area from Addis Ababa was more and more difficult. Visas requested to Sudan were suspect. Former missionaries from Ethiopia who had located in Sudan, along with

---

93. The fifth book of the New Testament, Acts recounts the history of the birth of the church in the first century and records the miracles and struggles which occurred during that period.

94. Cotterell (1988), *Ethiopia*, 122.

new ones from Austria, struggled with difficulties and needed direction. In Kenya, combined ministry between the Africa Inland Church and SIM was undertaken, particularly among Somali speaking peoples who had come across into Kenya from the Ogaden and Somalia. In Nairobi, former Ethiopian missionaries were heading up a Somali language radio ministry and persevering with their translation and distribution of the Scriptures in Somali. Work among Somalis was started near their border and outreach was begun in northern Kenya to the Boranas, an ethnic group which spread over into southern Ethiopia. Considering this broad spectrum, SIM International began to plan toward moving Mr. Cumbers to Kenya to facilitate directing work in the three countries. Alex Fellows was slated to transfer from Soddo to Addis, to superintend Ethiopia.

When the Cumbers' departure time came, leaving Ethiopia was difficult. John made a diary entry in his characteristic understatement: "The Kale Heywet Church arranged a very special occasion at the Genet Hotel. It was a touching scene as they presented us with several mementos and made speeches of appreciation. May 28th was the eve of our departure for service in Kenya. We had a delightful time of fellowship at Lakew's, and the next morning Tekle came at 7:30 for an emotional farewell. We took off for Nairobi—and many new experiences."[95]

More changes came to the Cumbers in 1984. John had such broad experience that he was asked to join the International Administration at SIM Headquarters in the United States. Personal factors played a part, as well. His heart problems would also be easier to monitor there. Naomi had lost her mother with heart failure in Cleveland just that year. As their plane climbed out of Nairobi in the darkness, they thought back over their years in Africa, 35 for Naomi, 27 for John, remembering scene after scene. They thanked God for all He'd done in their lives during those traumatic but marvelous years.

FROM AMERICA, THE CUMBERS kept monitoring events in the country so near to their hearts. Ethiopia continued to have a low human rights rating. The Lutheran World Federation in Geneva, Switzerland, was bold to keep exposing the situation in Ethiopia.

---

95. Cumbers (1996), *Terror,* 248.

The Lutherans had founded the Mekane Yesus national church. *Kes* ("Priest") Gudina Tumsa, General Secretary of the Evangelical Church Mekane Yesus, was thought to still be incarcerated after four and a half years when the Lutheran World Federation news service in 1983 printed this statement:

> The military government has repeatedly claimed that there is freedom of religion in Ethiopia. But it refuses to take any responsibility for repressive measures and allows its administrators to act against the church in contradiction to its own declaration. The local administrators again escape their responsibility by referring to directives they say they have received from the provincial representatives of the Party, i.e., COPWE.[96]

These frank objections kept a small window open on Ethiopian abuses. Many Mekane Yesus believers were among those incarcerated, and key prisoners became a rallying cry for reform.[97]

Negussie, of course, was not a famous prisoner. But down at "the end of the world," a few blocks below the KHC's new property, Negussie's band of believers at the prison was growing. Tadesse Ayissa, the young man who had been delivered from electrocution at Arba Minch, turned up in Addis Ababa. For giving out Christian literature, he was sent to Kerchele prison. There he shared in the ministry with Negussie and his co-workers. These earnest believers talked personally with others and offered Bible studies when they found interest. At one point they had to separate the one Bible they had into seventy parts. During Negussie's imprisonment, some 300 came to the Lord. Thus a church—a body of believers—was established within the prison. "The Invisible Fellowship Church" they called it. It was invisible to the world, but seen no doubt with pleasure, by their heavenly Father.

Fantaye continued to work for the Ministry of Health, coming home on weekends. Times were difficult, and travel tense. Still

---

96. Cumbers (1996), *Terror*, 252, quoting *News Analysis*, October 17, 1983.

97. Ø. Eide, *Revolution and Religion in Ethiopia* (James Currey, 1996), 178 reports that the government did not admit to *Kes* Gudina's death, but in 1992, an officer who was witness to it confirmed this heroic Christian's murder (by strangling with a wire) to have been in 1979, the day after the Orthodox Patriarch Tewoflos and 38 others were killed.

unknown to her family, she made her Sunday pilgrimage to Negussie before going to the underground fellowship. She took some small package of fruit, sugar, or tea. Those few minutes allowed to them, conversing over a fence between, were the highlight of her week and his.

Sometimes the tension of being connected to a prisoner overcame her. "Don't risk your own safety," a voice would say to her. If ever she missed a Sunday, it upset Negussie terribly. Once, a thief in the prison sadistically announced to Negussie that Fantaye had married, that she was pregnant. For Negussie, trapped and powerless, even the hint of such a possibility devastated him. The days before her next visit were agony to him, questioning, waiting, praying. He longed for assurance from her own lips.

Repeatedly she mentally went over her prayer, uttered long before, for a Christian to share her life with who truly followed the Lord… and then her surprising assurance a month later the very first night of their meeting, that Negussie was the person for her. I want only the one You want for me, she told the Lord again. As week after week ticked by, and then month after month, Fantaye held on. Other suitors sought her hand. Her family became impatient with her unwillingness, wondering why a lovely and educated young woman of marrying age would not agree to some arrangement. What will happen to us? she could whisper only to God.

Eventually Fantaye was switched to a Ministry of Health office in Addis Ababa, so she began living at home all the time. As months stretched into years, her age crept forward as the seasons passed. Negussie began to chastise himself for keeping her from a woman's normal entrance into marriage and motherhood.

Will he ever be released? she wondered. One day she finally suggested, hesitatingly, "Perhaps we should let the relationship go." He realized the reasonableness of her words. Yes, he knew he should allow her that freedom. He gave it.

But back home, Fantaye could not forget his having told her once, "Like the land was given to Abraham, God has told me you are to be mine." She thought about God's promises to the Patriarchs. How sovereignly her Lord had brought Isaac and Rebecca together. She prayed, she agonized, but could not bring herself to break off this most precious relationship in their lives. How very long Jacob and Rachel waited in their days, she thought, and how long must we wait?

> *I remember my affliction and my wandering,*
> *the bitterness and the gall. I remember them,*
> *and my soul is downcast within me.*
> *Yet this I call to mind and therefore I have hope:*
> *Because of the LORD's great love we are not consumed,*
> *for his compassions never fail.*
> *They are new every morning;*
> *great is your faithfulness.*
> *I say to myself, "the LORD is my portion;*
> *Therefore I will wait for him."*
>
> *(Lamentations 3:19–24)*

Chapter 20

ENCOUNTERS ALONG THE SIDAMO ROAD

"Please," the Dilla elders implored Gerhard Bössler, "could you help us get Ato Mamo's daughter out of here?" Mastewat had run away on foot from Chuko to Dilla, terrified to be hunted by Party people. Her father's pharmacy had already been taken and he was in prison. He couldn't protect her from her tormentors. She was seventeen, and knew what they sometimes did to a young woman, unspeakable things. She well remembered the humiliation she'd borne that day when the cadres held fifty-four Wendo Genet high school students in a schoolroom for over twenty-four hours—without permitting them to relieve themselves—and then whipped them until their bladders and bowels burst. She had heard about the sexual torture methods they sometimes used. Many a young person was left too mutilated to bring forth children.

"The girl is in real danger," the elders insisted. "We know it is risky, but could you try to drive her through to Addis?" Gerhard was the one missionary left who made rounds down the road through Sidamo. His wife and sons carried on in Addis Ababa, where Edith served as nurse at the mission school. From there he made periodic trips on motorcycle or by Land Rover southward through Debre Zeit, down to Shashamane, where the road forks west to Soddo or goes on south to the Sidamo capital at Hawassa, and on past Wendo Genet and Ato Mamo's Chuko town to the larger center at Dilla. Gerhard's usual destination, actually, was Gujji territory.

Near Dilla, the Gedeos and Gujjis bordered each other—the "coffee people" as opposed to the "cattle people"—they were called. The Gedeos had been reached by the Brants with the gospel in the 1950s. The Gujjis, however, had resisted the message all along. They

MAMO BELETE (ADDIS ABABA, 1994)

had killed a number of the messengers, both national and foreign. Gerhard kept trying to find a door of entrance into Gujji hearts. He was at the time working on a water project which would benefit the Gujjis, meanwhile hunting for a key to open their eyes to their spiritual need.

Along Gerhard's route, Dilla served as an oasis where he could get gas and food, but especially he could have contact with Christians. Werku had returned to Dilla after his time at Grace Bible Institute and led the national believers' youth movement from that base. The older Christians, first generation converts in the Brants' time, were mature elders in the area by now, men like Balcha Bore, Hordofa Gidecho, and Werassa Hokotay.[98] Chuko was not far from Dilla on the way to Addis Ababa, and Ato Mamo Belete, a Wolaittan dresser trained at Soddo, was their good friend. They wanted to help this imprisoned brother's family, and his daughter was at risk.

Gerhard thought through the possibilities. He had passed the fourteen checkpoints on his route so many times that he was usually waved on without question, unless a new guard was on duty. He

---

98. Accounts of early efforts to reach the Gedeo people can be found in chapter eight of Willmott (1961), *Doors*. A more detailed and extended record is available in Brant (1992), *Wake*.

WERASSA HOKOTAY AND HORDOFA GIDECHO (DILLA, 1994)

chatted in a friendly way at the lowered barriers with the guards, and had found that his German accent raised less suspicion than an American's. He knew night travel was banned. I can't get her through during the day, and we're not supposed to drive at night, he reasoned. Finally he formed a plan and agreed to try to make it past the Chuko area where she was being hunted in the early evening.

Mastewat Mamo lay covered on the floor between the front and back seat, trembling as they drove. As the barrier was lowered in Chuko, Gerhard pulled to a stop and paused to ask if they wanted to search his car. Thanks be to God, he was waved on. When they got well past the area where she was being hunted, the fugitive moved up to the front seat. As night came on, they had to stop. It was awkward, for they dared not involve anyone else in their situation. Gerhard pulled in at Lake Langano, crawled up on the roof of the car, and left Mastewat to sleep inside. They set out at dawn and finally reached Addis Ababa. Gerhard was able to turn her over to friends at the Kolfe church near Bingham.

THE DILLA CHURCH CENTER kept having trouble. Actually, it was coffee which stirred up one tense situation. Coffee grew wonderfully in Gedeo's lush climate. This crop had profited wealthy landowners in the past, and one reason the Revolution was welcomed by the farmers was the socialists' promise of more ownership for the peasants. At that stage, they didn't realize that "ownership" would be defined collectively.

One day, two trucks roared up to the Dilla church compound gate. Their drivers hardly knew what to do next when the surveyed the scene before them. In the lane between the trucks and the storage building from which they'd come to confiscate a huge supply of coffee, lay an array of human cobblestones, mostly women and children, stretched out across their path!

"The Coffee Affair" was coming to a head that day. The believers had gathered "as one man"—in this case mostly women—to protect their sacrificial gifts from government confiscation. The women had carried this coffee on their own heads as their personal offering to the Lord Jesus, to be stored and then sold to finance a new church center on the twenty-five acres of land which had been awarded them when the government took over their former church property. The wood for building the church would come from the believers' own trees, as well. When the government had sent them notice, Ato Hordofa, one of the leading elders, had called the believers together to discuss the matter. They drew up a response: "We want it to be known that this coffee was a voluntary donation, specifically given for the building of the church, and not for the personal gain of any individual."

The day of the stand-off, Ato Kursi's wife Tsehaynesh Dori, mother of six, stood facing the trucks. Although the authorities had removed the church sign at the compound gate, she had carried it back and set it into place. "We are not afraid; we came to die," she announced to the officials. The woman knew she was undergirded by an unseen army of praying believers who had been alerted far and wide. Visible to the police were the 500–800 or so women, children, and older people spread out all over the compound, standing, praying, and singing. Rows of them lay prostrate right in the access road.

Already, Werku Gole, their towering young leader, and Balcha, seasoned chairman of the 127 Gedeo churches, had been jailed over the matter. The other leading men, like Tsehaynesh's husband, Kursi Shefeno, were being tracked down for arrest. "You are accused of planning to sell coffee on the black market," the officials had announced. "Ownership" was being redefined according to the

Encounters along the Sidamo road   255

TSEHAYNESH DORI (DILLA, 1994)

communistic principle: crops belong to all the people, not to a private farmer. The believers knew to Whom the coffee was dedicated, and were not going to let their offering go. They had collected it berry by berry from their own bushes.

When the church people wouldn't budge, the local administrator went to Werku in prison. "They are breaking the law," he insisted, and indicated that the authorities would not refrain from shedding blood. Civil disobedience on principle could only be pushed so far. The church's appeals had proved fruitless and the money wasn't worth lives. Some thought their case slightly illegal. Finally, for the sake of peace there was nothing to do but turn over the coffee. Thereby their church building fund was confiscated. It amounted to 17,000 Birr, about $8,500 US dollars, much money for Ethiopia.

This skirmish led to more confrontations in Dilla and then in Yirga Cheffe, when sister churches were closed in that town farther south. Werku stormed. Balcha (or Deyasso he was sometimes called) tried to head off these closings. Sometimes recalcitrant church members were beaten and forced out, after which cadres destroyed the buildings. Restrictions were tightened, burial services forbidden, and Christians ordered to teach that the God they worshipped did not exist. "We would rather die than deny the Lord," said Balcha. "If you were to kill us, that would bring us all the quicker into the presence of the Lord." When word of arrests came, "we somehow were able to receive this news with joy," Balcha said, "remembering that the Apostle Paul had written to the Philippians, 'It has been granted to you on behalf of Christ not only to believe on Him but to suffer for Him.'"

Werku's rebuff had been a sore point with local Party leadership. After GBI graduation, he'd roved around Ethiopia building up the youth movement. The communists recognized his potential and wanted badly to get him to lead in their cause. The man was hard to deal with—huge, pleasant, but forceful when demanding justice or making a point. When they had asked him to take Party leadership, he responded genially, "Why would a man go from higher office to lower office? Why would I go from the office of the King of Kings to just the king's office?" "He is foolish!" they roared. Putting his influence out of circulation was their next step. A car-load of soldiers from Hawassa arrived at Werku's house and took him off to the police station.

Werku was imprisoned for a while, then released. By now it was 1983. Three weeks later Hordofa and Balcha were seized, along with all the other twenty-seven elders of the Gedeo church association. The twenty-seven were separated for a time, but eventually ended up at a jail improvised in a public building by the peasants association in Wenago, fourteen kilometers south of Dilla.

Most of these elders were among those who had heard Pastor Hsueh, with Werku translating, when he'd come to Dilla in 1978 and 1979. Hordofa, a tall man with a broad face, had done some studying and had realized better than most what might be coming. Trusted in the community, he had been asked right at the beginning of the Revolution to be chair of the peasants association. Now he was being paid for his refusal. Hordofa's wide forehead is still deeply scarred from a blow which split open his skull during a torture session at Wenago.

The day it happened, the local Party secretary arrived in a drunken state. He threatened various of the twenty-seven men with a huge cudgel, among them the elderly Atara, who'd been a witch doctor before his conversion. An accompanying party member yelled at Hordofa, "Kale Heywet—renounce your faith!" Hordofa returned, "I have not believed in Kale Heywet, I have believed in Jesus Christ." The drunken Party secretary was infuriated, and crashed the club down upon Hordofa's head. It split open. Blood sprayed out so shockingly, that the drunken secretary wheeled and stumbled out.

The twenty-seven men the Party people were trying to break had already withstood great difficulties throughout the years when their church was being born. They'd experienced persecution from their own parents and neighbors in the 1950s. Before communism had come, their landlords had resisted the gospel and expelled them off of their land. They'd seen their homes and churches burned by Gujjis. The Orthodox or the government, often the same, had jailed evangelical believers before. When the communist cadres urged them to go back to their traditional culture in the 1970s, the believers had already paid the price for laying aside those practices which they'd deemed unbiblical. "The Bible *is* our culture now," Werassa put it.[99] This Marxist hurdle was just one more lap in their race.

When the elders did not recant, a new tactic was tried—removal to a more persuasive, more miserable prison, way down in the parched lowlands, about 130 miles south of Dilla. The very name "Yabello" could make chills go up the spine. At first, the men did not know where they were being taken, perhaps even to execution. In the middle of the night they were summoned outside. Soldiers went down the line of prisoners smashing rifles on their heads and bodies. They were loaded into a truck at 4 AM, bleeding and cold. Their experience that night was a strange combination of submission and triumph. Although they were helpless, a triumphant sense of being in the will of God—of being empowered by His Spirit for this test—came over the group. They began to sing.

One of the songs addressed God, and translated into English meant something like this:

---

99. Ethiopian Christians do not leave what they see as their culture's admirable features, such as their graciousness, hospitality, and people-oriented culture. What believers lay aside are bondages such as interethnic warfare, murder, polygamy, dealing with Satan through witch doctors, and worship of spirits, snakes, trees, and the like.

With one aim in view we go where you decide;
Because of your leading, night and day,
all our enemies will be overcome, so
Nothing can cause your servants to fear! [100]

THE DILLA MEN ARRIVED at Yabello prison hungry, aching, and caked with blood from beatings and dust from the open road. They expected to know no one, but were greeted warmly by two Christians brothers from Burji, the area the Fellows opened up in the 1950s, followed by the Cumbers. Aberra Wata and Tirufat Arero were young men who had been arrested when traveling to a funeral. People were forbidden to cross the borders of the peasant associations, and the two were also incriminated by the contents of their briefcase—a Bible, and a report of young people's work. "You are poisoning the minds of our youth," the official had ranted, and sent them to the police station.

Repeatedly in the days that followed, these young Burji men used threats thrown at them to challenge their attackers with meaningful considerations. "Do you know what my gun is used for?" a soldier taunted. "Yes, it can kill people," Aberra replied. "Two would be sufficient to finish off me and my friend here. If that were to happen we would be immediately transported to be with the Lord."[101] Such answers infuriated, but they were meant as a testimony which might plant a hope or a warning, even in the subconscious.

Once in jail, the artificiality of their "criminal" designation sometimes surfaced in amusing ways. A respected woman who taught in the local Yabello school suddenly became ill, then began raving. She evidenced what the community recognized as demon possession. Even the witch doctor could do nothing with her, and suggested sending for some *amanyoch* ("believers"). Few people would admit to that designation in those days, but someone suggested there were two *amanyoch* in jail. Aberra and Tirufat were fetched for a few hours. A Bible was called for and found, the gospel was read from it,

---

100. Cumbers (1995), *Joy*, 52f.
101. Confident statements like these were not based upon self-confidence, thinking oneself to be "good," but Christ-confidence. His promise to his disciples, sinful though they were, was "because I live, you shall live also" (John 14:19). Ethiopian believers meant their confidence to point to the risen Christ, whose resurrection and whose promises could be relied upon.

after which the prisoners prayed in the name of Jesus for the afflicted woman's deliverance. What takes place at a scene like this is frightening to behold, but not uncommon in Ethiopia. The *amanyoch's* prayers availed. After the violent demonic manifestations left the teacher, she admitted she'd earlier declared herself to be a Christian. She had abandoned the faith and sold herself to Satan, she said. The family was so happy about her restoration and so impressed with the miracle they'd witnessed, that they invited the prisoners to eat with them. The word of what had happened spread abroad. The next day the prison was thronged with people who wanted to see "the men with the incredible power." Of course they pointed them to the One whose power had overcome Satan.

Party officials went on accusing the two men of this crime and that. "Go away and read this," one said, putting a book in their hands. "Bring it back tomorrow and tell me what you have learned." This ruse was commonly used by people asking for a bribe. The prisoner is to return the book with money inserted, a condition for dropping the case. Of course they didn't cooperate, so eventually they were sent from Soyama prison to Yabello's. They arrived there before the Dilla men came.

At first they found the place very difficult. Aberra became ill, and almost died. The daughter of a man from Soyama who was teaching in Yabello providentially discovered them, and began to send them food. Then word came that Party leaders had studied Aberra's file and had decided that he should be executed. The Commandant announced the alternatives:

"It's either execution, or you must deny you are one of the believers." "If they execute me," Aberra returned, "I'll be immediately with the Lord." "That's what we thought you'd say," the Commandant grumbled. The matter was dropped.

Aberra had not been musically gifted, but he began to be given songs. He was amazed at this gift of composing. One of the guards, however, delighted in creating filthy parodies to the believers' songs, grieving them deeply. One evening this ugly-spirited man announced to them, "Tomorrow morning at this time you won't be in the land of the living." A few hours later, after midnight a terrific hailstorm broke out. It thoroughly frightened the prisoners and the whole town. Wind and hail wrecked several of the prison roofs, including the parodying guard's, but not Tirufat and Aberra's cell. To their surprise, higher-ups came bursting in the next morning, lashing the guard. He was stripped of his uniform and beaten before them, then put in a cell, himself. Somehow his treatment of the Christians was being blamed for the storm. Aberra and his friends begged for mercy for the man. The prison head had him beaten again, but he finally got his uniform back. Prisoners saw the elders taking the guard's part. The forgiveness demonstrated spoke volumes about the life of Christ at work in these unconventional prisoners.

Water was a big problem at Yabello. Neither destructive hail nor blessed rain was received lightly. When the Dilla men arrived, water was so scarce at that season that townspeople had only one miserable hole left and the prisoners had to send out with their own money to buy what little they could get for themselves. Three days after the twenty-seven came, a heavy rainstorm storm broke over the town, saturating the earth. "The believers have brought rain with them from Gedeo," the townspeople declared.

But the pressures upon not only the prisoners, but also on their families, were great. Under duress, eventually ten of the twenty-seven men decided to sign papers which would facilitate their release, in spite of the others' entreaties. They rationalized it this way: "Why are we fighting with our government? Abraham even said that Sara was his sister in the Bible in order to have peace with the ruling king. Elijah fled from Jezebel. Why should we bring all this trouble upon ourselves and our families?" The ten told the warden they would cease propagating the gospel. "Why ever did you come all this way to deny your faith?" asked the warden. "You could have done that in Dilla, and saved yourself a journey."

When the ten made it back home, they found that the wives of the remaining seventeen were being harassed by Dilla *kebele* leaders. "Don't complain to us about your families being destitute," they said. "Your husbands could have signed the paper and become free like the ten." However, the church was upset with those who returned. Some went to other denominations; others were eventually received back into fellowship with the Kale Heywet Church. The incident was hard to put aside.

The prison wardens started choosing Dilla men for special responsibilities when they saw the diligence with which the seventeen attacked the hard labor assigned them. Many became "trustees" and Balcha served on the prison council. Alcohol was a problem among the prisoners, causing fights and thieving and sometimes murder. The Christians began to help settle disputes. They would kneel on the floor and pour out their hearts to God for the place. "We knew that only the gospel could cure all this evil," Balcha said. "Without waiting for permission, we believers set up programs in each cell for Bible teaching." The keeper of the prison was duly impressed by the gradual change in the overall atmosphere of the prison. "He knew how the transformation had come about, and praised the elders for the careful counseling," Balcha said, "but we would have preferred that he had given the glory to God."

So it was that the believers were eventually allowed to teach freely. They constructed a temporary meeting place, and held services in the prison. When the Christians started earning a little from handicraft work, they tithed it and collected money to send to the church in Dilla for the evangelists' fund. Balcha, a man of humor, smiled at the situation. "What irony! All the churches in the countryside are closed, but the one in the prison is alive and well!"

Dilla church people had been sending someone with food for their men to Yabello every other week. They in turn shared it widely among the other prisoners, many of whom were Muslims. Few had seen such generosity in the context of a prison. When Christmas came, the Christian prisoners bought a big goat, and with special foods sent from Dilla, threw a party. Of course they told the story of Jesus. An Amhara prisoner who had once been in training for the Orthodox priesthood trusted Christ. In prison, he grew in the faith, and upon his release started a church in Yabello town.

This kind of result was typical of what was happening across Ethiopia. Prisons became preaching places, but places where the message presented could be tested for its worth in the fires of a mean but shared ordeal. Did Christ really change lives? Obviously. Few microcosms could demonstrate the truth so conclusively, as we might word it in the West. But it would be the demonstration of power which spoke best to Ethiopians—power demonstrated through natural, physical, and spiritual deliverances, and also through servanthood. The power of love shone brightly behind those prison walls, pointing needy people to the only One who could conquer hate with love.

WERKU GOLE (DILLA, 1994)

WHILE THE TWENTY-SEVEN were at Yabello, Werku Gole was doing time again in the Dilla prison. For the first six months, he wasn't allowed even to see his wife. "At first it was solitary confinement from visitors," Werku said. They feared his influence. Once Ato Tekle made a trip from Addis Ababa and was able to get in. Gerhard often came through Dilla. "When Mr. Bössler came, he wept to see me there, doing nothing," Werku said. "We talked together. The prisoners were astonished to see him weep."

Later Werku sometimes got a few words with his wife, Hallelujah, through the prison fence, with the help of people who would stand between that spot and the guardhouse line of vision. By then Hallelujah was mothering five children. Werku was thankful for his preparation for prison through Pastor Hsueh's visit to Grace Bible Institute years before. Yu Kwong had helped to prepare them for persecution, suggesting how to stand firm, and how to meet underground. He had encouraged them with testimonies of Christian leaders like Wang Ming-Dao who had suffered greatly but been spiritually victorious in China. On a later trip, Yu Kwong had visited the church in Dilla, bringing his wife. Hsueh Lily had shared with the women and her wise advice strengthened Hallelujah now.

Werku's leadership gifts couldn't go unnoticed even in prison. He was eventually allowed to teach math to prisoners. A charismatic man who spoke good Amharic, he was also chosen to make the prison announcements. God reminded him as if to say, "Look, even in prison I give you this job. You stand here in front, leading." Gerhard observed as he came and went that this work helped Werku avoid becoming demoralized.

After a year, in November of 1984, Werku was released. "Just limit your religion to your own family and keep quiet now," the communists said, but Werku would not be silenced. "How could we keep quiet?" he gestured, palms upturned. "We have to speak to other people! It's like breathing!"

Werku's prison experience helped him identify with the men down at Yabello. "I was serving them and their families. I worked on their papers. The Lord was so gracious, so kind to us. When one door is closed, the Lord opens another. The families were not left unaided. The church took the men food every fifteen days—two hundred kilometers they had to travel." The communists expected their isolation to make them give up. Eventually, Werku helped secure the release of the Yabello men. They'd been separated from their families for two years.

When they were all free again, Werku set out with enthusiasm to "outproduce" the communists. "I like the communists," he would declare openly, "for if we watch them very carefully, we can learn much from them. They are working for their ideology, and dying for it. Are we working as strongly? Are we working that hard to spread our philosophy for the good of the country? What power is behind the communists? Do we have less? No, greater! We must give our lives to proclaim our message!"

In response to Ethiopia's troubles, relief funds were coming in from abroad. Werku was good at spearheading programs. The Gedeo church instigated rural development in the form of schools, clinics, and kindergartens. Note that while all this was developing, the churches had been closed. The church had often been insulted as worthless, so Werku sent an invitation to Party leaders: "Come and see!" When the official from Hawassa went to examine the projects in the rural areas, he was amazed. "How did you get this built way up here?" he asked, incredulous. He spoke to the crowd that day, Werku remembers, something like this: "For our Mother Ethiopia we need this kind of people! We don't want just empty slogans. These people are needed. We need the working hand!"

AT THE FAR END of Gerhard Bössler's route lay Gujjiland, still almost unreached by the gospel. He could not seem to rest until the Gujjis had really had a chance to hear the gospel. Clifford Mitchell and Thomas Devers had tried to reach them in Dr. Lambie's time before the Italian invasion, but had been killed in 1935 traveling through Arsi Oromo. Gujji territory is dangerous for any "foreigner," for Gujjis kill to prove their manhood. They are known for taking the genitals from their victims as proof. First-generation evangelicals from the Burji, Amaro, and Gedeo believers had tried to befriend the wild Gujjis, but were killed or driven out. Even the military regime feared to meddle with them. As Gerhard said, "It became more and more clear to me that the Gujjis would never receive Good News from enemy territory!" He determined to raise up Gujjis to reach Gujjis, if he ever got the opportunity.

There was one Gujji who had become a Christian in the early sixties while his child was being treated at a hospital at Yirga Alem. This Ato Dembi Edina's life was transformed. He dealt in a godly manner with his unbiblical situation of having three wives. Some believed as a result of Dembi's witness, but the Gujjis burned his home down and told him to stay away. After three years living near Dilla Hospital for the treatment of a sick son, the father had been strengthen by fellowship with Gedeo Christians, and returned home to rebuild his house. He made it available as a base from which Dilla evangelists could circulate, which of course cost him in many ways, including being stoned in the marketplace. Dembi and Gerhard encouraged each other. When famine conditions threatened Ethiopia again in the early eighties, Gerhard worked on ways to get wells dug and food supplies channeled in to the Gujjis. "Food for work" programs were being offered in Ethiopia, endeavoring to help people without causing a loss of dignity or initiative. The formula had weaknesses, but it was worth a try. Gerhard began to supervise a road building project, for which crews earned food for work.

At the height of the drought, the road project meant sometimes as many as four hundred Gujjis got food for their work as the trails were being chipped out of the hillsides. The local people came to call these torturous trails "the Road of God." Its undulating red dirt route eventually became studded with groups of believers who had carved out their portion of the road with picks and shovels by day, and gathered in the night hours around campfires, where they listened to the few first-generation Gujji believers tell them about God's amazing provision of forgiveness and reconciliation.

Unknown to the Gujjis, Christians had been praying for them for decades. The light of reconciliation was beginning to shine forth further down the Sidamo road.

I revealed myself to those who did not ask for me;
I was found by those who did not seek me.
To a nation that did not call on my name, I said,
"Here am I, here am I."

(Isaiah 65:1–2)

Chapter 21

EAST AFRICA WRITHING

While Negussie's years strung out at "the end of the world," and the Dilla elders continued in prison down in Yabello, life in the outside world was about as challenging. The four horsemen of the biblical Apocalypse[102] seemed to be thundering across Ethiopia in the eighties: war and death in battles, and famine and pestilence in the provinces hardest hit by drought. The Horn of Africa was a seething pot boiling over. People streamed out into homelessness in all directions. The famine drove people toward food sources. Government resettlement schemes were turning people into internal refugees. Secret escapes over borders turned people into external refugees.

People moved east and west across those borders. Eastward, in 1981, a million Somali-speaking Ethiopian refugees out of the Ogaden strife had set up camps in barren Somalia. As the eighties progressed, Tigrayan and Eritrean refugees poured westward over the Sudanese border, fleeing displacement, famine, and war. In turn, Sudan pursued its own civil war, scattering refugees the opposite direction into Ethiopia.

Irony of ironies, the very issue which was used to bring down the Emperor came back to discredit the new rulers when their government's expensive Tenth Year Anniversary celebration overlapped the 1984 famine, now making world news. Famine had struck the Wollo Province in the north and even areas of the south. From *The Kansas City Star* we picked up on headlines at home:

---

102. See the Book of Revelation, chapter 6.

7 million Ethiopians face starvation, U.N. says

> More than 7 million Africans face death by starvation in Ethiopia, where the worst drought in a decade has left rivers bone dry and turned the nation's breadbasket into a dust bowl. [...] UNICEF said relief efforts have been hampered by rebels in Eritrea and Tigre provinces and the remoteness of many affected areas. [...] The drought, once centered in the north but now spread to the south, is considered the worst in the east African nation since 1974. More than 200,000 Ethiopians died during the 1972–74 dry spell, which indirectly led to the fall of Emperor Haile Selassie's government. [...] The Relief and Rehabilitation Commission [...] estimates that the number of people affected by drought and famine has crept up from 4.8 million to 5.2 million. [...] Ethiopia, which spends 46 percent of its budget on defense and has the largest standing army in black Africa with 250,000 troops, has denied charges it spends food aid to buy Soviet weapons.

The USA was supplying 43,000 metric tons of grain. Appeals from World Vision and other aid agencies brought shocking images into American living rooms (between juicy hamburger commercials), pictures viewers remembered from a decade before. "Ethiopia" was becoming synonymous with disease, despair, and death. But our family still saw it as a lovely land full of vibrant life, although mortally threatened.

IN MID JUNE 1984, a phone call came to my husband in Kansas. "Charles, the famine is worsening in Ethiopia. SIM has asked us to locate an emergency medical team. Could you get free for a couple of months and go—immediately?" Emmanuel International was rounding up medical workers for a project in southern Ethiopia—near Soddo, our first Ethiopian home. Missions in Ethiopia were hard-put to staff feeding programs, since missionaries were virtually quarantined and weren't allowed to increase their personnel. They turned to aid agencies for short-term volunteers. Charles did go out with an Emmanuel team of seven, most of whom were old SIMers who were thankful to get this opportunity to serve in Ethiopia again. Since the governmental blockage of permanent visas, staying long was not possible, but relaying people in on three-month visitors' visas allowed short windows of opportunity.

Getting back to the Soddo area after a decade under the Marxist heel, the team became painfully aware of the burial of so much that had been—the bustling mission schools, the busy Soddo Hospital and medical training program, the outstation clinics, and of course the burgeoning Wolaitta churches. The very earth had dried up. A feeding station was created in the lowlands, where the team set up camp. The volunteers must keep their distance from the Wolaitta believers, who now would come under suspicion if they fraternized with foreigners.

THE TEAM HEARD ABOUT one last triumph for local believers before the mass church closure the year before. This oldest of the southern churches for forty-four years had held annual Spiritual Life Conferences at Soddo. Great numbers came, and great blessing was poured out. Although the local government administrator warned that he would not give permission for the conference in 1983, the leading elders declared they would proceed as usual. Nearly 10,000 people arrived the first day, a shock to the administrator, who promptly drove over to the church compound with a police escort, arrested three leaders, and took them to town.

Accompanied by five carloads of soldiers, the elders were sent back to dismiss the crowd. It was a massive although peaceful assemblage, with people seated on the ground, mostly clothed in the brilliant white of the national costume, the scene dotted with the bright scarves of women. Hands went up all over the assembly, objecting to the order to disperse. "Muslims are allowed to meet, Orthodox Christians are allowed to meet, what's different about our wanting to meet without hindrance?" a spokesman challenged. "You see these women with children in their arms. They and the rest of us will rather die than give up the right to worship God. We'll face your guns. Shoot us in the front; we won't turn our backs to you!" The crowd raised their Bibles in the air and echoed their spokesman's challenge: "We will continue to worship God. You have your guns, but our Bibles are more effective weapons."

Deterred temporarily, the authorities left but returned the next day, only to find even more people gathered. It seemed that those in attendance the previous day had been joined by people who had at one time made a profession of faith, but for one reason or another had not stood firm. During the night there had been a tremendous heart-searching on the part of those present. With loud weeping, hundreds of backsliders confessed their sins and now stood with the other believers to demand that they should enjoy freedom of religion like the Muslims and Orthodox. In the end, the administrator removed his soldiers. The day went down as a victory for the church, and a witness to the watching community.

But retaliation did not linger long. All 738 of the Wolaitta churches were soon sealed in a day. Even house meetings were banned. Only underground activities were left to the evangelicals.

EMMANUEL'S FEEDING CAMP, one under SIM / KHC's care allotment, was located about 40 kilometers from Soddo, down towards a lake known for its hippos. In the distance the outline of Humbo Mountain could be seen, home of Ato Wandaro Dabaro, a beloved patriarch among the first Wolaitta believers. He had been imprisoned by the Italians. Now younger Christian leaders who grew up on that mountain were among those being periodically imprisoned, as was Wandaro, again, himself.

During Charles' tenure that summer of 1984, other ex-missionaries or their sons or daughters filtered in from Canada, Australia, and the United States. It was like a family reunion! But the rest of the family were not well. Some 10,000 Wolaittans were affected badly enough to need supplementary feeding, which was organized in twenty-five locations. People were hungry and dying and crying out to God.

Veteran missionary nurses know how to run a tight ship and the Emmanuel camp was cited as one of the best. No water was available. It had to be hauled in for everything. "At first, silence was the key to grasping the condition of the camp's children," Charles said. "It was like a cancer ward when we started. But after just a week of feedings, children's voices began to be heard—they began playing a little, as children will. Then we knew we were winning."

When our family had been stationed at Soddo Hospital almost twenty years before, Charles operated more often on bowel obstructions than on any other condition. The blockage struck many in a certain season and was caused from eating raw corn. That summer of 1984, a man came to the feeding camp obstructed, but the camp had no operating room. Charles risked driving him to Soddo Hospital, now staffed by Cubans. It was night, and they found no doctors on duty. Charles and an Ethiopian relief worker got the man into a bed. Spontaneously without thinking, Charles raised his voice and called out in a voice the ward could hear, *"Wosanah!"* The word had remained in his mind, for it was often used in the hospital in former days to call Wolaittans to pray. Now the term was forbidden. Nevertheless, others did join in prayer with Charles and his helper. (Some days later Charles got word that the patient miraculously survived without surgery.)

The two slipped out of hospital, so run down now, and started to drive back to camp in the darkness. Charles allowed himself one swing down the road past our old home—Dr. Scheel's before us, and others after us. The front room window was uncurtained, and on the wall above a dim lamp a huge photo stared out: Che Guevara, hero of the Cuban revolution.

During the summer of 1984, Ato Fancho's evangelist son came down to speak about Jesus to those who came for grain. Go'iso was barefooted, and being blind, easily hurt his feet. How pleased Charles was to be able to give him a pair of his boots. Later, Charles got a chance to visit Go'iso's sister Marta's home. Marta, a student on the campus, had cared for our children when we'd first come to Soddo. She had become my closest Soddo friend. It was Go'iso and Marta's father, Ato Fancho, whose church the cadre had tangled with, the cadre who fell into a drunken stupor and was eaten by hyenas.

Across the lake from the feeding center lay Gujjiland. The government decided to forcibly resettle Wolaittans suffering from drought over there, but the Gujjis were a frightening community among whom to dwell. Their fear would prove to be well founded.

Christians were pondering the underlying reason for the famine, struggling to see the hand of God in the situation. How should they pray? "Some see it as a judgment upon the church," we were told, "some as the rise of evil and the resultant neglect of God's people, some as an incentive for the nation to return to God." Charles was struck by the stark encounter he'd seen with the realities of Romans 8:35, "Who shall separate us from the love of Christ? Shall trouble or hardship or persecution or famine or nakedness…?" Psalm 33:18–19 meant much to the community: "But the eyes of the Lord are on those who fear him, on those whose hope is in his unfailing love, to deliver them from death and keep them alive in famine."

Back in Addis Ababa on his way home in August, Charles compared notes with other famine workers at the mission headquarters. By then, John Cumbers had moved to Kenya, and then on to the United States, and Alex Fellows was directing the Ethiopian field. "Uncle Charlie" was disappointed not to have touched bases with our old friend, Sahle. Later Sahle told him that in this case, God had protected them from meeting. Great pressures were being put on the Pente teacher and his wife Aberash in Debre Zeit just then. Being seen with a foreigner would have surely meant his arrest.

Back home, Charles poured out the story to our family. His most enduring image was a little boy beside the road to the feeding camp who solemnly waved to the famine workers day by day. He never seemed to come to the camp. Later Charles wondered, was he too weak to make it? He could not forget the little sentinel who did what he could.

THE PROBLEMS OF RELIEF work in the north were more complex, for there it was impeded by war-zone dangers and the cutting of supply lines. Ethiopian forces attacked inland truck routes and the seaport, where tons of food aid intended for the north were intercepted and commandeered. "Reports persisted of EEC [European Economic Community] grain intended for Ethiopia being simply trans-shipped at the Ethiopian port of Massawa into a Russian vessel, to pay for Russian munitions," reported Peter Cotterell in his analysis of the causes of the catastrophe.[103]

Already the government had put "villagization" into effect, forcing peasants to move from their scattered homes into planned villages, supposedly to cluster them around more easily delivered community services, but ones which rarely materialized. By the end of 1988, over twelve million people were reportedly relocated in villages in twelve of the fourteen administrative regions of the country.[104] Villagization was criticized as simply a method of facilitating the regime's control over the population, cutting rebels off from

---

103. See Cotterell (1988), *Ethiopia*, 151.
104. See Ofcansky and Berry (1993), *Ethiopia,* 85.

peasant support, and discouraging dissident movements.[105] Many became refugees rather than be villagized. In the Harerge region of the Ogaden, 33,000 fled to Somalia.[106]

Whether this tactic of forced resettlement of people from famine areas was designed to improve food possibilities or to break up centers of protest was not clear. In 1985 and 1986 about 600,000 were uprooted from their home villages and farms by the military and deposited in various areas of the south.

Conflict escalated between Eritrean insurgents and the Mengistu regime. Sudan was amazingly gracious about hosting more and more "guests." By early 1985, more than 300,000 refugees from the drought or war had arrived on Sudanese soil. Meanwhile, the opposite situation occurred in the south of both countries, where thousands of Sudanese refugees fleeing the conflict between the Sudanese regime and the Southern People's Liberation Front had come over the border into western Ethiopia.

In May of 1985, Charles received another call from Emmanuel International, this time for a rescue operation involving Ethiopians in Sudan. The government resettlement schemes were proving disastrous, for whole populations were being dumped in areas that were strange to them, and without the start-up tools and supplies they would desperately need. I sent out a postcard to friends which said:

> Prayer alert, please. Charles had another quick request and left May 9th, this time for Sudan. About 1500 Ethiopians had come across the Sudanese border from the uninhabitable tsetse fly belt, where they government had "resettled" them. They wandered across the border into a civil war zone, and are about to be cut off by the rains. Sudan's government asked Emmanuel to send a doctor and nurse to escort these people (ill with sleeping sickness and malaria) north to the safer and more supplyable refugee camps. [...] Try to "wear the shoes" of these displaced people—widowed, orphaned, ill, hungry, and bereaved—some Muslim, some Marxist, some Christian. [...] Sudan is struggling for stability after a coup, has its own hunger problem, and is flooded with refugees.

---

105. Ofcansky and Berry (1993), *Ethiopia,* 86. See also R. Kaplan, *Surrender or Starve* (Westview Press, 1988), 120.

106. Ofcansky and Berry (1993), *Ethiopia,* 88.

How could we get people to identify with a situation so removed from our western affluence? We had worked in Sudan in 1977–79, and could picture the situation and the terrain. We could well remember the fiery sting of the tsetse fly, which we'd experienced in closed-cab travel through the Sudan. These Tigrayan refugees were on foot. The swampy *sudd* of Sudan is impassable for months, when the rains come. Up north, the camps were dry, though bleak. At least they were supplyable, hence the plan to move people north quickly. Tigrayans back in the homeland were harder to supply. In fact, food aid delivery was so blocked when routed inland from the east coast of Ethiopia, that whatever was to get through to Eritrea or Tigray had to be trucked in from the west through Sudan.

We understood little about the Tigrayan people at that juncture, except that their rebel forces were becoming more and more threatening to the Ethiopian government. We hardly had noticed that Ethiopia's ancient Axumite dynasty had been seated in Tigray Province. Tigray lay just below the Eritrean Province. The two were "cousins" who shared a common vernacular language, Tigrinya, instead of the Amhara's Amharic. The Eritrean insurgency had begun in the 1960s, but the Tigray People's Liberation Front (TPLF) did not form until 1975. The TPLF demanded social justice and self-determination for all Ethiopians.[107] The Eritrean–Ethiopian War dragged on for years. In spite of Ethiopia's military aid from the Soviet Union and its allies, the insurgents could not seem to be beat. In the early eighties, Eritrean and Tigrayan insurgents began to cooperate, the Eritrean People's Liberation Front providing training and equipment which helped to escalate the TPLF into a full-fledged fighting force.

Moving Tigrayans into the inhospitable tsetse fly belt in western Ethiopia turned them into wandering refugees struggling to get away from the death trap where they were left.

The team which Charles worked with received truck loads of parched and exhausted Tigrayans who were brought into the bare camp, just a flat field with nothing to offer but grain, water, plastic buckets and tin cooking pots. Thorn trees offered little shade, for their leaves were gone, and the heat was intense for anyone, especially people accustomed to the Ethiopian highlands. Each little

---

107. See Ofcansky and Berry (1993), *Ethiopia*, 60.

group—families had been decimated—gathered rocks for their cooking fire. Fareed, a Sudanese graduate from Grace Bible Institute in Ethiopia years ago, directed the proceedings from a tin shed which served as both office and clinic.

But in the big refugee camp whose stick houses could be seen just beyond the new arrivals, cholera had broken out. That news was terrifying. Had the Tigrayan wanderers been torn from their homes, moved south, wandered west, and been trucked north, for this vast U-turn only to lead to death anyway? Would they do better to face armed violence at home, than death in this desert?

Charlie was barely getting acclimated himself when the team was caught by total surprise. Early one evening, just as the sun was dimming, the team noticed massive movement, but little sound. They went to check, and found the whole Tigrayan community standing at attention. All their meager supplies were gathered up and hung on walking sticks over their shoulders. Without a word, in a long file they turned their faces east and headed into the darkening desert. Only tin clinked and babies cried. They had made their choice. Relief workers wept. Who made it home, the foreigners would never know, nor what of "home" was left.

Perhaps the price people were paying in situations like these explains why the Tigray People's Liberation Front surprised the world six years later by persevering southward again, this time to the very capital, to expel Mengistu's government.

Woe to those who make unjust laws,
to those who issue oppressive decrees, to deprive the poor of their rights
and withhold justice from the oppressed of my people,
making widows their prey and robbing the fatherless.
What will you do on the day of reckoning,
when disaster comes from afar?
To whom will you run for help?
Where will you leave your riches?

(Isaiah 10:1–3)

Chapter 22

THE "BLACK JEW" ENIGMA

While the Four Horsemen of Revelation were thundering over Ethiopia in the early eighties, a secret operation known only to the participants was being organized. It happened close to where Charles watched the Tigrayan refugees rise up as one man and head eastward to Ethiopia, a few months before.

Operation Moses was a drama reminiscent of the Hebrews' exodus out of Pharaoh's Egypt. This modern exodus, over 3,000 years later, was out of Muslim Sudan. Some 8,500 "black Jews" from an ancient community in Ethiopia had escaped from their homeland and had since been languishing in Sudanese refugee camps. These "black Jews" were called Falashas, but *Beta Israel* ("House of Israel") was their preferred title.

Their exodus would spirit them to Israel, not on foot, but by air. Journalist Ruth Gruber paints the scene the first night of the mass escape starting in 1984. Picture 250 tattered refugees, some not yet born and some barely alive, packed into four busses after dark and driven from their refugee camp near Gedaref to Sudan's capital at Khartoum.

> Midnight. The busses pulled over to the back entrance of the international airport and waited. Shortly after 1 A.M., the 707 landed. The busses rolled up to the tarmac. The people spilled out. Mothers carried their babies beneath their *shammas* in pouches on their backs. Nearly naked children clung to adults' hands. Precariously, they mounted the stairs. Inside the plane, kindly Belgian stewardesses helped them fasten their seat belts. A doctor moved among them, prepared for any emer-

gency. At 2:40 A.M., the engines roared, the plane raced along the runway, and flew into the African sky. Operation Moses was underway. It was dawn, November 22. Thanksgiving Day.[108]

All this had to be kept under wraps as the operation continued, load after load. Flights dared not be scheduled from Sudan to Israel, so transfers were made in Europe. Diverse collaborators were at risk in this whole process: Jews from Israel, Europe, and the United States who were engineering it, Presidents Mengistu of Ethiopia and Nimeiry of Sudan who were looking the other way, and the refugees themselves, desperate for its completion. People who knew about Operation Moses were beside themselves either with uneasiness, impatience, or exaltation.

The refugee camps of Sudan at that point reportedly held some 400,000 refugees, a mixture of Jews, Christians, Muslims, and primal groups. The Operation's hope was for the roughly nine thousand Jews interred to be selected out from the others and carried safely into Israel by mid-January, 1985. This vast movement was fired by the compelling plight of the Ethiopian Jews in famine-decimated Ethiopia, further fueled by Israel's passionate call for *aliya* (immigrate to Israel, literally "going up"). Jews from all over the world had been returning to their avowed homeland since the establishment of the State of Israel in 1948.

The Derg had little sympathy for a religiously-oriented community of any kind. Past rulers had forbade the Jews to own land, resulting in the pejorative name *Falasha* which meant "landless one" or "foreigner," even though their roots in Ethiopia apparently predated Christian ones. Some say the word was coined to designate Arabian Jewish immigrants in the Christian era.[109] Once estimated at half a million, the population of Beta Israel was thought in the 20th century to number about 28,000.[110] Although a handful had in recent years trickled out secretly, Chairman Mengistu, like his predecessor, barred emigration. If he were to let the Jews leave, he may have reasoned, tens of thousands of Christians and Muslims would take it as a precedent for their getting out too. In the wake of the 1984 disaster, with NBC exposing the famine and aid pouring in from the

---

108. Gruber (1987), *Rescue*, 168.
109. See Parfitt (1985), *Operation*, 18.
110. Gruber (1987), *Rescue*, 9.

West, the secret flight of thousands was embarrassing to Ethiopia's government, especially the huge Jewish exodus. Of course, once out, most refugees were stuck over a border with no place to go. "Of the thousands who had fled to the camps in Sudan, the Jews were the only ones who had a place to go—Israel—anathema to the Communist regime," as Ruth Gruber put it.[111]

Mengistu needed funds and arms for his own purposes. Military expenditures were a constant drain, and celebrations for the 10th anniversary of the Revolution would be costly—$100 million as it was later reported.[112] It would seem that Mengistu traded the Falashas for hidden benefits supplied through Israel.[113] Israel was paying heavily to redeem Beta Israel. The initial costs for the Ethiopian exodus plus the first year of absorption was estimated at $100 million. The United Jewish Appeal in America was expected to raise $60 million of that, and actually brought in $65 million.[114]

American Jews, especially the American Association for Ethiopian Jews were less patient than other advocacy groups. Too early, a leak occurred in Israel and was picked up and announced by the *New York Times* on January 4th: "Israel Has Airlifted 10,000 Ethiopians." Other newspapers responded with their own headlines. "Bravo, Israel!" the London *Sun* applauded. "Israel alone" wrote the *British Sunday Express*, "was capable of plucking a whole people from the nightmare of the Ethiopian famine with such brilliant elan." The *Guardian* editorialized:

> There are no lengths to which Israel will not go to protect its people, as in the raid on Entebbe, or to avenge them, as in the capture of Eichmann. No other country would have had the nerve, and the total indifference to international niceties, to grab many thousands of people from the mountains of East Africa and fly them to another continent.[115]

---

111. Gruber (1987), *Rescue*, 10.
112. Gruber (1987), *Rescue*, 162.
113. Ofcansky and Berry (1993), *Ethiopia*, 300 says, "In 1985 Tel Aviv reportedly sold Addis Ababa at least US $20 million in Soviet-made munitions and spare parts captured from Palestinians in Lebanon. According to the EPLF, the Mengistu regime received US $83 million worth of Israeli military aid in 1987, and Israel deployed some 300 military advisers to Ethiopia."
114. Gruber (1987), *Rescue*, 185.
115. Gruber (1987), *Rescue*, 188.

Sudan's Nimeiry could no longer shut his eyes; he canceled the airlift.[116] Fear swept through those left behind. Israel's distraught Prime Minister assured the stranded remnant that Israel would leave no stone unturned to save them. Jewish leadership in the United States got the ear of President Bush, who was on his way to Africa. He met with Nimeiry, who agreed to a quick completion of the rescue under complete blackout, with "considerations." The $15 million in aid to Sudan which the USA had been withholding was propitiously released.

Americans played the major role now, Charles and I later learned. Of course, the Jewish presence is large in America. We gleaned clues to their motivation through an insight shared by an American researcher studying Falasha liturgy and music in the seventies. She had contact with American Jews who came repeatedly during the earlier famine to Ethiopia to bring aid, while secretly working toward facilitating immigration to Israel.

> I liked many of these people personally and came to understand better their almost fanatical commitment to the Beta Israel. Several alluded to guilt over the inability of the American Jewish community to save European Jewry during the Holocaust. The Falasha cause, they felt, was a rare opportunity to in some way compensate for that earlier tragedy, a chance to rescue Jewish lives in jeopardy. Others had been activists in the American civil rights movement. Disillusioned by black radicalism in the 1960s, they had come to view the Ethiopian Jews as a cause that demonstrated their commitment to radical equality.[117]

Thus Operation Sheba, an attempt to complete the partly aborted airlift, presented American Jews with a golden opportunity. "The rescue of the remaining refugees was nearly an all-American operation," Gruber reveals, tracing the intricacies of cooperation between American, Sudanese, and Israeli agencies as C-130s ferried planeloads from Gedaref every half hour, flying directly to a military airport outside Eilat in Israel.[118]

Informed by background in the Bible and the Ethiopian epic, we

---

116. See Gruber (1987), *Rescue*, 213f. Actually Nimeiry was deposed in April of 1985. His Vice President was served a life sentence over the Operation Moses affair.
117. K. Shelemay, *A Song of Longing* (Univ. of Illinois Press, 1991), 147.
118. See Gruber (1987), *Rescue*, 190.

read between the lines, mulling over the rescue's significance. The event echoed back to King Solomon's seed, traditionally said to be given to the Queen who received "all her desire" (1 Kings 10:13), plus the stolen Ark, supposedly spirited off to Ethiopia. Symbolically it was as if Sheba were making another journey to Israel, bringing back Solomon's progeny, her most priceless gift. Surely Zionistic and nationalistic overtones competed. Had the royal seed been ransomed back 3,000 years later... or stolen from the homeland of the unique nation which claimed guardianship of the Ark? Or a third possibility, was this modern exchange, as materialists would say, simply a matter of economics?

THE JEWS OF ETHIOPIA belong in the Christian story for historical, spiritual, practical, and eschatological reasons. Their interwoven importance in Ethiopia's whole saga emerges out of past and present history. Their future bears watching, as well.

Skipping over earlier Falasha history to the 20th century, we find that Zionism abroad played a major role in Beta Israel's "displacement," or "return"—two ways of looking at the situation today. Soon after Haile Selassie's reconquest of Ethiopia in 1941, the era of Zionism flowered, including growing interest in the "black Jews." Efforts to gain *aliya* status were made. In 1975, the Chief Rabbis concurred in ruling that the Jews of Ethiopia were eligible for Israeli citizenship under the Law of Return. Ethiopia's new government forbade immigration. Like everyone else, Beta Israel was caught in the malaise of the Revolution, the dangers of the Eritrean–Ethiopian War, and the extremities of the famine. As Jews on the outside presented it, "Caught between government and anti-government forces, threatened by deteriorating security and a declining economy, the Beta Israel endured repeated atrocities in the mid 70s and early 80s."[119] Steeled by a host of "atrocity" memories, Jews abroad thought in terms of deliverance. They strategized. Of course non-Jewish Ethiopians in even larger numbers suffered similar atrocities, but they had few advocates and found no corporate way of escape.

So it was that mysteriously, some 10,000 Falashas abandoned their villages to make the torturous month-long trek to Sudan. Along the

---

119. Shelemay and Berger (1986), *Jews*, 23.

way, it is estimated that probably 1,000 perished from hardships at the hand of nature and men, whether bandits, Ethiopian troops, or Sudanese border guards. Of those who reached the camps alive, it is estimated that 2,000 to 3,000 Falashas died there from dehydration and disease while waiting for passage to Jerusalem.[120]

Such was the situation on the eve of Operation Moses. "It surely deserves a place in history," said Israel's Chaim Rosen, "along with other spectacular rescue operations that have been carried out by the Israelis since the founding of the State. The rescue involved sorting out some 7,000–8,000 Jews from among approximately half a million Christian refugees in a Muslim country that had no official diplomatic relations with Israel."[121] Three of "Abraham's sons" (Galatians 3:6–9), Christian, Muslim, and Jew, again intertwined!

We wonder what the significance of this event might be in God's eyes. After all these centuries, who could have foreseen the mass exodus accomplished by Operation Moses? Who but the eternal One, the God of Israel!

> *Ah, land of whirring wings which is beyond the rivers of Ethiopia,*
> *which sends ambassadors by the Nile,*
> *in vessels of papyrus upon the waters!*
> *Go, you swift messengers,*
> *to a nation, tall and smooth-skinned,*
> *to a people feared near and far,*
> *a nation mighty and conquering,*
> *whose land the rivers divide.*
> *All you inhabitants of the world, you who dwell on the earth,*
> *when a signal is raised on the mountains, you will see it,*
> *and when a banner is raised on the mountains, look!*
> *When a trumpet is blown, hear! [...]*
>
> *At that time gifts will be brought to the LORD of hosts*
> *from a people tall and smooth-skinned,*
> *from a people feared near and far, a nation mighty and conquering,*
> *whose land the rivers divide,*
> *to Mount Zion, the place of the name of the LORD of hosts.*
>   *(Isaiah 18:1–3, 7; RSV)*

---

120. Shelemay and Berger (1986), *Jews*, 77.
121. Shelemay and Berger (1986), *Jews*, 79.

Part VI

PRAYING WITH ALL PRAYER

(During 1985–89)

*And pray in the Spirit on all occasions
with all kinds of prayers and requests.
With this in mind, be alert and always keep on praying
for all the Lord's people.*

(Ephesians 6:18)

Chapter 23
FREE!

"Come to celebrate! Negussie has been freed!" Fantaye could hardly believe the message. "Come to celebrate?" Yes, yes, the community always greeted freed prisoners, sharing thanksgiving and praise. "Negussie has been freed?" Yes, no, yes, she thought, could it be that our prayers have finally been answered? Could it be that we will next face each other with no fence between?

Fantaye trembled as she approached Negussie's sister's home. Almaz still did not know about Fantaye's relationship with her brother. Negussie! He will be inside. How will I ever melt into the stream of visitors who will come all day to greet him? Can the weight of feeling between us be kept invisible?

People took their turns praising God and greeting the released prisoner. Her turn finally came. Fantaye found herself weeping as they embraced. It was alright, everybody embraced in Ethiopia. It was alright, everybody cried at such moments of emotion. It was alright, their secret could be kept.

Fantaye's life would take on a whole new pattern! No more Sunday trips to the prison. No more praying, When? she wondered. Well, not when the release, now it was when find a job, when be able to...? No, we must not think too far ahead. Negussie must build up his strength. Ex-prisoners have to learn to live in freedom again. They are still suspect. Work is hard to find even for people with no mark against them. How will Negussie support himself? Let alone anyone else...

But there was hope! There were times together! Had God not had been faithful every step of the way? Surely He could be counted upon during these special days, and for their future!

NEGUSSIE BEGAN TO MOVE around Addis, acquainting himself with how the city's life had changed out there beyond him those six years. Now he could stand outside the police station where he'd first been incarcerated in Addis near the Piazza. He could stand where Fantaye had stood, but he could look into the foreboding building with x-ray eyes, picturing the layout, identifying with the prisoners, smelling the very stench of the place. But Negussie was free. He could pay a visit to his old community, the "Invisible Fellowship Church" down at the "End of the World," his second Addis prison home for so long, but he was free to leave again. He revisited his old haunts, dropping in at the mission headquarters, the compound where the Colemans had lived, and the former academy where he'd once worked. The buildings were largely unchanged, but much had happened to people in his absence. Most of all, he had changed. He'd suffered, grown, shared life with people and in places unknown to his old friends, and in it all, he had found the Lord to have been his most faithful friend.

And Fantaye? She had been there with him as best she could. She was a bridge to his past and a bridge to his future. For the present, they still had much living and learning to do together in the now which was suddenly available to them.

He found Pastor Kedamo's Meserete Heywet church to be teeming with activity, offered a joyful opportunity for worship, fellowship, and service. The Girls Christian Academy as he had known it when he worked there had been phased out. At the mission, John Cumbers had gone and Alex Fellows had come up from Soddo to take his role.

Out at the Press, Negussie's old friends, the Colemans, had gone home to Canada. How he longed to see his beloved friend, John. The adjacent language school was still in operation. A few new people were being allowed into the country, so classes had to be arranged for them as well as for returning missionaries who needed refresher courses. After six months without work, Negussie began as an "informant," as they called an individual tutor at the language school. Students loved him. He treated them professionally, but was such a warm, cheerful fellow, that they may not have realized what he'd been through. Sometimes they would tease him about being a bachelor. He would smile, and say little in response to that subject.

War and famine and poverty swirled around outside of Addis Ababa, but the city was supplied. Government-controlled media reported some of the conditions, but state-censored news was often manipulative, and could be falsified. One might hear a truer report from BBC. What could not be hidden in Addis Ababa was the ever-increasing influx of the wounded into hospitals, the homeless setting up more and more plastic hovels on the streets, and the increasing number of street children begging at stop lights.

At the new KHC property close to Kerchele Prison, more and more railroad cars which had brought in supplies now lined the courtyard, having been converted to storage for equipment or office space for Community Development administration. The famine which had arisen in 1984 had not abated. Aid organizations focused more and more activity on Ethiopia. Hussein worked with KHC, and his wife, Belaynesh, was working in the World Vision office. The expatriate organizations could ship in the food, but efficient and fair distribution depended upon trustworthy nationals. Eventually Negussie decided to respond to the cry for help in the famine.

Once he had told Fantaye, "I have no wealth, not much knowledge, but I have Jesus Christ in my heart, so I have everything, really. This is all I can offer you." His wealth had not increased in prison, and establishing a home would take money. Again, they must wait. Before he left Addis Ababa, they let their families know about their hope to someday marry. Fantaye's parents were not pleased. The matter would take time—time to win her family's favor and time to afford a wedding. Meanwhile, Negussie would serve where he could. He signed on with World Vision, and was sent to Sokota, a town hundreds of miles north of the capital. Once again, Fantaye was out of reach. This time the vast expanse of the awesome Simien Mountains separated the two.

NEGUSSIE'S FIRST SIGHT OF Sokota emerged from below their Twin Otter as it approached a steep-sided butte. Like everything in the Simien Mountains, this landform was huge. A space photo of the wrinkled face of this vast terrain would show Sokota to be on the north–south road, halfway between Lalibela and Mekelle, capital of the Tigray Province. Across the mountains to the west, Lake Tana gleams, and to the east, the escarpment drops off abruptly into the

Danakil desert. Seeing the butte's drop off at the end of the landing strip, a passenger couldn't help fearing, how will we stop in time?

The World Vision feeding center was located west of the Dessie–Asmara Road midway between Wollo and Tigray Provinces. Negussie learned that over the mountains to the south was Lalibela, with its 12th century rock churches. To the west were the Falasha settlements—their population cut in half since the "Operation Moses" exodus to Israel. Whom should Negussie find to be the administrator in charge but the Sahle who had recently been a school director near Debre Zeit. As they spent time together, Negussie learned some of what had been going on in Sahle's life.

WHILE NEGUSSIE HAD BEEN in prison in Addis Ababa, Sahle had felt like a prisoner himself in his job at Dukem. Aberash managed her math teaching with less problems than Sahle, who had a higher profile as an administrator. Agitation to get rid of him had risen to a fever pitch in 1984. He was accused of "sowing a foreign commodity," and he was called to the Party office. The night before the appointment Sahle and Aberash pondered over their predicament. "I must be happy if they put me in prison, and be thankful to the Lord," he reminded them both. Aberash assured him she was proud of his faith, and encouraged him to be bold and not ashamed.

At the Party office, he was asked questions like, "Aren't you a follower of this newcomer religion? What about your bringing this into the school?" They quizzed him about his political consciousness. Sahle had a fairly clear knowledge of Marxism-Leninism. "I know it, I'm not ignorant of it," he insisted, challenging them in return.

Then a higher Party leader came and 4,000 people were assembled in a big warehouse for a meeting called to expose the "Pentes." After *kebele* reports, the harangue began. The ordeal lasted hours—from nine to three.

"What are the characteristics of this newcomer religion?" the leader asked. Response: "It fools students, tells them not to fight, to throw guns down and pray. They say if we pray, money will come through the roof of the house. But the Orthodox go to war and even take the *tabot* (replica of the Ark). They are patriots! This new religion is the opposite. Our school director invites students by night and indoctrinates them. He is our enemy! We can't separate him from the imperialists!"

Sahle had long had the habit of trusting God with childlike faith. He observed the vicissitudes of his own life with amusement, as if looking in from the outside. Here's how he tells the story of this occasion when he was squirming in the hot seat:

"I was fanning myself, sitting in the audience. Today I'm going to get it, I thought. Then I noticed I was fanning myself with a magazine… oh, oh…*Guideposts Magazine*. I thought, I can't swallow it! I can't throw it down. I brought my own evidence! I tell you I was really sweating.

"Aberash was not there in the meeting. She was at home trying to braid our daughter's hair. The Holy Spirit urged her to stop and go and pray. She did, for one hour. Then she tried to do the hair again. Again the Spirit seemed to say to pray about Sahle. She couldn't have peace, so she prayed another hour.

"Students were assigned to make accusations. 'He's done this, done that,' went on and on. 'Have him go to Marxist discussions,' was a recommendation. 'No,' they threw back, 'he knows, he's denied Marxism as a science. We can't say he's ignorant. You try to convince him!'"

The meeting ended with Sahle being condemned and publicly cursed aloud. After that, he had to move the family off the school compound. It was the rainy season and two of their five children had the measles. After managing that resettling with difficulty, they were told to move again. Alas, next Sahle was put in jail at the *kebele* prison. "It was really very funny," as he recalls it. "It was a shock for the town, having the principal sleeping on the ground in jail just when grade six and eight exams were given, and report cards were due. I had to pay bail and get out just to get my reports done!"

Things went from bad to worse. Where to live next? A Christian couple in Debre Zeit kindly offered the family of seven their small service house—two narrow rooms, one about nine foot square, the other slightly larger, with the usual cooking shed outside. Sahle loaded up their goods and settled the family there. They enrolled their children in the Debre Zeit schools. Meanwhile Sahle had to walk ten kilometers (6.2 miles) a day to work at Dukem. Next the educational and *kebele* officers decided to strip Sahle of his principalship. They arranged to send him to a common teacher's job at a small school in a distant area. He'd been director at Dukem for four years, where he'd directed two shifts of grades one to eight. "I tell you, we were broken into pieces. We'd just paid school fees for our own children to start the new term in Debre Zeit in September. How many times more with no house, no position? we wondered. We were utterly broken."

They went to appeal the matter to the *awraja* education office. Aberash was weeping as she faced the man in charge:

"If you can't decide the truth—if your decision is illegal and not right—then our heavenly Father will make the right decision," she flatly stated.

"It's Sahle's mistake," the manager said.

"How so?" she retorted.

"He didn't register as a Party member!"

"I'm very glad he isn't a registered member," she returned.

"Aberru (his loving nickname for her), let it be," Sahle hushed her. "Please cool down, relax, take it easy. It's not the end of our life!"

One Party man saw the truth of the situation and tried to intercede for them, but the thing was left hanging in the air.

In Debre Zeit, believers from a number of church groups were praying for this beleaguered couple, including Girma, Teshome, and Solomon's families, the Air Force officers whose homes sheltered the underground church and Bible school. Very soon, out of the blue, an unexpected message came. Sahle was asked to work with World Vision, and to start in two weeks! Had he been the Dukem director, getting a "free letter" would have been difficult. Jobless, he was free to go. God had turned the tables!

Sahle was not one to hold a grudge and he could always see the humor in a situation. "When I began working for World Vision in the south, I had to travel through Debre Zeit in a big car. 'We are ashamed,' they'd say as they'd see me drive through. I tried to pray for them instead of cursing them. I prayed especially for about ten Party people after I went north to Sokota. When I was home on leave, I even took bananas and went to visit them. Before we were quarreling. Now I was hugging them. We were reconciled. The Lord can change things. He is a miraculous God! Some of them admitted to me, 'Sahle's God is the true God.'"

Sahle worked with World Vision half a year in Wolaitta, then in Kambaata. Periodically he got a short leave to come home to his family in the tiny house in Debre Zeit. In 1986, he was sent north to the distribution center at Sakota, where he found Negussie.

Sokota's feeding center was circled by the Derg's army, and beyond them, circled again by forces of the Tigray People's Liberation Front (TPLF). World Vision distributed food from this site. Sahle was assigned to be Project Director and Negussie as Stock Control Manager, acting as cashier and bookkeeper. People in area were in pitiful shape, beset by war and drought. For three years there had been little rain. The Agaw people lived in this area. They are a distinct ethnic group who ruled Ethiopia before the Solomonic line, and include the Falashas. People would walk long distances to receive food aid from the center. The rebels needed supplies too, which put food stashes in jeopardy.

SINCE NEGUSSIE AND FANTAYE were newly engaged, it was finally arranged that she might visit him briefly. She was terrified as the Twin Otter nosed down to land on the 900-meter butte. Learning that their World Vision camp was doubly surrounded—by the Ethiopian Army and the ring of Tigrayan rebels—was threatening, too. Still, it was wonderful to be in the same location with Negussie. After her visit, letters followed.

One day, however, riveting news came over Fantaye's radio. And back in Addis Ababa on home leave that week, Sahle heard it too. "Sokota is ambushed," the news blared. "The TPLF has taken the town!" Sahle was shocked. He could hardly believe it. He'd missed being caught by only three days and was sitting safely at home!

Eventually they learned the details: The rebels had brought 500 mules and donkeys and carried off the relief effort's stores of wheat, flour, oil, and the like. The staff up on the butte were held under house arrest for fifteen days, while the Tigray People's Liberation Front enjoyed eating the food on hand. They needed cash, too. Negussie told Mulugeta Haile at World Vision's head office later that when they demanded the money, it came into his mind that this is God's money. It was given for the destitute. I don't want to give it to the rebels. Negussie boldly refused to hand anything over. "We have nothing to give you. You have taken all our supplies, and we don't have money to give to you." He refused to discuss it further, and was willing to take the consequences. They surprised him. They refrained from resorting to further pressure. During the two weeks, they gave the famine workers daily political consciousness classes, talking about democracy and their goals. Captives were given four rather magnanimous choices: go abroad, go back home, stay in the area, or join the Tigray People's Liberation Front. It seemed that the TPLF at first meant simply to get Tigray Province free from the Derg. That was their goal when Sahle and Negussie were at Sokota. Later *Yehadig* (their Amharic name) decided to try to defeat the Derg.

After fifteen days, the rebels escorted the workers out, walking with them three days, exhausting days of climbing up and down the rippling mountain expanse. Negussie had kept the money in hiding, and carried it out. He was not used to such physical exertion. It took all his strength. About three hours short of Korem, a town on the Dessie road which was under Derg control, the TPLF escort bid them a cordial good-bye and left the group to make their way on alone. In Korem, transport to Addis Ababa could be found.

Back in the capital, Negussie took every cent of the money he had carefully protected from capture to the World Vision office. "But his reward," his old Wolisso friend Mulugeta Haile lamented, "was just to end up jobless." Sokota was closed. Negussie was appreciated and respected, but his employment ceased.

For nearly six months, the ex-prisoner was again without work. At least he and Fantaye had more opportunity to see each other. Eventually he worked with the Southern Baptist mission in Addis Ababa for over a year. Still, he longed for further training. Negussie's old friend Alemu had been sent to Kenya for training a decade before, but found the material so repetitive of what he'd had at Grace Bible Institute that he had gone on for advanced work in America. Now, at last, Negussie's treasured opportunity came. Pastor Kedamo and other leaders recognized the young man's potential. Such men were rare. The Kale Heywet Church offered Negussie a scholarship to study at Scott College in Kenya. This would qualify him for further church leadership, a future to which he looked with great expectations. Those who got out of Ethiopia in these tense days could not help feeling a sudden surge of freedom. Negussie fully intended to return, but the fresh air of a stable country would be a refreshing experience for a time.

Again, it meant postponing marriage, but the promise of a settled career gave the couple hope. By now, they'd waited a decade. Again, they parted. Now he would try to remember Fantaye's rich soft voice as he read her letters. This time the barrier was not a fence, not a mountain range, but a national boundary.

My times are in your hands;
deliver me from my enemies and from those who pursue me.
Let your face shine on your servant;
save me in your unfailing love. [...]

How great is your goodness,
which you have stored up for those who fear you,
which you bestow in the sight of men
on those who take refuge in you.
In the shelter of your presence
you hide them from the intrigues of men;
in your dwelling you keep them safe from accusing tongues.
(Psalm 31:15–16, 19–20)

Chapter 24

DEATHS AND BIRTHS

When rains came and the drought abated, it was time to assess the damage. An Ethiopian official who had headed up the relief operation and defected to America in 1986 wrote a book. By his calculations in *Red Tears,* 1.2 million people had died, 400,000 refugees were displaced in Somalia and the Sudan, 2.5 million were internally displaced, and 200,000 unaccompanied children had been registered. These statistics, no matter how staggering, are impersonal numbers to the outside observer.

We can get a better grasp of the meaning of such uprooting through stories of individuals. One such account appeared under the title, *A Courageous Journey: The Story of a Family's Will to Survive.*[122] Publishing it in 1988 with no identifiable place names used, Patricia St. John tells the story of many a child through the eyes of Mehrit, a teenage girl wandering with her little brother while her parents make a courageous journey to find them.

In his final chapter, the author of *Red Tears* goes beyond statistics gathered by 1985 to assess the gravest damage:

> But the biggest toll of the famine was psychological. None of the survivors would ever be the same. The famine left behind a population terrorized by the uncertainties of nature and the ruthlessness of their government. Families had been torn apart by resettlement, community life disrupted by the famine and by villagization. The dead had neither been buried decently nor mourned properly. The sick and the dying had not been cared for according to tradition. The religious and moral values of the people were put to the severest test.

---

122. P. St. John, *A Courageous Journey* (Moody Press, 1988).

Many felt that they had sinned and that God had punished them. Others felt that God had forsaken them. Many victims I spoke with had left their loved ones dead or dying by the roadside. Their own struggle to survive had pushed these events out of their minds, but now as they recovered the memories came back to haunt them. Many wished they had died with their loved ones. They found no relief in the rains: they had been dulled by hunger and sickness; now they were overwhelmed by fear of the unknown that lay ahead of them. They were afraid of another drought and the government reaction that would follow. All of the possibilities seemed equally terrifying. Would there again be no action at all for month after month? Would there be more resettlement, villagization, and mass conscriptions?[123]

Exhausted and disillusioned, Ethiopian citizens and government troops as well found themselves dispirited for war. The Eritrean People's Liberation Front (EPLF) and the Tigray People's Liberation Front (TPLF), however, grew in determination to take down the Mengistu regime. In 1986, the EPLF celebrated their twenty-fifth year of resistance, and called upon the United Nations, the Arab League, and the Organization of African Unity to recognize the legitimacy of their claim to nationhood. Guerrilla activities, isolated battles, offensives, and counter-offensives ground on.

DOWN IN THE SOUTH, families grieved the loss of their sons who had been captured by force and taken to the front to be used like so much gun-fodder. Prayer was the weapon the church waged. Often limited to underground gatherings in little groups, Christians used the night hours to build arsenals of prayer.

By now the church in the south had worked through its initial loss of equilibrium and was developing a stability and maturity. New initiatives were being born. The conference center at Bishoftu was one place expatriates and nationals could share fellowship without caution, and its remaining open seemed an on-going miracle. The Borlases had come back and were hosting events there, providing warmth and Howard's unfailing humor! In spite of the religious issue, believers tended to cooperate with the government's economic and social programs. They proved to be reliable workers in the Community Development projects across the county, and were

---

123. Dawit G., *Red Tears* (Red Sea Press, 1989), 355f.

learning technical and leadership skills thereby. A new station was even opened at Kamba. Instead of complaining about the resettlement program supposedly devised to combat effects of the famine, Christian students prepared themselves to use the opportunity to bring hope in Christ and supply the Scriptures to new places. Groups of believers in a "church" area welcomed the opportunity to resettle en masse to an "unreached" area. For example, Kambaatans resettled in an area in the North took their relocation as a mandate from God to open the way for the gospel in a place to which few evangelists had been allowed to go. Churches were born.

Whereas so much dying had multiplied hopelessness in the wider community, one particular burial in Wolaitta rose like a beacon of hope. It was Wandaro's. Only a few weeks before, the dear old saint had walked down from Humbo Mountain to Soddo and back, but his strength was waning. Wandaro Dabaro had been among the very first Wolaittans introduced to Jesus in the late 1920s by missionary Earl Lewis.[124] Wandaro in turn was instrumental in leading Daanna Meja to put his faith in Jesus, and the chain of believers continued. In those pre-Italian days, Wandaro was treated roughly by his master and local authorities who were Wolaitta's Amhara overlords. He was repeatedly imprisoned, beaten with sticks, whipped with rhinoceros hide, and had his hair and beard pulled out. Nevertheless, he used these "opportunities" to spread the word of God and invite his persecutors to believe. Fellow-believers observed his fortitude, prayed for him, and were themselves emboldened. When the cadres ordered his congregation to tear down their church, Wandaro led them all carrying the wood to the government leader's home—singing! For sixty years after his conversion, Wandaro had lived out a humble, prayerful, gentle life, winning far-flung strangers and the people of his mountain to the Lord. During the Revolution, he had stood with the young people who refused to shout the communists' curses, and went to jail with them.

---

124. The first child of the Lewises died three days after birth. Davis (1966), *Fire,* 44f tells of the funeral, to which leaders came who had actively opposed the gospel. Local understanding was that one must attend the funeral service of even his enemy, or else be linked with the witchcraft that may have caused the death. The Lewises' sorrow was mingled with joy to be allowed to testify to their hope in Christ in the context of the funeral.

On the day of Wandaro's funeral, communists officials in Soddo town had called a big meeting to try to bring the rising Christian witness in the area to a stop. They were upset with a wedding concurrently going on in town, one of those occasions believers used to witness publicly. Under their open window, amidst the officials' vows to stamp out this Christian movement, cars were going by, filled with celebrants singing praises to God! So upset were they with the juxtaposition under their noses that the funeral out on Humbo Mountain escaped their notice.

Out there, the neck of Humbo Mountain was being encircled by human chains of believers winding their circular way around the steep incline, heading for Wandaro's church, bearing bouquets of flowers. Thousands of believers in their gleaming white *shammas* were coming to celebrate their dear friend's life on earth, and now his life in Heaven, the life they too would share with the One who called Himself "the resurrection and the life." They rejoiced in the confidence that death simply transfers into Heaven the spirit of those who die, if they have already begun their new life somewhere along their road, as Wandaro had so long ago. Jesus told Nicodemus, "You must be born again," and they believed him. Such a huge gathering had not been held in Wolaitta since the churches were closed in 1983. It was like a conference again! God must have rejoiced over his son as he received him Home, his body now bedecked with garlands of flowers and his friends expressing their own expectation of immortality. Might God have chuckled a bit over the fuming officials in Soddo? Or wept?

WHAT ELSE WAS HAPPENING among Christians in the south? Going back a couple of years, and over eastward, the Dilla elders had been released. But the church building project which the coffee offering had been confiscated lay idle. The foundation stones rose two and a half meters above engulfing grass. Like many educated Ethiopians, the Gedeo leader, Werku Gole, had experimented earlier with the possibility of studying abroad, but government permission had been denied. Nine months after his release from prison, he was surprised to receive clearance to leave the country. Perhaps they thought his leadership would be less disturbing to the area if he could be removed from the Ethiopian scene.

Werku headed for LeTourneau College in Texas, leaving the family at home. Such a separation perhaps seems strange in our Western perspective, but it is something Africans have often had to do to further their education. Wives and children make the sacrifice and seem to count the price as a justified investment for the church and for the future for the whole family.

Werku later told the story of what happened in his case. At first all was new. He was enjoying the experience in the United States and was doing well in his studies. "But after a few weeks, the Lord spoke to my heart," he relates. I have done something wrong with the Lord, I thought, not with my family. What have I done against you? Please show me! I need peace in my heart. He seemed to answer me, 'You inaugurated all those projects. But what have you done with my church? Sheep and goats are wandering through the church foundation. There is no Bible teaching, it is a time of persecution.'

Werku pondered the Scriptures and found Jeremiah 45:5. "It speaks of 'seeking great things for yourself.' I wept. I knew it would be hard. I pleaded, If we build, won't the government take it? The door has finally opened to come here. What shall I do? 'Stop school. Start building, start teaching the Bible,' I felt He was saying to me.

"My hair was wet with perspiration. I was crying. Fortunately my roommate was gone. What shall I do? Who will understand me? How would people at home understand my quitting here? 'Go, it's enough that I understand you. This is between you and Me' the Father seemed to be saying. Can't I stay here and raise money?" Werku had effectively raised money to support the church. But the answer he got was no.

"I consulted the advisor in Longview, and he said, 'Let someone else do that, Werku.' God said, 'Listen to me, not others.' I sat down and wrote explanations to the school and to KHC, saying, 'I have a mission. The Lord has spoken to my heart.' I asked my professor to write a letter to the KHC office (who had sent me on scholarship) testifying that I'd been an outstanding summer school student, and had left of my own will. When I returned, they were astonished."

Big Werku loves to tell the story, gesturing widely. "I'm Werku-from-America now," he joked as he re-enacted it, "and I've come here to do things!" He surely did. He had come back to the schools, clinics, and kindergartens which they'd started earlier, now ready for more. He said the Dilla believers admitted, "Our heart wasn't with you. Only our lips. We didn't speak for we might have offended you. We believe it is the Lord who has done it. The Lord will reward you highly. We will stand with you. Lead us!"

By the time of Werku's return, the churches in Gedeo had opened again. So they all put their hands to the work and went on to build the big church and conference hall, an Amharic-language Bible school, and the first Kale Heywet Ministry Training Center (KMTC). The KMTC, a vision of Paul Balisky, was designed to fill the hole left by GBI's closing. It took students at the upper-level for theological training offered in English, combined with practical skills deemed valuable to the country. In Gedeo the church was marching forward again.

CONCURRENTLY, THE BIGGEST BREAKTHROUGH among unreached peoples was happening in Gujjiland. Werku's old friend, Gerhard Bössler, had carried a burden for the Gujjis for years. Even though he'd won a hearing by years of helpfulness to them through the road and water projects, and even though the Gujji king was willing for the Bösslers to live among them, government red tape blocked permission for a clinic station for several years. In 1985 they almost gave up and moved to Kenya to approach the Borana people, a related Oromo group over the border. Permission to build a clinic among the Gujjis finally came at Christmas time, 1985. They wasted no time moving into a remote location called Biyo.

The Enemy was not quick to let them in. Just when a German builder had arrived, Gerhard's car slipped over the edge of a mountain road, hurling hundreds of feet below. The Ethiopian passenger was killed instantly, and Gerhard was barely alive when his wife Edith arrived. As Gerhard healed, Edith carried on in the next months, doing the lifting and the driving. Her frustration nearly reached breaking point when trying to get out to their son's high school graduation in Kenya. That trip necessitated her getting letters from seven levels of clearance—traveling from office to office, local and regional and national—to allow exit and re-entry! Such were the nightmares of bureaucracy.

By means of Biyo station, medical care, a grain mill, and other community helps were brought in. After the Gujjis' long history of killing people from the outside, Gerhard did not forget that his plan was "to raise up Gujjis to win Gujjis." Their oral culture needed to have the language reduced to writing, materials prepared, literacy taught, and the Bible translated. Leadership must be raised up. A church was being born!

Although thousands of these fierce people came to faith in the God of the whole earth, they were still in the minority. Life among the Gujjis is never "safe." Edith saw this regularly as she treated speared or mutilated patients, treated gunshot wounds, and sometimes had to give up the mortally wounded for dead. Once in awhile the Bösslers were warned of intentions to kill them. A few tense nights were spent in the car, ready to try an escape if attacked. They always decided to stay and take what came. In the final analysis, what came after decades of praying and dying was glorious birth. The Spirit of God was moving in Gujjiland.

For you know that it was not with perishable things
such as silver or gold that you were redeemed
from the empty way of life handed down to you from your ancestors,
but with the precious blood of Christ,
a lamb without blemish or defect. [...]

Now that you have purified yourselves by obeying the truth
so that you have sincere love for each other,
love one another deeply, from the heart.
For you have been born again,
not of perishable seed, but of imperishable,
through the living and enduring word of God.
                          (1 Peter 1:18–19, 22–23)

Chapter 25

TWO SAGAS IN BALE

Women's stories in Ethiopia generally remain hidden. Wives' experiences run parallel with their husbands, but are usually told through their husband's mouths. One woman's saga stands out like Deborah's in the Old Testament or Priscilla's in the Book of Acts.[125] Yeshi Belachew's story stretches over long years of faithfulness, and was set in the scene of the Bale mountains. Bale lies on the edge of the Kale Heywet body of believers, east of the Sidamo road. As a woman, Yeshi did not travel to KHC elders' meetings. She lived in quiet obscurity, but what a swath this lone woman cut!

A second story of long faithfulness in Bale Province is that of Ato Asfaw Demisse. He would occasionally make the trip down to Addis Ababa or to an annual KHC meeting somewhere in the heart of southern Ethiopia, bringing word of the state of the believers in his area. It was he who begged for help at the leaders' meeting at Langano when the Revolution was new. Often communities like Yeshi's or Asfaw's knew little of sister fellowships in each other's areas. The terrain was rough to travel, but harder than nature's obstacles was the mindset of human authorities with an eye quick to accuse or find fault. Eventually, Ato Asfaw and *Woizero* ("Mrs.") Yeshi did meet in 1978. By the close of the eighties, both their groups in Bale were knowing and appreciating each other.

As the reader hears their stories and their struggles with the Orthodox community, it would be natural to wonder how Christians of two different stripes could understand each other so little. Of course, we could ask that same question of similar Christian divisions

---

125. See Judges 4 and 5 regarding Deborah; and Acts 18, Romans 16:3, and 1 Corinthians 16:19 regarding Priscilla, wife of Aquila.

YESHI BELACHEW (ADDIS ABABA, 1996)

in the world, outside of Ethiopia. This chapter will conclude with observations about Ethiopia's unique faith community situation.

YESHI BELACHEW WAS BORN to Amhara parents in 1947. In spite of their Orthodox orientation, Yeshi said her family was tied up with evil spirits. "Ten demons lived in my mother." Yeshi was a tall girl with almond-shaped eyes. She too was sometimes troubled by the demons. At about thirteen, she was given in marriage to Tesfaye Wundgerod.

At a time when the couple and their children were living together with Yeshi's mother in Addis Ababa, Yeshi's brother worked in the capital at the Commercial Bank of Ethiopia. When Yeshi was twenty-one, her brother showed her from the Word of God how to acknowledge Jesus Christ as her own savior. She feared her Orthodox husband, if she were to do so. He was unhappy when he found her reading a Bible, but eventually she did receive Christ as her Lord. Within six months, so did he. It was five years later in a time of illness that Yeshi and Mulatu's mother was healed, renounced Satan, and was delivered from long bondage.

Tesfaye worked in a government office in Addis Ababa, but decided to go into business way out in Bale Province many kilometers east of Shashamane. The town was largely Oromo and Muslim along with Amhara and Orthodox Christian people. The Orthodox priests in the area were bitterly opposed to other forms of Christian belief. From the start, the new family was labeled as "Protestant"—simply meaning non-Orthodox—and shunned. Just before the Revolution, a few people came to Jesus through this couple, and the Orthodox and government united to put them in prison, calling them the despised name, "Pentes." An SIM missionary was working at the time in Bale, and traveled to Tesfaye and Yeshi's area to encourage the handful of believers there. As they gathered, police and Orthodox priests surrounded their house and took the whole group to the police station. "They asked us why we were teaching the gospel of God," Yeshi recounts, "because they said they were the only apostles authorized to teach." Eight priests testified against the arrested group. However, they became so embroiled in an argument among themselves that they forgot the reason they'd come was to condemn the Protestants. The foreigner was eventually released, but the others had to find guarantors for bail in order to get out.

They rented a building for worship, but again it was surrounded one day by the police and the urban community, and the sixteen Christians were taken off to the police station. One woman among the little handful being arrested remarked, "It is not our number that they fear, but the power of God in us, which is great." The officials separated and interrogated them like criminals. When Tesfaye came home from a trip and discovered what was happening, he told their accusers that following the Protestant religion was not a crime. He requested and got their release, but they were ordered not to leave town.

During these days, a few believers among people from other areas of Ethiopia were assigned to Bale during the *zemecha* literacy campaign. They encouraged the struggling fellowship. Local believers were subjected to economic pressures next, for all their domestic animals were stolen. In Yeshi's husband's absence on another business trip, their eleven month old child suddenly died. The cold rejection of the town was hard for the grieving mother to bear, and quite un-Ethiopian. "Orthodox parish members complained they could not bury my child because I did not have the so-called 'Father of the Soul' among the priests. Even if the community wanted to help me, the priests did not. A neighbor who was a military man went to the police station and told the priests that if they had any accusation, to handle it by law, not by keeping a dead child unburied." He brought prisoners to dig a grave in common land, that the body might not have to rot in the field.

Believers are not ignorant of the Enemy's devices. He divides through suspicion, distrust, and hate. The next attack was framed in the context of the Somali struggle. Control of the lowland Ogaden was a recurring issue between Ethiopia and Somalia. In 1976 Somalis were plundering property and taking grazing cattle from the people of Bale. In 1977, fighting nearly reached Yeshi's town. "Pentes do not want to go to war," accused the little flock's attackers. They took Yeshi's husband to the battle one Tuesday. On Wednesday, Tesfaye was shot. "When they came back from the place and told me—happily—that he was shot in the forest," Yeshi remembers, "everything was out of my control. I cried to the Lord. Their hearts did not feel hurt for him who left his old mother, six children and nine people in the family to me. They were quarreling with each other over who and where to bury him. I was hurt inside and prayed to God to take care of everything. I also decided not to go and get the dead body of the husband whom I did not even like to be without for five minutes, because I did not want to be a cause for the community to laugh at me (by taunting her and denying her husband burial in the Orthodox cemetery). My God heard my prayer. When the dead bodies of seven other people were brought to the town, my husband's had disappeared." There was no body to bury.

Yeshi struggled to keep the family fed with no income. She was nine months pregnant when her husband was taken, and two weeks after his death, she delivered her last child. Christian friends had gone away because of persecution, and she was left to deliver alone. Only one military person in the area briefly came forth to help. Many tried to convince her to go back to Orthodoxy, to Mary, and to angels as her intercessors. She refused to leave the Lord Jesus Christ as her only mediator.

She and the children struggled to survive. She taught them the Bible and Christian ethics faithfully, and the townspeople could not deny they were a good influence on other children. There were five sons left, and one little daughter. The latter came to the attention of the cadres who staged celebrations for the Revolution. "Then Satan started to attack me again. They took my only daughter to sing in a music band. When she told them she couldn't sing for them, they beat and stoned her terribly. All my children had the same problem." Little Genet was only about eight at the time, but made her own decision. "If she won't sing, there'll be no school exams for her," they threatened Yeshi. Kassu's oldest was taken to jail for a week. Yeshi appealed to the authorities for his release, reminding them she had no husband, and that his father had died in the war. They released him, but would periodically come and ask for her boys. Like so many young men, they would have to keep moving around outside the city to avoid being registered and taken to one of the fronts.

At that time Yeshi was meeting secretly with four Christians who mutually comforted each other. Before long, they dared not come to her. She actually knew of more believers in the town, but they could not risk being associated with her. Her home was right in front of the political offices, so everyone who came or went or stood talking outside her home was watched.

"Three believers who transferred in from Kambaata joined me in praying earnestly about the situation in 1986. We were encouraged by Jeremiah 33:3: 'Ask me and I will tell you some remarkable secrets about what is going to happen here.' I stuck to God, because I had taken Jesus like my husband, my Lord, my God, and I continued to raise my children to depend upon Him." As they prayed and fasted, God worked. Fifteen more believed.

Woizero Yeshi used caution in conducting their underground fellowship. She divided them into three groups who did not even know about the other two. The firm Christians met inside her home secretly, the growing believers met outside her home, and those who had very recently come to the Lord were each discipled separately. Often two believers simply appeared to be chatting casually on the street, but they were in fact encouraging each other spiritually. She didn't let them know about each other, lest the weak ones would break down and become informers.[126]

Orthodox leadership stepped up persecution in the eighties. Believers were driven out from social affairs of the town. They forbid their members to patronize Woizero Yeshi's small shop, a business her brothers had helped her set up. Kassu, her oldest, would come home day after day, saying, "Mom, no sales today." She and Kassu told God they wouldn't leave, considering the shepherding she was doing. People accused her falsely of "cajoling children with candies and clothes." They killed her two goats and threw them in the middle of the marketplace so that everyone would see them. They blacklisted every believer they could identify, and even named some as having Orthodox approval to be destroyed. But in spite of the pressures, more and more came to Jesus. They kept affirming God's deliverances, claiming his promise in Romans 8:28, "that in all things God works for the good of those who love him, who have been called according to his purpose." Although the townspeople shunned the shop, the rural people came, and when they came, they heard about Jesus the Christ.

Yeshi's group banded with believers in two nearby towns, choosing three elders for each group. Woizero Yeshi was chosen as one of the three in hers. She agonized very early about what her church leadership role should be as a woman. "I had some fear before God," she admitted, "but I told Him these were special circumstances in a time of persecution." Ceremonies normally enjoyed by the Christians were difficult to arrange. When elders from elsewhere visited the area, a baptism was arranged far from town, at nine at night, and another time just before dawn. When any such gathering was impossible, a water tank sufficed in her home. Having no place for burial was one of the hardest deprivations facing evangelicals. Eventually a place was located and was received with deep thanksgiving as a gift from God.

Yeshi said God showed his righteousness to her enemies, recalling words of the 6th Psalm: "Go, leave me now, you men of evil deeds, for the Lord has heard my weeping and my pleading. He will answer all my prayers. All my enemies shall be suddenly dishonored,

---

126. When the pressure finally lifted a few years later they were introduced to each other and found themselves to be in a fellowship of eighty.

terror-stricken, and disgraced. God will turn them back in shame." Even without a father, her children grew up and did well in their education. (Three completed twelfth grade by the close of the Revolution, and the other three were progressing in their studies.) She claimed the promise of the Lord to Zion, "For the mountains may depart and the hills disappear, but my kindness shall not leave you. My promise of peace for you will never be broken, says the Lord who has mercy upon you" (Isaiah 54:10).

Out of her prayers and faithful leadership grew a whole community of people who knew their God. Psalm 126 expresses what she says she has seen in her experience: "Those who sow in tears will reap with song of joy. He who goes out weeping, carrying seed to sow, will return with songs of joy, carrying sheaves with him."

ASFAW DEMISSE'S TOWN WAS some eighty kilometers from Yeshi's area. Oromo and Somali Muslims dominate the area. Four famous Islamic shrines nearby are involved with the occult and demonism. Asfaw came from the Shewa Oromo and his family "wore the thread" around their necks, designating them to be Orthodox Christians. Since his parents spoke Oromo and the priests conduct services in Ge'ez or Amharic, they were not well taught. Asfaw heard the gospel from an Ethiopian believer when he was about sixteen. He was thrown out of his home when he believed, but after a year was allowed back. Asfaw was a winsome boy, stocky built with a wide forehead and a dimple in his chin.

Asfaw's knowledge of the Oromo language led to his translating for nurses in an SIM clinic. His warm and gentle earnestness equipped him for spiritual ministry and so after a year in Durame Bible School, he returned home as a clinic evangelist with Chris Lund. The Somali war soon caused the clinic to close. Kambaatan evangelists had come to the area, but along with the missionaries were removed during the Revolution. Asfaw was pushed into church leadership. With his lovely wife, Tedebaba, and the four children born to them, he continued ministry there throughout the Revolution.

In 1977, at the annual meeting held at Langano he asked the Kale Heywet Church to help them build a small church. Opposition from the Orthodox priests and Muslim leadership was strong. Then the communists added more. These pressures caused so many to fall away that finally only five were meeting together.

Prayer became the driving force of Asfaw's life. When militants threatened to kill him in 1978, he spent a whole night in a church praying. "It was a lovely night," he recalls. He had a dream or vision which was so wonderful he cried when it was over. From then on, he stayed in the church all night every Friday. Among his fellow believers a pattern developed thereafter which has become perpetual. They pray from about eight to midnight; they sleep on the floor till about 4 AM, the women on one side, men on the other; then they rise and pray, slipping out when the rooster crows before dawn.

Sometimes defeats are turned into victories years later. Disappointed with a loss in 1974, Asfaw saw an unusual outworking in 1989. It seems Al and his son Howie Brant drove to Asfaw's town in 1974 just as the Revolution was beginning and also went to visit a distant place called Jara. Jara had once been Asfaw's hometown, and so he interpreted for Al as he showed a Christian film in the market place there. Many people responded by saying they were receiving Christ as their Savior, but no missionaries came again. Time passed, with little fruit seen in Jara.

Fifteen years later an eleventh-grade student from Jara suddenly began displaying signs of insanity. He went to Asfaw, who prayed for him, and the symptoms went away. Later he met with Asfaw from time to time, and one day received Christ as his Savior. The next day when the boy's relatives arrived from Jara, his previous symptoms returned as soon as he saw them. They thought the boy should go to a mental hospital in Addis Ababa, and Asfaw agreed to go with them to the capital. The hospital which treated mental illness refused admittance, saying they could do nothing for him. The Black Lion Hospital gave them the same response. It was getting late and so they crossed the street to SIM Headquarters and got permission to stretch out on the benches in the chapel. At 5:30 AM the boy awoke and said to his relatives, "I accepted Christ as my Savior; you have to do the same." Within two hours, he died. Asfaw had hoped his concern for the lad would open the way for discussing new life with the relatives, but instead, death had won.

Burial at home is important to Ethiopians, and so mission and church people in Addis Ababa collected money and arranged a

ASFAW DEMISSE (ADDIS ABABA, 1996)

vehicle to take the corpse and the relatives and Asfaw back to Bale. At the funeral, Asfaw testified to the good news of new life offered by receiving the resurrected Christ, as he always did. Eighteen heads of houses trusted Christ as their savior! Some of the relatives who came from Jara came to Asfaw and said, "Fifteen years ago we saw a film about Jesus Christ which, as far as we can remember, told us the same things that you are teaching us. Is this so?" "Yes!" Asfaw answered, overcome with joy. "Nobody visited us to tell us any more. Will you come to Jara and instruct us further?"

A small fellowship was born in Jara, but there was no one to teach them regularly. So the believers in the larger town collected money among themselves and sent them a short-wave radio to hear Christian programs in the Oromo language aired by the Far East Broadcasting Association. Unfortunately, when a corporate witness became evident, the Oromo community's Orthodox priests threatened to excommunicate any who showed the believers the usual social courtesies, such as help in time of sickness or death. A home was burned, an ox was lost, and so forth. It was Asfaw's community of believers who manifested a loving spirit again and sent funds for replacement.

Asfaw has a peace and joy about him which quietly radiates even in spite of repeated suffering. That glow was there when he brought his grown son to Charles for treatment. He'd been stabbed by an irate Muslim, almost severing his arm. "The Lord chose the weak and the foolish to confound the wise," he told me with humility, describing the unusual opportunities he's been given to reach individuals among the rich and empowered as well as the poor and disenfranchised. If evangelicals canonized "saints," this man of prayer would seem to qualify.

Outsiders are puzzled by the way these two groups who claim allegiance to the same Lord speak on wavelengths that barely receive one another. Those listening in from the outside could contribute missiological insights which might clarify and encourage both arms of the Ethiopian Christian body. Both groups have wonderful gifts with which to bless each other, if only they could begin to do so.

Must denominational communities repeat the mistake which Christ prepared the early church to expect from established believers in Yahweh? "They will put you out of the synagogue; in fact, a time is coming when anyone who kills you will think he is offering a service to God" (John 16:2). The Lord Jesus, Lord of the Orthodox as well as the Pentes, said, "As I have loved you, so you must love one another. By this will all men know that you are my disciples, if you love one another" (John 13:34–35). This is our God-appointed task. If we identify who the Enemy really is, then understanding, healing, and love can come.

Therefore, remember that formerly you
who are Gentiles by birth and called "uncircumcised" by those
who call themselves "the circumcision"
(that done in the body by the hands of men)—
remember that at that time you were separate from Christ,
excluded from citizenship in Israel and
foreigners to the covenants of the promise,
without hope and without God in the world.

But now in Christ Jesus you who once were far away
have been brought near through the blood of Christ.
For he himself is our peace,
who has made the two one and has destroyed the barrier,
the dividing wall of hostility,
by abolishing in his flesh the law
with its commandments and regulations.
His purpose was to create in himself one new man out of the two,
thus making peace,
and in this one body to reconcile
both of them to God through the cross,
by which he put to death their hostility.
      (Ephesians 2:11–16)

Chapter 26

GLIMPSING THE KINSHIP OF GRIEF AND GLORY

My heart raced as our Ethiopian Airlines jet began its descent to Addis Ababa. It was 1988, and I had last left that runway in 1977, weeping. We had gone on to Kenya and Sudan, from which our family had last left African soil in 1979. Charles had been back to Africa from the United States three times in the interim, without me. This time, we'd found care for my mother, and I had come back too. What would we find, eleven years after the scattering of the majority of missionaries out of Ethiopia?

As we came down the ramp, blinking into the brilliant sunlight of Ethiopia, another plane had just landed, bringing passengers from Israel. In that line we spotted—could it be?—Pastor Kedamo. Like most Ethiopian Christians, the desire to go to Israel was a given, and we learned later that friends abroad had arranged this opportunity. How wonderful at that moment to meet this dear Kambaatan whose family we'd met in our early Leimo Hospital days and later in Addis Ababa as Kedamo became the beloved "country-to-city pastor" during the Revolution!

Headquarters looked so much like it had when we'd first arrived, the rains washing sheet-like across the asphalt drive as they always had, bougainvillea brightening the old gray shingled exterior, the dining room the same, except for a change of curtains. We set down our bags in the room we were assigned. It was among many rooms we'd occupied along with our three boys in past years as we'd come and gone. We stared at the walls and at each other, overwhelmed by a flood of memories. We sorely missed our sons.

Thursday afternoon brought the same Inter-Mission prayer meeting that had begun in the 1950s. Attending it helped to bring us together with a few of the faithful still left in the country, grayer and wiser. Like the nationals, expatriates of different denominational hues had drawn closer together as they'd shared the trials of the Revolution. The sense of unity, of caring for one another, was deep.

Although we used the SIM guesthouse when we were in the capital, that summer we were not serving under the sponsorship of the mission, but the national church. Having no hospitals left, SIM had no place to use us. Emmanuel International was sending no doctors to Ethiopia that year, for the "emergency" element had waned. However, Dr. Mulatu Baffa had told World Medical Missions in the United States that the church could use Charles to encourage the few struggling KHC clinics in the countryside.

In the first interview with our "boss" at KHC Headquarters, we realized we were an anomaly. Dr. Mulatu had directed countless expatriate volunteers by now, often field representatives from well-established aid organizations like World Vision or Tearfund. They came with full funding, their own cars, and the like. We, on the other hand, had just barely scraped up enough money for our plane tickets, and had to look to the Kale Heywet Church even for transportation to wherever they sent us. Now the shoe was on the other foot—we were begging rides from nationals, rather than giving them. Some things had changed, and really, for the better!

THREE THINGS REMAIN IN my memory of our first trip down-country to Hossana: the pleasure of riding with our Ethiopian brothers, the beauty of the countryside in spite of its ominous cracked soil, and the surprise stop after dark just short of Hossana. (Whether it was a scheduled stop or a special gift to us, we never learned.) In a small town with no electricity, the Land Rover pulled up quietly to the gate of a compound. My back was so sore from hours of pounding that I could hardly climb out of the vehicle. "Come," they urged us, a certain light in their eyes.

We were cautioned to make no noise as we were guided through a yard past the shape of a kiln, stacks of firewood, the large-leafed outlines of banana-like *ensete* plants, through a back entrance of a simple home of mud and tin construction. Inside all seemed dark, until our traveling companions drew us around a corner into a second room, where one single light shone. Above the candle a huge man stood, his face bent over the Scriptures in his hands. A cough awakened us to the presence of a couple dozen men and women around the circumference of the room, looking at us questioningly, for interruptions of secret meetings were rare, and sometimes signaled danger. Our hosts drew us up to the towering shepherd and presented us to each other. I drew in my breath, exclaiming "Abba Gole!" With formal warmth, the patriarch embraced us in Ethiopian fashion, kissing first one side and then the other of our faces. Such was our welcome to an underground fellowship, one of thousands of such groups among Christians in Ethiopia.

The weeks in Hossana were graced with elements that never change—the winsomeness of the people and the beauty of the countryside. The compound now belonged to the Church, not SIM, and we were the only foreigners there. We'd never seen beet *wat* before—not meat but beet. With wonderful spicing it was good, but it was a sign of lean times.

We were warmed by a sense of spiritual reality in the fellowship we were privileged to share with the community while living on the church compound. Their gatherings a couple nights a week awakened us to one clear difference between American and Ethiopian Christians. Americans had more personal "power" (through money, cars, goods, freedoms) and less sense of need. These Ethiopian brothers and sisters were powerless to make things happen, so literally depended on God for everything. One result was deep and sustained prayerfulness, an orientation we independent Westerners often lack.

Charles keenly remembers the effect upon him of a study one night on the "seventh trumpet" in Revelation. He kept thinking, "How differently one reads the passage when sitting with a suffering community on wooden stools in a mud-walled home, rather than in a Western church with padded seats, air-conditioning, and a parking lot filled with cars."

> The seventh angel sounded his trumpet, and there were loud voices in heaven, which said:
>
> "The kingdom of the world has become the kingdom of our Lord and of his Christ, and he will reign for ever and ever."

> And the twenty-four elders, who were seated on their thrones before God, fell on their faces and worshipped God, saying:
>
> "We give thanks to you, Lord God Almighty, the One who is and who was, because you have taken your great power and have begun to reign. The nations were angry; and your wrath has come. The time has come for judging the dead, and for rewarding your servants the prophets and your saints and those who reverence your name, both small and great—and for destroying those who destroy the earth." (Revelation 11:15–18)

This is the dark side of the moon, Charles thought, the other side of the sun. God means business. For those who abuse others, their time is coming. What powerful people do to defenseless ones should make somebody angry... And who is better qualified than God?

CHARLES WORKED WITH Ato Paulos, a dresser trained at Soddo Hospital years before, who supervised two clinics, one there on the KHC compound and another at a World Vision-funded center in a area hit hard by drought. The Kambaatan and Hadiyyan churches' emphasis on Community Development was contributing orphan care, grain supplements, reforestation and the like to the society. Churches were still allowed open outside Hossana town proper, so we enjoyed well-attended services in the building shared by the Bible School which was still operating. Ato Girma Hanano was the director. He'd been through rough waters in Jimma, but remained a man of joy with a family who loved to sing.

But there were puzzling aspects, the clearest of which involved the chasm between funding of "development" and "spiritual" arms of the local ministry, and the resultant threat to relationships between those who worked in those two areas. The Bible School was in short supply of everything. Students slept on rough bunks in the school attic and cooked their own meager food over stick fires. On the same compound, Community Development (CD) workers got the best housing and roared in and out of the compound in aid-contributed Land Rovers. One day the head of the CD ministries gave us a ride to town and stopped at the local bank to get some aid money. Out of the bank he came with his arms brim full of packets of green bills, which he threw nonchalantly into the front seat. We'd never seen so much Ethiopian money. Ato Girma, heading up spiritual ministries, probably hadn't either. Those in his branch wondered why

Christians abroad were seemingly so much more devoted to physical than spiritual aid.

While passing through Headquarters in Addis Ababa that summer, who should we meet but Malcolm Hunter, back briefly after years of absence from Ethiopia. Having done graduate studies in Community Development, Malcolm had clear ideas of the direction he thought Christian development should take. Although happy to be back with the people he loved, he was not pleased with the CD trend which he observed to be unfolding, nor were some others of the mission staff. His first love was the national church, and he did not think the trend bode well for the church. The trend might be called "Project Missions." In earlier days when missionaries were scattered over the country, CD was done with modest appropriate technology and administered on a local level. Now money was pouring in from huge aid organizations with little staff on the field to administer the actual services. Malcolm observed factors which promoted a trend which posed new problems: "the inevitable pressure to undertake projects which meet the requirements of large funding agencies as well as the expectations of the Ethiopian government." Technologically sophisticated programs were thrown into operation, large amounts pumped in, and then suddenly removed on the donor's timetable. One of Ethiopia's sayings, "once a friend, always a friend," was not a presupposition of the aid industry.

WE HEADED DOWN THE Sidamo road next. While visiting a clinic at Dilla—hardly functioning for lack of medicines—we happened in on a striking example of relationships which had grown over decades between Ethiopians and expatriate Christians. That particular day of our visit, literally hundreds of Gedeo choir members were gathering outside the huge church which Ato Werku Gole had come back from Texas to build, giving up his studies abroad. The varied colors of their robes distinguished them as being from many different congregations. Ato Werku towered above the crowd, using a cam-recorder. Word had reached Gedeo that Al Brant, who had brought the message of Christ to them in the 1950s, was dying at home in Canada. His spiritual children and grandchildren had decided to send Ato Werku to his side, with tokens of their love and esteem. Imagine the joy of the old warrior on his deathbed seeing a video of representatives of the multitude who had come out of their darkness to the Lord, and hearing hymns of praise to their God from their lips. While in Canada, Werku would arrange for a number of young Gedeo church leaders to go there for study. Let them study; his gift was promotion.

Charles made the rounds of a few other KHC-related clinics. At Durame, the foreigner's presence was met with strong antagonism from local communist officials and put the clinic dresser in an awkward position. This gave Charles a taste of the vulnerability Ethiopian Christians regularly risked.

MEANWHILE, I HAD STAYED at Lake Bishoftu. The ancient crater lake was as beautiful as ever, unchanged by much except for deforestation and now reforestation—a project Bruce Bond had come back from New Zealand to initiate on the east side of the lake. This was a "food for work" project meant to employ people and raise their standard of living, while building up self-sustainability. The Debre Zeit church which had been born in the little thatched Sharon Cottage down by the lake had grown from those nine people to hundreds of members. Now it operated an underground night Bible school housed inconspicuously in the homes of the three Air Force officers, Girma, Solomon, and Teshome.

What had radically changed at Bishoftu was the clientele. While the buildings were much the same, the menu was more Ethiopian. No longer thronged as a vacation and "relief and rehabilitation" place for hundreds of missionaries of various denominations—since most were gone—Bishoftu had thrown open its arms to nationals. It provided a rare place of rest from the constant surveillance Christians were subjected to in the outside world. A dozen or more national church groups scheduled meeting after meeting at this oasis: elders' conferences, student conferences, women's conferences, interdenominational conferences, leadership conferences, spiritual life conferences, Community Development conferences, and so on. These drew nationals into opportunities for growth and training, especially the students of the Evangelical Student Union.[127] Years later an Ethiopian leader told me, "SIM's greatest contribution during the

---

127. EVASU is related to the International Fellowship of Evangelical Students.

Revolution was Bishoftu, a God-send to the national church—all the churches—the one protected place we found to gather, grow, and become one."

One weekday afternoon after a conference had closed, I asked a student who had stayed over for a day to rest, to meet with me. By talking with the conference center's guests, I was trying to get a sense of what God was doing. We took two chairs out into the sunshine on the porch of my one-room cabin. For the next two hours, the older expatriate learned from the national who was probably about twenty in age but much older in experience. With few pastors and only an occasional church allowed open, the laity of Ethiopia had become an active "priesthood of all believers." Students often took heavy leadership.

This poised but very tired young woman talked matter-of-factly about pressures on students known as Christians, which often included relegation to second-class status at the university, displacement to remote *zemecha* assignments, and prison terms. With so many seeking entrance, and so few places in Addis Ababa's one university, only the top students got in. I asked how beleaguered Christian students "kept alive spiritually" in the atheist ethos of a communist-dominated faculty. I was amazed as she listed an array of responsibilities the believers embraced as they very purposely organized networks complicated by necessary concealment underground. They maintained (at carefully worked out "coded" times and places) regular study, discipleship, worship, and training opportunities which demanded a commitment and developed a depth beyond any I'd seen in America. I could sense in this young woman that in the process, the high cost of discipleship was reaping dividends—serious biblical growth, intimate fellowship, and mature leadership training. I realized that this little time apart at Bishoftu had been a key link in her group's "body life"—not just a vacation. And her extra day of rest without tension was badly needed. Christian students in Ethiopia carried a very adult load of leadership at a very young age. Ethiopian children had long taken adult roles as tenders of children and the family animals, but harder tasks had been forced upon them by the role young people were forced to play in "the vanguard of the

Revolution," sent out on *zemecha*, assigned as Marxist-Leninist cadres, or sent off to a war front. They needed all the spiritual reserves they could build.

WE LEARNED THAT Sahle Tilahun's family no longer lived in the Debre Zeit area, where they'd suffered difficulties with his principalship for years. He'd worked with World Vision for awhile. After Sahle and Negussie's assignment with World Vision at Sokota was cut short by the TPLF rebels, Sahle had begun working with a publishing house. He had also seen a dream come true—getting a home of their own. With deep joy they invited us to visit it, still in construction, out on Addis Ababa's fringe.

Turning off the tarmac onto a rough cobblestone road, we arrived at their hilltop compound. Their tin roof shone in the sunlight, and spanned a much wider dwelling than the tiny quarters in which they'd managed for so many years near Debre Zeit. The brown mud-and-wattle walls still smelled new. Passion fruit vines hung over the entrance and pungent aroma of eucalyptus trees wafted on a refreshing breeze. They were overjoyed that the Lord had given them such a palace, and we rejoiced with them.

Inside, peace reigned. Wedding pictures and embroidered Bible verses hung on the walls. Ethiopian children customarily do not eat with company. However, their shy and respectful children came out and sang to us—more exposure than children usually get. Sahle and Aberash rehearsed God's goodness to them over the years. By now, Sahle was in publishing Christian materials, a restricted but much-needed ministry in Ethiopia. Aberash continued teaching math in Addis Ababa. Both took leadership in their church fellowship. At the close of a wonderful *injera* and *wat* feast, as we talked Aberash performed the traditional hour-long coffee ceremony, which includes grinding, roasting, boiling, and serving Ethiopia's famous specialty. Such times with Ethiopian friends were priceless. We knew we'd continue to long for this quality of fellowship when we got back to production-centered America.

IN ADDIS ABABA WE experienced another night to remember in the home of a modern Abraham and Sara. Abraham Yosef, we learned, was the leader of the Great Commission work in Addis Ababa,

Glimpsing the kinship of grief and glory   323

ABERASH TAKELE AND SAHLE TILAHUN (ADDIS ABABA, 1994)

initiated by Campus Crusade's overseas ministries. Seeing this beautiful family (this modern Abraham had eleven children!) and hearing about what God was doing throughout the city was moving. The capital had the advantage of trained or trainable leadership. In the countryside, that lack posed deep problems in this time when in spite of persecution, thousands were believing, but there were not enough shepherds of the flocks. As our new friend Abraham drove us back to the SIM compound through the dark empty streets of Addis Ababa, our questions drew him out further.

"How many small groups meet in Addis underground?," we asked. "Within the Great Commission network, about a thousand groups."

"Amazing! And where did you come from, Abraham?" "Eritrea," he answered.

"Did we hear you right?" "Yes, Eritrea."

God works in amazing ways, his wonders to perform.

WHILE WE WERE STAYING at Headquarters, one day two guests arrived (each with one small suitcase) after attending a pastors' conference in Kenya. They were Sudanese, and we'd known the one named Timothy Niwar in Sudan years before. Christians have a hard time getting exit permits in Muslim Sudan. The conference had become their "cover" for quickly detouring over to Ethiopia to look for their lost people—their wives and children who had disappeared from their homes two years before during an ambush while the fathers were away in Khartoum. Sudanese government soldiers had come to their Uduk settlement shooting and burning and capturing. Those who could flee ran for their lives, ran eastward, ran until they dropped, and then struggled on. Timothy had come to find out whether their missing people might be in Ethiopia. They'd been lost for two years. Would the Ethiopian government allow the men to search to find them—or what was left of them—and to help them?

We drove the two Sudanese to the church Kedamo Mechato pastored that Sunday. In the packed service inside, I was deeply moved as hundreds of worshippers began to sing in spite of their suffering, and to pray corporately but also individually to the Lord, in a soft hum all over the room. Few white faces were visible and we felt deeply privileged to be there. In fact, we wept, identifying with their sorrows, but also with their joy.

Between services, we were allowed to join a meeting where the elders gathered together to welcome the men from Sudan. The Ethiopians knew little about what was happening to Christians in the vast, landlocked nation next door. Why? Because since African media networks are limited and censored, Ethiopians could learn more about Sudan from BBC than from their own media. However, BBC didn't major on the suffering of remote Christians. We happened to know these men's story, because missionaries had been sharing prayer information between the countries to try to uphold the beleaguered Uduks.

This interlacing takes some explanation: Missions in East Africa have had a history of going in and out of "revolving doors." When the Italian war pushed missionaries out of Ethiopia in 1936, some went to Sudan. When Sudan's civil war pushed missions out in 1961, many went back to Ethiopia. When Ethiopia's Revolution pushed expatriates out in 1977, a block of missionaries switched to Sudan. Don Stilwell of SIM became an advocate for the Sudanese Uduks and kept in touch with others who had worked among them over the last fifty years. Uduks had the misfortune of being located on the border between northern and southern Sudan, both sides of which either commandeered their allegiance, or distrusted their loyalties.

Glimpsing the kinship of grief and glory 325

TIMOTHY NIWAR (ADDIS ABABA, 1988)

Being Christianized, they were automatically considered suspect by their Islamic government and were brutally attacked. They had fled eastward into Ethiopia. Theirs was a no-win situation, and resulted in tragic human loss.

Timothy Niwar rose to speak. He was a small man and very dark skinned, similar to the looked-down upon ethnic groups way out on Ethiopia's western border. He chose a scripture close to the hearts of Ethiopian Christians as they'd faced their ordeal, but his listeners did not know much about the Sudanese ordeal. Before sharing that story with them, Timothy set the tone with a passage which opens 1 Peter (chapter 1:3–9). He read without ceremony, but I read between the lines. My heart was stabbed as I applied each phrase to the Uduks:

> Praise be to the God and Father of our Lord Jesus Christ! In his great mercy he has given us new birth into a living hope through the resurrection of Jesus Christ from the dead, and into an inheritance that can never perish, spoil or fade. This inheritance is kept in heaven for you, who through faith are shielded by God's power until the coming of the salvation that is ready to be revealed in the last time.

> In all this you greatly rejoice, though now for a little while you may have had to suffer grief in all kinds of trials. These have come so that the proven genuineness of your faith—of greater worth than gold, which perishes even though refined by fire—may result in praise, glory and honor when Jesus Christ is revealed. Though you have not seen him, you love him; and even though you do not see him now, you believe in him and are filled with an inexpressible and glorious joy, for you are receiving the goal of your faith, the salvation of your souls.

Timothy smiled kindly at his listening brothers, and then quietly sympathized with what they had been suffering in Ethiopia. Then he shared what the Sudanese Christians had been suffering. Perhaps no Christians in our world today have suffered as severely as the Sudanese. Timothy spoke simply, but their own experiences of hunger and war and separation and death caused the elders to read between the lines of his story and identify deeply. The racial barrier evaporated into fervent prayer. In the days ahead, those prayers for locating the Uduk remnant were answered.

They found their missing community out in western Ethiopia. However, return home still was not safe. The Sudanese Christian story is a tragic one. Those of the body of Christ who are alert to their plight continue to pray for their fortitude, and that their ongoing agony and displacement may be used in God's mysterious purposes.

WHEN OUR THREE-MONTH visa ran out, we did not want to leave. But we had promised our son, Johnathan, and his wife, Betsy, to meet them in Israel as we returned from Ethiopia, and they from John's research on refugees in Sudan. We found them to be wan and twenty pounds lighter, but eager to see the land of our Lord's incarnation together.

Each morning with a lunch Betsy packed, we headed out for some area of Jerusalem or beyond. I kept praying we could make contact with some Falasha Jews. We found one Ethiopian Orthodox family running an art shop in the town of Safed. The father showed us a big poster of Amharic's 250-character alphabet, which he was teaching his children. "How can they hold on to their native language when they must learn in Hebrew?" he lamented. In Jerusalem, we met a

Glimpsing the kinship of grief and glory 327

ETHIOPIAN JEWISH REGIMENT (JERUSALEM, 1988)

few Ethiopians in their two Orthodox churches, one in the Old City, and one outside. But no Falashas.

Then came our day to go to the Wailing Wall. We descended the steps and stood at a distance watching black-coated Jews bobbing their heads toward the wall as they prayed below the Temple Mount.

This usual order of the day was suddenly interrupted by the arrival of what looked like an Israeli army event. Brilliant sunlight poured down on detachment after detachment of Israeli youth who marched down into the courtyard to come to attention before the most sacred stones left to Israel, the Wailing Wall. High above the lip of this wall where the Hebrews could only weep, gleamed the Dome of the Rock, Islam's triumphant shrine, dominating the great enclosure where once stood Solomon's Temple. From the Chapel of Tears across the Kidron Valley we had seen the golden Dome framed by the chapel's focal window a few days before. The window looks out on Jerusalem from just about the location where on the day of the Triumphal Entry, Jesus would have stopped and wept. His words constitute the chapel's inscription: "Oh Jerusalem, Jerusalem, you who kill the prophets and stone those sent to you, how often I have longed to gather your children together, as a hen gathers her chicks under her wings, but you were not willing" (Matthew 23:37). Two centuries later, the Messiah's people still weep.

As tourists who just happened to be at the Wall at that historic moment of vow-taking, we stood transfixed. Masada had become a new reality to us now that we had that week visited that impregnable butte where the last bastion of Jews had stood against the Romans in 73 AD, and had chosen mass suicide to captivity. Now these khaki-uniformed trainees were ready to vow "Masada, never again!" Some were Sabres, native-born Israelis, we learned, and others were immigrants from far-flung nations from China to Australia. We gasped as our eyes were riveted on a detachment standing on the steps in the southwest most corner of the whole expanse... a regiment of handsome recruits with high cheekbones and narrow noses, men and women, and not white.

All week I had prayed to come into contact with Falasha Jews in Israel. Suddenly 250 Ethiopian troops stood before us. When the ceremony was completed, and they relaxed at ease, we drew near and searched their faces. Pride, yes, but Ethiopians are always proud. Dignity, yes, but Ethiopians are always dignified. What was new? Their military tams at cocky tilts, their lighted cigarettes, their quiet isolation, their long looks into the past or perhaps the future, playing over faces at repose.

We had heard that the Falashas were not entirely happy in Israel. Their absorption and integration into society had not been easy for them or for their new nation. Both were paying a high price. To be stripped of all that was familiar, including one's native language, was frightening and disorienting. Living in hotels and city flats and rural kibbutz and military barracks was all new to a people accustomed to family solidarity in a one-room mud hut without electricity or running water. So this was Israel, 20th century.

They had come heralded as the last of the lost tribes and had been redeemed at high cost. Many were the surprises, but none so disturbing as a process to which they were asked to submit, ritual circumcision (just one drop of blood). Were they not already circumcised? Had they not guarded their community from adulteration all these centuries? Had they not kept alive perhaps the oldest of Jewish expressions left in the world, originating before the Babylonian exile? What was the nature of this Judaism being practiced 2400 years later?

The Ethiopian resistance over this circumcision matter was not making the Falashas popular in Israel. Furthermore, they were unusual beyond their color, for they had come out of a situation which had sent an unbalanced community to Israel, an unusually young group, for the old had not been strong enough to come. Sixty-five percent were under 25 years.[128] The Amharic-speaking elders who did make it were being rendered powerless, for they had been stripped of their authority to guide the young, replaced by absorption leaders and teachers of Hebrew and company commanders. Most formidable of all, their priests had been de-legitimized by the power of the rabbinate.

Angry young men who were almost the first of their people to have the tools to communicate with the outside world put up a fight. In Israel they were introduced to public dispute, to strikes. After all, they were the marrying age, and the rabbinate was withholding marriage certificates from them if they did not submit to the ritual circumcision.

---

128. Shelemay and Berger (1986), *Jews*, 82.

Shmuel Avraham was a respected educator and political leader in Ethiopia, a Falasha who survived the anti-intellectual campaign of the Derg and had made the treacherous journey to Israel in 1981. In 1986 he published a book about his community, as an active participant in the Falasha cause. "What was required of me and the others was a *tipat dam*—the ritual drawing of a drop of blood—and immersion in *mikvah—t'villah*," he explained. "This had been the rule since Ethiopian Jews were first included under the Law of Return. The process was called *hidush* ('renewal')."

By 1985, undergoing *tipat dam* in order to be considered Jewish had been waived, but the question was pushed to another level, the time of marriage. Women had always been required to immerse in the *Mikvah* before marriage, but not men. "If an Ethiopian couple is told that the man must also immerse in order to confirm his Jewishness, there is a definite implication of conversion that is offensive to us." Avraham goes on to express the frustration and disappointment that was actually leading some to suicide:

> The absorption workers who brought us the news about our questionable status as Jews were themselves not truly observant Jews; for us this was incredibly ironic. In Ethiopia, we didn't have secular Jews, religious Jews, or orthodox, conservative, and reform Jews. Everyone was simply Jewish. In the villages this meant that everyone went to synagogue, observed Shabbat, read the Torah, and prayed—all were Jews.
>
> When we arrived in Israel, we found that some people smoke and ride cars in Jerusalem on Shabbat. Our elders were greatly angered. Our people are forbidden even to walk long distances on Shabbat. "Where are we now" our elders asked. "It can't be Jerusalem."
>
> The Ethiopians came wanting to live Jewish lives, and ready to learn whatever is taught in Jerusalem. If there was a gap between what they knew and rabbinic Judaism, that was something beyond their control, which they were willing to correct. Treated with respect, they would have accepted all of rabbinic halakha. But being told that we weren't really Jewish destroyed our positive, eager attitude.[129]

---

129. Sh. Avraham and A. Kushner, *Treacherous Journey* (Shapolsky Publ., 1986), 167f.

Glimpsing the kinship of grief and glory   331

When we left Tel Aviv for America, we were heavy hearted for Beta Israel. It is not that Israeli officials haven't struggled mightily with this community's integration. Israel is what Israel is, and that is also a problem. One of their interpreters put the Falasha situation this way as of 1986:

> At this point in their absorption process, tension continues to prevail between their primordial sentiments—those feelings that still tie them to their former ways of life in Ethiopia—and their stated desire to be like other Israelis. This tension is bounded on the one hand by the specter of their becoming a totally separate group, and on the other hand by the vision that the Ethiopians will renounce all their traditions and, apart from color, become indistinguishable from the majority of other Israelis.[130]

Perhaps there is a third possibility down the path of their pilgrimage.

ON WE FLEW TO poor rich America. There we struggled to debrief personally and tried to answer questions about what we'd found. "Egypt is ruined," we'd heard Ato Seyoum summarize in words echoing Pharaoh's counselors during Moses' Ten Plagues. (Ato Seyoum was a professor who had returned to Ethiopia after years away.) So much that had built up over centuries, and particularly the 20th century, had been smashed. On many levels, Ethiopia, like Egypt long ago, seemed ruined—on physical, economic, social, political, and cultural levels. Even the ground had seemed cursed.

Was there nothing hopeful to report? Nothing good to say? Well, for those with eyes to see, there was another level, one which Ato Seyoum, and we, and many were driven to explore. What had happened to the remnant community who had held tightly to God in Jesus the Christ?

They had been mercilessly pursued by the Enemy of God, who is always devising new ways to destroy. He'd tried famine and war. Now he would push bitterness, greed, and jealousy. He would use cults to confuse the untaught thousands who had come to faith. The Enemy would keep putting the pressure on, but during this Derg-time lap of their race, the believers had proven Jesus' promise that "the gates of Hell shall not prevail against the church" (Matthew 16:18, KJV).

---

130. Shelemay and Berger (1986), *Jews*, 84.

How greatly they had suffered; yet their Lord had told them to expect to suffer. And to expect glory along with the grief. Glory was peeking out from the dark clouds over Ethiopia. The church was coming forth in strength. She had been indigenized, sifted, purified, humbled, unified, exercised, charismatized, multiplied, and glorified. A remnant of this generation had been faithful, to the praise of God's glory. Those who could see, could see the ongoing triumph of a higher Sovereign.

> *Dear friends, do not be surprised at the fiery ordeal*
> *that has come on you to test you,*
> *as though something strange were happening to you.*
> *But rejoice inasmuch as you participate in the sufferings of Christ,*
> *so that you may be overjoyed when his glory is revealed.*
> *If you are insulted because of the name of Christ, you are blessed,*
> *for the Spirit of glory and of God rests on you. [...]*
>
> *And the God of all grace, who called you to his eternal glory in Christ,*
> *after you have suffered a little while,*
> *will himself restore you and make you strong, firm and steadfast.*
> *To him be the power for ever and ever. Amen.*
>
> (1 Peter 4:12–14; 5:10–11)

Part VII

TROPHIES OF VICTORY

(During 1989–94)

For those who sow in tears will reap with songs of joy.
He who goes out weeping, carrying seed to sow,
will return with songs of joy, carrying sheaves with him.
                (Psalm 126:5–6)

Chapter 27

SURROUNDED

Over the communist world in the late eighties, confidence in their ideology was waning, but fear was used to hold people in check. The deep longing for freedom sent more and more shoots of green up through the concrete grayness. The monolith began to crack. First came Poland's Solidarity movement, fueled by a strong Catholic base. After Brezhnev's death, Gorbachev's *glasnost* opened the way for long suppressed nationalism to spring into expression in country after country. The year 1989 was pivotal. Symbol of the system, the Berlin Wall between East and West Germany went down. Czechoslovakia's "velvet revolution" freed another people. While Chinese students demonstrated in Tiananmen Square, a coup almost succeeded in Ethiopia. In Romania, a revolution of prayer brought down Ceauşescu during Christmas week. By 1991, even Russia would tear down the symbols of a failed ideology. All over the world, people watched their televisions in amazement as Lenin's mute and prone statue was lifted by helicopter, and dumped. It seemed the unbelievable had occurred.

In the light of what was happening in the communist bloc, military funding was drying up for Ethiopia. As early as 1988, Gorbachev began to pull back military assistance to Ethiopia, asking for a "just solution" to the disputes in the north.[131] He told Mengistu that the Kremlin, which from 1977 to 1989 had poured a total of eleven billion dollars into his war economy, would not renew its military treaty with Addis Ababa was to expire in 1991.[132] Meanwhile Cuba had reduced its troops after the Ogaden War, and in 1989 terminated

---

131. Ofcansky and Berry (1993), *Ethiopia*, 296.
132. *Insight*, June 12, 1989, 38.

twelve years of military cooperation. Even after their break in diplomatic relations in 1973, Israel had quietly continued to supply various sorts of military aid, spurred on by their stake in the strategic Red Sea region, as well as by Zionist hopes for rescuing Beta Israel.

In Ethiopia as the 1980s closed, a light at the end of the Revolution's tunnel was beginning to gleam in the distance. Opposition to Mengistu's government began to unite. The estrangement between the Eritrean People's Liberation Front and the Tigray People's Liberation Front (TPLF) began to dissipate. The TPLF destroyed a 20,000 Ethiopian army force in Tigray in 1989.[133] An alliance was formed when the TPLF held its third congress, which subsequently united a number of fronts (including Amhara and Oromo factions) which became known as the Ethiopian People's Revolutionary Democratic Front (EPRDF). Working under the framework of the EPRDF, the Tigray People's Liberation Front in 1989 moved south into Wollo, winning victories in Dessie and Debre Tabor, which cut the road between the cities of Gondar and Bahir Dar, allowing the insurgents to get into northern Shewa, less than 160 kilometers from Addis Ababa. Mengistu stepped up mobilization and resistance. In 1990, the Ethiopian People's Revolutionary Democratic Front controlled most of Tigray, and in 1991, launched three offensives that destroyed the Ethiopian army.

In February of 1991, Operation Tewodros drove the government out of Gondar and Gojjam in two weeks. In March, other operations resulted in the capture of military headquarters at Nekemte in Wollega, and overran Dessie and Kombolcha in Wollo. By May 20th, the EPRDF had captured all the government positions in northern Shewa, had taken Ambo, and were advancing on the capital from the west. Little but demoralized and fleeing troops lay between the EPRDF forces and the capital.

During this buildup, British, Canadian, and US Embassies urged nonessential government personnel and dependents to leave.[134] Evacuations began. Missions took necessary steps, like backing up

---

133. A fuller account of the end of this struggle can be found in the final chapters of Ofcansky and Berry (1993), *Ethiopia*.

134. Many of these details about the last few weeks before Addis Ababa fell came from a report by Jean Sokvitne and from interviews with others on the scene.

computer systems, sending out copies of important documents with travelers, and having wages for employees prepared and on hand. Ethiopian Airlines planes were being flown out of the country to avoid capture, while Lufthansa and the United Nations were sending in emergency flights.

Reportedly, the EPRDF was asking the government to form a coalition which could comprise transitional rule until a more permanent government could be established. On April 19th, President Mengistu's speech had sounded more ready to talk. His exit was regarded as essential for the upcoming negotiations to succeed. In May, the US Assistant Secretary of State was able to persuade Mengistu to resign the presidency and accept exile in Zimbabwe. He fled the country by small plane on the 21st. On the 23rd, Lenin's statue was removed from its imposing place, the red flag with its hammer and sickle was removed from Revolution Square, and Mengistu's picture disappeared from government offices. In the midst of this vast turnaround, the Ethiopian armed forces disintegrated and began selling their weapons and robbing civilians. Some soldiers went home. Many officers fled to Sudan, Djibouti, or Kenya. Naval units dispersed across the Red Sea.

That last week, the EPRDF dealt strategically with the seat of government, capturing the air force base at Debre Zeit first. For three days, Addis Ababa was left untouched. In their houses, people waited in fear of what was coming, many fervent in prayer. Overhead, hour after hour the scream of jet after jet split the sky. Why? In that strange pause between Friday May 24 and Sunday the 26th, an operation code-named "Solomon" was taking place. To the Falasha saga was being added another astounding chapter. Israel had been furnishing an array of military assistance to Ethiopia in exchange for permitting the emigration of the Beta Israel. That month of May, Israel had paid Mengistu US $35 million in cash for his clearance to fly the gathered Falashas from Addis Ababa to Israel. Only an estimated 5,000 were left behind, mostly near Gondar. When the last of forty plane sorties had landed, the lid came off in Israel:

The Jerusalem Post (Sunday, May 26, 1991)

Ethiopian Jewry Rescued—14,400 are flown here in a 24-hour lift
Israel made history yesterday completing a massive lightning airlift that carried some 14,400 beleaguered Ethiopian Jews from Addis Ababa to their ancestral homeland in a breathtaking 24 hours. "Operation Solomon," conducted by the Israel Defense Forces in coordination with the Jewish Agency, [...] as well as the Ethiopian government [...] brought tears to the eyes of many of the thousands of Israelis who took part in the reunification of Jews with 20,000 of their family members already in Israel. [...] "This is the reason why Israel exists!" said one *El Al* ground crew member.

Such was the announcement of a most unusually engineered flight of that ancient Jewish community over the Red Sea—at the breathtaking moment of Addis Ababa's capture. Yet the operation was accomplished without panic. While government troops guarded the perimeter of Addis Ababa's international airport, rebel forces had halted in a circle eighteen kilometers outside the capital. As if guided by a master plan, the TPLF paused outside its target for three disciplined days, long enough for this historic event to be completed. What a strange day in Ethiopian history.

And what a triumphant day in Israeli history. The rescue plane loads included a reported world record of 1,000 passengers on one Jumbo jet, a cargo flight with no seats. "You could never do it with pudgy Russians and Israelis with five suitcases in each hand," a bus driver told the *Post.* "They are thin, these Ethiopians."

The new arrivees were met by family members who had long awaited their arrival, but were stunned at its sudden accomplishment. Six years before, Operation Moses had airlifted some 8,500 from the Sudanese refugee camps. It was the strong who had lived through the 170 mile trek out of Ethiopia through mountains and deserts and survived death-trap internment camps in Sudan, finally to be rescued in the unbelievable operation. Now those 8,500 were being joined by 14,400 who had been waiting in Ethiopia. They'd long been dreaming of Jerusalem. Said their proverb: "The hungry go to food, the thirsty go to water, but I go to Jerusalem." This last Operation included may of the old who had remained behind, and the young—some so young that seven were born during the flight!

Wrapped in their *shammas*, the travelers hobbled down the ramp with stunned faces. In the next few days, families members hunted through their forty absorption centers for loved ones. Most were rewarded with the poignant joy of reunion.

What a day was May 26, 1991, in world history, too, for those who thought globally—in World Jewry, in the Arab world, and the Christian world, as well. Symbolically, the Queen of Sheba's descendants had been captured. What might the next moves on the chessboard be? Challenging new options emerged for every group. Those unique Jewish clusters left behind in Ethiopia faced unusual new problems as well.

Some fumed over the whole sticky issue. Was this a matter of buying and selling a community? Was this really "redemption of the lost tribe of Dan"? Was this flood of foreigners coming into Israel under the Law of Return simply the result of political Zionism? Time may tell.

ON MONDAY THE 27th, while peace talks were being held in London, law and order was breaking down in the capital. Armed government soldiers roamed the city. Prison doors were opened, releasing 2,000 incarcerated political detainees, thieves, and murderers. A thorough EPRDF takeover begged for doing, if only to maintain law and order. At SIM Headquarters, the staff hunkered down in the lower storey, and nurse Jean Sokvitne prepared emergency medical supplies in case they came under siege.

Preliminary to surrounding Addis Ababa, the TPLF swung east around Bishoftu Mountain to come up behind the Ethiopian Air Base at Debre Zeit. John Dakins, who was running Bishoftu then, quite innocently drove right into the forces moving straight along the Bishoftu road. John was ordered to drive back down the road they'd taken and to spend the night in a little village, until Debre Zeit was secured. The cheerful New Zealander was not mistreated. Most of the "conquerors" were well-disciplined teenage troops, he said, some of the toughest of whom were women.[135]

---

135. In Eritrea's long guerrilla war, women played significant roles, as women did in the Tigrayan liberation effort, also. A. Wilson, *The Challenge Road* (Red Sea Press, 1991), provides profiles of the roles played and conditions experienced by women fighters.

When the TPLF swept on through and surrounded the base, Ethiopian airmen feared for their lives. Sixty officers were rounded up in the middle of Debre Zeit town, awaiting their fate. Believers took pity on them and began supplying the prisoners with food. Many expected to be killed and were uniquely open to hearing the risen Lord's invitation to believe in him. "Because I live, you shall live" (John 14:19). Among those being held were the three Air Force officers, Girma Abebe, Solomon Beyene, and Teshome Haile. After a few days, junior officers were sorted out and given permission to go. The fate of senior officers remained unknown. So many had been converted in those short days, that by their own choice Girma, Solomon, and Teshome took the risk of remaining among the waiting prisoners, in order to strengthen and tend to their new brothers' needs.

Around Addis Ababa, the noose tightened. Those two days are indelible in the minds of those on the scene. Out on the west edge of town, Sahle Tilahun and Aberash Takele were surprised to sight tanks in their area. They feared their home would be demolished. They watched and prayed as the tense hours ticked past. At dawn of the 28th, Sahle noticed the Ethiopian troops moving about their nearby encampment peacefully, impotently shaving and combing their hair as smoke arose in the distance from the palace. Later in the day, they'd fire straight up in the air to get the attention of those passing by. "You want to buy something? A door? A fridge for 400 Birr? An AK–47 automatic rifle or a hand grenade for a bargain price? Come and buy!" As the battle-weary TPLF swept in, Sahle noticed long, uncombed hair framing determined faces.

When the fireworks really let loose, Sahle and Aberash gathered their children under the bed. The whole world seemed to be collapsing, with Derg tanks shooting in every direction and rifle fire ripping the air. Theirs had consistently been a praying and singing family. They'd not prayed and sung in this context before! Singing steadied their hearts and helped to drown out the three or four hour din. "The Lord is my shepherd..." they read from Psalm 23, words they had never experienced in such a setting.

Bruce Adams by then had taken over the reins of the mission from Alex Fellows. He remembers it all happening so much more quickly and neatly than could have been anticipated. The battle for the city that morning of May 28th, was accomplished with little resistance. At 5 AM, the TPLF's tanks with big guns started moving up Churchill Boulevard toward the Old Palace grounds, where the Derg people took their last stand. Of course Mengistu had been gone a week. It was uncanny, Bruce said, for the Mission compound community to hear the gunfire while gathered around a radio listening to a BBC correspondent who was broadcasting from the Hilton Hotel just across the city in plain view.

Huge blasts rocked the city when ammunition stashes were hit. Windows were blown out everywhere, including those at SIM Headquarters. By eleven that morning, quietness reigned. The takeover was finished. On street corners, TPLF soldiers, male and female, and very young, maintained disciplined order. Most spoke Tigrinya, few knew Amharic. A few more gigantic blasts struck subsequently. From out on the Debre Zeit road south of Addis, an isolated blast flattened "armory hill," where a huge supply of arms had been stashed underground. Actually, except for 2–3,000 deaths from the explosions, reportedly only 600–800 people were actually killed in battle. It had been a long road from Tigray to Addis, but victory had come.

As news spread across the realm, reactions varied. Some thanked God the ordeal was over. The brutal tyrant, Ali Musa, shot himself. Up north in Eritrea, the Eritrean People's Liberation Front (EPLF) had taken Dekemhare, Keren, Asmara and the port at Assab. With the fall of Addis Ababa to the Ethiopian People's Revolutionary Democratic Front, the EPLF announced they now considered Eritrea to be a self-government region. A referendum regarding secession would be conducted, they said. The unity of Ethiopia was cracking.

The Ethiopian People's Revolutionary Democratic Front (EPRDF) called in various diplomats, nongovernmental organizations, the United Nations and the European Economic Community to the Hilton Hotel to discuss vast relief needs in the country, and pledged to honor agreements made with the past government. Periodic incidents kept the city tense. Out in an area where people were pillaging an ammunition dump, suddenly it caught fire, exploding wildly. Many were killed or badly burned. Hearing later that many of those who were burned were afraid to go to a clinic lest they be accused, nurse Jean Sokvitne ventured out from the mission property to find and treat people.

The city began again to resume some normality, but was rocked by a mighty blast on June 4th at 4:30 in the morning, when another large ammunition dump near the old Girls Christian Academy was set on fire. The Pepsi plant (with its carbon dioxide supply) went up in a raging inferno, but the fuel tanks and large grain storage silos adjacent, mercifully, were left in tact. Windows were shattered all over town, and an estimated one thousand nearby homes were damaged. Mengistu-sympathizing arsonists were suspected.

Down in the wilds of Gamo Gofa retreating toward the Sudan border, some Ethiopian soldiers hid out and lived by pillaging. The Gujjis invited the Wolaittan settlers who had been forcibly transplanted to the settlement on the east side of Lake Abaya to meet for a "good-bye feast." It surely was. The few who had come to Christ among the Gujjis caught wind of their community's intentions, and warned whatever Wolaittans they could. Gerhard and Edith Bössler were caught in the tense situation. At the close of the feast, the Gujjis rose up and slaughtered 300 of their guests. Hardly touched by the vicissitudes of the Revolution, it seemed to be "business as usual" in Gujjiland.

In June, the Worker's Party of Ethiopia was no longer functioning. Meles Zenawi, the EPRDF's leader, had put an Amhara in as Prime Minister of the interim government. The temporary government promised elections within two years, and agreed that a UN sponsored referendum on Eritrean independence should be held in 1993. A few confiscated properties began to be returned to citizens and churches. Ethiopian Airlines resumed flights again; the Assab road opened; busses started running even to Asmara, something that hadn't happened for eleven years.

When "reckoning time" inevitably arrived in the long established communities across the land, crooked officials during the Marxist-Leninist regime were sometimes exposed. A rare "Joseph" stood out. A young Christian named Desalegn Tesemma had come into much persecution while a high school student at home and then a university in Addis Ababa, but on return to Hadiyya he'd been appointed as the Deputy Subregion administrator. That was in 1989. His parents were distressed that he would work for an atheistic government. "I assured them that this was from the Lord, just like Joseph had known that his appointment in Pharaoh's court was designed by God. My parents were persuaded, and the elders of the church met to commend me to God in my new job, vowing to keep me in their prayers every day." From the very first, Desalegn declared himself openly as a practicing Bible-believing Christian. Accusations were gathered against him, listing all sorts of "crimes" but somehow he stayed on duty.

"When the TPLF overpowered the Mengistu government in 1991," Desalegn recounted later, "all the administrators ran away, fearing reprisals from the people. I stayed where I was. Some friends asked me, 'Why don't you take your family and flee for your life?' I replied that the Lord had called me to this job and was able to protect me under any circumstances. When the new government finally got around to investigating me they asked the people of the district what sort of administrator I had been, and not one person testified against me."

Such was a loving God's answer to the praying community who had undergirded the administrator. Lives of faithful men like Desalegn pointed to the One who really could enable a weak human to become the sterling "new man" Marxism-Leninism had so confidently hoped to create. As a Bulgarian believer had written from prison years before, although derided, persecuted, and hidden away, the Christian in a socialist society is simply to *be* the new man—a man whom only Christ can produce.

Praise our God, O peoples, let the sound of his praise be heard;
he has preserved our lives and kept our feet from slipping.
For you, O God, tested us; you refined us like silver.
You brought us into prison and laid burdens on our backs.
You let men ride over our heads; we went through fire and water,
but you brought us to a place of abundance. [...]

Come and listen, all you who fear God;
let me tell you what he has done for me.
                    (Psalm 66:8–12, 16)

Chapter 28

BREAKING FORTH

The Addis Ababa stadium had never seen anything like it. The stands and playing field were packed, and there wasn't even a soccer game. Thousands of Christians were gathered for a public "Praise Giving Day." Their songs split the skies. Tesfaye's son, Theophilos, reared in Chencha, had returned from England only twenty days before. He stood on the playing field, trying to take it all in. In every corner groups of people were singing, bowing, praying, weeping, lifting their hands in praise. Fifteen hundred choirs from all over the city, from every denomination, were leading in worship.

Theophilos was in such a state of awe that he couldn't even remember later who preached. "Pastor Kedamo maybe," he said. "Heaven came down that day!" Childhood memories in Chencha must have come back… his father and uncles and other elders taken to prison… his own suffering as the child of a "criminal" in the cadres' eyes… his mother's struggle to keep the family fed and clothed and brought up "in the nurture and admonition of the Lord"… his father's illness in jail and his mother's bold plea for hospitalization… the elders' release after two long years… yet Tesfaye's being hounded by Ali Musa… keeping his father away for years… on the run, or working in Hossana or Addis Ababa or elsewhere… and then his sudden, brief reappearance in their home under cover of night. It was all over now! By God's grace, they'd all survived, and grown, and could even affirm what Tesfaye had deeply learned over these rough years: "We know that in all things God works for the good of those who love him, who have been called according to his purpose." All over the stadium, people were reliving their own memories, reawakening their pain, and savoring the comfort and deliverance their Lord provided. Truly, "Great is thy faithfulness!"

Passersby must have wondered at the stadium's sounds that night, and the size of the crowd. Can there be so many of these Pentes? Where have they all come from? We thought they'd been stamped out! Painted on the wall above the main entrance gate, Marx, Lenin, and Engels still gazed down upon the event. Their two-dimensional faces paled in comparison with the crowd who vibrated with another dimension. Since Dialectical Materialism had been swept away, great surges of spiritual expression kept surfacing every time a church door opened. KHC's largest church, *Meserete Heywet* ("Foundation of Life"), had so many coming that they multiplied into eleven congregations, meeting wherever they could find to congregate, all over town. When the *Mulu Wongel* ("Full Gospel") church opened its doors the first time after the Revolution, 15,000 people arrived. Churches of *Meserete Kristos* ("Christ the Foundation"), the Mennonite-founded group, once with 200, now were 2,000. The Lutheran-initiated church, *Mekane Yesus* ("the Place Where Jesus Dwells"), had burgeoned just like SIM's congregations had. And so it was all over the capital and beyond. The number of believers had grown, often tenfold, whether they'd operated underground or above.

After the euphoria of celebrating the victory of their mutual Sovereign, and recognizing their unity in his service, the various evangelical groups began to take stock. Now that they had the freedom to choose a course, what should their priorities be? What had God been preparing them for during this long period of pruning? What fruit did He wish to bring forth? Although they might have varied in ways of baptizing or interpretations of communion or styles of church government, the dozen or so evangelical-spirited groups found they were of one mind on the main thing—people needed to know Jesus the Christ. Lives which had been demolished needed comfort, strength, hope, rebuilding. As they took stock of the new government's attitude, they were amazed to find little blockage of requests for return of property, or purchase of new, or permits for building churches and schools.

All over the south, believers reclaimed churches and took stock of the vast number of new members of the family who needed to be grounded and strengthened in their faith. Training became the watchword of the decade. In Addis Ababa, new Christian magazines appeared, added to the few which had been maintained underground during the Revolution. At Debre Zeit, the underground Bible school blossomed in the open. At Kuriftu lake, over the hill from Bishoftu, a large church building arose. Community development projects and the orphanage which the Bonds had helped the KHC plant out at Kuriftu expanded further.[136] Vegetable gardening, cattle breeding, chicken farming—all sorts of new or expanded projects took off. In Gamo Gofa, Bible schools opened, scripture translation continued, and the Aari and Maale believers partnered with missionaries among the Banna and Mursi. At Hossana, a second Kale Heywet Ministry Training Center was begun, and at Soddo, community health projects were undertaken. At Dilla, Ato Werku organized an evangelism conference, calling in leaders from all the country's evangelical groups. People of vision raised the banner for moving out. "Let's reach the rest of the country while we can. This is our hour! Let's get going!"

The various missions were rejuvenated as well. They rose to the occasion by sending in new recruits and many old-timers made their way back. SIM's leadership passed to Bruce Bond, the New Zealand horticulturist who had first done plantings at Shashemane Leprosarium's agricultural program in the 1950s. Mr. Bond had spearheaded the Bishoftu reforestation project during the famine and helped the Kale Heywet Church to create Kuriftu's agricultural / horticultural project. Now he was asked to tend the mission's spiritual planting in a new era. The national church was calling loud for help with training. Establishing more Bible schools was given top priority, although 4,000 students were already in session. Training was needed in areas that ranged from computer operation to crop management. The national leaders who had been seasoned throughout the Revolution were now mature men. They were equipped to work shoulder to shoulder with the mission. Now, however, it was the church rather than the mission which must take the lead. January of 1992 saw the foundation stone of a large KHC office complex go into place. Within a few years, the old compound which had been expanded by using boxcar sized shipping containers would be replaced by a modern four-storey office building as the hub of

---

136. See Bruce and Norene Bond's *When Spider Webs Unite* (Bond, 2005).

KHC operations, from which Dr. Mulatu and Ato Shiferaw Wolde Michael would direct the whole denomination. Ato Shiferaw would head up Compassion International's broad work in Ethiopia with children as well.

SIM headquarters, once jammed with a thousand worshippers on Sundays, and hundreds of students in night school, soon grew sedate. It seemed a bit lonely without all the bustle of students and church leaders coming and going as they had before. The International Evangelical Church which had nearly burst the SIM compound chapel seams on Sundays moved into a beautiful new facility designed by Malcom McGregor shared with the Evangelical Theological College (ETC). ETC was like a wide-leafed tree grown out of its Grace Bible Institute root which SIM had planted three decades before in Jimma, but now was serving many denominations. On the university and medical school campuses, EVASU, the evangelical student movement, became bold in its witness. Christians drew questioning students in to investigate the previously forbidden option in their life search.

WHAT OF THOSE WHO were still reeling from the collapse of the system in which they had put their trust? So many had hoped communist promises would deliver a new society. They too had paid a heavy price. Perhaps Meresse's story can communicate one thoughtful man's summary of what the Revolution's experiment boiled down to.

We got to know Meresse Abraham among a group of seven into whose fellowship we were drawn when we returned to Ethiopia, three years after the Revolution collapsed. The group had come into being right after the change, and had been handed on from Joe Harding's leadership to others, and eventually to Dr. Bascom. The group was made up of business and professional people, all of whom knew English well. In past years, any Bible study leadership we'd done in the countryside had to be conducted in Amharic.

On Tuesday nights, in the Mission living room after their work we met with them for two years. Never had we had such consistent, mind-to-mind and heart-to-heart contact with a group of Ethiopians. Considering their ethnic diversity and former animosities, such a group could only have been held together by the Spirit of the living Lord. Their provincial homes ranged from Eritrea to

SHIFERAW WOLDE MICHAEL (ADDIS ABABA, 1994)

Tigray to Shewa to Gamo Gofa, and religious backgrounds ranged from Orthodox family background to primal religions. Six were men, one a woman. Among them was a school administrator, a teacher, a clinic supervisor, a plant manager, and a telecommunications trouble shooter. Three were married, one had lost his wife, one married while we were all together, one shortly after we left, and two remain single. From their individual stories, we learned that three had been in prison, one had been an alcoholic, one a confirmed Marxist. One had studied abroad in America, another had done six years training in Russia. One had lived with Peace Corps teachers in Ethiopia, had longed to emigrate, but never managed to do so. Politically, some were from "the winners" in this latest conflict, some from "the losers," and others from the community caught in between. What sort of rough edges and heated discussions might we expect? Strangely, warmth consistently flowed from their shared Lord.

The second year into our studies together in our living room, we took a few weeks to share our life stories—one each evening. Every one of those nights left us informed, deeply touched, and drawn ever closer to them all. Ato Meresse was the one who had been a hard-line communist. He was the tallest of the group, always neatly dressed with dress shirt, suit and tie, closing a day's work in labor relations in a skyscraper down on Churchill Avenue. He walked to the mission, owning no car. A real gentleman, he emanated humility, and attitude which had probably developed recently. He chose his words carefully, often gesturing with his long hands. His forehead was high, his face fine-featured, and his hair was touched with gray. I guessed him to be about forty-five. His manner was serious but pleasant, and a joyful light in his eyes often revealed keen perception, deep thought, and kindly empathy with the group as we interacted. This is the story he told us—supplemented by some questions I later asked him:

I'VE COME FROM AN Orthodox family—as most of us have. At that time to me religion was mostly from watching my mother, who was a devoted follower of the Orthodox Church. I was the third oldest.

After grade school in Asmara, I came to Addis for high school. There I had a chance to read about Dialectical Materialism and was highly impressed by it. Dialectical Materialism talks a lot about "Mother Nature." Theoretically it is based in science with all the mathematical calculations, etc. Although it was strictly forbidden by the government of Haile Selassie, no matter how risky it might be, I kept learning it secretly in places—like toilet rooms and dormitories. I went head on for it, and the deeper I became in it, the more I felt I was close to understanding "Mother Nature." Communism has its own "trinity." I worshipped Marx, Lenin, and Engels, and became their disciple.

However, my higher education in the late 1960s was interrupted. I was caught with political pamphlets in the university. The fourth and fifth year students were agitating. I was more interested in their leadership than their doctrine, but the leader of the underground movement (anti-Haile Selassie) gave me four pads of printed letters (400 sheets each) and said, "Go and hide them in your dormitory." (They were to be distributed in the streets at night.) I got caught by security red handed. They took me to jail in a military camp with forty students, mostly men. It was a horrible experience, and lasted forty-three days. Finally parliament asked His Imperial Majesty for our forgiveness. Some of the ministers' sons and high officials were involved. We were "forgiven"—a category of judgment—all forty of us. Three were allowed back to the university, eleven to fifteen were not allowed to return or to hold any government post. The rest were now allowed back, but could join a government office. That ended my college education, which lasted only half a year.

In jail I was sick. I liked to play basketball. When I went to the camp I weighed 89–90 kilos; after forty-three days I weighed 60. There was little food, we underwent physical torture. At five in the morning we were made to run barefoot in sand—till we had bloody feet; we had to walk kneeling—it was planned demoralization. I had to spend six months in the hospital afterward. I never recovered in weight.

When I got out of Balcha hospital, I saw two announcements: Telecommunication and Civil Aviation. I passed both tests. I went to Telecommunications the next week, and was sent to Dire Dawa. I wanted to get away from Addis. I was demoralized. After two years the revolution came. I met my wife in Dire Dawa. We were married a month after the revolution. When it erupted—it seemed to me "a blessing in disguise"—a dream to see His Imperial Majesty destroyed. He'd destroyed my education. With all my heart I joined the Party. I was a devoted anti-imperialist.

I was fascinated with Marxism. I even tried to translate Castro, the *Communist Manifesto*, and Ho Chi Minh into Amharic. It taught "dog eat dog." You know, the Revolution eats its children. This is a law of the revolution and people accept it. In 1974 the revolution erupted. When the military regime took over and proclaimed socialism, I saw it as a blessing for me. I did not hesitate to join in one of the political parties which the junta established. In the beginning I thought all was going well and smoothly. No. Nothing went well and smoothly, for shortly after the organization of the parties there came this fight for power among them. To make a long story short, the military crushed all the parties and banned them.

During this transitional period, many were killed and arrested and I was one of those arrested for political reasons. I was an Eritrean. My younger brother was with the Eritrean People's Liberation Front in the field. They wanted to isolate me. It made me bitter. I was taken to the police and was held twenty-three days in jail underground,

MERESSE ABRAHAM (ADDIS ABABA, 1996)

in dark solitary confinement. It is a story which I do not choose to go into now. For the first few weeks, no one knew where I was, and this shook my wife. Later I found out that because of this rumor my wife had some mental trauma. My wife didn't know where I was. She thought I'd been killed. She never recovered from that trauma. When she died a year later, I almost went crazy. I connected her death to the shock of my disappearance.

The incident of my arrest brought confrontation. I went totally against the people in local Party leadership—but not against Marxism-Leninism. I started to attack them. I was bitter. I'd been lucky enough to be released from prison, but the loss of my wife was something I could not bear. I hated the city I lived in. I was totally demoralized; everything was dark around me. I was not even sure what to do with my three children who were fourteen, nine, and five years old. The first step I took was to apply for transfer. My application was accepted and six months later at the end of the year 1990, I left Dire Dawa for Addis.

In Addis nothing changed, in fact, it was the other way around—more frustration. I was restless and unstable. So I thought drinking maybe would help and I drank a lot. But things went from bad to worse. Drinking was no solution. Yet the hunger to find a remedy kept boiling within me.

I'd had a friend for years, a close friend who had stayed in Addis Ababa while I went to Dire Dawa. I had become a communist, he a Christian (not realized by me). We began to meet, and each time I suggested meeting Sunday morning, he never wanted to meet me then. He'd say "afternoon." It took him time to tell me his position. "I have a place to go every Sunday morning, but you won't like it," he said. I asked "Why not?" Eventually he said, "Come see for yourself." "I'll see where he goes," I thought.

He brought me to the International Evangelical Church (IEC) building. I found it to be an international group. There were young and old and well-to-do people. Kind of a club, I thought, a social gathering. "Are you a member of this group?" I asked my friend. I had no idea it was a church. I'd thought church people were all poor, sick, crying people in difficulty. These people were not that type.

The first Sunday the talk was meaningless to me, although in English. Afterwards, I asked my friend, "What was he talking about?" "The Bible," he said. "He was preaching." "Preaching!" I exclaimed. "Is this a church? Did you understand it?" I was confused. How come I didn't understand, I asked myself when alone. I'll give it one more chance, I thought.

We met again. I learned later that it was a Pastor Bark who was speaking. He was speaking from the book of Matthew, something about hypocrisy. I thought he was talking only to me. I couldn't even look to left or right. I felt I must leave that place, but I had no power to get up. He was hammering me! "Is this magic?" I asked myself. "Is he a magician?" I was a man of forty, but I felt four or five there, totally zero. It was very painful. "You're a hypocrite," he was saying, as if to me. It was one of the longest hours of my life—in my heart, my mind, my soul. I had seen painful things—I'd seen torture—and heard painful things, but this was the most painful of all. He talked only twenty-five to thirty minutes, but it seemed like the whole day. "Stop!" I was thinking, "When will it stop?!"

Afterwards I asked my friend, "Is he a magician?" "No, the Holy Spirit leads him," he answered. "Who is the Holy Spirit?" I asked.

I wanted to grasp this. "Come next week and you'll find out," was his answer.

That week from Monday to Saturday I couldn't sleep, couldn't work normally. His words came back. I was restless. I had no one to ask advice of. "I'm not normal," I thought. "That magician did something to me." I couldn't sleep or eat and I told my friend how bad I was feeling. "Come Sunday and you'll find some answers," he said. "You can talk to him after the meeting."

I was thinking about it. "Did he say I can meet that man and ask him questions?" What I wanted was revenge. "I can shame him! I thought, ridicule him like he did to me—by my knowledge of Marxist-Leninism!" (Except he did it before the whole congregation, and I couldn't do that.) If God laughs, He must have been laughing, so childish and stupid I was.

On the next Sunday that I went, I was restless, just waiting to meet him. There was singing, and then a younger man came to speak, a pastor Steve. I was more angry. He's really a magician, I thought. He knew I was ready for him and so he didn't come!

The message from the younger man was on love. He even touched on the marriage relationship. I almost cried. The younger one was not like that hard man the time before. He didn't hate, I thought. He was gentle and kind. I told my friend, "If that hard man is not coming next week, I'll come." The Holy Spirit was cooling me down.

The third Sunday I attended it was Pastor Bark speaking again. I thought he was going to expose my secrets and talk to me again. But he was gentler, kind. I thought it was my first time to see him. Magicians are all ugly in my mind. Now this man was being gentle. I listened. What's going on? I asked my self. He was tough last time, he exposed my secrets. The first Sunday was hard, the next was about love, now this third time I've come, he's changed.

I decided that on the next Sunday I'd talk to whoever was in the pulpit. I was planning, I'll shake his hand and then I'll say, "Can I talk to you?' The next Sunday, pastor Steve came again. I was more relaxed. But I just had no understanding spiritually. Is he talking to me or not? I asked myself. As we were walking out, a black American was just in front of me. I was waiting for that handshake. When I came to the speaker, he was talking to this man who he seemed to have known in America. Steve Strauss gave me his hand, but he kept talking to the other man. It broke me! It shocked me. He was not even looking at me. I was totally shattered! My friend asked, "How did you find the message?" "Do these people discriminate?" I fumed. "He refused to even look at me!"

For three or four Sundays I refused to go. For two Sundays my friend stayed away with me. The third week he went alone to the church, and came to me after the ceremony. "That church is for Americans or white people," I said—although I had seen many Africans. The forth Sunday he came early and said, "Please, let's go to the church. We'll see it, then go somewhere together afterward." "Okay," I said.

Bark was preaching. For the first time, I tried to understand. He was talking about John 8:31–32, Christ's words about how to find truth. I had attended about eight Sundays by then, and that was the first meaningful speech which got through to me. I thought I understood. "What is the truth?" was the question. It seemed elementary to me. "Without Christ, a person is in darkness, is dead, is in bondage," he said. My mind started to catch up. I had always had this hunger for truth.

We went home and I read the Bible with my friend. I read John 8:31–32 in Amharic. That was the door—that was how my mind was opened. I had questions, was in confusion, had problems, but a kind of change was going on inside myself.

A few months later, after one ceremony I went to talk to Pastor Joe. I approached him systematically, not directly. "I want to know more. Are there books? A library I could visit?" I asked him. "Before I answer that," Pastor Joe said, "can you and I talk some time this week?" That was what I really wanted! I came Tuesday and we met in the big living room here at the mission compound. "First of all," he asked me, "have you accepted Jesus as your Savior?" "Where? How? What's that?" I asked. He gave me a testimony. He used Bible verses. He was tactful, spoke with simplicity. "Let's meet once or twice a week," he said. "Are you willing?" I said "Yes!"

A few months later the Derg collapsed and the Ethiopian People's Revolutionary Democratic Front came in. By then I'd joined with some group that met (five or six people) with Pastor Joe. I think we were all beginners. He started to teach us. I am still learning.

The churches had been closed during the Derg regime, but now they were opened. I was so thirsty, so hungry, that I went with a friend who had been in the Full Gospel church before it was closed. He went, and I did too. The Amharic version of worship and teaching was even more wonderful than the English! There I accepted Jesus as my Savior and my Lord. I got a Bible, was baptized, and a tremendous change came in my life.

Physically, all was not smooth, but I had peace inside and more patience in my character. I stopped drinking. I don't know how. It went out of my life. There were changes. I found out that receiving Jesus as Savior meant coming from darkness to light.

Now I understand how the devil worked through Marxism. The devil likes to copy the Bible, to run parallel to Christianity. I also know that Dialectical Materialism has its own trinity. The Bible reveals God as the Father, the creator. In Dialectical Materialism, Marx is the father, the founder. Biblically, God the Son sacrifices Himself on the cross. In Dialectical Materialism, Frederic Engels sacrificed his finances to finance Karl Marx in London in his exile. In the Bible, God the Holy Spirit does the work of God in our lives. In Dialectical Materialism, Lenin was the one who put the theory into practice. Communism's three disciples of the devil were my idols. In Marxism-Leninism you don't have hope. People live and die and that's all. Mother Nature. Nothing to hope for. There's a time limit. You run when your age allows but when you grow old and are decaying, you become meaningless—like garbage. The ideology stops somewhere, and it has a dying, too; then it is all dark. In Christ you can hope. Age doesn't matter. Life doesn't decay.

In Dialectical Materialism you have to read, memorize, and then scientifically practice it. In the Bible, you can read it, but it also reads you. Dialectical Materialism doesn't talk to you, answer you, read you. I found out that the Bible has already read me! I came more and more close to the spiritual life. In Dialectical Materialism, matter remains just the same, dead. The Bible is new, it's alive. Every morning the word of God is new. In matter, you don't experience these things; with matter you get tired of it; you may even dislike it. If you read Genesis 4, every time you read it, there will be a new revelation. This is mysterious to me! I'd had a restless mind since childhood, always looking for new things. I thought materialism was the best I could find. I was wrong. The Bible is the best of them all!

My life has changed. Of course, I have flesh and blood, but the Lord is always at hand. He can solve things. I'm a member now in the Full Gospel church. I am serving part time, teaching newcomers before baptism. Praise the Lord, I have brought three groups up to baptism, and now I'm meeting with a fourth group. Life with Jesus is wonderful!

My daughters have all three become saved and baptized. Yes, all since 1992. I hope my mother will yet be saved. When we are together, it's a kind of warfare. But I think and hope and pray she'll yet come to trust in Jesus.

Finally, let me tell you one key to how my life turned around. Remember, I was one of those people trying to stop the Bible. I was working in Dire Dawa when big demonstrations were held, I sometimes was a speaker for the Marxist party line. But let me skip on to after I had received the Lord and tell you what happened to me here in Addis just a few years ago:

I was walking outside the Telecommunications building when I saw a woman in the distance with her face in tears. I was puzzled. I didn't think I recognized her but she kept focused right on me, weeping. "Do I know her? From where?" I asked myself. I was embarrassed and couldn't place her. She kept walking straight toward me and finally she was right before me. We embraced, kissing as Ethiopians customarily greet. But she held me tight. She was crying. I finally had to admit I didn't know where we had met. "Yes, we haven't met," she admitted. That puzzled me all the more! She was so moved. "Give me a few moments to compose myself," she said. My heart was beating hard. Finally she told me this story:

> Ten years ago I flew to Dire Dawa to visit my mother. It was a Sunday. The plane was late. The *kebele* had announced a meeting in the stadium at seven in the morning. Mother said we must go. She was old. It was hot. I asked, why must we go. "If I don't, the *kebele* will send me to jail," she answered. We went to the stadium with 40–50,000 other people. A message was given by some VIPs, political propaganda about Marx, Lenin, Somali and Eritrean wars, etc. You were one of the speakers that day. Somehow, I focused upon you. That day I prayed to the Lord, "Never let me be killed before you bring this man to Jesus."

For ten years that woman had prayed! One Sunday morning shortly before this meeting we experienced outside of the Telecommunications building, this lady had spotted my face in an Addis church. She hurried toward me, but I became lost in the crowd. She went back again, but didn't see me at that church. She began going from church to church to find me. She'd almost given up when she spotted me that day we met, in the crowd near the Telecommunications, where she'd come to use the phone booth.

It was a miracle meeting. "Jesus has done his homework!" she told me. "I don't mind if He takes me now." You know, it doesn't take the CIA or the KGB. It was the Lord who found me.[137]

"Did you ever see her again?" we couldn't help asking. Meresse seemed deep in thought. "This woman's face was alight, like an angel," he said. After that day, I kept looking for her. I only saw her twice. The first was the day when she was crying. The second time I traced her in the church. I'd looked for her many Sundays—as if she herself had done it for me. I greeted her and asked for her address. She smiled and said, "No. Don't worry—Christ has taken over. It's his responsibility now."

I suppose she didn't want me to worship or idolize her. She wanted to give the praise to Christ. "Christ answered my prayer. I've proved it. I've witnessed to it," she seemed to communicate. In her sight the matter was complete. She did not choose to make more of it. Perhaps she has gone from Addis. She left me alone, to give praise to Jesus.

Meresse looked into the distance and said, "Her example still encourages me. I say to Jesus, remembering my sister, She waited ten years. You are the God who can be an answer even after ten years." Meresse bowed his dear head and simply whispered, "This helps me to pray."

To you, O LORD, I lift up my soul; in you I trust, O my God.
(Psalm 25:1)

---

137. Handwritten document submitted to the author, *Merissa's testimony.*

Chapter 29

CONSUMMATION

What had been happening in Negussie and Fantaye's lives during this time when Ethiopia was awakening out of her nightmare? They had waited for the consummation of their marriage for eleven years, six of them divided by prison walls, and after Negussie went to Kenya, they'd had to live a thousand miles apart. At Christmas time of 1990, Fantaye bravely took leave of her family and flew unattended to Kenya. For a month she lived in an apartment in Nairobi. Then the day arrived.

There is something about an Ethiopian wedding ceremony, even when performed in a foreign country, which defies description. It's not the ceremony itself, it is the majestic grace with which Ethiopians tend to carry themselves, almost as if King Solomon and the Queen of Sheba's court were at hand. The traditional Ethiopian bride's cape is embroidered with gold and her dignified head is crowned with gold as well. She is clothed in spotless white.

Not one member of their families was able to be present for this Nairobi wedding, although Negussie's brother had been commissioned to take three community elders to Fantaye's parents in Ethiopia to secure their permission. Many Ethiopians knew one another through the Ethiopian Fellowship Church which met in the Kenya International Conference Center, but a larger place was needed for the wedding. Pastor Berhanu Deresse arranged for it to be held in the large Nairobi Baptist sanctuary. Negussie had often assisted Pastor Berhanu by giving testimony in Christian meetings. Negussie was well-known and deeply loved. Everyone wanted to come—business and professional people, students, refugees—a huge group came to rejoice with the bride and groom that day. They came bearing gifts, film for the photos, food for the reception,

NEGUSSIE KUMBI AND FANTAYE MOGUS (ABOUT 1990)

cars for the parade, whatever was needed for the all-day celebration an Ethiopian wedding involves. "We've never seen such a wedding," they said afterward.

For Christians, a wedding points forward to the ultimate marriage toward which history is moving. That consummation is issued in by the Marriage Feast of the Lamb and is glimpsed in the book of Revelation. The Son of God receives his Bride, whom he has purchased with his own blood and has been preparing to enter into this new phase of life. All the peoples of the earth are invited to this wedding which will draw people together from all time and space.

Fantaye herself really knew almost no one at her wedding, except the groom and Pastor Berhanu, and yes, Sahle. Typical of Sahle's happy fortune, he happened to be sent to a conference in Nairobi just at the right time.

Finally the newlyweds set up a home together. Negussie was in the midst of his second year at Scott Theological College, sixty-five miles out of Nairobi. Theirs was an unusually close relationship, something not always enjoyed in Ethiopian marriages. Aydeko from Wolaitta was studying at Daystar in Nairobi, and the young couple would sometimes come to the city and visit the apartment Aydeko shared with two other Ethiopians. Aydeko would get up to prepare tea, and Fantaye would tease him, "Ethiopian men don't prepare tea!" "But you don't know where the supplies are," he'd counter. "Oh yes I do!" she'd insist, and take over in the kitchen, where on special days, the delicious aroma of *wat* began to come forth, and *injera* sour-bread would be sent for. This was the spicy meal which meant "home" to Ethiopians. "How we enjoyed being with them," Aydeko remembers. "Their relationship was beautiful—words can't express it. You know, she'd gone against her family and lost her good job to marry Negussie. Her brothers found it hard to accept a deformed person and they tried to isolate her if she married him. Losing her job was costly, but she said she preferred being Negussie's wife to her position at the Ministry of Health." In the long hours of visiting, sometimes Negussie would reveal to them glimpses of what he had passed through during his years in prison in Wolisso and the two places in Addis Ababa—how he was tortured bodily and mentally, and how God had sustained him, even used him, through it all.

One of the couple's great joys was being visited by Alemu Beeftu when he came to Kenya. Research for his work in America or conference speaking invitations brought him to Nairobi from time to time. These brief meetings brought back memories of their youth, renewed their friendship, and gave them all cause to praise God for what he was doing in their lives.

NEGUSSIE KUMBI (ABOUT 1990)

These were happy days. After classes, sometimes Negussie and Fantaye would take walks or picnics in the cool of the evening. At home, he would strum his guitar and sing in the night hours, enjoying Fantaye's presence. He loved a song of an Ethiopian singer named Derege Kebede, about God as *El–Shaddai*. Translated into English it said, "In my own strength, I'd not have gotten through. God's grace got me through." He would sing, remembering all he had been through. The decade before, his guitar had brought difficulty, for they tried to force him to sing for the Revolution. Now he could sing to his God and his wife, in peace. "The difficult days are over," he would say to Fantaye. "The future is ahead. Don't be afraid. A time of blessing is ahead of us."

Back in Ethiopia, a new day was about to dawn. Restrictions on worship were loosening up, but they couldn't have guessed that six months after their wedding, the Derg government would collapse. When the fall came, that thrilling news filled them with hope for a new kind of life in Ethiopia, resplendent with new freedoms.

Negussie was midway in his preparation for a life of service. It was fitting that the German nurse who had awarded Negussie his first Bible in Wolisso should visit Kenya. Chris Ott had treasured Negussie's letters from prison, especially the one in which he said, "I have chosen the path of the cross, to glory." Now she rejoiced with him. She met his bride. His suffering was over and was now replaced with opportunities for meaningful service and graced with the joys of married life.

When into his third year of studies, in March of 1992 the fruit of Fantaye and Negussie's love brought forth a son, whom they named *Natnael (Nathanael)*, which means "God gave." Aydeko was among those who brought gifts. The little family returned for five months to Ethiopia for an internship with Pastor Kedamo at the Meserete Heywet Church. Ato Shiferaw Wolde Michael, a lawyer from Debre Berhan, was among the strong leaders in that congregation, men who had served the Christian community strategically during the Derg days. Negussie learned from these leaders. He left home early and came home late, working with small groups and doing personal counseling. It was good to have fellowship with old friends from Wolisso, too, like Mulugeta Haile, who worked with World Vision. With him Negussie shared the vision for service which was developing in his mind. He felt there was a lack of counseling in the church. From youth to the elderly, people struggled with spiritual and material problems. Evangelists preach and then leave, but Negussie was concerned for someone to pay attention to people's problems, to listen to them, help them, pray with them, and for them afterwards.

At Easter of Negussie's final year, French-speaking SIM representatives contacted Negussie when passing through Nairobi on their way to Pakistan. Immanuel and Soula Isch had been challenged by Negussie's testimony, which they heard of from the Colemans in Canada. The hat Negussie had made for John Coleman was somehow a symbol which stuck in their minds. They were thrilled to meet Negussie and Fantaye in Kenya. Negussie was coughing though, not seeming to be really well. *Nebeyu* ("the prophet"), a second son, had just been born. The daughter of Daniel, Soddo Hospital's administrator, broke away from her own studies at Moffatt College near the hospital and came to care for the lonely mother when she delivered, while Negussie cared for Natnael and kept up his studies at home.

As the time to return to Ethiopia drew near, Fantaye found herself wishing they could somehow stay away. The suggestion that they remain abroad, taking further studies, had to be weighed. Many a bright seminarian had done that, but Negussie could not bring himself to do so. Still, he wondered if he should help his wife obtain some skills while out of the country—like learning to type and use a computer so as to prepare her to help him in his ministry. It happened that Negussie's childhood friend, Alemu, came from America to visit them while he was doing doctoral research in Nairobi. Alemu had stayed on in the United States for additional years of graduate work. His long absence from Ethiopia caused mistrust from some of the church and mission community. It had been very painful for Alemu. To spare Negussie that, he recommended, frankly, that Negussie return home and serve, at least for a while. Perhaps Fantaye's getting those skills could wait till the children were older.

The final term was a difficult one, for their second child was born, right during Negussie's exams, right when he was pushing hard to finish his course. His desire to begin serving in Ethiopia was passionate. He longed to receive fuller power for service. He planned to take a month there, he told Fantaye, "just to go before the Lord." But a few weeks before graduation, he became so ill that he had to be hospitalized. It was diagnosed as typhoid. Struggling to carry through with graduation, he got up too soon. Aydeko observed how very ill he was, and with Fantaye, felt they must not leave, but must get him well in Kenya. Negussie's legs were swollen more and more, and even walking became difficult. Unfortunately, scholarship money had run out and so they left, Fantaye weeping with apprehension. When they arrived in Ethiopia, her husband went straight to the hospital. Negussie was sick, sicker than anyone knew.

He spent a little time at his brother's home in Addis Ababa, but the next two months were a blur of transfers to clinics and hospitals. When Mulugeta heard of his illness, he rushed to him. "It was heartbreaking to me," Mulugeta remembers, "that after his graduation… that this should be. I could tell he was really sick, but we talked; he even teased a little. He told me he had a breathing problem, that he was very tired, had lost his appetite, was under treatment. They took him to Universal Clinic, where he was an in patient for a week. His body was swelling. 'Well, if I die, I have no fear at all,' he said. 'Just pray for me. If I die, I'll go to face my Lord.' But he loved his wife like anything. When he thought of her, it brought tears."

By then, Murray and Bea Coleman had returned to work in Ethiopia. With their son Dan and his wife who were visiting from Canada, they came up from Hossana to see Negussie. His condition was sobering. They were very distressed to find him so ill.

"Why have the sufferings of Job come upon me?" he asked once in his pain. With medication he got relief, but Fantaye was horrified when she got a look at his bloated body. Trying to protect her from concern, he told her good night in the normal way, but to a nurse after she was gone, he whispered, "I won't last the night."

"The doctor advised his brother to take him to the Black Lion Hospital to get oxygen assistance," Mulugeta remembers. "He took him. But before they gave the oxygen, Negussie went to be with the Lord. Kidney failure after earlier typhoid complications, they wrote down as the cause of death. Negussie was only forty one. We were all in shock. We took his body to his brother's home, and people started coming from Addis Ababa and Wolisso. We all went to Pastor Kedamo's church. Negussie's body was buried at St. Joseph's cemetery on Debre Zeit road. No one was prepared for his death."

TO NEARLY EVERYONE WHO knew their story, this ending seemed incredible. It was inscrutable to Fantaye most of all. She had waited eleven years. Now in her mid thirties, overnight she had become a widow with two little sons, one two and a half, the other five months old. She was stunned. Natnael cried continually for his daddy. Weeping, she nursed Nebie, hardly able to bear the grief.

Over in Canada, John Coleman put down the phone after his parents called, devastated. By now John had a family. Eventually, he poured out his grief on paper:

> Negussie, how can I say what you meant to us? You were like a big brother to us when we were kids. I could say that you were the first and best friend I ever had, but you were more than that. You were family. You embraced us and we embraced you. A thousand memories flood my mind as I think of the years we had together. You were so gentle and patient with us when we were little. You were like a guide to us in more than one way. Not just showing us the path to the spring or the bridge (or the "spridge" when we were being crazy!) and teaching us the best games

like stone tag, but you were a role model and mentor to us—just enough older to be our leader but young enough or humble enough was it, to be a peer too. We learned so many things from you. Graciousness, contentment, simplicity, thankfulness… is there a word for the attitude you took toward life? You were certainly full of joy and so much fun to be with!

You didn't talk to us that much about yourself—your own family, life at school, and such. Maybe you talked with Mom and Dad more about those things. I remember Mom saying that whenever you were asked about your back and having TB of the spine, you would respond by thanking God that because of that illness you heard the good news about Christ and became God's child.

I remember some of the talks we used to have together when I would walk to the big *zigaba* tree with you when it was time for you to go home. You had wonderful dreams about the future, of getting an education and doing something for your country. Every time we had to come home to Canada, we would pledge our friendship to each other. I will never forget the last time that I saw you in the summer of 1975. We were living at the Press and I walked to the gate with you and said good-bye, I think in both Ethiopian fashion and with a big hug. Little did I know that I would have to wait until heaven to see you again.

But you wrote me so many letters. I'm glad I saved most of them. They are full of praises to God despite difficulties that you faced, encouragements to me to love the Lord with all my heart. I have letters from you from… and all of them radiate with that same sincere love for the Lord and His people. You guys, you and Alemu and Tesfaye and the others really stuck together and urged one another on to love the Lord and live for him. Your dedication and sincere love just radiated from your lives. What a privilege it is to have known you and been your friend!

John would never be the same.

Pastor Kedamo's expectations for the ministry of his new colleague was crushed. Ato Tekle Wolde Giorgis, who had followed so many prisoners' sagas, sat in mourning along with his son-in-law, Mulugeta. Negussie's mourners ranged from family to friends, from Wolisso to Asmara, from Kenya to America, from pastors to prisoners, from students to teachers, from old to young. Crowds came to the funeral at the Meserete Heywet church, during which Ato Kedamo spoke and Ato Shiferaw led in prayer. With the Apostle Paul they affirmed that believers need not "grieve like the rest of men, who have no hope" (1 Thessalonians 4:13). The word of God gives glimpses of the magnificent life into which we enter when we step into His presence. The Savior explained his own death in terms of a principle which would work out in His people's lives: "Very truly I tell you, unless a kernel of wheat falls to the ground and dies, it remains only a single seed. But if it dies, it produces many seeds." (John 12:24). The believing community could count on God's faithfulness. New seeds would spring forth from Negussie's planting.

This death stirred deep thought. In some ways death by disease is harder to fathom than heroic martyrdom. In some ways, sudden martyrdom was not more costly than the grueling daily price people like Negussie chose to pay. People tried to deal with Negussie's untimely death, trying to absorb its meaning.

Derege Abebe, who published a Christian magazine underground during the Derg, interviewed many and put together a powerful summary of Negussie's life testimony. Now above ground, the *Word of Life* magazine was read by thousands. Negussie's sister Almaz shared memories from their childhood, saying that as she pondered his life, "He seemed to be a man created for suffering… and yet, he was always smiling." She perceived that her brother was a man of God, quite early in his life. "The secret things of God were revealed to him. He was a thankful person, a loving person, a humble person. Until the end, he was a man of praise."

Fantaye was still struggling to trust God in this loss. She tried to relate to Derege a few significant segments of their life story for the article he was writing. This was being a terrific test of her own faith. She could hardly speak of Negussie without tearing up. Little things would undo her. Someone asked for his guitar. It was to her a symbol of his suffering, and she could not give it up. She was honest about her deep grief, with which many could identify. She shared a passage from Isaiah 57 which someone had given her and which especially helped her: "The righteous perish, and no one ponders it in his heart; devout men are taken away, and no one understands that the righteous are taken away to be spared from evil. Those who walk uprightly enter into peace; they find rest as they lie in death." Through Derege's publishing a testimony of Negussie's life, many who did not even know him were edified.

Like many who loved him, Mulugeta kept mulling over the tragedy. He finally settled it in his mind. "God has his own plan. Negussie had contributed his life for the gospel of Jesus Christ in a communist state. He'd been naked, beaten, tortured. He'd shouldered that great responsibility with the Lord's assistance. We used to think, If Negussie is able to shoulder this, though weak, what about those of us who are stronger? Even after his graduation, what more did the Lord want? He had completed his task. The Lord gave him rest."

In America, Alemu Beeftu was torn asunder. Childhood memories came back—Negussie rarely without a smile... his gracious spirit, his joy, even when subjected to so much pain. He remembered their discussion only a year before, in Nairobi. Had he advised them wrongly... to return home? The thought tortured him. What was God doing? "Except for the question which led me to the Lord, the question of Negussie's death was the hardest question of my life," he said years later. He kept asking the Lord, What's behind this? One day, as he was driving along a road, the answer came. He had been reading the book of Acts, chapter 12, wherein the Apostle James (son of Zebedee) was killed by King Herod Agrippa I. On the other hand, the Apostle Peter was sent to prison, and soon escaped. One was killed, the other let out. That's my right, the Lord seemed to be saying to Alemu, It was not that James or Peter was better. That's my choice, my purpose.

As Alemu pondered the meaning of Negussie's life and death, a profound understanding came to him, one which was to change his life. "All this caused me to face a realistic assessment of what ministry is about." Alemu had been a fruitful man strongly dedicated to spiritual productivity. In that moment, he felt God was revealing to him a truth: "Ministry is not an activity, it is total obedience to my revealed will for your life as long as you live, not what you produce. Negussie finished his service. He was not to teach and preach, he was just to obey, without title, without pay. He accomplished his ministry."

Responsible for the care of their two sons, Fantaye looked to her heavenly Bridegroom. By the time the youngest, Nebie, was three, the boy received a new name. "Because of what I've been through," she said, "I've changed his name to "Mikias." *Mikias* means "There is no one like God."

When the crippled "king" from Wolisso arrived in Glory, it would seem that on the altar of his life lay a shining summation—uncluttered, it seemed, with much wood, hay, or stubble. Like his Savior, the Lamb of God, Negussie had chosen the path of the cross to glory. God be praised.

Many Ethiopian believers chose the path of the cross in their own ways. It would seem that they, and we, are the richer for what they brought forth from the circumstances of their short appearance on the stage of history. Why it all happened is beyond our ability to know. But world wide, believers press on, reminded that "today" is all we have, and life is short, even if it is long. People in a fallen world do not just "live happily ever after" following each phase of history. But the table for the Wedding Feast is being set. Everyone is invited, and needs to know so. Anyone may choose to live happily ever after, in Glory. God be praised!

They overcame him by the blood of the Lamb
and by the word of their testimony
(Revelation 12:11a)

Glossary

(Amharic to English, except where noted)

adhari   one who pulls back (from the Revolution)
alem   world
aliya   return (Hebrew)
amanyoch   believers
amlak   God
amlakachin hoy   Oh our God
andinet   General Assembly (of the Kale Heywet Church)
ato   Mr.
awraja   subregion
baka   enough
bet   house
Beta Israel   House of Israel
birr   Ethiopian monetary unit
cadre   young person assigned by the Party to promote Marxism-Leninism
dass   temporary roofing structure for big meetings
daanna   title of honor (Wolaitta; from Amharic *danya,* "judge, leader")
dem   blood
den-dah-nah   he will arise (in Wolaittan language)
Derg   "Committee of Equals" (Provisional Military Administrative Council)
desita or *des*   joy (*des yelal* "it says joy!"—an idiom expressing happiness)
egziabihir yemesgen   God be praised!
ensete   false banana plant
Ethiopia tikdem   "Ethiopia first" (Revolution's slogan)
falasha   "landless" or "foreigner" (term for the Black Jews)
falashmura   Falashas converted to Christianity
ferenji   non-Ethiopian, foreigner
fidel   alphabet
fokere   "to boast" (to shout communist slogans)

Ge'ez holy language of worship in the Ethiopian Orthodox Tewahedo Church
Haile Selassie "power of the Trinity"; last Emperor of Ethiopia
hazen sadness
hig law
injera and wat flat bread dipped in spiced gravy (national food)
kalicha witch doctor
Kale Heywet (KHC) "Word of Life" Church (SIM background)
Kay Shibbir Red Terror
kebele smallest urban administrative unit
Kebra Negest "Glory / Nobility of the Kings" (historical novel)
kes priest or pastor
lekso literally "weeping," the communal bereavement process
mahiber fellowship, association, council
Mekane Yesus (EECMY) "Place where Jesus dwells" Church (Lutheran)
Meserete Kristos (MKC) "Christ the Foundation" Church (Mennonite)
Meserete Heywet "Foundation of Life" (a KHC church in Addis Ababa)
meskel cross; celebration of the finding of the True Cross
mikvah ritual bath (Hebrew)
misganah praise
Mulu Wongel "Full Gospel" Church
negus King (***Negussie*** my king)
Nigusa Negest King of Kings
Pentes short for "Pentecostals" (in Ethiopia: not Orthodox or Catholic)
ras second highest rank in the feudal-military hierarchy ("head, governor")
Saitan Satan
sefir area, neighborhood
sefi hizb wide masses ("broad masses")
sudd the vast swamp in southern Sudan
tabot consecrated replica of the Ark of the Covenant
teff a cereal indigenous to Ethiopia, the flour used in making *injera*
tella locally brewed beer
timket Orthodox holiday commemorating Christ's baptism
tipat-dam ritual drawing of a drop of blood (in Israel)
wass security (a deposit to make certain the fulfillment of an obligation)
woizero Mrs.
Yehadig coalition of fronts who drove out the Derg in 1991
zemecha "campaign" (Development Through Cooperation Campaign)

List of Informants and Recorded Testimonies

(Ethiopian informants are listed under their forenames)

Key:

ARI = Audio Recorded Interview
CRI = Computer Recorded Interview
WT = Written Testimonial (first person quotation)
HN = Handwritten Notes of author (notes still available)
MO = Memory Only (notes not found)

Aberash Takele [Sahle's wife] (see pp. 53f, 73, 101, 149f, 272, 288–290, 322, 340). Interviews in Addis Ababa, e.g. 1995/8/30 and 1996/4f. CRI.

Adams, Bruce A. (see pp. 155, 185, 213f, 340f). Addis Ababa, 1996/4/18 and 20. CRI.

Alemu Beeftu [modern spelling: Biftu] (see pp. 12–15, 51, 142f, 172, 292, 361, 364, 366, 368). Colorado Springs, USA, between 1997–99. MO.

Asfaw Demisse (see 128, 245, 303, 309–312). Addis Ababa, 1994/10/4. CRI.

Balcha [aka Deyasso] Bore (see pp. 252, 254–256, 261). Dilla, 1994/11. ARI, HN.

Balisky, E. Paul & Lila W. (see pp. 107, 127, 153–158, 185, 214, 300). Trip to Langano and Dilla (with Colemans), 1995/7. CRI.

Bassa Dea (see pp. 197–199, 202, 204f, 244). Addis Ababa, 1994/10/7 (transl. Daanna Dadino Dager). CRI.

Belaynesh Dindamo [Hussein's wife] (see pp. 57f, 93, 106, 140–142, 287). Addis Ababa, 1995/5 (end of month). CRI.

Bössler, Gerhard & Edith (see pp. 185, 246, 251–253, 262–264, 300f, 342). Addis Ababa, 1996/4 or 5. CRI.

Brant, Howard (see pp. 107, 127–129, 156, 200, 310). Addis Ababa, 1995/2/24. CRI.

Buchay [Wandaro's wife] (see p. 213). Soddo, 1994/9/7 (transl. Yemisrach Waja). ARI, CRI.

Carlson, Gerald & May. Maaki, 1994/6/23. ARI.

Coleman, John (see pp. 9–15, 91–93, 177, 182, 365f). Addis Ababa, 1994/9/2. ARI [together with Murray Coleman].
Coleman, Murray & Beatrice (see pp. xii, 9f, 51, 108, 154f, 185, 188, 365). 1995/6/20. ARI, CRI.
Degu Deklaabo (see pp. 128, 194–198, 204, 244). Addis Ababa, 1994/8/13 and 1995/3/6 (transl. Ruth Cremer). CRI.
Desalegn Enaro (see p. 218). Addis Ababa, 1994/6/26. CRI.
Desalegn Tesemma (see pp. 342f). Durame, 1994/11/20. CRI.
Ekaso Eybero (see pp. 219f). Soddo, 1994/9/7. CRI.
Emmanuel Abraham (see pp. 75–77). Bishoftu, 1995/10/20. CRI.
Entz, Paul. Addis Ababa, 1994/7/23. CRI.
Fantaye Mogus [Negussie's wife] (see pp. 171–174, 176, 181f, 189f, 248–250, 285–287, 291–293, 359–365, 367–368). Addis Ababa, several times, e.g. 1995/8/9 (transl. Haregewoin). CRI.
Girma Abebe (see pp. 91, 99–101, 290, 320, 340). Bishoftu, 1995/1/16. CRI.
Girma Deresse [Werkwuha's husband] (see pp. 229–231). Hossana, 1994/11/20 (transl. Bea Coleman). ARI, CRI.
Girma Hanano (see pp. 57f, 157, 227f, 236, 318f). Addis Ababa, 1995/6. ARI.
Hagen, Johannes [aka Hans] (see p. 57). Addis Ababa, 1995/7/17. CRI.
Hordofa Gidecho (see pp. 252, 254, 256f). Dilla, 1994/7/27f (transl. Melesse Kebede). ARI, CRI.
Hsueh, Yu Kwong & Lily (see pp. 153–156, 188, 245f, 256, 262f). Addis Ababa, 1994/12/23. ARI, CRI.
Hunter, Malcolm (see pp. 101f, 129–133, 198, 200, 319). Addis Ababa, 1995/2 (beginning of month) and Bishoftu, 1995/3/1. ARI, CRI.
Hussein Yusef [Belaynesh's husband] (see pp. 57f, 93, 106, 140–142, 244, 287). Addis Ababa, 1995/5 (end of month). CRI.
Isaias Roba. Dilla, 1994/7/29. HN, CRI.
Kedamo Mechato (see pp. 6, 14f, 71f, 129, 143, 188, 200, 231f, 244, 286, 315, 363, 366). Addis Ababa, 1995/7/18 (transl. Bea Coleman). CRI.
Kursi Shefeno [Tsehaynesh's husband] (see p. 254). Dilla, 1994/7/28. HN.
Lacy, Doris. Addis Ababa, 1995/8/8. CRI.
Lakew Tesemma (see pp. 63, 142, 155, 188, 209, 247). Addis Ababa, 1995/3/21. ARI, CRI.
L'ool [pseudonym] (see pp. 165–168). Addis Ababa, 1978 and in Khartoum, 1979. MO.
Mahey [aka Mahare] Choramo (see pp. 195, 219–221). Soddo, 1994/9/8 (transl. Seta Wotango). ARI, CRI.

List of informants and recorded testimonies   375

Makebo Wadolo (see p. 225). Hossana, 1994/11/20 (together with Admasu Dotamo, Demisse Doliso, Girma Deresse & Werkwuha, Tenkir Teni, Teshale Sabiro, and Zenebech Laka; transl. Bea Coleman). CRI.

Mamo Belete (see pp. 140, 142, 251–253 [mentioned together with his daughter, *Mastewat*]). Addis Ababa, 1994/9/30. CRI.

Markina Meja (see pp. 208, 214–216, 221). Soddo, 1994/9/8. CRI.

Maunsell, Colin & Hazel. Bishoftu, 1995/7/1, 3f, 7, 12f, and 15. CRI.

Meresse Abraham (see pp. 348–358). Addis Ababa, 1995f. MO, WT.

Mesghina Gebre Medhin (see p. 90). USA 1985, HN, and Addis Ababa, 1995/7/25, CRI.

Mulatu Baffa, D.C. (see pp. 116–118, 129, 188f, 235–237, 243, 316, 348). Addis Ababa, 1994/12 and 1996/5/2. CRI, WT.

Mulugeta Haile (see pp. 177, 291f, 363–366, 368). Addis Ababa, 1996/4/22. CRI.

Negussie Kumbi [Fantaye's husband] (see pp. 3, 6–15, 38, 51, 89, 91–93, 113, 171–178, 181f, 189–192, 248f, 285–288, 291–293, 359–369). In his words: various letters and "hat" note to John Coleman. Information largely from Colemans, Fantaye M., Mulugeta H., C. Ott, Derege Abebe's magazine article, and Kay Bascom's CRI called *Negussie timeline*.

Ott [married: Weber-Ott], Christraude (see pp. 11, 174, 363). Addis Ababa, 1994/8/29. CRI.

Sahle Tilahun [Aberash's husband] (see pp. 33–35, 52–54, 73, 99–104, 149f, 272, 288–292, 322, 340, 361). Interviews in Addis Ababa, e.g. 1995/8/30 and 1996/4f. CRI.

Scheel, Kim. Langano, 1994/9/2. ARI.

Seta Wotango (see pp. 211–213). Soddo, 1994/9/8. ARI, CRI.

Shiferaw Wolde Michael (see pp. 348, 363, 366). Interviews in Addis Ababa, e.g. 1996/5/6. CRI.

Solomon Abate (see pp. 143, 151, 165). Summary of interaction at Addis Ababa, 1977 and Nairobi, 1978/7. CRI.

Solomon Beyene (see pp. 91, 99–101, 290, 320, 340). Debre Zeit, 1995/1/16. CRI.

Stilwell, Donald & Muriel (see p. 324). Addis Ababa, 1995/1/3 and Bonga, 1995/9/23. CRI.

Tadesse Ayissa (see pp. 119–123, 248). Addis Ababa, 1994/9/17 (transl. Degene Gide). ARI, CRI.

Tekle Wolde Giorgis (see pp. 57f, 69, 79–81, 93, 100, 106, 127f, 140, 182, 188f, 193, 203, 244, 247, 262, 366). Interviews in Addis Ababa, e.g. 1995/2/14 and 1995/9/23. CRI, WT.

Terefe Alsi (see pp. 204, 244). Jinka, 1994/11/12 (transl. John Coleman and Demisse Doliso). CRI.

Tesfaye Tole (see pp. 56–58, 83, 85, 93, 194, 196, 199–201, 203f, 217, 244, 345, 366). Addis Ababa, 1994/8/16 and 1995/1. ARI, CRI.

Teshome Haile (see pp. 91, 99–101, 290, 320, 340). Debre Zeit, 1995/1/16 and Addis Ababa, 1996/4/30. CRI.

Timothy Niwar (see pp. 323–326). Addis Ababa, 1998/6 or 7. MO.

Tsehaynesh Dori [Kursi's wife] (see p. 254). Dilla, 1994/7/28. HN.

Volkmann, Arthur D. & Susan (see pp. 54–58, 93–95, 156). Addis Ababa, 1995/3/27. ARI, CRI.

Waja Kabeto (see pp. 132, 207, 217f, 244). Addis Ababa, 1994/6/24 and 28 (with Desalegn Enaro and Dr. Dietrich Schmoll). ARI, CRI.

Werassa Hokotay (see pp. 252, 257). Dilla, 1994/7/27f (transl. Melesse Kebede). ARI, HN, CRI.

Werkwuha Makuria [Girma Deresse's wife] (see pp. 229–231). Hossana, 1994/11/20 (transl. Bea Coleman). ARI, CRI.

Werku Gole (see pp. 56, 82, 127, 155, 245, 252, 254–256, 262f, 298–300, 319f, 347). Addis Ababa, 1995/2/7. ARI, CRI.

Wisner, Roy H. (see pp. 83–86, 200). Addis Ababa, 1996/1/30. CRI.

Yeshi Belachew (see pp. 303–309). Addis Ababa, 1995/8/16 and early 1996 (transl. Haregewoin). CRI.

Yoel Fughi (see pp. 233–235). Durame, 1995/11/24 (together with Segaro Seleto, Tadesse Handetto, et al. CRI.

Yohannes Bosana (see pp. 99, 207, 210, 213). Soddo, 1994/9. CRI.

Yosef Yirba. Dilla, 1994/9/27f. CRI.

Zealot [pseudonym] (see pp. 161–163). Nairobi (Kenya), late 1977. MO.

Unnamed Ethiopian business man (see pp. 163–165). Nairobi (Kenya), late 1977. MO.

Unnamed young female student (see pp. 321f). Babogaya, 1988/7 or 8. MO.

Bibliography

UNPUBLISHED SOURCES

Private Collection of Kay Bascom (Manhattan, Kansas, USA)

Audio tape recorded interviews (ARI):
[Buchay, et al.] Wolayitta women Wandaro-s wife Buchay_and Seta-s mother • Hordofa Gidecho_Deyaso Bore_Werassa Hokotay • Carlson • [John Coleman] On Negussie Kumbi (1994/7/18) • *Murray and John Coleman [on roadtrip] • [Girma Deresse] Girma Hanano [!], Tape 1 • [Girma Deresse] Girma • [Girma Hanano] Girma,* Side A • *Hsuehs* [6 tapes] • *Malcolm Hunter* [2 tapes] • *Lakew Tessema • Mahey Choramo • Kim Scheel • Seta Watango • Tadersse Ayessa* [4 tapes] • *Tesfaye Tole* [2 tapes] • *Volkmann* (recorded 1995/8/10) • *Waja Kabetto • Werkwuha & Zenebech Laka,* side A • *Werku Golle* [2 tapes]

Computer recorded interviews (CRI):
Bruce Adams; *Bruce Adams VCR, Ato Fancho; Wandaro's funeral • Asfaw Demissie_Ginir • [Balisky & Coleman] Langano_Dilla trip notes • Bassa Dea_Gamo Gofa • Belaynesh Dindamo [and Hussein Yusef] • Gerhard Bossler • Howie Brant 2-24-95 • Buchay_Wandaro's wife • Coleman story • Degu Deklabo_Aari • Waja [Kabeto] and Desalyn [Enaro] • Desalyn Tesemme • Immanuel Abraham • L. from Paul Entz • Fantaye expansion Aug • [Girma Abebe, Solomon Beyene, Teshome Haile] DZ Airforce Men • [Girma Deresse, Makebo Wadolo, et al.] G & G - Hadiya • Hagen Interview • Hordofa Gidecho_Gedeo • Hsuehs* [transcription corrected by Hsueh L.] • *Malcolm Hunter; Malcolm Hunter II • Icasso Eberro_Wolaitta • Isaias Roba_ Yirga Chaffee • Kaydamo Macheto • Doris Lacy; Doris Lacy_Tesfaye Tole • Lakew Tessema-Shewa • Mahare Choramo_Wolaitta-Hammer • Mamo Belete, Sidamo • Markena_Wolaitta • Maunsell discussions • Mesghina Gebre Medhin • Dr. Mulatu Baffa • Mulu Geta Haile • Chris [Ott] on Negussie • Sahle Tilahun and Aberash; Sahle Tilahun # 33; Sahle Tilahun additional • Seta [Wotango]_ Wolaita • Ato Shiferaw W_Michael • Solomon Abate • Don Stilwell; Stillwell gleanings • Tadesse Ayesa_Arba Minch • Teferra/Wolde Michael (from Desse) • Tekle Wolde Giorgos; Gleanings at Tekle W_G Sept • Terefa Alsi _ GG • Tesfaye Tole_ Chencha • Teshoma Haile 96 • Art Volkmann; Volkmann's tape answers • Ato Waja Kabeto; Waja [Kabeto] and Desalyn*

[Enaro] • *Werasa Hokote_Gedeo* • *Werku Golle* • *Roy Wisner 1-30-96* • *[David Yap] On Pastor Hsueh* • *Yeshi Belacho* • *[Yoel Fughi et al.] Kambatta, XIII B* • *Yohanes Bosano_Wolaitta* • *Yosef Yirba (& Kukebo Oda)_Ged*

Written Testimonies and Reports (WT):
[Meresse Abraham] Merissa's testimony • *[Mulatu Baffa] Dr. Mulatu's personal testimony* • *[Tekle Wolde Giorgis] Tekle W_G letter* (transl. Kinday)

In addition, hundreds of photographs and negatives (especially from the summer of 1988, and from 1994 to 1996), diaries kept at various periods between 1965–1996, audio and computer recorded interviews not used in the final version of this book, as well as letters, newsletters, and newspapers.

PUBLISHED SOURCES AND LITERATURE
(Ethiopian authors are listed under their forenames)

Andrew, Brother and Charles Paul Conn (1977). *Battle for Africa.* Old Tappan: Fleming H. Revell.

Andrew, Brother, ed. (1979). *Destined to Suffer?* Orange: Open Doors with Brother Andrew.

Arén, Gustav (1978). *Evangelical Pioneers in Ethiopia: Origins of the Evangelical Church Mekane Yesus* (Studia Missionalia Upsaliensia 32). Stockholm: EFS förlaget; Addis Ababa: The Evangelical Church Mekane Yesus.

— (1999). *Envoys of the Gospel in Ethiopia: In the Steps of The Evangelical Pioneers, 1898–1936* (Studia Missionalia Upsaliensia 75). Stockholm: EFS forlaget.

Aymro Wondmagegnehu and Joachim Motovu, eds. (1970). *The Ethiopian Orthodox Church.* Addis Ababa: Ethiopian Orthodox Mission.

Avraham, Shmuel and Arlene Kushner (1986). *Treacherous Journey: My Escape from Ethiopia.* New York: Shapolsky Publishing.

Bahru Zewde (2001). *A History of Modern Ethiopia, 1855–1991* (Eastern African Studies). 2nd ed. Oxford: James Curry; Athens: Ohio Univ. Press; Addis Ababa: Addis Ababa Univ. Press.

Balisky, E. Paul (2009). *Wolaitta Evangelists: A Study of Religious Innovation in Southern Ethiopia, 1937–1975* (ASM Monograph Series 6). Eugene: Pickwick Publications.

Bascom, Kay (2001). *Hidden Triumph in Ethiopia.* Pasadena: William Carey Library.

Bascom, Tim (2015). *Running to the Fire: An American Missionary Comes of Age in Revolutionary Ethiopia* (Sightline Books). Iowa City: Univ. of Iowa Press.

Belai Giday (1992). *Ethiopian Civilization: In Memory of the 2500 Victims Killed in Hauzien, 1988.* Addis Ababa: Belai Giday.

Bond, Bruce and Norene Bond (2005). *When Spider Webs Unite They Can Tie Up a Lion.* Auckland: B. and N. Bond.

Brant, Albert E. (1992). *In the Wake of Martyrs: A Modern Saga in Ancient Ethiopia.* Langley: Omega Publications.

Cannata, Sam *et al.* (1978). *Truth on Trial.* Nashville: Broadman Press.

Cotterell, F. Peter (1973). *Born at Midnight.* Chicago: Moody Press.

— (1988). *Cry Ethiopia.* Eastbourne: MARC.

Cumbers, John B. (1995). *Count It All Joy: Testimonies from a Persecuted Church.* Kearney: Morris Publishing. [Reprinted 2012 in Addis Ababa by SIM Press.]

— (1996). *Living with the Red Terror: Missionary Experiences in Communist Ethiopia.* Kearney: Morris Publishing.

Davis, Raymond J. (1966). *Fire on the Mountains: The Story of a Miracle—The Church in Ethiopia.* New York: Sudan Interior Mission.

— (1984). *The Winds of God.* Summer Hill, Cedar Grove: SIM International Publications.

Dawit Wolde Giorgis (1989). *Red Tears: War, Famine and Revolution in Ethiopia.* Trenton: The Red Sea Press.

Duff, Clarence W. (1980). *Cords of Love: A Testimony to God's Grace in Pre-Italian Ethiopia—As recorded in memorabilia of one of the Sudan Interior Mission's "C.O.D. Boys."* Phillipsburg: Presbyterian and Reformed Publishing Co.

Eide, Øyvind M. (2000). *Revolution and Religion in Ethiopia: Growth and Persecution of the Mekane Yesus Church, 1974–85* (Eastern African Studies). Oxford: James Currey.

Emmanuel Abraham (1995). *Reminiscences of My Life.* Oslo: Lunde forlag.

Fargher, Brian L. (1996). *The Origins of the New Churches Movement in Southern Ethiopia 1927–1944* (Studies of Religion in Africa 16). Leiden etc.: E. J. Brill.

Fekadu Gurmessa (2009). *Evangelical Faith Movement in Ethiopia: Origins and Establishment of the Ethiopian Evangelical Church Mekane Yesus.* Transl. and ed. by Ezekiel Gebissa. Minneapolis: Lutheran Univ. Press.

Forsberg, Malcolm and Enid Forsberg (1975). *In Famine He Shall Redeem Thee: Famine Relief and Rehabilitation in Ethiopia.* Summer Hill: Sudan Interior Mission.

Fuller, W. Harold (1968). *Run While the Sun Is Hot* (Moody diamonds 21). New York: Moody Press.

Grierson, Roderick *et al.*, eds. (1993). *African Zion: The Sacred Art of Ethiopia.* New Haven: Yale Univ. Press.

Gruber, Ruth (1987). *Rescue: The Exodus of the Ethiopians.* New York: Atheneum.

Hancock, Graham (1993). *The Sign and the Seal: The Quest for the Lost Ark of the Covenant.* New York: Simon & Schuster.

Hege, Nathan B. (1998). *Beyond Our Prayers: Anabaptist Church Growth in Ethiopia, 1948–1998.* Scottdale, Waterloo: Herald Press.

Jones, E. Stanley (1963). *The Word Became Flesh.* New York: Abingdon Press.

Kaplan, Robert D. (1988). *Surrender or Starve: The Wars behind the Famine.* Boulder: Westview Press.

Lyall, Leslie T. (1960). *Come Wind, Come Weather: The Present Experience of the Church in China.* Chicago: Moody Press.

Markina Meja Madero (2008). *Unbroken Covenant with God: An Autobiography in the Context of the Wolaitta Kale Heywet Church, Ethiopia.* Translated by Haile Jenai. Belleville: Guardian Books.

McLellan, Dick (2013). *Warriors of Ethiopia.* 2nd edition. Epsom: Lost Coin Books.

— (2013). *Messengers of Ethiopia: Extraordinary Stories of Men and Women Who Suffered and Died for the Gospel.* 2nd edition. Epsom: Lost Coin Books.

Mehari Choramo and Brian L. Fargher (1997). *Ethiopian Revivalist: Autobiography of Evangelist Mehari Choramo.* Edmonton: Enterprise Publications.

Mesghina Gebre Medhin (1989). *Eritrea: The Agony of My People.* Shippensburg: Companion Press.

Mockler, Anthony (1984). *Haile Selassie's War: The Italian–Ethiopian Campaign, 1935–1941.* New York: Random House.

Nee, Watchman (1980). *The Normal Christian Life.* 8th print. Wheaton: Tyndale House Publ. [1st English ed. 1957]

Nelson, Harold D. and Irving Kaplan, eds. (1981). *Ethiopia: A Country Study* (American Univ. Foreign Area Studies). 3rd ed. Washington: Headquarters, Dept. of the Army.

Ofcansky, Thomas P. and LaVerle Bennette Berry, eds. (1993). *Ethiopia: A Country Study* (Area Handbook Series). 4th ed. Washington: Federal Research Division, Library of Congress.

Parffit, Tudor (1985). *Operation Moses: The Story of the Exodus of the Falasha Jews from Ethiopia.* London: Weidenfeld and Nicolson [American ed.: New York: Stein and Day].

Parker, Ben (1995). *Ethiopia: Breaking New Ground* (Oxfam country profiles). Oxford: Oxfam.

Partee, Charles (2000). *Adventure in Africa: The Story of Don McClure from Khartoum to Addis Ababa in Five Decades.* Lanham: Univ. Press of America.

Shelemay, Kay Kaufman (1991). *A Song of Longing: An Ethiopian Journey.* Urbana, Chicago: Univ. of Illinois Press.

Shelemay, Kay Kaufman and Natalia Berger, eds. (1986). *The Jews of Ethiopia: A People in Transition.* New York: Jewish Museum; Tel Aviv: Beth Hatefutsoth.

St. John, Patricia M. (1988). *A Courageous Journey: The Story of a Family's Will to Survive.* Chicago: Moody Press.

Taylor, Rhena, ed. (1987). *The Prisoner and Other Stories.* London: MARC Europe.

Temesgen Sahle (2016). *"Come and See His Works": Biography of Evangelist Kedamo Mechato.* Addis Ababa: Ethiopian Kale Heywet Church Communications and Literature Department. [Amharic]

Thomson, Blair (1975). *Ethiopia: The Country That Cut Off Its Head–A Diary of the Revolution.* London: Robson Books.

Tibebe Eshete (2009). *The Evangelical Movement in Ethiopia: Resistance and Resilience.* Waco: Baylor Univ. Press.

Wilmott, Helen M. J. (1961).*The Doors Were Opened: The Remarkable Advance of the Gospel in Ethiopia.* London: Sudan Interior Mission.

Wilson, Amrit (1991). *The Challenge Road: Women and the Eritrean Revolution.* Trenton: Red Sea Press.

For Further Reading

Afework Hailu Beyene (2014). *The Shaping of Judaic Identity of the Ethiopian Orthodox Tawahado Church: Historical and Literary Evidence*. Ph.D. dissertation. London: School of Oriental and African Studies.

Alemayehu Mekonnen (2013). *Culture Change in Ethiopia: An Evangelical Perspective* (Regnum Studies in Mission). Oxford: Regnum Books International.

Andargachew Tiruneh (1993). *The Ethiopian Revolution 1974–1987: A Transformation from an Aristocratic to a Totalitarian Autocracy* (LSE Monographs in International Studies). Cambridge: Cambridge Univ. Press.

Balisky, E. Paul and Lila W. Balisky (2008). "The Ethiopian Church and Mission in Contexts of Violence: Four Historical Episodes," in: Keith E. Eitel (ed.), *Missions in Contexts of Violence* (Evangelical Missiological Society Series 15). Pasadena: William Carey Library, pp. 201–212.

Balisky, Lila W. (2015). *Songs of Ethiopia's Tesfaye Gabbiso: Singing with Understanding in Babylon, the Meantime and Zion*. D. ICS dissertation. Pasadena: Fuller Theological Seminary.

Clapham, Christopher (1988). *Transformation and Continuity in Revolutionary Ethiopia* (African Studies Series 61). Cambridge: Cambridge Univ. Press.

Donham, Donald L. (1999). *Marxist Modern: An Ethnographic History of the Ethiopian Revolution*. Berkeley and Los Angeles: Univ. of California Press, Oxford: James Currey.

Egeland, Erik (2016). *Christianity, Generation and Narrative: Religious Conversion and Change in Sidama, Ethiopia, 1974–2012* (Studia Missionalia Svecana 116). Uppsala: Uppsala Univ.

Fargher, Brian L. (2002). *Bivocational Missionary Evangelist: The Story of the Itinerant Evangelist Sorsa Sumamo of Northern Sidama*. Edmonton: Enterprise Publications.

Getachew Bellete (2000). *Agonies and Hallelujahs* (The Story of the Kale Heywet Church in Ethiopia, vol. 3: 1974–2000). Addis Ababa: Kale Heywet Church, Literature Department. [Amharic]

Getachew Haile et al. (2005). "Ethiopian Orthodox (Täwaḥədo) Church," in: S. Uhlig (ed.), *Encyclopaedia Aethiopica*, vol. 2. Wiesbaden: Harrassowitz Verlag, pp. 414–432.

Getie Gelaye (2000). *Peasants and the Ethiopian State: Agricultural Producers' Cooperatives and their Reflections in Amharic Oral Poetry – A Case Study in Yetnora, East Gojjam, 1975-1991* (Forschungen zu Sprachen und Kulturen Afrikas 7). Hamburg: Lit Verlag.

Haustein, Jörg (2011). *Writing Religious History: The Historiography of Ethiopian Pentecostalism* (Studien zur Außereuropäischen Christentumsgeschichte 17). Wiesbaden: Harrassowitz Verlag.

Henze, Paul P. (2007). *Ethiopia in Mengistu's Final Years: The Derg in Decline*. Vol. 1. Addis Ababa: Shama Books.

James, Wendy et al., eds. (2002). *Remapping Ethiopia: Socialism and After* (Eastern African Studies). Oxford: James Currey, Athens: Ohio Univ. Press, Addis Ababa: Addis Ababa Univ. Press.

Kaplan, Steven (2003). "Betä Ǝsra'el," in: S. Uhlig (ed.), *Encyclopaedia Aethiopica*, vol. 1. Wiesbaden: Harrassowitz Verlag, pp. 552–559.

Kipfer, Brent L. (2017). *Persecuted and Thriving: Meserete Kristos Church Leadership during the Ethiopian Revolution (1974-1991)*. D. Min. thesis. South Hamilton: Gordon-Conwell Theological Seminary.

Launhardt, Johannes (2004). *Evangelicals in Addis Ababa (1919–1991): With Special Reference to the Ethiopian Evangelical Church Mekane Yesus and the Addis Ababa Synod* (Studien zur Orientalischen Kirchengeschichte 31). Münster: Lit Verlag.

Markakis, John (2011). *Ethiopia: The Last Two Frontiers* (Eastern Africa Series). Suffolk and New York: James Currey.

Messay Kebede (2011). *Ideology and Elite Conflicts: Autopsy of the Ethiopian Revolution*. Lanham, etc.: Lexington Books.

Mohammed Girma (2012). *Understanding Religion and Social Change in Ethiopia: Toward a Hermeneutic of Covenant*. Basingstoke: Palgrave Macmillan.

Provisional Office for Mass Organizational Affairs; Agitation, Propaganda and Education Committee, ed. (1977). *Basic Documents of the Ethiopian Revolution*. Addis Ababa.

Prunier, Gérard (2015). "The Ethiopian Revolution and the Derg Regime," in: G. Prunier and E. Ficquet (eds.), *Understanding Contemporary Ethiopia*. London: Hurst & Company, pp. 209–232.

Samuel Yonas Deressa and Sarah Hinlicky Wilson, eds. (2017). *The Life, Works, and Witness of Tsehay Tolessa and Gudina Tumsa, the Ethiopian Bonhoeffer* (Lutheran Quarterly Books). Lanham: Fortress Press.

Sauer, Christof, ed. (2012). *Bad Urach Statement: Towards an Evangelical Theology of Suffering, Persecution and Martyrdom for the Global Church in Mission* (The WEA Global Issues Series 9). Bonn: Verlag für Kultur und Wissenschaft. [Digital copy available at www.wordevangelicals.org]

Teferra Haile-Selassie (1997). *The Ethiopian Revolution 1974-1991: From a Monarchical Autocracy to a Military Oligarchy.* London and New York: Kegan Paul International.

Tibebe Eshete (2010). "Evangelical Christians and Indirect Resistance to Religious Persecution in Ethiopia," *The Review of Faith & International Affairs* 8, no. 1, pp. 13–21.

— (2013). "The Early Charismatic Movement in the Ethiopian Kale Heywet Church," *PentecoStudies* 12, no. 2, pp. 162–182.

— (2015). "Marxism and Religion: The Paradox of Church Growth in Ethiopia, 1974–1991," in: H. A. Gravaas, C. Sauer, T. Engelsviken, M. Kamil, and K. Jørgensen (eds.), *Freedom of Belief and Christian Mission* (Regnum Edinburgh Centenary Series 28). Oxford: Regnum Books International, pp. 242–258.

Wiebel, Jacob (2014). *Revolutionary Terror Campaigns in Addis Ababa, 1976–1978.* Ph. D. dissertation. Oxford: University of Oxford.

INTERNET RESOURCES

Dictionary of African Christian Biography, entry on Ethiopia
www.dacb.org/stories/ethiopia/ethiopia.html

Good Amharic Books [Lapsley/Brook Foundation]
www.good-amharic-books.com

www.ingramcontent.com/pod-product-compliance
Lightning Source LLC
Chambersburg PA
CBHW071238300426
44116CB00008B/1085